DIALOGUE with the DEAD

DIALOGUE with the DEAD

A Racist Colonialist Economic Cannibal, Sir Charles Phillip Haddon-Cave

"An odd thought strikes me:
– we shall receive no letters in the grave"

Dr. Samuel Johnson

By

Dr. Olayinka Bamgbelu

WORKBOOK PRESS LLC
187 E Warm Springs Rd,
Suite B285 Las Vegas NV 89119 USA

Website: https://workbookpress.com/
Hotline: 1-888-818-4856
Email: admin@workbookpress.com

Ordering Information:

Quantity sales. Special discounts are available on quantity purchases by corporations, associations, and others. For details, contact the publisher at the address above.

Library of Congress Control Number:

ISBN-13: 978-1-965732-18-2 Paperback Version
978-1-965732-24-3 Digital Version

REV. DATE: 03/03/2026

Table of Contents

DEDICATION

Dedicated to Omopenu Adenike Olusoga (1935-2020), the source of the principal X Chromosome. I shall come to you, for you shall never return to me – **2 Samuel 12:23**.

"Every man has a right to utter what he thinks is true, and every other man has a right to knock him down for it, martyrdom is the test." Dr Samuel Johnson (1709-1784).

President Trump, a genetic Briton, implied that Britons are excessively STUPID.

"There is no sin except stupidity." Wilde (1854-1900).

"Freedom to report the truth is a basic right to which the court gives a high level of protection, and the author's right to his story includes the right to tell it as he wishes." Lord Toulson (1946-2017).

If King's School and Oxbridge-Educated, Pure White, Lord Justice Charles Anthony Haddon-Cave, KC, a very hardened CLOSETED RACIST first son of a very rich (**Mark 10:25**) Pure White Hereditary White Supremacist Oxbridge-Educated Tasmanian Colonialist Economic Cannibal, Sir Charles Phillip Haddon-Cave (1925-1999) could disprove the truth, which is that his own pure white kindred, British Soldier, Stephanie Twidale (TD), unrelentingly lied under oath and on record – **Habakkuk 1:4**, he will concomitantly disprove the implied belief of a genetic Briton, albeit a son of a mere Scottish domestic servant (kitchen-hand), President Trump, which is that Britons are excessively stupid, and he will also disprove the belief of some Nigerians, from shit hole Africa, which is that he is a closeted OPPORTUNIST RACIST pure white supremacist bastard.

"The highest reach of injustice is to be deemed just when you are not." Plato

Hereditary white supremacist bastards JAILED Quasi-Mulatto (impure Black), 'Ugly' Constance Briscoe, for a lesser offence - **Habakkuk 1:4.**

Why is lying to liars an offence?

Hypocrisy is by far the greater offence.

Psalm 53: No one is good, not even one.

John 8:7, Matthew 7:1-6: All liars are GUILTY, so liars should not Judge liars. Only He who has no sin has the MORAL RIGHT to Judge Sinners - **John 5:22, Matthew 25:31-46, Revelation 3:21**. RACIST descendants of THIEVES and owners of stolen lives do not have the MORAL RIGHT to Judge Sinners.

"Blue-eyed devils." Elijah Mohammed (1897-1975).

Matthew 12:27: Devils cannot cast out demons.

It is not the TRUTH that impure Black, 'Ugly' Constance Briscoe is the only incompetent liar in Great Britain.

Psalm 116:11: "Lies are told all the time." Sir Robert Michael Havers (1923 -1992), QC, Attorney General. Elitist Oxbridge-Educated Pure White Son of a Pure White Rich Man (Mark 10:25), Sir Cecil Robert Havers (1889-1977), QC.

When their own people commit RACIST CRIMES against our own people, from shit hole Africa, their own people who oversee the administration of their own law will investigate allegations of RACIST EVIL against their own people, and when they find that they are based on TRUTHS, hereditary white supremacist bastards will BURY Merciless Racist Evil – **Habakkuk 1:4.**

Matthew 2:16: They deceive their own mentally gentler white children (OECD) and the pure white IMBECILES they shepherd (predominantly but not exclusively pure white) that they are very highly civilised, super-enlightened, and ultra-righteous geniuses who do everything LEGALLY: Rules-based procedures, precedent statute etcetera, including RACIAL HATRED and FRAUD, and they destroy all self-educated NIGERIANS, from shit hole Africa, who know that they are brainless hereditary RACIST pure white bastards.

ONLY HYPOCRISY IS THE GUILTY CRIMINAL: A pure white OPPORTUNIST RACIST descendant of pure white THIEVES - **Exodus 20:15**, extremely nasty RACIST KILLERS - **Exodus 20:13**, and owners of stolen lives, sat on the BONES of stolen children of poor people and Judged SINNERS – **Matthew 7:1-6, John 8:7.**

King's School and Oxbridge-educated very rich man's son (**Mark 10:25**), Lord Justice Charles Anthony Haddon-Cave, KC, a RACIST first son of a Tasmanian Colonialist Economic Cannibal, which part of the Royal Courts of Justice, WC2A 2LL, was not STOLEN, or which part did your own pure white mother and father buy, or which part preceded SLAVERY: The grand building or its chattels?

An ignorant hereditary RACIST direct descendant of THIEVES and owners of stolen and destroyed lives – **Habakkuk.**

SLAVERY rebuilt everything it succeeded and paid for everything it preceded, including Freemasonry Quasi-Religion (1717), the Royal College of Surgeons (1880), The Royal Courts of Justice (1882), the Old Bailey (1907), The NHS (1948), the GDC (1956), and absolutely everything else, including Industrial Revolution.

Those who know the TRUTH dissent the most. Those who know the least dissent the least. Those who know the truth obey the least.

Ignorance is bliss: "Those who know the least obey the best." George Farquhar (1677-1707).

Ignorant opportunist racist pure white bastards (predominantly but not exclusively pure white), descendants of ultra-righteous pure white THIEVES and owners of stolen lives – **Exodus 20:15, Habakkuk 2:6-9.**

"The supreme vice is shallowness." Wilde (1854-1900).

If skin colour that one neither made nor chose is universally acknowledged to be irrefutably superior, but if one's intellect is not, it is plainly deductible that Freedom of Expression is not one's friend.

"Freedom of Expression is a basic right." Lady Hale.

"Sometimes people don't want to hear the truth because they don't want their illusions destroyed." Friedrich Nietzsche (1844-1900).

The Ne Plus Ultra of Slimy Hypocrisy: BEDFORD, ENGLAND: Pure White Senior District Judge: Poly-educated (not Russell Group Lower-Class Alternative Education - **Proverbs 17:16**) son of a pure white plebeian hoe ultra-righteously sat on a very expensive highchair that his pure white mother and father could not afford, and which the pure white IMBECILES (predominantly but not exclusively pure white) who sat before him could not, and did not, buy, and the opportunist RACIST pure white bastard Judged SINNERS – **John 8:7, Matthew 7:1-6**. Only SAINTS have the Moral Right to Judge Sinners – **John 5:22**. Hereditary RACIST direct descendants of THIEVES – **Exodus 20:15,**

Racist Murderers – **Exodus 20:13**, and owners of stolen and destroyed lives do not have the Moral Right to Judge SINNERS. Blue-eyed devils cannot cast out green-eyed demons – **Matthew 12:27**. Facts are sacred and cannot be overstated.

"Find the truth and tell it." Harold Pinter (1930-2008).

Hereditary RACIST pure white bastards (predominantly but not exclusively pure white) dress up interracial intellectual envy and call it a different name. They do not want their own mentally gentler white children (OECD) and the pure white IMBECILES they shepherd (predominantly but not exclusively pure white) to know the TRUTH, which is that apart from our inferior skin colour, which we neither made nor chose, and our more inferior accent when speaking their own language, a foreign language (omo ale ti ko gbo ede awon baba nla re) our own people, from shit hole Africa, are human beings too, and we are also properly created by Almighty God, and to conceal these DIVINE TRUTHS, hereditary RACIST pure white bastards (predominantly but not exclusively pure white) resort to RACIST CRIMINALITY, secure in the knowledge that all Judges will be PURE WHITE and their hope is that they would all be hereditary RACIST pure white bastards too – **Habakkuk 1:4.**

"Could you face the Russians by yourselves?" President Trump.

Pure White President Trump, a genetic Briton, put Great Britain in her natural place. They are bullies too, and they do not deserve anyone's sympathy when they are bullied by their own pure white genetic kindred.

BEDFORD, ENGLAND: Pure White Senior District Judge Paul Robert Ayers, our own Senior Vice President of the Association of Her Majesty's District Judges, which part of UNNATURAL EXCESSIVE STUPIDITY is Great?

"Why, Sir, Sherry is dull, naturally dull; but it must have taken him a great deal of pains to become what we now see him. Such an excess of stupidity, Sir, is not in Nature." Dr Samuel Johnson (1709-1784).

"Negro is a stage in the slow evolution from monkeys to man." Quasi-Mulatto (impure Black), Dr Frantz Fanon (1925-1961)

"We are no longer your monkeys." Patrice Lumumba (1925-1961): Fed CIA issued bullets spat out by CIA issued guns.

BRISTOL, ENGLAND: Based on available evidence, the entire foundation of BRISTOL, including Bristol University where Helen Falcon (MBE) studied mere dmf, is BONES, more BONES than the millions of skulls at the doorstep of Pol Pot (1925-1998).

INNATE INTERRACIAL INTELLECTUAL ENVY.

If President Trump, a pure white genetic Briton (Archie is impure, <43% Nigerian), could disprove the TRUTH, which is that his own pure white kindred, Pure White Briton, Senior Bedford's District Judge Paul Robert Ayers, our Senior Vice President of the Association of Her Majesty's District Judges, unrelentingly lied under oath (approved Judgement) and on record – **Habakkuk 1:4**, he will confirm the belief of hereditary white supremacist bastards, which is that interracial intellectual jealousy is a baseless myth.

If as they vulgarly brag, it is the TRUTH that hereditary RACIST pure white bastards (predominantly but not exclusively pure white) are Superior Creations of Almighty God, why do opportunist RACIST pure white bastard cretins resort to RACIST CRIMINALITY to defeat self-educated Nigerians, from shit hole Africa, in open debates?

BARAWO/OYINBO OLE/ODE: King's School and Oxbridge-educated Wellborn Born fool (stolen hereditary advantages, unearned patronages, and undeserved privileges), Lord Justice Charles Anthony Haddon-Cave, KC, a RACIST first son of a very rich Tasmanian Colonialist ECONOMIC CANNIBAL (**Mark 10:25**), let me tell you, the pure white ancestors of your pure white mother and father were THIEVES – **Exodus 20:15, Habakkuk 2:6-9,** and owners of stolen children of defenceless poor people, including the African ancestors of the QUASI-MULATTO, impure Black/impure White, <43% Nigerian, grandchildren of HRH King Charles.

Facts are sacred: "The truth allows no choice." Dr Samuel Johnson (1709-1784).

Reasoning and vision do not have finite boundaries, and the fellow is who He says He is – **John 14:6**, and He told Jews and Gentiles, only TRUTHS, in the Council, when He disclosed pictures His unbounded mind painted.

King's School and Oxbridge-educated Lord Justice Charles Anthony Haddon-Cave, KC, a closeted hereditary white supremacist very rich Colonialist Economic Cannibal's son (**Mark 10:25**), let me tell you, the mind that I did not choose is FINER that your indiscreetly crooked, unashamedly mediocre, vindictive, potently weaponised, and institutionally RACIST waste of money

Fish and Chips Justice System, and I do not believe in any part of your SHIT, as no part of your SHIT is good, not even one – **Psalm 53,** and I have the POWER to use cogent facts and irrefutable evidence to irreparably destroy you and every part of your SHIT – **Habakkuk 1:4.**

The pure white European is only interested in MONEY, and if you did not know that truth, it is proof that you could not see him as he truly is. An ignorant hereditary RACIST pure white bastard. An opportunist RACIST direct descendant of ultra-righteous PROFESSIONAL THIEVES – **Exodus 20:15**, extremely nasty RACIST KILLERS – **Exodus 20:13**, and owners of stolen and destroyed children of defenceless poor people (AFRICANS).

Hereditary RACIST pure white bastards (predominantly but not exclusively pure white) spin everything, including themselves. **Psalm 116:11**: They tell lies all the time, but they lie that they don't lie – **Psalm 144**.

Exodus 20:13-15: OYINBO OLE/ODE/BARAWO: "The colonialists care nothing for Africa for her own sake. They are attracted by African riches, and their actions are guided by the desire to preserve their interests in Africa against the wishes of the African people. For the colonialists all means are good if they help them to possess these riches." Patrice Lumumba (1925-1961), Assassinated, indirectly killed by the CIA; the Negro was fed European made bullets spat out by European made guns. DEVILS.

BEDFORD, ENGLAND: Pure White, Indiscreetly Crooked, and Hereditary White Supremacist Senior District Judge Paul Robert Ayers, our own Senior Vice President of the Association of Her Majesty's District Judges, let me tell you, the most important part of the matter is MONEY, and it is not the yield of your Christ-granted talent and/or land; your land yields only FOOD. Your pure white ancestors were THIEVES – **Exodus 20:15, Habakkuk 2:6-9.** Unlike PUTIN'S SIBERIA, there are no gas fields in Bedfordshire and where your own pure white father and mother were born. You are worthy only because you are pure white and Great Britain is very rich (the sixth largest economy on earth), and apart from those, you are PURIFIED NOTHING (Froth).

Robert Hibbert (1769-1849) should confirm that prior to SLAVERY, there weren't very many proper houses in Tommy Robinson's LUTON. Slavery rebuilt everything it succeeded and paid for everything it preceded. An ignorant hereditary RACIST descendant of PURE WHITE THIEVES – BARAWO – **Habakkuk.**

Your brain is not good. You are very lucky that you are PURE WHITE. Had you been BLACK, you wouldn't have been our Judge in BEDFORD.

BARAWO/OYINBO OLE/ODE: They hate us, and we know, and if you did not know, it is proof that you could not see them as they truly are.

When their own people commit RACIST CRIMES against our own people, their own people who oversee the administration of their own law criminally BURY RACIAL HATRED. Their unassailable overwhelming leverage is the certainty that all Judges will be PURE WHITE, and their hope is that they would be hereditary RACIST pure white bastards too – **Habakkuk 1:4.**

BEDFORD, ENGLAND: Our Own Indiscreetly Crooked, Unashamedly Mediocre, and Hereditary Racist pure white bastard, albeit a Senior District Judge within one of the dullest adult populations in the industrialised world (OECD), Pure White, Indiscreetly Crooked, and unashamedly closeted hereditary white supremacist Officer of the Most Excellent Order of our own Empire of Stolen Inheritance (gigantic yields of several continuous centuries of ancestral theft – **Habakkuk 2:6-9, Exodus 20:15**, Sue Gregory (OBE), and Freemason, Brother Richard William Hill, Bedfordshire's Class Senior NHS Postgraduate Tutor, fabricated reports, and/or unrelentingly lied under oath, including approved Judgements, and/or on record. They are all PURE WHITE, and their pure white ancestors were incompetent RACIST LIARS too, they were THIEVES and owners of stolen children of defenceless poor people, including the AFRICAN ANCESTORS of the Quasi-Mulatto, impure Black/impure White (<43% Nigerian) niece and nephew of the Prince of Wales.

BEDFORD, ENGLAND: Our Own Indiscreetly Crooked, Unashamedly Mediocre, and Hereditary Racist pure white bastard, albeit a Pure White Senior District Judge within one of the dullest adult populations in the industrialised world (OECD), it is impossible, absolutely impossible, to COMPETE on a colour-blind level intellectual playing field without resorting to RACIST CRIMINALITY; they are INFERIOR: We think it, we believe it, and we can prove it. Sincere immodesty is sincerer than insincere modesty.

"We shall forge a colour-blind society based on merit." President Trump

Brainless Hereditary White Supremacist Nonsense: Words, mere words.

Facta Non Verba.

It is impossible, absolutely impossible, for a hereditary white supremacist bastard to be colour-blind and transparently impartial.

Only very stupid Negurs expect descendants of Slave-owners to voluntarily relinquish several centuries-old inherited advantageous positions in exchange for NOTHING. Who does that? President Thomas Jefferson's transparent, equal, and exact law – is an unrealistic aspiration. We are SLAVES: Only our visible chains are off; our true will never be voluntarily removed. Change occurs by steps not by giant leaps. Maafa (1445-1888) ended <200 years ago. Substitution is fraudulent emancipation. Slavery preceded Colonisation. Neo-Colonialism is the New Slavery.

"Moderation is a virtue only among those who are thought to have found alternatives." Dr Henry Kissinger (1923-2023).

"Knowledge advances by steps, and not by leaps." Thomas Babington Macaulay (1800-1859), Former Secretary at War of Great Britain

BARAWO/OYINBO OLE/ODE: BEDFORD, ENGLAND: Pure White, Indiscreetly Crooked, and Hereditary White Supremacist Senior District Judge Paul Robert Ayers, our brainless hereditary RACIST pure white bastard FAILED in practice (loads did), and he parked his liability at the public till, and the opportunist RACIST pure white bastard sold unashamed mediocrity and confusion to the undiscerning. Unlike PUTIN'S RUSSIA, there are no gas fields in John Bunyan's Bedford and where his pure white father and mother were born.

BARAWO/OYINBO OLE/ODE: Our own IMBECILE Pure White Senior District Judge Paul Robert Ayers of our own Empire of Stolen Inheritance – **Exodus 20:15, Habakkuk 2:6-9:** The land on which his pure white mother and father were born yields only FOOD, he is verifiably a functional semi-illiterate, he is rich, and the opportunist RACIST pure white bastard DISHONESTLY implied that he did not know that the pure white ancestors of his pure white mother and father were THIEVES and owners of stolen children of defenceless poor people, including the African ancestors of the QUASI-MULATTO (impure White/impure Black, <43% Nigerian) grandniece and grandnephew of Major Andrew Mountbatten Windsor.

"Freedom of Expression is a basic right." Lady Hale.

'Judiciary in England and Wales 'institutionally racist', says https://www.theguardian.com › law › oct › judiciary-[i…18 Oct 2022—Exclusive: more than half of legal professionals in survey said they saw a judge acting in a racially biased way.

If all Pure White Legal Professionals in their Godforsaken Racist Hell Hole were excluded from the Guardian Survey, 50% will become 100%.

BARAWO/OYINBO OLE/ODE: BEDFORD, ENGLAND: Pure White, Indiscreetly Crooked, and Hereditary White Supremacist Senior District Judge Paul Robert Ayers, 'Bro', let me tell you, the most important part of the matter is MONEY, and it is not yours. Your land yields only FOOD and you are a functional semi-illiterate. You are worthy only because you are pure white, and you are RICH only because the pure white ancestors of your pure white mother and father were THIEVES and owners of stolen children of defenceless poor people, including the AFRICAN ANCESTORS of the impure Black/impure White, Quasi-Mulatto (<43% Nigerian) great grandchildren of the Duke of Edinburgh of Blessed Memory, Prince Phillip (1921-2021), and the grandniece and grandnephew of the Duke of Edinburgh.

Philippians 1:21: Phillip was a 33rd Degree Freemason (Scottish Rite).

Our own NIGERIA (oil/gas) is by far more relevant to the economic survival of all your own mentally gentler white children (OECD), your pure white mother, your pure white father, and your pure white spouse than Robert Hibbert (1769-1849) and Tommy Robinson's LUTON. Unlike PUTIN'S SIBERIA, there are no gas fields in Northamptonshire and where the pure white father and mother of Pure White, Indiscreetly Crooked, and Hereditary White Supremacist Senior District Judge Paul Robert Ayers, were born, and the very highly luxuriant soil of Bishop's Stortford yields only FOOD. Bishop's Stortford's Cecil Rhodes (1853-1902) was an insatiably greedy RACIST pure white bastard and a PROFESSIONAL THIEF – **Exodus 20:15, Habakkuk 2:6-9.**

"I prefer land to Nigg*rs." Cecil Rhodes (1877).

"We shall deal with the racist bastards when we get out of prison." Comrade Robert Mugabe (1924-2019).

BARAWO/OYINBO OLE/ODE: BEDFORD, ENGLAND: Pure White, Indiscreetly Crooked, and Hereditary White Supremacist Senior District Judge Paul Robert Ayers, 'Bro', let me tell you, the Nigerian, from shit hole Africa, is a FOETUS (**Acts 2:17**), as what he can vividly see is clearer than dreams, visions, and prophecies, and the mind that he did not choose is finer than yours, and he has the power to use cogent facts and irrefutable evidence to irreparably destroy you and your indiscreetly crooked, VINDICTIVE, potently weaponised, unashamedly mediocre, and institutionally RACIST waste of money Fish and Chips Justice System – **Habakkuk 1:4.**

BEDFORD, ENGLAND: GDC, Pure White, Indiscreetly Crooked, and Hereditary White Supremacist Sue Gregory (OBE) our own Officer of the

Most Excellent Order of our own Empire of Stolen Inheritance – **Exodus 20:15, Habakkuk 2:6-9**, unrelentingly lied under implied oath and on record – **Habakkuk 1:4.** Constance Briscoe was JAILED for a lesser offence: Apartheid by stealth.

Sue Gregory (OBE), our Officer of the Most Excellent Order of our Empire of Stolen Inheritance – **Exodus 20:15, Habakkuk 2: 6-9**, the opportunist RACIST pure white bastard spun everything, including herself. They tell incompetent RACIST LIES all the time, and they lie that they don't lie – **Psalm 116:11, Psalm 144.**

Habakkuk: The nemesis is not extinct, and it has inevitably caught up with Great Britain, and she is dying: Based on several decades of very proximate observations and direct experiences, their Country is SHIT, and they are worse than SHIT, and the Quality of Human Beings in their Godforsaken Racist Hell Hole, including Sue Gregory (OBE) – is very poor (OECD). Pure White, Indiscreetly Crooked, Mediocre (a mere dmf), and Hereditary White Supremacist Bastard, Sue Gregory (OBE) - is our own Officer of the Most Excellent Order of our own Empire of Stolen Inheritance – **Exodus 20:15, Habakkuk 2:6-9.**

Pure white RACIST criminality guarded by pure white RACIST Judicial Power is a very efficient pathway to stolen victory in interracial intellectual contests, but it is retrogressive because it stifles natural selection, and reverses progressive evolution, cages individual development, and arrests overall growth.

BEDFORD, ENGLAND: GDC, Pure White, Indiscreetly Crooked, and Hereditary White Supremacist Freemason, Brother Richard William Hill, Senior NHS Postgraduate Tutor, albeit Bedfordshire's Class, fabricated reports and unrelentingly lied under oath and on record – **Habakkuk 1:4.**

PERCEPTION IS GRANDER THAN REALITY: If as opportunist RACIST pure white bastards vulgarly brag, they are truly SUPERIORLY CREATED by Almighty God, why do hereditary RACIST pure white cretins need RACIST CRIMINALITY to defeat self-educated Nigerians, from shit hole Africa, in open debates? Based on several decades of very proximate observations and direct experiences, the pure white man is grossly overrated.

They desire INTELLECTUAL SUPERIORITY, but He hates them, so He gave them superior skin colour and superior posh accent when speaking their own language, and in protest, they criminally steal yields of Christ-granted talents of self-educated NIGERIANS, from shit hole Africa, secure in the knowledge that all Judges will be PURE WHITE and their hope is that they would be hereditary RACIST pure white bastards too – **Habakkuk 1:4.**

BEDFORD, ENGLAND: Pure White, Indiscreetly Crooked, and Hereditary White Supremacist Senior District Judge Paul Robert Ayers, unrelentingly lied under oath (approved judgement) – **Habakkuk 1:4.**

Impure White/impure Black (Quasi-Mulatto), 'UGLY', Constance Briscoe was JAILED for a lesser offence.

BARAWO/OYINBO OLE/ODE: Hereditary RACIST pure white bastards think SUPREME KNOWLEDGE is their birth right, but if a mere NEGRO, from shithole Africa, proves to them that they are brainless pure white RACIST BASTARDS, they would resort to RACIST CRIMINALITY, secure in the knowledge that all Judges will be hereditary RACIST pure white bastards too.

BARAWO/OYINBO OLE/ODE: They were all members of their brainlessly and baselessly self-awarded pure white superior race: Homogeneity in the administration of their law is an impregnable secure mask of Merciless Racist Evil, a very potent weapon of RACE WAR.

"Trump's administration parked courts with white Judges." Kamala Harris

BEDFORD, ENGLAND: The Serengeti of pure white racist bastards (predominantly but not exclusively pure white). They hate us, and we know.

Leviticus 19:33-34: Hereditary RACIST pure white bastards kill foreigners, albeit remotely. Their type killed the NIGERIAN General Medical Practitioner, Dr Richard Bamgboye, only 56, and the INDIAN Dentist, Dr Anand Kamath, only 42, albeit hands-off, with the mens rea hidden in the belly of the actus reus – **Exodus 20:15.**

BARAWO/OYINBO OLEW/ODE: BEDFORD, ENGLAND: Pure White, Indiscreetly crooked, and hereditary white supremacist Pure White Senior District Judge Paul Robert Ayers, a Senior Vice President of the Association of Her Majesty's District Judges, you are a very powerful RACIST DUNCE, and to live in your world, one needs to feign ignorance, conceal the TRUTH, and live like an actor; life is not that precious, so do your worst.

Kings School and Oxbridge-educated, Lord Justice Charles Anthony Haddon-Cave, KC, a RACIST first son of Tasmania University and Oxbridge-educated Tasmanian Colonialist Economic Cannibal, Pure White European Christians are killing each other in Eastern Europe. Why should Nigerians and their children fight and die - in defence of Great Britain, against Russia, when they are treated inferiorly under English law? Any action, direct or indirect, which punishes our own people for the dark coat that we neither made nor chose – is intellectually incompetent and Antichrist.

BARAWO/OYINBO OLE/ODE: Uncontrollable Transparent Hereditary Racial Hatred: If Pure White, Indiscreetly Crooked, and Hereditary White Supremacist Bedford's District Judge Paul Robert Ayers, the Senior Vice President of the Association of Her Majesty's District Judges, could disprove the truth, which is that he and his own pure white kindred, Sue Gregory (OBE), and Richard Hill (Freemason) are OPPORTUNIST RACIST CRIMINALS, he will concomitantly disprove the TRUTH, which is that the administration of English Law is a Negrophobic charade; an indiscreet RACIST SCAM – **Habakkuk 1:4.**

"He has refused to submit to a medical examination." Kings School and Oxbridge-educated, Lord Justice Charles Anthony Haddon-Cave, KC, a RACIST first son of Tasmania University and Oxbridge-educated Tasmanian Colonialist Economic Cannibal.

Brainless Nonsense: An ignorant one-dimensionally educated hereditary RACIST pure white bastard, and an ultra-righteous descendant of THIEVES, Racist Killers, and owners of stolen children of defenceless poor people, including the African ancestors of the impure white (57%)/impure Black (43% Nigerian, Mulatto Duchess of Sussex.

"The supreme vice is shallowness." Wilde (1854-1900).

Matthew 27:32-56: Kings School and Oxbridge-educated, Lord Justice Charles Anthony Haddon-Cave, KC, a RACIST first son of Tasmania University and Oxbridge-educated Tasmanian Colonialist Economic Cannibal, was Christ kidnapped and lynched like Gadhafi because He lied, or was He crucified because He was a lunatic?

Matthew 14: BEDFORD, ENGLAND: Pure White Poly-educated son of a relatively poor man, albeit England's Class Senior District Judge Paul Robert Ayers, alleged 33rd Degree Freemason (Scottish Rite), the archetypal pure white Englishman, and the Senior Vice President of the Association of Her Majesty's District Judges, was John Jailed because he lied, or did the intolerant lunatic Jew remove his head because he was a lunatic – **Matthew 14**? Which part of Bedfordshire Masonic Centre, MK42 8AH, and Bedford County Court, MK 40

1SQ, was not STOLEN, or which part did your own pure white mother and father buy, or which part preceded SLAVERY: The grand buildings or their very expensive chattels?

AFRICANS who know the TRUTH obey the least: "Those who know the least obey the best." George Farquhar (1677-1707).

Then, all Judges in Great Britain, including Lord Denning (1899-1999), were pure white Freemasons, and most of them were thicker than a gross of planks – **Habakkuk 1:4.**

BARAWO/OYINBO OLE/ODE: BEDFORD, ENGLAND: Pure White Poly-educated son of a relatively poor man, albeit England's Class Senior District Judge Paul Robert Ayers, alleged 33rd Degree Freemason (Scottish Rite), the archetypal pure white Englishman, and the Senior Vice President of the Association of Her Majesty's District Judges, your pure white ancestors were THIEVES. The brain that you inherited from your pure white father and mother is, evidently, not good. The most important part of the matter is MONEY, and it was STOLEN. John Foster (1759-1832) of Brickhill will confirm that prior to SLAVERY, there weren't very many proper houses in Bedford. One-dimensionally educated, hereditary white supremacist, and ultra-righteous descendants of THIEVES – **Exodus 20:15, Habakkuk 2:6-9.**

BARAWO/OYINBO OLE/ODE: Our own direct ancestors were never CARRIED - during the CARRYING TRADE (Maafa, 1445-1888); they killed many in our tribe in the African bush, but they did not carry any. They are more familiar with AFROCARIBBEAN, David Lammy, Diane Abbott, and their type, Genetic Plantation Negroes; direct descendants of stolen African children who were unnaturally selected, genetical reversed, artificially paired up, deliberately bred for hard labour, and reared like cattle, on stolen land – by very highly civilised, super-enlightened, and ultra-righteous pure white European Christians.

Genetic mix is the Holy Grail: Weakening of the common genetic pool. The quality of human beings in their Godforsaken RACIST HELL HOLE is very poor, and that is why a functional semi-illiterate hereditary RACIST pure white bastard was a Senior District Judge, albeit within one of the dullest adult populations in the industrialised world (OECD).

"The best opportunity of developing academically and emotional." England's Class Pure White Senior Bedford's District Judge Paul Robert Ayers, alleged Freemason, and the Senior Vice President of the Association of Her Majesty District Judges.

BRAINLESS NONSENSE: His pure white skin concealed his impure dark black brain. His spinal cord was his highest centre.

"Yes, Sir, it does her honour, but it would do nobody else honour. I have indeed not read it all. But when I take up the end of a web, and find a packthread, I do not expect, by looking further, to find embroidery." Dr Samuel Johnson (1709-1784).

ACCURATE SEERS: They foresaw that a functional semi-illiterate hereditary RACIST pure white bastard will FAIL in practice and park his liability at the public till by becoming a Senior District Judge in BEDFORD, albeit within one of the dullest adult populations in the industrialised world, so they looted AFRICA (Maafa, 1445-1888: Wherever they mercilessly slaughtered Africans, they dispossessed them, and whenever they robbed our own direct ancestors, they took possession. They are no longer here, but their SADISTIC GENES continue to flow through the veins of their direct descendants who remain here.

BARAWO/OYINBO OLE/ODE: Ignorant direct descendants of THIEVES – **Exodus 20:15, Habakkuk 2: 6-9**. Colonisation replaced slavery, and Neo-colonialism is the New SLAVERY. Substitution is fraudulent emancipation.

"Moderation is a virtue only among those who are thought to have found alternatives." Dr Henry Kissinger (1923-2023).

BARAWO/OYINBO OLE/ODE: **Exodus 20:15, Habakkuk 2:6-9**: They are THIEVES, period!

BARAWO/OYINBO OLE/ODE: Ignorant descendants of THIEVES and owners of stolen African children cannot FOOL us, and they cannot school us because we have minds of our own, and they should go to Al Jahannam, and stay there, if they choose to talk only rot –Bob Marley (1945-1981).

If the hereditary RACIST pure white bastard read his approved Judgement, he was a FOOL, and if he did not, he lied as he implied that he did. We are all who we are, the inheritors of our inheritances, the genes of our individual ancestors. The pure white ancestors of his pure white mother and father were incompetent RACIST LIARS too, they were THIEVES and owners of stolen children of defenceless poor people, including the African ancestors of QUASI-MULATTO, impure White/impure Black (<43% Nigerian), grandniece and grandnephew of Major Andrew Mountbatten Windsor.

Based on several decades of very proximate observations and direct experiences, the pure white man is grossly overrated.

BEDFORD, ENGLAND: Pure White Senior District Judge Paul Robert Ayers: "He is a typical Englishman, usually violent and always dull." Wilde (1854-1900).

Poly-educated, unashamedly functional semi-illiterate, and hereditary RACIST pure white bastard. The only evidence of his HIGHER IQ is the gigantic stolen inheritance that his thoroughly wretched pure white ancestors crossed the English Channel, not that long ago, without luggage or decent shoes, to latch onto. No brain. Poor natural resources. Several continuous centuries of stealing and slavery preceded their huge stolen heritance. Unlike PUTIN'S SIBERIA, there are no gas fields in Freemasons' Kempston.

1976-2022: Our opportunist RACIST pure white bastard of our own Empire of Stolen inheritance was granted the platform to display hereditary prejudice, so while the thoroughly stupid pure white man was supposedly diligently performing his legitimate duties, the hereditary RACIST pure white bastard set traps, and the sole purpose of the pure white direct descendant of the father of lies – **John 8:44, John 10:10,** was to steal and/or destroy yields of self-educated NIGERIANS Christ-granted talents. Having FAILED in practice, loads did, the closeted pure white supremacist bastard parked his liability at the public till and sold unashamed mediocrity and confusion to the undiscerning – in exchange for very valuable consideration. Perception is grander than reality. Everything, absolutely everything, is brainlessly and baselessly assumed in favour of the universally acknowledged irrefutably SUPERIOR SKIN COLOUR that the very fortunate wearer neither made nor chose.

"When a stupid man is doing what he is ashamed of, he always declares that it is his duty." George Bernard Shaw (1856-1950).

BARAWO/OYINBO OLE/ODE: BEDFORD, ENGLAND: Pure White Poly-educated son of a relatively poor man, albeit England's Class Senior District Judge Paul Robert Ayers, alleged 33rd Degree Freemason (Scottish Rite), the archetypal pure white Englishman, and the Senior Vice President of the Association of Her Majesty's District Judges, 'Bro', let me tell you, the pure white ancestors of your pure white mother and father were Armed Industrial Scale Professional THIEVES – **Exodus 20:15, Habakkuk 2: 6-9.** I am what I got, and unsolicited: 'The blame is his who chooses. God is blameless.' Plato. I do not believe in any part of your indiscreetly crooked, vindictive, potently weaponised, unashamedly mediocre, and institutionally RACIST Waste of Money Fish and Chips JUSTICE SYSTEM, as no part of SHIT is good, not even one – **Psalm 53**, and I have the

POWER to use cogent facts and irrefutable evidence to irreparably destroy you and it – **Habakkuk 1:4**.

"British Justice is racist and should not be trusted by members of ethnic minorities." Peter Herbert, OBE, an Expert of their Law – **Luke 11:52.**

APARTHEID LAW: "The highest reach of injustice is to be deemed just when you are not." Plato

"Michael Jackson would have been found guilty if he'd been black." Jo Brand.

Constance Briscoe was JAILED for a lesser offence; had she been white or had the Judges been BLACK, she might have 'WALKED', and better still, had she been pure white, male, English, and Freemason, all for one, and one for all might have saved her. Their people are everywhere in their Godforsaken Racist Hell Hole, and they control almost everything, including RACIAL HATRED and FRAUD – **Habakkuk 1:4:** Integrity, friendship, respect, and charity.

Hereditary RACIST pure white bastards (predominantly but not exclusively pure white) do not want self-educated Nigerians in their world, and they fear the untamed minds of our own people more than PUTIN'S POISONS. They want a world where all Nigerians are one-dimensionally educated Born-Again Christians who have been systematically brainwashed to believe that the brain is part of the universally acknowledged irrefutably superior skin colour and that Freemasons are the New Truly Good God – **Mark 10:18.**

'Bro'. let me tell you, Supernatural exists and it is consistently accessible to those who stand where it can come – **John 14:26.**

BARAWO/OYINBO OLE/ODE: If Pure White King's School and Oxbridge-educated Lord Justice Charles Anthony Haddon-Cave, KC, a RACIST first son of a very, very, very, very, very, very, RICH (**Mark 10:25**), and insatiably greedy (**Habakkuk 2:5)** Tasmanian Colonialist Economic Cannibal, Tasmania University and Oxbridge-educated very, very, very, rich man's son (**Mark 10:25**), Sir Charles Phillip Haddon-Cave (1925–1999), and the grandson of Francis Haddon-Cave, born in Hobart in early 20th-century Australian settlement; a properly schooled impostor and an expert of deception (perception is grander than reality), and a direct descendant of genocidal pure white RACIST BASTARDS, the decimators of Native Tasmanians (Black Wars, 1827-1832), a closeted white supremacist descendant of DRUG LORDS (opium merchants of the Qing Dynasty), and a homie of Eton and Oxbridge-educated very, very, very, rich men's son, Archbishop Justin Welby (**Mark 10:25**), could use cogent facts and irrefutable evidence to disprove the TRUTH, which is that his own pure white kindred, GDC, Pure White Sue Gregory, OBE, our own Officer of the Most Excellent Order of our own Empire of Stolen Inheritance – **Exodus 20:15, Habakkuk 2:6-9**, and the archetypal pure white Englishwoman, unrelentingly lied under implied oath and on record – **Habakkuk 1:4,** and GDC, Pure White British Soldier, Stephanie Twidale (TD), unrelentingly lied under oath and on record – **Habakkuk 1:4**, and GDC, Pure White Mrs Helen Falcon, MBE, our own Member of the Most Excellent Order of our own Empire of Stolen Inheritance, the typical pure white Englishwoman, the archetypal Mediocre Member of the Mediocre GDC Committee, a ROTARIAN (vulgarly charitable Freemasonry Quasi-Religion, albeit without Voodoo or Occultists' Rituals), England's Class Postgraduate Dean, Oxford, and the spouse of Mr Falcon, unrelentingly lied under oath and on record, and GDC, Pure White Freemason, Brother Richard William Hill fabricated reports and unrelentingly lied under oath and on record – **Habakkuk 1:4**, he will disprove the open advice of Peter Herbert (OBE), our own Officer of the Most Excellent Order of our own Empire of Stolen Inheritance (gigantic yields of several continuous centuries of ancestral theft – **Exodus 20:15, Habakkuk 2:6-9**), a Quasi-Mulatto (impure White/impure Black), albeit an expert of their law – **Luke 11:52**, which is that English Law is transparently equal for Blacks and Whites, but its administration is not – **Habakkuk 1:4**, and he will also confirm the believe of scores of millions of pure white Britons (predominantly but not exclusively pure white), which is that Antichrist Islam, Antichrist Judaism, Antichrist Freemasonry Quasi-Religion (Mediocre Mafia, Experts of their Law (New Pharisees) – **Luke 11:52**, New Good Samaritan (**Luke 10:25-37**), New Good Shepherd – **John 10:11-18,** and New Truly Good God – **Mark 10:18,** Defenders of Faiths, and Dissenters of the Faiths), and all other motley assemblies of exotic religions and faiths, including those associated the 15 Holy Books in the HOUSE OF COMMONS – are not intellectually flawed Satanic Mumbo Jumbo, and He will also confirm that reasoning and vision have finite boundaries, and if reasoning and vision have finite boundaries, the fellow must have LIED when He disclosed pictures His purportedly unbounded mind painted – **John 14:6,** but if the fellow told Jews and Gentiles the TRUTH – in the Council, we are all FORKED, as his knights attack all Kings and Queens simultaneously, and only the Queens could move (CHECKMATE), and everything that is not aligned with the Divine Exceptionalism of the fellow is travelling in the wrong direction and heading straight for the ROCKS.

“It does no harm to throw the occasional man overboard, but it does not do much good if you are steering full speed ahead for the rocks.” Sir Ian Gilmour (1926-2007), Eton and Oxbridge-educated very rich man’s son (**Mark 10:25**).

CHAPTER ONE

Yinka Bamgbelu: King's School and Oxbridge-educated Lord Justice Charles Anthony Haddon-Cave, KC, Royal Courts of Justice, Strand, WC2A 2LL, London, a closeted RACIST first son of a very, very, very, very, RICH (**Mark 10:25**) Tasmania University and Oxbridge-educated insatiably greedy hereditary white supremacist Tasmanian Colonialist Economic Cannibal, Sir Charles Phillip Haddon-Cave (1925-1999), bro', let me tell you, like your Eton and Oxbridge-educated homie, Archbishop Justin Welby, your pure white ancestors were INDUSTRIAL-SCALE PROFESSIONAL THIEVES – **Exodus 20:15, Habakkuk 2:6-9**.

"The truth allows no choice." Dr Samuel Johnson (1709-1784)

Karen Kwamboka: Based on decades of proximate observations, they, nearly all, are pure white straight-faced RACIST CRIMINALS: 1976-2022: Our brainless hereditary RACIST pure white bastard of our own Empire of Stolen Inheritance. Having FAILED in practice, loads did, the opportunist RACIST pure white bastard parked his liability at the public till and sold unashamed mediocrity and confusion to undiscerning IMBECILES – in exchange for very valuable considerations. Based on cogent, irrefutable, and available evidence, it is not the TRUTH that the appointment of Judges, in Great Britain, is based on progressive, transparent, colour-blind, and measurable objectivity.

Yinka Bamgbelu: Equitable and fair justice: A tooth for a tooth: The pure white bastard should FU*K OFF; our over promoted waste of money FAKE JUDGE. The opportunist RACIST pure white bastard should go to hell and stay there. The bro' should fu*king stay here; it is safer than NIGERIA – **Exodus 21:23-27.** In our own NIGERIA, the probability that the opportunist RACIST pure white bastard would be found and summarily dealt with is > - 100% (greater than minus 100%).

"We shall deal with the racist bastards when we get out of prison." Comrade Robert Mugabe (1924-2019).

Karen Kwamboka: COLOURISM/WHITE PRIVILEGE: Our own IMBECILE Freemason Senior District Judge of our own Empire of Stolen Inheritance, you are very special only because you are PURE WHITE and Great Britain is very rich (the sixth largest economy on earth), apart from those, you are NOTHING, PURIFIED NOTHING. It is absolutely impossible for your Christ-granted talent and yields of the land on which your own pure white mother and father were born to sustain your very high standard of living. Unlike PUTIN'S SIBERIA, there are no gas fields Robert Hibbert (1769-1849) and Tommy Robinson's LUTON and where your own pure white mother and father were born. No brain. Poor natural resources. Several centuries of THIEVERY and SLAVERY preceded their huge stolen inheritance (gigantic yields of several continuous centuries of ancestral theft – **Exodus 20:15, Habakkuk 2:6-9**). Facts are sacred and cannot be overstated.

Yinka Bamgbelu: BARAWO/OYINBO OLE/ODE: BEDFORD, ENGLAND: Pure White Poly-educated son of a relatively poor man, albeit England's Class Senior District Judge Paul Robert Ayers, alleged 33rd Degree Freemason (Scottish Rite), the archetypal pure white Englishman, and the Senior Vice President of the Association of Her Majesty's District Judges, bro', let me tell you, again, based on cogent, irrefutable, and available evidence, the pure white ancestors of your pure white mother and father were INDUSTRIAL-SCALE PROFESSIONAL THIEVES and owners of stolen and destroyed lives of stolen children of defenceless poor Africans – **Exodus 20:15, Habakkuk 2:6-9,** so you are not a SAINT and a SINNER who is a direct descendant of THIEVES and owners of stolen lives does not have the Moral Right to Judge Sinners – **Matthew 7:1-6, John 8:7.**

Karen Kwamboka: "The white man was created a devil, to bring chaos upon the earth." Malcolm X (1925-1965), assassinated, fed bullets made by pure white European Christians – spat out by GUNS made by pure white European Christians.

GREENLAND: Yanks will do whatever they need to do to survive. Pure White European Christians, including Danes, visited North America, and things did not turn out well for Native Americans - Stephen Hawking (1942-2018) paraphrased.

Yinka Bamgbelu: Armed hereditary RACIST pure white bastards became ultra-righteous and highly civilised, but only after several continuous centuries of MERCILESS RACIST EVIL.

Properly rehearsed ultra-righteousness and deceptively schooled civilised decorum were preceded by several continuous centuries of Merciless RACIST EVIL: The greediest economic cannibalism and the evilest RACIST TERRORISM the world will ever know - **Habakkuk 2:5.**

Karen Kwamboka: Based on decades of observations, hereditary RACIST pure white bastard (predominantly but not exclusively pure white) love skin colour superiority, but they hate Freemason of Expression because they don't want their mentally gentler white children (OECD) and the pure white imbeciles they shepherd (predominantly but not exclusively pure white) to know the TRUTH, which is that only their superior skin colour and Almighty God are truly good - **Mark 10:18.**

Yinka Bamgbelu: BARAWO/OYINBO OLE/ODE: Pure White Unashamedly Hereditary White Supremacist Lord Justice Charles Anthony Haddon-Cave, KC, a RACIST first son of a Tasmanian Colonialist Economic Cannibal, and a direct descendant of genocidal pure white RACIST bastards; his armed direct ancestors used disease, overwork, and very violent armed robbery (land grab) - to decimate the population of Native Tasmanians, they directly and indirectly KILLED >90 % of Native Tasmanians, and dispossessed them. and evil RACIST pure white bastard Christians directly and indirectly KILLED >90% of Native Americans and dispossessed them, and after several centuries of the Carrying Trade (Maafa, 1445-1888), in 1884 his evil pure white hereditary RACIST European Christian ancestors partitioned AFRICA and looted her; what the fu*k is civilised about killing and stealing?

"How Europe underdeveloped Africa." Dr Walter Rodney (1942-1980).

Karen Kwamboka: RACIST SHIT PEOPLE. The sole evidence of their very High IQ is the stolen inheritance that their pure white ancestors crossed seas to latch onto. They stole the land, and stolen Africans worked it. What did the Scottish domestic servant and the working-class German take to North America, and what did they find there that was not stolen?

Yinka Bamgbelu: BARAWO/OYINBO OLE/ODE: Bro', let me tell you, sincere immodesty is sincerer than insincere modesty, you are intellectually INFERIOR. It is impossible, absolutely impossible, for you and your pure white type to COMPETE on a colour-blind level intellectual playing field without resorting to RACIST CRIMINALITY – **Habakkuk 1:4.**

Karen Kwamboka: Ignorant hereditary RACIST pure white bastards (predominantly but not exclusively pure white), and ultra-righteous descendants of THIEVES – **Habakkuk 2:6-9, Exodus 20:15**. Facts are sacred and cannot be overstated. BEDFORD, ENGLAND: Our own indiscreetly crooked, unashamedly functional semi-illiterate, and hereditary white supremacist Senior District Judge

Paul Robert Ayers, albeit England's Class Senior Judge, Sue Gregory (OBE),our own Officer of the Most Excellent Order of our own Empire of Stolen Inheritance – **Exodus 20:15, Habakkuk 2:6-9**, and Pure White Freemason, Brother Richard William Hill, Senior NHS Postgraduate Tutor, albeit Bedfordshire's Class, fabricated reports and/or unrelentingly LIED under oath and/or on record – **Habakkuk 1:4**. They were all PURE WHITE. Dark Black Constance Briscoe was JAILED for a lesser offence.

Yinka Bamgbelu: I am aware of the existence of a consistently accessible supernatural. If I tell you, you have the power to section me, but if I show you, you will bury the TRUTH as the IMBECILES you shepherd must not know that you do not have SUPREME KNOWLEDGE.

Karen Kwamboka: BEDFORD, ENGLAND: Based on cogent, irrefutable, and available evidence, our pure white Senior District Judge Paul Robert Ayers of our own Empire of Stolen, lowlife poly-educated hereditary RACIST pure white bastard. No brain. Poor natural resources, several centuries of stealing and slavery preceded their huge stolen inheritance – **Exodus 20:15, Habakkuk 2:6-9**, unrelentingly LIED under oath (approved judgement) and on record. The Pure white ancestors of his pure white mother and father were incompetent RACIST LIARS too; they were THIEVES and owners of stolen children of defenceless poor people, including the African of the QUASI-MULATTO (impure Black/ impure White), <43% Nigerian, grandniece and grandnephew of Major Andrew Mountbatten. The hereditary RACIST pure white bastard should stay here; it is safer than NIGERIA – **Exodus 21:23-27.** In NIGERIA, the probability that the opportunist RACIST pure white bastard would be found and summarily dealt with, but only under due process, our own Native and customary laws, is > 100%.

Dark Black Constance Briscoe was Jailed for a lesser offence. Facts are sacred and cannot be overstated.

Yinka Bamgbelu: 1940: France, a Great Military power on paper, but spineless without the support of the YANKS, surrendered within 6/52.

2026: It would take <6 hours to convert Europe into NUCLEAR ASH.

2026: In the same position as UKRAINE, but without the support of the YANKS, Great Britain would surrender within 6/7.

Karen Kwamboka: 'Pure White British Judges, nearly all, are INNATELY RACIST BASTARDS, and should not be trusted by Africans." Peter Herbert (OBE) paraphrased

"Someone must be trusted. Let it be the Judges." Oxbridge-educated rich man's son **(Mark 10:25)**, Lord Denning (1899-1999).

Yinka Bamgbelu: Hereditary RACIST pure white bastards do not want to pay equitable, fair, and just REPARATION, but they love gigantic yields of involuntary mass emigration, at GUNPOINT, Slavery (Maafa,1445-1888), partition, colonisation, and neo-colonisation (1884 – to date), but insatiably greedy pure white bastards (predominantly but not exclusively pure white) hate mass migration.

Karen Kwamboka: King's School and Oxbridge-educated Lord Justice Charles Anthony Haddon-Cave, KC, Royal Courts of Justice, Strand, WC2A 2LL, London, a closeted RACIST first son of a very, very, very, very, RICH (Mark 10:25) Tasmania University and Oxbridge-educated insatiably greedy hereditary white supremacist Tasmanian Colonialist Economic Cannibal, Sir Charles Phillip Haddon-Cave (1925-1999), based on cogent, irrefutable, and available evidence, it was absolutely impossible for your pure white ancestors to survive without STEALING - **Exodus 20:15, Habakkuk 2:6-9**. Carrying and selling millions of stolen children of defenceless poor Africans was the Ne Plus Ultra of THIEVERY. It is absolutely impossible for you to survive without stealing and/or cheating. Omi eko, eko ni: Nothing has changed, only the style of THIEVERY has mutated. Colonisation succeeded Slavery, and Neo-colonialism is the New Slavery: Substitution is fraudulent emancipation: "Moderation is a virtue only among those who are thought to have found alternatives." Dr Henry Kissinger (1923-2023).

Yinka Bamgbelu: BEDFORD, ENGLAND: Pure White Poly-educated son of a relatively poor man, albeit England's Class Senior District Judge Paul Robert Ayers, alleged 33rd Degree Freemason (Scottish Rite), the archetypal pure white Englishman, and the Senior Vice President of the Association of Her Majesty's District Judges, based on irrefutable evidence, the pure white ancestors of your pure white mother and father were THIEVES (BARAWO); theirs were unparalleled acts of theft opportunistically aimed at unarmed and defenceless AFRICANS. The entire foundation of your civilisation is RACIST EVIL. You do not have the MORAL RIGHT to Judge Sinners – **John 8:7, Matthew 7:1-6.**

Karen Kwamboka: NUCLEAR WAR will favour Africa and Africans because in Wars settled with only sticks and stones, our hardier people will always win.

"I know not with what weapons World War III will be fought, but World War IV will be fought with sticks and stones" Albert Einstein (1879-1955).

Yinka Bamgbelu: BEDFORD, ENGLAND: Pure White Poly-educated son of a relatively poor man, albeit England's Class Senior District Judge Paul Robert Ayers, alleged 33rd Degree Freemason (Scottish Rite), the archetypal pure white Englishman, and the Senior Vice President of the Association of Her Majesty's District Judges, what do you have that is truly good – **Mark 10:18**? You do not have anything that was not directly or indirectly STOLEN and/or is the yield of transparent virtue. You are very lucky that AFRICAN DESCENDANTS of the robbed do not, currently, have overwhelming leverage (NUKES) necessary to demand, and if need be, violently extract equitable, fair, and Just REPARATION: Bi igba ba da oju de, a o si, bi o se si, a o fo: BARAWO (RACIST BASTARD THIEVES).

Karen Kwamboka: THEIR WEAPONISED RACIST JUSTICE SYSTEM: Based on available evidence, their indiscreetly crooked, VINDICTIVE, unashamedly mediocre, potently weaponised, and institutionally RACIST waste of MONEY Fish and Chips Justice System is FU*KED, irreparably FU*KED, as it has foreseeably succumbed to INCEST, weakening of their common genetic pool, and associated physical and/or mental wonkiness, and hereditary white supremacist Freemason Senior Judges, and others, who make loads of money from their unashamed mediocrity and CONFUSION – prop shit up: Conflict of interest.

"A government that robs Peter to pay Paul can always depend on the support of Paul." George Bernard Shaw (1856-1950).

Yinka Bamgbelu: Corinthians 5:8: Sincerity and modesty are attributes of Christ, but modesty is subservient to sincerity, as TRUTH is the prime attribute of Jesus, and no one, including Christ, is TRULY good - **Mark 10:18.**

"I believe truth, the prime attribute of the Deity; and death an eternal sleep, at least of the body." Lord Byron (1788-1824).

Karen Kwamboka: "The United States is falling into temptation and turning away from some of its allies." President Macron.

President Trump needs deliverance - Matthew 6:13. I know a MAN OF GOD in Lagos who could deliver him, but not for NOTHING.

"Those who have the power to do wrong with impunity seldom wait long for the will." Dr Samuel Johnson (1709-1784).

Yinka Bamgbelu: BEDFORD, ENGLAND: Pure White Poly-educated son of a relatively poor man, albeit England's Class Senior District Judge Paul Robert Ayers, alleged 33rd Degree Freemason (Scottish Rite), the archetypal pure white Englishman, and the Senior Vice President of the Association of Her Majesty's District Judges, you an ignorant hereditary RACIST pure white bastard, and an ultra-righteous descendant of THIEVES; your skin colour is SUPERIOR, and your accent when speaking your own language is even more SUPERIOR, but your intellect is not. It is ABSOLUTELY IMPOSSIBLE for you and your pure white type to COMPETE on a colour-blind level intellectual playing field without resorting to RACIST CRIMINALITY – **Habakkuk 1:4.** You are INFERIOR, certainly intellectually: We believe it, and we can prove it. Sincere immodesty is sincerer than insincere modesty. Your land yields only FOOD. Unlike PUTIN'S SIBERIA, there are no gas fields in Freemasons' KEMPSTON and where your own pure white mother and father were born. OYINBO OLE/ODE/BARAWO: An ignorant descendant of ultra-righteous pure white THIEVES and owners of stolen children of defenceless poor people, including the African ancestors of the QUASI-MULATTO, impure White/impure Black, <43% Nigerian, grandniece and grandnephew of the Duke of Edinburgh.

"Sometimes people don't want to hear the truth because they don't want their illusions destroyed." Friedrich Nietzsche (1844-1900).

Karen Kwamboka: The YANKS are NATO, and absolutely everything else is an auxiliary bluff.

OXFORD, ENGLAND: GDC, British Soldier, Stephanie Twidale (TD) unrelentingly lied under oath and on record - **Habakkuk 1:4**. The pure white ancestors of her pure white father and mother were incompetent RACIST LIARS too, they were THIEVES and owners of stolen children of defenceless poor people, including the African ancestors of impure White/impure Black, QUASI-MULATTO, <43% Nigerian, grandniece and grandnephew of Major Andrew Mountbatten Windsor.

Yinka Bamgbelu: Hereditary RACIST pure white bastards tried to SECTION me, not because I am a LUNATIC, but because I know TRUTHS that the PURE WHITE IMBECILES they shepherd (predominantly but not exclusively pure white) must not know.

BARAWO/OYINBO OLE/ODE: BEDFORD, ENGLAND: Indiscreetly crooked, verifiably functional semi-illiterate, and hereditary RACIST pure white

Senior District Judge Paul Robert Ayers, albeit England Class, if as you implicitly vulgarly brag, you and your pure white type are intellectually superiorly created by Almighty God, why the fu*k do you need blatant RACIST CRIMINALITY to defeat a self-educated Nigerian in a open debate? No brain. Poor natural resources. Several centuries of stealing and slavery preceded their huge stolen inheritance (gigantic yields of several continuous centuries of ancestral theft – **Exodus 20:15, Habakkuk 2:6-9**). Facts are sacred and cannot be overstated.

BEDFORD, ENGLAND: GDC, Pure White, Sue Gregory (OBE) lied under implied oath and on record – **Habakkuk 1:4.**

OXFORD, ENGLAND: Pure White, Helen Falcon (MBE) lied under oath and on record – **Habakkuk 1:4.**

'UGLY' Dark Black Constance Briscoe was JAILED for a lesser offence.

Karen Kwamboka: Pure white civilised people do not tell lies and they do not steal except by mistake. Ignorant hereditary RACIST descendants of THIEVES and owners of stolen lives – **Exodus 20:15, Habakkuk 2:6-9.**

Yinka Bamgbelu: It is absolutely impossible for VERY HIGHLY CIVILISED, SUPER-ENLIGHTED, AND INNATELY SUPERIOR PURE WHITE PEOPLE, Helen Falcon (MBE) and SUE GREGORY(OBE), to tell lies, so the Nigerian, from shit hole Africa, is mental: Certum est quia impossibile est.

Karen Kwamboka: THEY ARE INSATIABLY GREEDY, HEREDITARY RACIST, AND INNATE THIEVES - **EXODUS 20:15**: CARRYING TRADE: CARRYING AND SELLING MILLIONS OF STOLEN CHILDREN OF DEFENCELESS POOR PEOPLE, INCLUDING THE ANCESTORS OF MEGHAN MARKLE WAS THE NE PLUS ULTRA OF STEALING – **Habakkuk 2:6-9.**

Yinka Bamgbelu: If you know that one's ancestors were PROFESSIONAL THIEVES and owners of stolen and destroyed lives of the children of defenceless poor people (Africans), and you accept stolen money from the inheritors of stolen money, infinite sojourn inside Al Jahannam is your destiny.

Karen Kwamboka: Was Jesus lynched like Gadhafi because He lied, or was He crucified because He was a LUNATIC - **Matthew 27:32-56**? When it became apparent to Jews and Gentiles that the fellow was intellectually unplayable, He was kidnapped and KILLED – **Exodus 20:15.** He was not punished for speaking but was KILLED solely to prevent him from speaking.

Yinka Bamgbelu: Was John JAILED because he lied, or did the intolerant LUNATIC JEWISH BASTARD remove his head because he was mental - **Matthew 14**? Like Trump, Xi, Putin, MBS, Kim, Babies Etcetera, the intolerant lunatic Jewish bastard, King Herod, wanted everyone to love him unconditionally, and demanded that everyone must say only what he loved to hear.

Karen Kwamboka: Opportunist RACIST pure white bastards, descendants of ultra-righteous PURE WHITE PROFESSIONAL THIEVES – **Exodus 20:15**, and owners of stolen lives brainlessly and baselessly self-awarded SUPREME KNOWLEDGE, and they lie that they don't lie - **Psalm 144.**

Yinka Bamgbelu: ACCURATE PURE WHITE RACIST SEERS: They foresaw that a functional semi-illiterate hereditary RACIST pure white bastard will be our Senior District Judge in Bedford, England, so they looted AFRICA: Wherever the insatiably greedy opportunist RACIST pure white bastards mercilessly slaughtered AFRICANS, they dispossessed them, and whenever they robbed our own African ancestors, they took possession – **Exodus 20:15, Habakkuk 2: 6-9.**

Karen Kwamboka; INTERRACIAL INTELLECTUAL PURE WHITE ENVY DRESSED UP AS IMMIGRATION ENFORCEMENT: ICE AGENTS, HALF-EDUCATED SCHOOL DROPOUTS, AND THEIR GED TYPE. If President Trump, a pure white genetic Briton (Archie is impure, <43% Nigerian),could disprove the TRUTH, which is that his own pure white kindred, British Soldier, Stephanie Twiddle (TD), unrelentingly lied under oath – **Habakkuk 1:4**, he would concomitantly confirm the belief of hereditary white supremacist bastards, which is that interracial intellectual jealousy is a baseless myth.

Yinka Bamgbelu: The nemesis is not extinct, and it has inevitably caught up with Great Britain, she is dying: Pure White, indiscreetly crooked, and an opportunist RACIST pure white bastard was our British Soldier, albeit our Territorial Defender of our own Empire of Stolen Inheritance – **Exodus 20:15, Habakkuk 2:6-9.** The YANKS are NATO, and absolutely everything else is an auxiliary bluff.

Karen Kwamboka: The pattern of MERCILESS RACIST EVIL is the same everywhere in their Godforsaken Racist Hell Hole: Pure white RACIST criminality guarded by pure white RACIST Judicial Power is a very efficient pathway to stolen victory in interracial contests, but it is retrogressive because it stifles natural selection, reverses progressive evolution, cages individual development, and arrests overall growth.

Yinka Bamgbelu: Racist pure white bastards (predominantly but not exclusively pure white) steal power (usurp), and ignorant RACIST BASTARDS use stolen power to BURY RACIST EVIL: Persecutory Negrophobia guarded by Negrophobic Perjury. Pure white skin conceals an impure dark black brain.

OXFORD, ENGLAND: GDC, Mrs Helen Falcon (MBE), the archetypal pure white Englishwoman (perception is grander than reality), our own Member of the Most Excellent Order of our own Empire of Stolen Inheritance (gigantic yields of several continuous centuries of ancestral theft – **Exodus 20:15, Habakkuk 2:6-9)**, a ROTARIAN (vulgarly charitable, Antichrist, and Hereditary White Supremacist Freemasonry Quasi-Religion, but without VOODOO – **Revelation 21:8**, or occultists' rituals, our typical Committee Member our own GDC, England's Class Postgraduate Dean, Oxford, and the Spouse of Mr Falcon, unrelentingly lied under oath and on record- **Habakkuk 1:4.** The pure white ancestors of her pure white father and mother were incompetent RACIST LIARS too, they were THIEVES and owners of stolen children of defenceless poor people, including the African ancestors of the QUASI-MULATTO, impure Black/impure White (<43% Nigerian), grandchildren of HRH King Charles.

"Find the truth and tell it." Harold Pinter (1930-2008).

Karen Kwamboka: OYINBO OLE/ODE/BARAWO: The entire foundation of BRISTOL, including BRISTOL UNIVERSITY, where Mrs Helen Falcon, MBE, alleged genetic Czechoslovakian Jew, studied mere dmf or tooth science, was built on a foundation of BONES, BONES of stolen children of defenceless poor people, including the African ancestors of the impure White/impure Black Duchess of Sussex, 43% Nigerian, and more BONES than the millions of skulls at the doorstep of Pol Pot (1925-1998).

Yinka Bamgbelu: Irreparable intellectual degradation of the RACIST THINKING CLASS. The nemesis is not extinct, and it has inevitably caught up with Great Britain, she is dying: Pure White Mrs Helen Falcon (MBE), a verifiably crooked and unashamedly indiscreetly opportunist RACIST pure white bastard is our own Member of the Most Excellent Order of our own Empire of STOLEN INHERITANCE – **Exodus 20:15, Habakkuk 2:6-9.**

Karen Kwamboka: He is uglier than his pure white father, Sir Charles Phillip Haddon-Cave (1925-1999), a Tasmanian Colonialist Economic Cannibal, so his pure white mother must also be physically ill-favoured too.

"He has refused to submit to a medical examination." King's School and Oxbridge-educated Lord Justice Charles Anthony Haddon-Cave, KC, Royal Courts of Justice, Strand, WC2A 2LL, London, a closeted RACIST first son of a very, very, very, very, RICH (**Mark 10:25**) Tasmania University and Oxbridge-educated insatiably greedy hereditary white supremacist Tasmanian Colonialist Economic Cannibal, Sir Charles Phillip Haddon-Cave (1925-1999).

BRAINLESS RACIST NONSENSE!

Yinka Bamgbelu: England is dying: Irreversible Intellectual Decline among Members of the Higher Upper-Classes (Pure White Privileged Dullards). Our brainless pure white bastard of our own Empire of Stolen Inheritance – **Exodus 20:15, Habakkuk 2:6-9**. Our ultra-righteous opportunist RACIST pure white privileged dullard was granted the platform to display hereditary prejudice. A RACIST first son of a very, very, very, rich, insatiably greedy Colonialist Economic Cannibal – **Habakkuk 2:5.**

Karen Kwamboka: Their indiscreetly RACIST and potently weaponised administration of their Fish and Chips Law.

Based on several decades of very proximate observations and direct experiences, the pure white man is grossly overrated.

Facts are sacred and cannot be overstated.

"The truth allows no choice." Dr Samuel Johnson (1709-1784).

Yinka Bamgbelu: **John 14:26**: When the Divine Helper unravels hereditary RACIAL HATRED, to save face, and to conceal PURIFIED TRUTH, hereditary RACIST pure white bastards (predominantly but not exclusively pure white), members of their brainlessly and baselessly self-awarded SUPERIOR RACE, resort to RACIST CRIMINALITY, and they unleash their THUNDER, the Lunatic Negro Card: Any Negro who disagrees with any member of their brainlessly and baselessly self-awarded superior race – is a LUNATIC, for sure: Certum est quia impossible est.

Karen Kwamboka: In more homogenous countries such as RUSSIA and CHINA, progress is driven by measurable objectivity (natural selection).

In Multi-ethnic Britain/USA, members of the thinking class are almost exclusively pure white, as colour-blind Christ-granted talent is retrogressively subservient to the universally acknowledged irrefutably superior skin colour that the fortunate wearer neither made nor chose.

Yinka Bamgbelu: "I emphasis the point." Pure White Senior Bedford's District Judge Paul Robert Ayers.

"I don't want to talk grammar. I want to talk like a lady." George Bernard Shaw (1856-1950).

Our own brainless hereditary RACIST pure white bastard of our own Empire of Stolen Inheritance - **Exodus 20:15, Habakkuk 2:6-9,** it is not the TRUTH that daily dialogues with PURE WHITE IMBECILES (predominantly but not exclusively pure white) is a proper job that is worthwhile and manly.

Karen Kwamboka: Hereditary Racist descendants of THIEVES and owners of stolen lives do not have the 'cards' necessary to resist the absolutely inevitable land grab of Greenland, so they should FU*KING stop moaning; actions, not words.

Following centuries of extortionately profitable MAAFA (1445-1888), in 1884, armed European Christians partitioned Africa and looted her

The YANKS and RUSSIANS are in the mood for armed land grab.

Yinka Bamgbelu: Racist descendants of ultra-righteous pure white THIEVES and owners of stolen lives – **Exodus 20:15, Habakkuk 2:6-9.** IMAGBON, 1892. BENIN, 1897. FLAT TRACK BULLIES. TRUMP'S POODLES.

"Ethical foreign policy." Robin Cook (1946-2005).

If hereditary RACIST pure white bastards (predominantly but not exclusively pure white) are as ethical, and as brave, as vulgarly brag, they must directly use GUNS to evict Putin from Crimea, he stole it with guns – **Exodus 20:15.**

Karen Kwamboka: King's School and Oxbridge-educated Lord Justice Charles Anthony Haddon-Cave, KC, Royal Courts of Justice, Strand, WC2A 2LL, London, a closeted RACIST first son of a very, very, very, very, RICH (**Mark 10:25**) Tasmania University and Oxbridge-educated insatiably greedy hereditary white supremacist Tasmanian Colonialist Economic Cannibal, Sir Charles Phillip Haddon-Cave (1925-1999),: The mind that I did not choose is FINER than your Fish and Chips Waste of Money Fake Justice System, and I do not believe in any part of your SHIT, and I have the POWER to use facts and evidence to destroy you and your SHIT. Reasoning and vision do not have finite boundaries. The only sinless Judge that was exclusively appointed by Almighty God – **John 5:22**, will Judge all, including hereditary white supremacist Freemason Bastard

Judges, with the sword of transparent TRUTH, not Jonathan Aitken's, but the Divine Sword of Transparent Truth – **Matthew 25:31-46, Revelation 3:21.**

Yinka Bamgbelu: Proverbs 20:15: Their universally acknowledged irrefutably SUPERIOR pure white skin colour that they neither made nor chose is indisputably a great creation of Almighty God, but it is not the GREATEST.

If skin colour that one neither made nor chose is universally acknowledged to be irrefutably SUPERIOR, but if one's intellect is not, it is plainly deductible that Freedom of Expression is not one's friend.

Our own unashamedly functional semi-illiterate, opportunist RACIST, and ignorant pure white bastard of our own Empire of STOLEN INHERITANCE - **Exodus 20:15, Habakkuk 2:6-9**, if as he vulgarly implied, he and his pure white kindred are SUPERIOR creations of Almighty God, why did they need RACIST CRIMINALITY to defeat a mere Negro, from shithole Africa in an open debate?

Karen Kwamboka: BEDFORD, ENGLAND: Pure White Poly-educated son of a relatively poor man, albeit England's Class Senior District Judge Paul Robert Ayers, alleged 33rd Degree Freemason (Scottish Rite), the archetypal pure white Englishman, and the Senior Vice President of the Association of Her Majesty's District Judges, our own NIGERIA (gigantic and varying natural resources) is by far more relevant to the economic survival of all your own mentally gentler (OECD) white children than Masons' Kempston. Unlike PUTIN'S SIBERIA, there are no gas fields in Tommy Robinson's Luton and where your own pure white mother and father were born. Facts are sacred and cannot be overstated. No brain. Poor natural resources. Several centuries of stealing and slavery preceded their huge stolen inheritance – **Exodus 20:15, Habakkuk 2:6-9.**

Yinka Bamgbelu: OYINBO OLE/ODE/BARAWO: The functional semi-illiterate opportunist RACIST pure white bastard should FU*K OFF. The land on which he was born yields only FOOD, he is verifiably a functional semi-illiterate, he is RICH, and he dishonestly implied that he didn't know that the pure white ancestors of his pure white mother and father were THIEVES (**Exodus 20:15, Habakkuk 2:6-9**) and owners of stolen children of defenceless poor people, including the African ancestors of the Mulatto Duchess of Sussex (Impure White/impure Black, 43% Nigerian).

Karen Kwamboka: UNITED STATES OF AMERICA: A RACIST HELL HOLE.

Slimy Hypocrisy: Armed Racist European Christian Bastards dispossessed unarmed and defenceless Native Americans, and stole their land - **Exodus 20:15, Habakkuk 2:6-9.** If it was okay for Racist Pure White Danes to take part in land theft in defenceless Africa (1884), why should it be wrong for the YANKS to steal land in absolutely defenceless Greenland? Hypocritical defendants of extremely nasty RACIST THIEVES, looters of AFRICA.

Yinka Bamgbelu: Our New Demi-God fears only Russia and China: A Pure White Supremacist Genetic Scottish RACIST THUGGISH BASTARD, a beneficiary of armed land grab: His thoroughly wretched grandad, an abjectly poor pure white German Serf, disembarked in North America, without luggage or decent shoes, and uninvited, not that long ago, 1885, and his mumsy, a plebeian Scottish wench, a mere kitchen hand, landed in North America, uninvited, in 1930.

Karen Kwamboka: OYINBO OLE/ODE/BARAWO: They hate us, and we know. The only BLACK opportunist RACIST pure white bastards (predominantly but not exclusively pure white) truly love is our own MONEY (Africa's vast and varying natural resources), and absolutely everything else is DECEIT. A Racist descendant of very violent and RACIST grabbers of Tasmanians' land. XY: His Principal X Chromosome is derived from his bland, colourless, and absolutely unremarkable pure white mother, and the Y Chromosome from his more remarkable father, Tasmanian Colonialist Economic Cannibal, Sir Phillip Hadden-Cave (1925-1999), has very little genetic material, and is essentially the source of masculinity, especially his prick.

Yinka Bamgbelu: Their Country is SHIT, and they are worse than SHIT. They are extremely powerful pure white bastards (predominantly but not exclusively pure white). It is absolutely impossible for them to COMPETE on a colour-blind level intellectual playing field without resorting to RACIST CRIMINALITY.

BEDFORD, ENGLAND: District Judge unrelentingly lied under oath and on record (approved Judgement) – **Habakkuk 1:4,** the Senior Vice President of the Association of Her Majesty's District Judge, and a mere poly-educated functional semi-illiterate pure white son of pure white lowlife plebeian nobodies. GDC/NHS: Sue Gregory (OBE), our own Officer of the Most Excellent Order of our own Empire of STOLEN INHERITANCE (**Exodus 20:15, Habakkuk 2:6-9**).

Karen Kwamboka: Their SHIT COUNTRY where a functional semi-illiterate pure white bastard was a Senior District Judge. Genetics mix is the Holy Grail, and there is considerably more to it than their SUPERIOR SKIN COLOUR.

They are not the only creation of Almighty God, and they are not IMMORTAL, and the universally acknowledged irrefutably SUPERIOR SKIN COLOUR that the very fortunate wearer neither made nor chose is not the only wonder of our world.

Yinka Bamgbelu: Rule-based procedures, precedent, and statute are subservient to the MORALITY of a dementing or demented (Alzheimer's disease/ atypical dementia) unapologetic hereditary pure white supremacist bastard and thuggish genetic Scottish bully.

Necessitas vincit legem: "In no government power can be abused long. Mankind will not bear it. If a sovereign oppresses his people to a great degree, they will rise and cut off his head. There is a remedy in human nature against tyranny, that will keep us safe under every form of government." Dr Samuel Johnson (1709-1784).

Karen Kwamboka: OYINBO OLE/ODE/BARAWO: Hereditary RACIST pure white son of a pure white plebeian hoe, albeit Bedford's Class Senior District Judge, based on available evidence, the brain that you inherited from your pure white parents is not good. Your skin colour is SUPERIOR, but your intellect is not. You are RELEVANT only because you are pure white. You are RICH only because the pure white ancestors of your pure white mother and father were THIEVES and owners of stolen children of defenceless poor people, including the African ancestors of the QUASI-MULATTO, impure Black, impure White, <43% Nigerian – grandchildren of HRH King Charles.

Yinka Bamgbelu: "The supreme vice is shallowness." Wilde (1854-1900).

Had the appointment of PRESIDENTS been based on measurable objectivity, the hereditary pure white supremacist bastard, a very shallow son of a Scottish domestic servant, would not have had a look in.

"We shall forge a colour-blind society based on merit." President Trump.

Karen Kwamboka: HEREDITARY WHITE SUPREMACIST BASTARDS, QUASI-DALITS IN EUROPE, LOWLIFE SHIT PEOPLE, BECAME RACIST MAHARAJAHS ON STOLEN NATIVE AMERICANS' LAND, IN NORTH AMERICA.

OYINBO OLE/ODE/BARAWO: A RACIST direct descendant of thoroughly wretched lowlife Scots, abjectly poor pure white fishermen, cleaners, kitchen hands, and general domestic servants - in the households of Robber Barons/ Upper-Classes.

Yinka Bamgbelu: Racist pure white bastards (predominantly but not exclusively pure white) fear PUTIN'S POISONS more ORESHNIK MISSILES, and they hate immortal sarcasm more than insults.

"The first human who hurled a curse instead of a weapon against his adversary was the founder of civilization." 1856-1939.

Hereditary RACIST pure white bastards invite us to defend ourselves against pure white Mason Racist Criminals before pure white Freemason Criminal Racist Judges, in their Godforsaken RACIST HELL HOLE. Devils cannot cast out demons – **Matthew 12:27.**

Then, all Judges were pure white Freemasons, and most of them were thicker than a gross of planks.

BEDFORD, ENGLAND. GDC, Pure White Freemason, Brother Richard William Hill, Senior NHS Postgraduate Tutor, Bedfordshire, fabricated reports and unrelentingly lied under oath – Habakkuk 1:4. Dark Black Mulatto (Impure Black/impure White) direct descendant of plantation Negroes, Constance Briscoe, was JAILED for a lesser offence. Facts are sacred and cannot be overstated.

Karen Kwamboka: Hereditary RACIST pure white bastards, SUPERIORITY is their birth right. Skin colour that they neither made nor chose is universally acknowledged to irrefutably SUPERIOR, so SUPERIOR PEOPLE must 'run' faster than NEGROES, but they cannot, so they steal our running shoes, secure in the knowledge that all Judges will be pure white, and their hope is that they would be hereditary RACIST pure white bastards too. Oxford, England: MPS/GDC/NHS/BDA, Pure White British Soldier of our own Empire of Stolen Inheritance – **Exodus 20:15, Habakkuk 2:6-9**, Stephanie Twidale (TD) unrelentingly lied under oath and on record – **Habakkuk 1:4**. The pure white ancestors of her pure white father and mother were incompetent RACIST LIARS too, they were THIEVES and owners of stolen children of defenceless poor people, including the African ancestors of the QUASI-MULATTO, impure Black/impure White, <43% Nigerian, grandniece and grandnephew of Major Andrew Mountbatten Windsor.

Dark Black Constance Briscoe was Jailed for a lesser offence – **Habakkuk 1:4**. Facts are sacred and cannot be overstated.

Yinka Bamgbelu: Based on observations and direct experiences, functional semi-illiterate Mason Senior District Judges, nearly all, are hereditary RACIST bastards.

"The best opportunity of developing academically and emotional." Pure White Poly-educated son of a relatively poor man, albeit England's Class Senior District Judge Paul Robert Ayers, alleged 33rd Degree Freemason (Scottish Rite), the archetypal pure white Englishman, and the Senior Vice President of the Association of Her Majesty's District Judges.

OYINBO ODE/OYINBO OLODO/ OYINBO MUGU: OUR BRAINLESS PURE WHITE FOOL OF OUR OWN EMPIRE OF STOLEN INHERITANCE – **EXODUS 20:15, HABAKKUK 2:6-9.**

"I don't want to talk grammar. I want to talk like a lady." George Bernard Shaw (1856-1950).

Our brainless opportunist RACIST pure white bastard of our own Empire of STOLEN INHERITANCE – **Exodus 20:15, Habakkuk 2:6-9**, was granted the platform to display hereditary prejudice. The opportunist RACIST pure white bastard rode on the back of a very powerful tiger, and he thought he was it, disappointed, the poly-educated pure white rubbish would have instantly reverted to NOTHING. His pure white skin concealed his impure dark black brain. His spinal cord was his highest centre.

If the hereditary RACIST pure white bastard, albeit England's Class Senior District Judge, read his approved judgement, he was a FOOL, and if he did not, he lied as he implied that he did.

Karen Kwamboka: BEDFORD, ENGLAND: Pure White Poly-educated son of a relatively poor man, albeit England's Class Senior District Judge Paul Robert Ayers, alleged 33rd Degree Freemason (Scottish Rite), the archetypal pure white Englishman, and the Senior Vice President of the Association of Her Majesty's District Judges,, the poly-educated hereditary RACIST pure white son of pure white plebeian nobodies was admitted as a Solicitor in 1976, and having FAILED in practice, loads did, the OPPORTUNIST RACIST pure white bastard parked his liability at the public till, and other people paid loads of other people's money in exchange for unashamed mediocrity and confusion (QUASI-COMMUNISM). From 1976-1992, our opportunist RACIST and verifiably unashamedly functional semi-illiterate pure white bastard of our own Empire of STOLEN INHERITANCE – **Exodus 20:15, Habakkuk 2:6-9**, sold mediocrity and confusion to those who had the power to choose, and he FAILED, loads did, and from 1992-2022, the poly-educated pure white son of pure white plebeian nobodies secured a very cushy salaried job that rewarded FAILURE and SUCCESS alike (QUASI-COMMUNISM) as an apprentice Judge (Deputy District Judge), from 1992-2000, when he became a District Judge, albeit Bedfordshire Class, and from 2000 – 2022, the ignorant INNATELY RACIST pure white bastard, a descendant of THIEVES Judged Sinners.

Yinka Bamgbelu: OYINBO OLE/ODE/BARAWO: BEDFORD, ENGLAND: Pure White District Judge Paul Robert Ayers, our brainless hereditary RACIST pure white bastard of our own Empire of STOLEN INHERITANCE. The pure white ancestors of your pure white mother and father were THIEVES – **Exodus 20:15, Habakkuk 2:6-9**. Facts are sacred and cannot be overstated. Without the support of the YANKS, your Country is a sitting duck. A 5th Military Power Impersonates a SUPERPOWER: Delusional Grandeur of the Stolen Past. The only evidence of his brainlessly and baselessly SELF-AWARDED Higher IQ, which his thoroughly wretched pure white ancestors crossed the English Channel, not that long ago, without luggage or decent shoes to latch onto.

Karen Kwamboka: Our brainless hereditary RACIST pure white bastard of our own Empire of Stolen Inheritance - **Exodus 20:15, Habakkuk 2:6-9,** a QUASI-ICE AGENT impersonated a Senior District Judge, albeit Bedford's Class. No brain. Poor natural resources. Several centuries of STEALING and SLAVERY preceded their huge stolen inheritance (gigantic yields of several continuous centuries of ancestral theft – **Exodus 20:15, Habakkuk 2:6-9**).

Yinka Bamgbelu: Pure White Mark Fuhrman, a mere GED, looked like a RACIST ICE AGENT: A half-educated school dropout, and his type, lowlife (GED), and hereditary white supremacist pure white bastard (disproportionately but not exclusively pure white) who has been systematically brainwashed to believe that the greatest creation of Almighty is skin colour.

"I have seen evil, and it has the face of Mark Fuhrman." Johnnie Cochran (1937-2005).

Karen Kwamboka: President Trump, hereditary RACIST pure white bastards (disproportionately but not exclusively pure white) want SUPERIORITY, their brainless and baseless birthright, and they can have it, but based only on MERIT, what is wrong with that?

"We shall forge a colour-blind society based on merit." President Trump

Yinka Bamgbelu: OYINBO OLE/ODE/BARAWO: Based on available evidence, the pure white ancestors of his pure white mother and father were

THIEVES. If our hereditary RACIST pure white bastard of our own Empire of Stolen Inheritance – **Exodus 20:15, abakkuk 2Hhhhh Habakkuk 2:6-9,** read his own approved Judgement, he was DEMENTED (Alzheimer's disease/ atypical dementia) pure white bastard, and a functional semi-illiterate pure white FOOL, and if he did not, he LIED as he implied that he did. The pure white ancestors of his pure white mother and father were incompetent RACIST LIARS too, and they were THIEVES and owners of stolen children of poor people, including the QUASI-MULATTO, impure Black/impure White, <43% Nigerian, grandniece and grandnephew of Major Andrew Mountbatten Windsor.

CHAPTER TWO

Karen Kwamboka: Our RACIST pure white bastard cannot speak German, not one word: Omo ale ti ko gbo ede baba re. Your German ancestors were THIEVES, they disembarked in NORTH AMERICA in 1885, without luggage or decent shoes, and uninvited, and only a year after Pure White European Christian THIEVES partitioned Africa (1884). What was the real name of your German Patriarch? The real name of GHISLAINE MAXWELL'S father was Ján Ludvík Hyman Binyamin Hoch, the Czechoslovakian Jew crossed the English Channel in 1940, without luggage or decent shoes.

BEDFORD, ENGLAND: Pure White Poly-educated son of a relatively poor man, albeit England's Class Senior District Judge Paul Robert Ayers, alleged 33rd Degree Freemason (Scottish Rite), the archetypal pure white Englishman, and the Senior Vice President of the Association of Her Majesty's District Judges, what is the real name of your own pure white father, where did he come from, when, and did he arbitrarily acquire a camouflage English name? Or did your ancestors evolve from MAMI WATA in the River Great Ouse? A BRAINLESS POOR PURE WHITE FOOL.

Yinka Bamgbelu: BEDFORD, ENGLAND: Pure White Poly-educated son of a relatively poor man, albeit England's Class Senior District Judge Paul Robert Ayers, alleged 33rd Degree Freemason (Scottish Rite), the archetypal pure white Englishman, and the Senior Vice President of the Association of Her Majesty's District Judges, you are not a SAINT because the pure white ancestors of your pure white father and mother were opportunist RACIST pure white bastards, industrial-scale PROFESSIONAL THIEVES, extremely nasty RACIST KILLERS, insatiably greedy evil bastards, and owners of stolen children of defenceless poor people, including the AFRICA ancestors of the Mulatto, impure White/impure Black, 43% Nigerian, Duchess of Sussex.

Karen Kwamboka: Slavery rebuilt everything it succeeded and paid for everything it preceded, including the GDC (1956) and the NHS (1948). Our own Hereditary RACIST pure white bastard of our own Empire of STOLEN INHERITANCE - **Exodus 20:15, Habakkuk 2:6-9**, was granted the platform to display hereditary prejudice.

Our own MONEY. Our own NIGERIA, Shell's docile cash cow since 1956 (OLOIBIRI). GDC was established in 1956. Facts are sacred and cannot be overstated.

Yinka Bamgbelu: BEDFORD, ENGLAND: Pure White Poly-educated son of a relatively poor man, albeit England's Class Senior District Judge Paul Robert Ayers, alleged 33rd Degree Freemason (Scottish Rite), the archetypal pure white Englishman, and the Senior Vice President of the Association of Her Majesty's District Judges, the most important part of the matter is MONEY, and it is not yours. Your ancestors were THIEVES. NIGERIA (oil/gas) is by far more relevant to the economic survival of all your own white children, your pure white father, your pure white mother, and your pure white spouse than Freemasons' Kempston. Unlike PUTIN'S SIBERIA, there are no gas fields in bland, colourless, and almost lifeless NORFOLK/NORWICH (Coastal Dole/the Departure Lounge of life) and where your own pure white mother and father were born. Facts are sacred and cannot be overstated.

Karen Kwamboka: If hereditary RACIST pure white bastards (disproportionately but not exclusively pure white) are as brave as they vulgarly brag, they MUST DIRECTLY, not by proxy, use overwhelming extreme violence to evict PUTIN from Crimea, he used extreme overwhelming violence to convert Bakhmut and Avdiivka from bricks to rubble and stole them – **Exodus 20:15.**

Yinka Bamgbelu: OYINBO OLE/ODE/BARAWO: BEDFORD, ENGLAND: Pure White Poly-educated son of a relatively poor man, albeit England's Class Senior District Judge Paul Robert Ayers, alleged 33rd Degree Freemason (Scottish Rite), the archetypal pure white Englishman, and the Senior Vice President of the Association of Her Majesty's District Judges, there is no LAW in your Shit Country. Yours is a Godforsaken RACIST HELL HOLE. You and all your type are all Racist Criminals, including all Pure White Supremacist Freemason Judges. You are in trouble, big trouble. You have picked on the wrong person. You are INFERIOR; inferiorly created by Almighty God. Sincere immodesty is sincerer than insincere modesty. I do not believe in any part of your waste of MONEY Fish and Chips Justice System, and I shall use cogent facts and irrefutable evidence to destroy you and SHIT – **Habakkuk 1:4.**

Karen Kwamboka: Pure White Privilege: One rule for Pure Whites and a different rule for all others. Dark Black Constance Briscoe was JAILED for a lesser offence. BEDFORD, ENGLAND: GDC/NHS, Sue Gregory (OBE) our own Officer of the Most Excellent Order of our own Empire of Stolen Inheritance – **Habakkuk 2:6-9, Exodus 20:15**, unrelentingly lied implied under oath and on record – **Habakkuk 1:4.** The pure white ancestors of her pure white father and mother were incompetent RACIST LIARS too, they were THIEVES and owners of stolen children of defenceless poor people, including the African ancestors of the QUASI-MULATTO , impure Black/impure White niece and nephew of our Pure White Prince of Wales.

Facts are sacred: "The truth allows no choice." Dr Samuel Johnson (1709-1784).

Yinka Bamgbelu: An ignorant hereditary RACIST pure white bastard, a one dimensionally educated functional semi-illiterate pure white son of a pure white plebeian hoe, and a direct descendant of THIEVES and owners of stolen and destroyed lives - who is drowning in personal in personal and inherited sins did not have the MORAL RIGHT to Judge SINNERS - **John 8:7, Matthew 7:1-6.**

Karen Kwamboka: "I emphasis the point." Pure White Poly-educated son of a relatively poor man, albeit England's Class Senior District Judge Paul Robert Ayers, alleged 33rd Degree Freemason (Scottish Rite), the archetypal pure white Englishman, and the Senior Vice President of the Association of Her Majesty's District Judges.

A BRAINLESS PURE WHITE FOOL.

"Yes, Sir, it does her honour, but it would do nobody else honour. I have indeed not read it all. But when I take up the end of a web, and find a packthread, I do not expect, by looking further, to find embroidery." Dr Samuel Johnson (1709-1784).

Our very, very, very, highly respected functional semi-illiterate pure white bastard of our own Empire of Stolen Inheritance. The respect is wholly assumed: Perception is grander than reality. Why should NEGROES respect a verifiably crooked opportunist RACIST pure white bastard?

Our own NIGERIAN BABIES with huge oil wells and gigantic gas fields near their huts eat only 1.5/day in our own NIGERIA, a very bellyful opportunist RACIST pure white bastard who pure white mother and father have never seen CRUDE OIL was our Senior District Judge in our Bedford, Great Britain. Which part of our own shit hole Africa is GREAT?

OYINBO OLE/BARAWO (**EXODUS 20:15, HABAKKUK 2:6-9**): "How Europe underdeveloped Africa." Dr Walter Rodney (1942-1980).

Yinka Bamgbelu: Hereditary RACIST pure white bastards want all NIGERIANS to be Born-Again Christians, historical imbeciles, who have been systematically brainwashed to believe that Hereditary White Supremacist

Freemasons (disproportionately but not exclusively pure white) are the New Truly Good God (**Mark 10:18**)

Karen Kwamboka: Our misfortunes, nearly all, are intelligently designed by hereditary white supremacist Freemason Bastards.

BEDFORD, ENGLAND: Freemason, Brother Richard William Hill, Senior NHS Postgraduate Tutor, albeit Bedfordshire Class, fabricated reports and unrelentingly lied under oath and on record – **Habakkuk 1:4.**

Yinka Bamgbelu: Hereditary RACIST pure white bastards (disproportionately but not exclusively pure white) will investigate allegations of RACIST EVIL against their own pure white kindred, and when they find that they are based on PURIFIED TRUTHS, they will try to justify RACIAL HATRED, if they can't, they will bury it, and if they can't bury it, they will kill the witnesses and/or victims.

Karen Kwamboka: Leviticus 19:33-34: They are worse than hereditary white supremacist bastards, TRUMP'S THUGS (ICE AGENTS), half-educated school dropouts, lowlife mere GED, who wear camouflage uniform as the Mask of RACIAL EVIL, and stifle progressive colour-blind competition. RACIST KILLERS OF ALIENS. Trump's ICE Agents evict foreigners; they also kill people, but rarely.

Yinka Bamgbelu: Nigerian, Dr Richard Bamgboye, a Medical Practitioner, only 56, and INDIAN DENTIST, Dr Anand Kamath,only 42, came to Great Britain for a better life; they are in the afterlife - **Exodus 20:13.** They were unlawfully killed by hereditary RACIST pure white bastards (predominantly but not exclusively pure white), albeit hands-off, with the mens rea hidden in the belly of the actus reus.

Karen Kwamboka: The Conservative Leader, the 100% genetic Nigerian, and the Pure White Labour leader - are lawyers, but Nigel Farage is a mere pure white school dropout who makes end meet by being paid loads of other people's money by other people in exchange for inciting white supremacist bastard thugs.

Yinka Bamgbelu: OYINBO OLE/ODE/BARAWO: Then, when Pure White Solicitors and Barristers (disproportionately but not exclusively pure white) FAILED IN PRACTICE, loads did, if they were FREEMASONS, they became Judges or something else, and if not, they became POLITICIANS or something else – **Habakkuk 1:4**. It is absolutely impossible for lecherous pure white bastards (disproportionately but not exclusively pure white) to survive without parking their liabilities at the public till.

Karen Kwamboka: BARAWO/OYINBO OLE/ODE: BEDFORD, ENGLAND: Pure White Poly-educated son of a relatively poor man, albeit England's Class Senior District Judge Paul Robert Ayers, alleged 33rd Degree Freemason (Scottish Rite), the archetypal pure white Englishman, and the Senior Vice President of the Association of Her Majesty's District Judges, ngbo, you were well respected by all in BEDFORD, including Negroes, is this true, and do you have proof? An ignorant hereditary RACIST descendant of pure white THIEVES and owners of stolen children of defenceless poor people, including the AFRICAN ANCESTORS of the Quasi-Mulatto, impure White, impure Black, <43% Nigerian, grandniece and grandnephew of Major Andrew Mountbatten Windsor.

Yinka Bamgbelu: Our opportunist RACIST pure white bastard of our own Empire of Stolen Inheritance – **Exodus 20:15, Habakkuk 2:6-9**, an unashamedly functional semi-illiterate Poly-educated pure white son of pure white plebeian nobodies, and a mere former debt-collector Solicitor in NORWICH (5th Rate Partner). He was a Judge only because he fu*king could not do anything else. Apart from debt-collection, what was in bland, colourless, and almost life NORFOLK/NORWICH (Coastal Dole/the Departure Lounge of Life) for a functional semi-illiterate Freemason Solicitor to do?

Karen Kwamboka: They are not the only creation of Almighty God, and their supposedly HIGHER IQs are brainlessly and baselessly assumed. Is our genetic Scottish bastard a THIEF - **Exodus 20:15**; an armed land grabber A grossly overrated genetic Cuban, infra dignitatem, gangs up with a Racist son of a Scottish domestic servant and oppresses Europeans. RACIST THIEVES AND SLAVE-MERCHANTS:

"Those who have robbed have also lied." Samuel Johnson (1709-1784).

Yinka Bamgbelu: 1976-1992: Our most highly respected hereditary RACIST pure white bastard nearly succeeded in the real world where people were free to 'vote' with their cash 1992-2000: Our pure white RACIST crap was an apprentice Judge for about a decade

2000-2022: He was carried by the PUBLIC: Privileged Dullards' Quasi-Dole.

Karen Kwamboka: President Zelensky: Mutated from a pure white supremacist homunculus Jewish comedian to a torchbearer.

President Trump: Mutated from a hereditary RACIST, very shallow, and grossly incompetent apprentice to a DEMIGOD, the New Truly Good Shepherd - **John 10:11-18.**

Yinka Bamgbelu: "The white man is the devil." Elijah Mohammed (1897-1975).

Based on several decades of very proximate observations and direct experiences, he is not only a devil, but he is also a THIEF. If one's ancestors were THIEVES, stealing must be one of one's inheritances – **Exodus 20:15.**

Karen Kwamboka: You are a pure white RACIST TRAMP. Your pure white ancestors were THIEVES and owners and/or beneficiaries of stolen children of defenceless poor AFRICANS. You have all the characteristics of an impudent genetic Scottish leech.

'The impudence of an Irishman is the impudence of a fly, that buzzes about you, and you put it away, but it returns and flutters and teases you. The impudence of a Scotsman is the impudence of a leech, that fixes and sucks your blood.' Dr Samuel Johnson (1709-1784).

Yinka Bamgbelu: Our brainless hereditary RACIST pure white bastard sold grand deception for value. He constructively LIED that the appointment of Judges by dementing or demented pure white Masons Lords, was based on colour-blind and measurable objectivity, if that were the TRUTH, why was the opportunist RACIST pure white bastard an apprentice Judge (Deputy District Judge) for eight years?

Karen Kwamboka: "The attached book cover for "The White Judge Lied" by Yinka Bankole-Bulu visually reinforces the theme of judicial deception, highlighting alleged lies by white judges that undermine objectivity in the legal system." AI

AI is a White Supremacist Scam, and a Liar: Not all liars are RACISTS, but all racists are maliciously liars.

Yinka Bamgbelu: Our own, very, very, very, highly respected White Mason Senior District Judge of our own Empire of Stolen Inheritance. Pure White Skin, a Huge Stolen Inheritance, and what else?

Karen Kwamboka: Proverbs 20:15: The most important creation of Almighty God is intellect, and it is absolutely unrelated to the universally acknowledged irrefutably superior skin colour that the wearer neither made nor chose.

OXFORD, ENGLAND: GDC, Pure White Mrs Helen Falcon, MBE, Member of the Most Excellent Order of our own Empire of Stolen Inheritance – Exodus 20:15, Habakkuk 2:6-9, a very high ranking ROTARIAN (vulgarly charitable, hereditary white supremacist, and Antichrist Freemasonry Quasi-Religion without Voodoo or Occultists' Rituals), the archetypal Member of the GDC Committee, England's Class Postgraduate Dean, Oxford, and the spouse of Mr Falcon – unrelentingly lied under oath and on record – **Habakkuk 1:4.** Constance Briscoe was JAILED for a lesser offence. Facts are sacred and cannot be overstated.

Abuse of temporary power is the fullest definition of evil. There can be a SPECIAL RELATIONSHIP only among equals. A joje ko dun bi enikan ko ni: The pattern of MERCILESS RACIST EVIL is the same everywhere in their Godforsaken Racist Hell Hole: Pure white RACIST criminality guarded by pure white RACIST Judicial Power is a very efficient pathway to stolen victory in interracial contests, but it is retrogressive because it stifles natural selection, reverses progressive evolution, cages individual development, and arrests overall growth.

Yinka Bamgbelu: OYINBO OLE/ODE/BARAWO: Our own MONEY: Our own NIGERIA, Shell's docile cash cow since 1956 (OLOIBIRI). GDC was established in 1956. Facts are sacred and cannot be overstated.

Unlike PUTIN'S SIBERIA, there are no gas fields in Masons' Kempston and where the pure white father and mother of our own highly respected Pure White Poly-educated son of a relatively poor man, albeit England's Class Senior District Judge Paul Robert Ayers, alleged 33rd Degree Freemason (Scottish Rite), the archetypal pure white Englishman, and the Senior Vice President of the Association of Her Majesty's District Judges, were born, and the very highly luxuriant soil of Bishop's Stortford yields only FOOD. Bishop's Stortford's very highly respected Cecil Rhodes (1853-1902) was a RACIST pure white bastard and a THIEF – **Exodus 20:15.** Facts are sacred and cannot be overstated.

Karen Kwamboka: If the hereditary RACIST pure white genetic Scottish bastard, an unapologetic white supremacist thug, is the torchbearer for Americans, it is proof that their Godforsaken Racist Hell Hole is SHIT, and they are worse than SHIT. Hereditary RACIST pure white bastards, disproportionately but not exclusively pure white, must do their WORST, and we shall do ours.

Yinka Bamgbelu: OYINBO OLE/ODE/BARAWO: Our very highly respected hereditary RACIST pure white bastard of our own Empire of Stolen

Inheritance – **Exodus 20:15, Habakkuk 2:6-9**. 1976-1992, he FAILED in practice, loads did. 1992-2000, (Apprentice Judge) Deputy District Judge. 2000-2022, District Judge.

Bedford, England: Pure White SEnior District Judge Paul Robert Ayers, what were you respected for, and provide cogent and irrefutable objective evidence that you were truly respected by all, including NEGROES? A brainless hereditary RACIST pure white bastard: Perception is grander than reality. A RACIST descendant of THIEVES and owners of stolen children of defenceless poor people, including the African ancestors of the QUASI-MULATTO, impure Black/impure White (<43% Nigerian) grand children of HRH King Charles.

Karen Kwamboka: 1976-2022: Our IMBECILE Freemason Senior District Judge of our own Empire of Stolen Inheritance – **Exodus 20:15, Habakkuk 2:6-9,** was alleged to be well respected in BEDFORD; Assumed, brainless, baseless, and unverifiable respect. Even if it can be objectively verified that the hereditary RACIST purer white bastard was very highly respected, what the fu*k is the value of opinions of pure white IMBECILES (disproportionately but not exclusively pure white)?

Yinka Bamgbelu: Ignorant hereditary RACIST pure white bastards (disproportionately but not exclusively pure white) , thoroughly STUPID ultra-righteous descendants of THIEVES and owners of stolen defenceless poor children of defenceless poor people, including the African ancestors of our MULATTO (impure White/impure Black, 43% Nigerian), Duchess of Sussex.

"There is no sin except stupidity." Wilde (1854-1900).

Sheep unnaturally shepherd sheep. Shepherds know that their sheep are MORONS, but sheep do not know that their shepherds are MORONS too.

"Mediocrity weighing mediocrity in the balance, and incompetence applauding its brother……." Wilde (1854-1900).

Karen Kwamboka: BARAWO/OYINBO OLE/ODE: HEREDITARY RACIST PURE WHITE BASTARD SCAMMERS (PREDOMINANTLY BUT NOT EXCLUSIVELY PURE WHITE): SUPERFLUOUS SUPERIORITY (SKIN COLOUR/ACCENT), THE COLLECTIVE REFUGE OF THE INTELLECTUALLY DISFAVOURED.

The centuries-old unspoken myth, which is that Christ-granted talent is related to the universally acknowledged irrefutably superior skin colour that the very fortunate wearer neither made nor chose – is the mother of all RACIST SCAMS.

Yinka Bamgbelu: Based on very proximate contacts, in a very poorly aerated courtroom, the hereditary RACIST pure white bastard, albeit England's Class Senior District Judge, had a very distinct body odour; the pure white Briton stank.

"Britons stank." Wole Soyinka.

55 BC onwards (400 years): Britain was owned by the Romans. Romans built many baths in Bath. Prior, Britons had never seen baths, so they stank. The Upper Classes concealed body odour with lavender. Romans left 400years later, prior, stinking lowlife Britons were not allowed to have baths in Roman baths in Bath.

Karen Kwamboka: "Jews are good with money." President Trump.

Of course, they are - but whose cash.

President Trump, their talentless billionaire (**Mark 10:25**) newest truly good God-like (**Mark 10:18**) knows all and sees all - **Psalm 15:3**.

Ivanka and Jared Kushner are Pure White Good Jews. Judas Iscariot, Ghislaine Maxwell's dad, and Bernard Madoff were Pure White Bad Jews.

"The Pure White Bad Jew, not the Jew, is the devil." Khalid Abdul Mohammad paraphrased.

"The white man is not only practicing Racism and Zionism, and with the prostitution ring, the so-called Jew man with the Jew woman all over the world to make a few dollars, he is also practicing sexism. He's a racist, he's a Zionist, an imperialist. He's a no-good bastard. He's not a devil, the white man is the Devil. " Khalid Abdul Mohammad (1948–2001), San Francisco State University, May 21, 1997

Karen Kwamboka: OYINBO OLE/ODE/BARAWO: BEDFORD, ENGLAND: Pure White Poly-educated son of a relatively poor man, albeit England's Class Senior District Judge Paul Robert Ayers, alleged 33rd Degree Freemason (Scottish Rite), the archetypal pure white Englishman, and the Senior Vice President of the Association of Her Majesty's District Judges, our brainless hereditary RACIST pure white bastard, our ultra-righteous descendant of THIEVES and owners of stolen children of poor people – **Exodus 20:15, Habakkuk 2:6-9**; our ugly tall-dwarf, taller than physically ill-favoured, homunculus Jew, President Zelensky, thinks he is a genius because he was our Senior District Judge, in BEDFORD, albeit within one of the dullest adult populations in the industrialised world (OECD).

CHAPTER THREE

Yinka Bamgbelu: OYINBO OLE/ODE/BARAWO: BEDFORD, ENGLAND: Pure White Poly-educated son of a relatively poor man, albeit England's Class Senior District Judge Paul Robert Ayers, alleged 33rd Degree Freemason (Scottish Rite), the archetypal pure white Englishman, and the Senior Vice President of the Association of Her Majesty's District Judges, you are leech. You are RICH (the sixth largest economy on earth) only because the pure white ancestors of your pure white mother and father were THIEVES and owners of stolen children of poor, including the African ancestors of the QUASI-MULATTO (impure White/impure Black) < 43% Nigerian, grandniece and grandnephew of Major Andrew Mountbatten Windsor.

Karen Kwamboka: A genetic Cuban is the neck that moves the head (elementary mind) of the Ruler of the World. Without the support of the YANKS, Europe, including Great Britain, is a sitting duck.

"Putin fears the US, but not Europe." President Trump.

Proverbs 9:10: Reasonable Putin fears God, and the end of the world.

Yinka Bamgbelu: "Envy is weak." Yul Brynner (1920-1985).

Interracial Envy is not a Myth: When Hereditary Racial Hatred and Envy Copulate, insanity is their Offspring.

BEDFORD, ENGLAND: Pure White Poly-educated son of a relatively poor man, albeit England's Class Senior District Judge Paul Robert Ayers, alleged 33rd Degree Freemason (Scottish Rite), the archetypal pure white Englishman, and the Senior Vice President of the Association of Her Majesty's District Judges, our own brainless hereditary RACIST pure white bastard of our own Empire of Stolen Inheritance – **Exodus 20:15, Habakkuk 2:6-9**, ultra-righteously sat on a very expensive HIGHCHAIR that his own pure white father and mother could not afford, which the pure white IMBECILES (disproportionately but not exclusively pure white) who sat before him could not, and did not buy, and the pure white RACIST bastard Judged SINNERS – **John 8:7, Matthew 7:1-6.**

Karen Kwamboka: "Treating your irreconcilable enemy with respect is striking soft in a battle." Dr Samuel Johnson (1709-1784) paraphrased

BEDFORD, ENGLAND: Pure White Poly-educated son of a relatively poor man, albeit England's Class Senior District Judge Paul Robert Ayers, alleged 33rd Degree Freemason (Scottish Rite), the archetypal pure white Englishman, and the Senior Vice President of the Association of Her Majesty's District Judges, your pure white ancestors were THIEVES – **Exodus 20:15, Habakkuk 2:6-9.**

Yinka Bamgbelu: Hereditary RACIST pure white bastards are more familiar with Negroes of Afro-Caribbean extraction, such as David Lammy, Diane Abbott, and their type, direct descendants of Stolen African Children (Plantation Negroes, who were unnaturally selected, genetically reversed, paired up, deliberately bed for hard labour by hereditary RACIST pure white bastards, albeit very highly civilised, ultra-righteous, and highly respected European Christians.

Facts are sacred and cannot be overstated.

Karen Kwamboka: "You have enemies? Good. That means you've stood up for something, sometime in your life." Sir Winston Churchill (1874-1965).

THEY ARE OUR IMMORTAL ENEMIES: OUR POSITIONS ARE ABSOLUTELY IRRECONCILABLE.

Racial Hatred: The most important part of RACIAL HATRED is Racist Lies guarded by Racist Judges. Persecutory Negrophobia guarded by Negrophobic Perjury – **Habakkuk 1:4.**

Yinka Bamgbelu: OYINBO OLE/ODE/BARAWO: BEDFORD, ENGLAND: GDC/NHS, Pure White Sue Gregory (OBE) our own Officer of the Most Excellent Order of our own Empire of Stolen Inheritance (**Exodus 20:15, Habakkuk 2:6-9**) unrelentingly lied under implied oath and on record. Pure White Senior Bedford's District Judge lied under oath (approved judgement) and on record – **Habakkuk 1:4.** Dark Black Constance Briscoe was JAILED for a lesser offence: Apartheid Law by Stealth. Facts are sacred and cannot be overstated.

OYINBO OLE/ODE/ BARAWO: Our brainless hereditary RACIST pure white bastard of our own Empire of Stolen Inheritance (**Exodus 20:15, Habakkuk 2:6-9**) ultra-righteously sat on the BONES of stolen children of defenceless poor people, including the African ancestors of the QUASI-MULATTO, impure White/impure Black, <43 % Nigerian, grandniece and grandnephew of the Duke of Edinburgh, and the opportunist RACIST pure white bastard, neck deep in inherited and personal sins - Judged SINNERS - **John 8:7,Matthew 7:1-6**:

Slimy Hypocrisy Ne Plus Ultra. Only He who has no sin has the moral right to Judge SINNERS – **John 5:22**.

Karen Kwamboka: Unlike PUTIN'S SIBERIA, there are no GAS FIELDS in bland, colourless, and almost lifeless Robert Hibbert (1769-1849) and Tommy Robinson's LUTON, and where the pure white mother and father of Pure White Bedford's District Judge Paul Robert Ayers, our Senior Vice President of the Association of Her Majesty's District Judges, were born.

Yinka Bamgbelu: Asymmetric Mutual Race Hate: They hate us, all of us, and they have unbounded and unaccountable power, and we know; we hate them more, all of them, and they know, but we are powerless and have been robbed to penniless since their armed ancestors found our defenceless ancestors in the African bush, in the 15th century. Institutional RACIAL HATRED in Great Britain is worse, by far worse, than RACIAL HATRED in North America.

Karen Kwamboka: Ti a ba ka eru, inu eru a ba je: If we tell you what we truly feel, the TRUTH, you will be very sad, and to bury TRUTHS, you have unbounded and uncountable powers to do RACIST EVIL with impunity.

"Those who have the power to do wrong with impunity seldom wait long for the will." Dr Samuel Johnson (1709-1784).

Yinka Bamgbelu: OYINBO OLE/ODE/BARAWO: BEDFORD, ENGLAND: Pure White Poly-educated son of a relatively poor man, albeit England's Class Senior District Judge Paul Robert Ayers, alleged 33rd Degree Freemason (Scottish Rite), the archetypal pure white Englishman, and the Senior Vice President of the Association of Her Majesty's District Judges, you are a pure white descendant of pure white THIEVES – **Exodus 20:15, Habakkuk 2:6-9,** because the pure white ancestors of your pure white father and mother were THIEVES and owners of stolen children of defenceless poor people (AFRICANS). It is absolutely impossible for your Christ-granted talent and yields of the land on which your own pure white mother and father were born. Unlike PUTIN'S RUSSIA, there are no oil wells or gas fields in Bedfordshire, and the very highly luxuriant soil of Bishop's Stortford yields only FOOD. Bishop's Stortford's Cecil Rhodes (1853-1902) was a RACIST pure white bastard and a very hardened PROFESSIONAL THIEF – **Exodus 20:15, Habakkuk 2:6-9.**

Karen Kwamboka: Ignorant RACIST descendants of THIEVES – **Exodus 20:15, Habakkuk 2:6-9**: Superior skin colour, and more superior accent: The collective haven for intellectually disfavoured pure white bastards (disproportionately but not exclusively pure white).

BEDFORD, ENGLAND: Pure White Poly-educated son of a relatively poor man, albeit England's Class Senior District Judge Paul Robert Ayers, alleged 33rd Degree Freemason (Scottish Rite), the archetypal pure white Englishman, and the Senior Vice President of the Association of Her Majesty's District Judges, it is not the TRUTH that daily dialogues with pure white IMBECILES (disproportionately but not exclusively pure white) is a proper Job that is worthwhile and manly, albeit within one of the dullest adult populations in the industrialised world (OECD).

Yinka Bamgbelu: "British Justice is RACIST and should not be trusted by ethnic minorities." An expert of their law (**Luke 11:52**), a Quasi-Mulatto (impure Black/impure white) direct descendant of plantation Negroes (Stolen African Children, Peter Herbert (OBE), our own Officer of the Most Excellent Order of our own Empire of Stolen Inheritance – **Exodus 20:15, Habakkuk 2:6-9.**

Karen Kwamboka: I do not believe that there is a part of their waste of money FISH AND CHIPS JUSTICE SYSTEM that is not RACIST; no part of their SHIT is good, not even one – **Psalm 53.** Theirs is not an apple with a few worms, theirs is an irreparably FU*KED ball of worms. Devils cannot cast out demons: **Matthew 12:27.**

Yinka Bamgbelu: Reporting a pure white Mason crooked bastard to a pure white crooked Mason Bastard Judge is a barren exercise: Integrity, friendship, respect, and charity: All for one, and one for all. Their people are everywhere, in their GODFORSAKEN RACIST HELL HOLE, and they control almost everything, including RACIAL HATRED and FRAUD - **Habakkuk 1:4.**

Karen Kwamboka: CIVILISATION ERASURE. The pure white ancestors of their pure white mother and father were THIEVES – **Exodus 20:15, Habakkuk 2:6-9**, and their civilisation was essentially based on STEALING. 1824-1832, extremely nasty genocidal pure white bastards killed plenty of Native Tasmanians (>97% were unlawfully killed, under God's Law – Exodus 2013). In 1833, greedy RACIST pure white bastards shared STOLEN MONEY (yields of millions of stolen and destroyed lives of stolen children of defenceless poor Africans), among scores of thousands of EVIL RACIST pure white bastards. They hate us, and they are very powerful; we hate them more, but we are powerless: UNBALANCED MUTUAL RACE HATE.

Yinka Bamgbelu: Ignorant RACIST descendants of THIEVES. The fellow is who He says He is – **John 14:6.** Reasoning and vision do not have finite boundaries. **John 14:26:** Supernatural exists and it is consistently accessible to those who stand where it can come. If we disclose TRUTHS to them, they will be VERY AFRAID, and when they are frightened, they are VERY DANGEROUS.

Karen Kwamboka: The fellow was kidnapped and killed only because He spoke, and He was not punished for speaking, but was killed solely to prevent Him from speaking – **Matthew 27:32-56.**

"Freedom of Expression is a basic right." Lady Hale

"There is not a truth existing which I fear or would wish unknown to the whole world." President Thomas Jefferson (1743-1826).

Yinka Bamgbelu: "Freedom of expression is the cornerstone of our democracy." Pure White, Eton and Oxbridge-educated Very Rich Man's Son (**Mark 10:25**), Lord Jacob Rees-Mogg.

A nrin nile, inu nbi elesin: A njefo sun, inu nbi eleran. Mo kuku ti ri omo Oba to di eru ri, mo si tun ti ri iwofa to di alaso. They hate us, and we know.

Karen Kwamboka: Their Country is SHIT, they are worse than SHIT, and they know.

BEDFORD, ENGLAND: District Judge, our ignorant hereditary RACIST descendant of PURE WHITE THIEVES – **Exodus 20:15, Habakkuk 2:6-9,** let me tell you, it is not the TRUTH that daily dialogues with pure white IMBECILES (predominantly but not exclusively pure white) is a proper job that is worthwhile and manly.

OYINBO OLE/ODE/BARAWO: "They may not have been well written from a grammatical point of view but I am confident I had not forgotten any of the facts." Pure White Geraint Evans, England's Class Welsh Postgraduate Tutor, Oxford.

Yinka Bamgbelu: Our own NIGERIAN BABIES with gigantic oil wells and gas fields near their huts eat only 1.5/day in our own NIGERIA, a verifiable functional semi-illiterate hereditary RACIST pure white bastard, a mere former debt-collector Solicitor in NORWICH (5th Rate Partner) whose pure white father and mother have never seen CRUDE OIL, and whose pure white ancestors, including John Foster (1759-1832) of Brickhill, Bedford, were fed like battery hens with gigantic yields of millions of stolen and destroyed children of defenceless poor people, including the AFRICAN ANCESTORS of the Quasi-

Mulatto, impure White/impure Black, <43% Nigerian, grandchildren of HRH, King Charles.

Karen Kwamboka: Unlike PUTIN'S RUSSIA, there are no oil wells or gas fields in bland, colourless, and almost lifeless Freemasons' Bedfordshire, and the very highly luxuriant soil of Bishop's Stortford yields only FOOD. Bishop's Stortford's Cecil Rhodes (1853-1902) was a RACIST pure white bastard and a very hardened highly respected PROFESSIONAL THIEF – **Exodus 20:15.**

Yinka Bamgbelu: Their hairs stand on end when they are challenged by self-educated NIGERIANS, we and our type are the ones hereditary RACIST pure white bastards (predominantly but not exclusively pure white) would beat up without the support of the YANKS.

Karen Kwamboka: ICE: Half-educated school dropouts, pure white RACIST bastards (predominantly but not exclusively pure), mere GED, and their type, who desire a world where substance is subservient to superfluous and where universally acknowledged irrefutably SUPERIOR SKIN COLOUR that the very fortunate wearer neither made nor chose, and their more superior accent when speaking their own language, which is wired to their highest centre, their spinal cords, not their brains.

Yinka Bamgbelu: "Agriculture not only gives riches to a nation, but the only one she can call her own." Dr Samuel Johnson (1709-1784).

Then, there was only subsistence feudal agriculture.

Gigantic yields of millions of stolen and destroyed AFRICAN CHILDREN, not feudal agriculture, lured JEWS to Great Britain.

Hereditary RACIST insatiably greedy pure white bastards shipped millions of GUNS to Africa in exchange for Cargoes of scores of thousands of stolen children of defenceless poor people. Ignorant RACIST pure white bastards weren't deterred by His Justice - **John 5:22, Matthew 25:31-46, Revelation 3:21**, because they did not believe in His exceptionalism – **John 14:6.**

Karen Kwamboka: Our brainless hereditary RACIST pure white bastard. Our ultra-righteous descendant of pure white THIEVES, with an arbitrarily acquired camouflage English name. The only evidence of the self-awarded HIGHER IQ of the opportunist RACIST pure white bastard is the HUGE STOLEN INHERITANCE that his thoroughly wretched pure white ancestors crossed the English Channel, not that long ago, without luggage or decent shoes, to latch onto – **Habakkuk 2:6-9.**

Yinka Bamgbelu: Devils cannot cast out demons – **Matthew 12:27.**

"Those who have robbed have also lied." Dr Samuel Johnson (1709-1784).

Based on available evidence, Police Officers, not all, are LIARS. Hereditary pure white supremacist Freemason Bastard Judges (predominantly but not exclusively pure white), ultra-righteous descendants of THIEVES (BARAWO), Jailed Constance Briscoe for lying to descendants of CLOSETED RACIST LIARS, THIEVES, and owners of her direct ancestors: Reductio ad absurdum.

Psalm 116:11: "Lies are told all the time." Sir Michael Havers (1923-1932), Attorney General, 1980.

Karen Kwamboka: OYINBO OLE/ODE/BARAWO: BEDFORD, ENGLAND: Based on cogent, irrefutable, and available evidence, Pure White Freemason, Brother Senior District Judge unrelentingly lied under oath (approved Judgement) on record - **Habakkuk 1:4.** GDC: Pure White Freemason, Brother Richard William Hill fabricated reports and unrelentingly lied under oath and on record. GDC, Sue Gregory (OBE) our own Officer of the Most Excellent Order of our own Empire of STOLEN INHERITANCE, gigantic yields of several continuous centuries of ancestral theft - **Exodus 20:15, Habakkuk 2:6-9**), alleged genetic LITHUANIAN JEW, unrelentingly lied under implied oath and on record – **Habakkuk 1:4**. The pure white ancestors of her pure white father and mother and father were THIEVES: They were incompetent RACIST LIARS too, professional armed robbers, armed land grabbers, and owners of stolen of children of defenceless poor people, including the African ancestors of the QUASI-MULATTO, impure White/impure Black, 43% Nigeria, Duchess of Sussex, the grand-daughter-in law of the Duke of Edinburgh of Blessed Memory, Prince Phillip (1921-2021).

Philippians 1:21: Phillip was a 33rd Degree Freemason, Scottish Rite. Facts are sacred and cannot be overstated.

Yinka Bamgbelu: BEDFORD, ENGLAND: Pure White Poly-educated son of a relatively poor man, albeit England's Class Senior District Judge Paul Robert Ayers, alleged 33rd Degree Freemason (Scottish Rite), the archetypal pure white Englishman, and the Senior Vice President of the Association of Her Majesty's District Judges,, immodesty apart, and sincere immodesty is sincerer than insincere modesty, I am overwhelmingly intellectually DOMINANT, I shall prove it by using cogent facts and irrefutable evidence to irreparably destroy you and your Fish and Chips Justice System. You are PURIFIED SHIT. Your pure white ancestors were THIEVES – **Exodus 20:15, Habakkuk 2:6-9.** Facts are sacred and cannot be overstated.

Karen Kwamboka: NORTHAMPTONSHIRE ENGLAND: Pure White Senior NHS Nurse, Rachael Bishop unrelentingly lied under oath and on record – Habakkuk 1:4. Had she been BLACK, or had the Judges been BLACK, she would have been in trouble. Constance Briscoe was JAILED for a lesser offence.

"Michael Jackson would have been found guilty if he'd been black." Jo Brand

Yinka Bamgbelu: "Saving for retirement would soon be irrelevant." Elon Musk, a closeted white supremacist beneficiary of Apartheid.

BRAINLESS NONSENSE.

Because everywhere will soon be NUCLEAR ASH.

Hereditary white supremacist pure white bastard whose ancestors emigrated to SOUTH AFRICA, uninvited, and without luggage or decent shoes, and whose passports were European made GUNS, and their Visas were European made BULLETS. Lecherous pure white bastards.

Karen Kwamboka: **Habakkuk 1:4:** Freemasons' Ritualists' Racist Administration of their law - **Revelation 21:8:** Constance Briscoe was JAILED for a lesser offence

Mediocre GDC, ENCOUNTERS: A NEGRO'S TRUE STORY. Thuggery is not law -Abiodun Olayinka Bamgbelu

Yinka Bamgbelu: Matthew 26:59-60: GDC hired Racist Liars. **Revelation 21:8**: If RACIST GDC could disprove the truth, which is that pure white British Soldier, Stephanie Twidale (TD) unrelenting lied under oath and on record, it will confirm that a RACIST CROOK was not hired – **Habakkuk 1:4.**

Karen Kwamboka: You are an opportunist pure white RACIST CRIMINAL; I have evidence. The mind that I did not choose is FINER than your unashamedly mediocre waste of Money FISH and CHIPS Justice System, and I have the POWER to use cogent facts and irreversibly evidence to irreparably destroy you and your MEDIOCRE PURE WHITE SHIT – **Habakkuk 1:4.** Supernatural exists and it is consistently accessible to those who stand where it can come – **John 14:26.** Their indiscreetly corrupt Justice system that is overseen by the Freemasons, essentially, for the benefit of pure white people (disproportionately but not exclusively pure white). They hate us, and we know.

Yinka Bamgbelu: The hereditary RACIST pure white bastard, albeit Bedford's Class Senior District Judge, was obsessed with me. He should fu*king stay here; it is safer than NIGERIA - **Exodus 21:23-27.**

Had the opportunist RACIST pure white bastard not been our Senior District Judge in BEDFORD, one wouldn't know him. What can a functional semi-illiterate opportunist RACIST pure white bastard, a poly-educated pure white son of pure white plebeian nobodies – have that self-educated NIGERIANS would voluntarily buy?

Karen Kwamboka: Hereditary RACIST pure white bastards. Spineless Wimps. Trump's Poodles. Delusional Grandeur of the Stolen Past. A mere 5th Rate Military Power impersonates a SUPERPOWER. If hereditary RACIST pure white bastards are as BRAVE as they vulgarly brag, they MUST DIRECTLY, not through gullible proxies, use GUNS to evict Putin from Mariupol, he stole it with GUNS – **Exodus 20:15**

Yinka Bamgbelu: Which part of HEREDITARY RACIAL HATRED is the administration of English Law – **Habakkuk 1:4**?

BEDFORD, ENGLAND: Based on available evidence, Pure White Poly-educated son of a relatively poor man, albeit England's Class Senior District Judge Paul Robert Ayers, alleged 33rd Degree Freemason (Scottish Rite), the archetypal pure white Englishman, and the Senior Vice President of the Association of Her Majesty's District Judges, lied under oath (approved Judgement). GDC: Sue Gregory (OBE) lied on record. GDC: Mason, Richard Hill fabricated reports and lied under oath. Constance Briscoe was JAILED for a lesser offence. Facts are sacred and cannot be overstated.

Karen Kwamboka: Exodus 21:23-27: In our own NIGERIA, in our own shit hole AFRICA, the probability that hereditary RACIST pure white bastards would be found and fed bullets is greater than minus 100% (> - 100%).

"We shall deal with the racist bastards when we get out of prison." Comrade Robert Mugabe (1924-2019).

Yinka Bamgbelu: Apartheid Law: One Rule for Pure Whites, and another Rule for all others. GDC: British Soldier, Stephanie Twidale (TD) unrelentingly lied under oath and on record – **Habakkuk 1:4**.

Karen Kwamboka: Psalm 116:11: "Lies are told all the time." Sir Michael Havers (1923-1992), QC. Dark Black Constance Briscoe is not the only incompetent LIAR in Great Britain, but she was JAILED for a lesser offence.

Yinka Bamgbelu: Our Poly-educated, unashamedly functional semi-illiterate pure white rubbish of our own Empire of Stolen Inheritance – **Exodus 20:15, Habakkuk 2:6-9,** and a hereditary RACIST pure white son of a pure white plebeian hoe ultra-righteously sat on the BONES of stolen African children, more BONES than the millions of skulls at the doorstep of Pol Pot (1925-1998), and the ignorant opportunist RACIST descendant of ULTRA-RIGHTEOUS RACIST THIEVES Judged SINNERS – **John 8:7, Matthew 7:1-6.**

Karen Kwamboka; Immodesty apart: Sincere immodesty is sincerer than insincere modesty. Bedford's Freemason Senior District Judge, albeit England's Class, I am overwhelmingly intellectually dominant, and I know, and I have the power to use facts and evidence to absolutely irreparably destroy you and your indiscreetly crooked, unashamedly MEDIOCRE, vindictive, potently weaponised, and institutionally RACIST waste of money fish and chips Justice System that you serve: No brain. Poor natural resources. Several centuries of stealing and slavery preceded their huge stolen inheritance (gigantic yields of several continuous centuries of ancestral theft – **Exodus 20:15, Habakkuk 2:6-9**: OYINBO OLE/ODE/BARAWO.

Yinka Bamgbelu: White Privilege is Apartheid by Stealth:

"Negro is a stage in the slow evolution from monkeys to man." Dr Frantz Fanon (1925-1961).

Karen Kwamboka: 1967: Six Days War.

2026: In the same position as the UKRAINE, but without the support of the YANKS, Great Britain will surrender within 6/7.

"Could you face the Russians by yourselves?" President Trump.

1940: Without the support of the YANKS, France surrendered within 6/52.

Yinka Bamgbelu: Hereditary RACIST pure white bastards should fu*king fu*k off. They should fu*king stay here; it is safer than NIGERIA. A tooth for a tooth: **Exodus 21:23-27**. Let me tell you, based on several decades of very proximate observations and direct experiences, your Country is SHIT, and you are worse than SHIT. Perception is grander than reality.

Karen Kwamboka: They hate us, and we know. Philosophy is not the remedy if a Negro is cornered in an alley by dozens of pure white supremacist bastards - with cricket bats in their hands.

"The white man is the devil." Elijah Mohammad (1897-1975).

'Why, Sir; to be sure when you wish a man to have that belief which you think is of infinite advantage, you wish well to him, but your primary consideration is your own quiet. If a madman were to come into this room with a stick in his hand, no doubt we should pity the state of his mind; but our primary consideration would be to take care of ourselves. We should knock him down first, and pity him afterwards." Dr Samuel Johnson (1709-1784).

Yinka Bamgbelu: "We are no longer your monkeys." Patrice Lumumba (1925-1961).

Patrice Lumumba, Steve Biko, Jamal Khashoggi, John (**Matthew 14**), and Christ (**Matthew 27:32-56**), were killed solely to prevent them from speaking.

"Where the press is free and every man is able to read, all is safe." President Thomas Jefferson (1743-1826).

Karen Kwamboka: An ignorant poly-educated pure white RACIST son of a pure white plebeian hoe. A mere former debt-collector Solicitor in NORWICH. Hereditary RACIST pure white bastards love fighting, and AFRICANS are their preferred opponents. If hereditary RACIST pure white bastards are as BRAVE, as they vulgarly brag, they must DIRECTLY use GUNS to evict PUTIN from Crimea, he stole it with GUNS - **Exodus 20:15.**

Yinka Bamgbelu: Our grossly overrated pure white rubbish of our own Empire of Stolen Inheritance – **Exodus 20:15, Habakkuk 2:6-9**. Superior pure white skin colour, a gigantic stolen inheritance, and what else? Before Slavery, what?

Karen Kwamboka: Of course, the stereotypical Negur is a LUNATIC.

OXFORD, ENGLAND: GDC, British Soldier, Stephanie Twidale (TD) unrelentingly lied under oath and on record – **Habakkuk 1:4**.

They are a properly organised GANG of Racist Criminals, and the administration of their law is a weapon of RACE WAR.

The Negro, from shit hole AFRICA, must be a LUNATIC because a pure white British Soldier can never be a RACIST CRIMINAL.

Yinka Bamgbelu: An ignorant descendant of ultra-righteous pure white THIEVES. "He has refused to submit to a medical examination." Lord Justice Haddon-Cave, KC.

A scatter-head hereditary RACIST PURE WHITE BASTARD. A direct descendant of THIEVES, armed land grabbers (**Habakkuk 2:6-9, Exodus 20:15**). His direct ancestors, genocidal pure white racist bastards – directly or indirectly killed >97% Native Tasmanians.

Karen Kwamboka: Our grossly overrated hereditary RACIST pure white bastard of our own Empire of Stolen Inheritance - **Habakkuk 2:6-9, Exodus 20:15,** was granted the platform to display hereditary PREJUDICE. The most important part of the matter is MONEY, and it is not yours. Unlike PUTIN'S SIBERIA, there are no gas fields in Bishop's Stortford. The highly luxuriant soil of Bishop's Stortford yields only FOOD. Bishop's Stortford's Cecil Rhodes (1853-1902) was a pure white RACIST BASTARD and a Professional Armed Robber.

Yinka Bamgbelu: Hereditary RACIST pure white bastards dress up RACIAL HATRED and INTERRACIAL ENVY, the evilest combination, and they call RACIST EVIL impartial, colour-blind, and competent administration of English Law - **Habakkuk 1:4.**

Karen Kwamboka: Ignorant descendants of ultra-righteous pure white professional armed robbers. Hereditary RACIST pure white bastards love fighting, and AFRICANS are their preferred opponents. If hereditary RACIST pure white bastards are as BRAVE, as they vulgarly brag, they must DIRECTLY use GUNS to evict PUTIN from Crimea, he stole it with GUNS - **Exodus 20:15.**

Yinka Bamgbelu: We do not believe in any part of your laws, but we are bound by them. We do not believe that hereditary RACIST descendants of THIEVES and owners of stolen children of defenceless poor people have the MORAL RIGHT to Judge sinners – **Matthew 7:1-6, John 8:7**, while sitting on THRONES of Bones of stolen children of poor people– **Revelation 3:21.**

Karen Kwamboka: BEDFORD, ENGLAND: District Judge, our very, very, very, highly respected, poly-educated, hereditary RACIST, unashamedly functional semi-illiterate, a properly schooled impostor, a deceptive expert of their law (**Luke 11:52**), and a waste of money FAKE JUDGE – **Habakkuk 1:4**, it is absolutely impossible for you and your own pure white kindred, including Richard Hill, to COMPETE on a colour-blind level intellectual playing field without resorting to RACIST CRIMINALITY. You are an INFERIOR creation of Almighty God; we shall prove it.

Yinka Bamgbelu: Our brainless hereditary RACIST pure white bastard of our own Empire of Stolen Inheritance – **Habakkuk 2:6-9, Exodus 20:15,** if you were not a Judge, apart from being a POLITICIAN, what else could you do? 1976-2022: Our brainless hereditary RACIST pure white bastard, having FAILED in Legal Practice, loads did, our hereditary RACIST pure white bastard parked his liability at the public till, and sold MEDIOCRITY and confusion to the undiscerning in exchange for very valuable consideration – QUASI-COMMUNISM.

Karen Kwamboka: IRREVERSIBLE CIVILISATION ERASURE: Their indiscreetly crooked, VINDICTIVE, unashamedly mediocre, potently weaponised, and institutionally RACIST Justice System is FU*KED, irreparably FU*KED, as it has foreseeably succumbed to INCEST, weakening of the common genetic pool, and associated physical and mental wonkiness, and hereditary white supremacist Freemason Judges, and others, who make loads of MONEY from unashamed mediocrity and confusion prop SHIT UP: Conflict of interest.

"A government that robs Peter to pay Paul can always depend on the support of Paul." George Bernard Shaw (1856-1950).

Yinka Bamgbelu: Castrate violent rapists – Giorgia Meloni. Castrate all IMBECILES, including hereditary white supremacist pure white Freemason Judges. Enduring Residues of Historical Power Imbalance: Asymmetric Mutual Race Hate: Then, on Cane/Cotton/Tobacco Plantations, Negroes who non-violently bedded devout Christian seductress, libidinous pure white European women, were violently castrated with very sharp knives

"The white man is the devil." Khalid Abdul Mohammad (1948-2001).

Karen Kwamboka: Norman Tebbit (1931-2025): Cricket Test. Millions of Ukrainians dodged the draft. Motivation is the most important part of close contact violence. Why should Negroes fight and die for the continuing propagation of a RACIST JUSTICE SYSTEM that treats one race superior and another inferior?

Yinka Bamgbelu: Homogeneity in the administration of their law is a very potent weapon of RACE WAR – **Habakkuk 1:4.**

Unapologetic hereditary white supremacist pure white bastard: Homogeneity in the administration of their LAW is a very potent weapon of WAR, A LATENT, BUT RAGING RACE WAR.

Karen Kwamboka: Kamala Harris did not say that Trump's administration packed courts with functional semi-illiterate pure white Freemason Judges – **Habakkuk 1:4.**

IRRECONCILABLE MUTUAL RACE HATE: They hate us, and they are very POWERFUL, and we know. We hate them more, but we are POWERLESS, and they know.

CHAPTER FOUR

Yinka Bamgbelu: True feelings rarely disclose true intentions, so shun display. They hate us, and we know.

Their Country is SHIT, and they are worse than SHIT, and their people, not all, are absolutely worthless, certainly intellectually (OECD).

"To disagree with three-fourths of the British public on all points is one of the first requisites of sanity, one of the deepest consolations in all moments of spiritual doubt." Wilde (1854-1900).

Karen Kwamboka: Pure White Racist Senior District Judge Paul Robert Ayers, albeit Bedford's Class, the BRAIN that you inherited from your pure white father and mother is BAD.

Their properly organised Masons' Crime Syndicate Criminally Impersonates the Competent Impartial Administration of English Law – **Habakkuk 1:4.**

Yinka Bamgbelu: To survive, even pure white Freemason Judges (disproportionately but not exclusively pure white) must tell stories (INCOMPETENT LIES OR DECAYING LIES - WILDE). Evil RACIST pure white bastards ((disproportionately but not exclusively pure white) always lie that they don't lie - **Psalm 144.**

"To survive, you must tell stories." Umberto Eco (1932-2016).

Karen Kwamboka: Their Country is SHIT, and they are worse than SHIT, and they know, but they don't know that we know too.

Yinka Bamgbelu: Those who nearly passed or just passed the A/Level could do law in Great Britain, one of the dullest adult populations in the industrialised world (OECD). Their Godforsaken RACIST HELL HOLE Shit Country where a poly-educated son of plebeian nobodies, a mere former debt-collector Solicitor, was a Senior District Judge, albeit Bedford's Class.

Karen Kwamba: It is possible to pay the Taliban, but only God Almighty can defeat the Taliban.

"We cannot defeat the Taliban by force. We must negotiate with them" Pervez Musharraf (1943-2023).

Yinka Bamgbelu: Delusional grandeur of the Stolen Past: A 5th Rate Military Power Impersonates a SUPERPOWER. The quality of the average human being in their Godforsaken Racist Hell Hole Shit Country is very poor, so a crooked hereditary RACIST pure white bastard was a soldier, Stephanie Twidale (TD).

Karen Kwamboka: OXFORD, ENGLAND: Pure White British Soldier, Stephanie Twidale (TD), unrelentingly lied under oath and on record - **Habakkuk 1:4**. Dark Black, Quasi-Mulatto (impure Black), Constance Briscoe was JAILED for a lesser offence: APARTHEID LAW. Facts are sacred and cannot be overstated.

Yinka Bamgbelu: BEDFORD, ENGLAND: Pure White Racist Senior District Judge Paul Robert Ayers, albeit Bedford's Class, our brainless hereditary RACIST pure white bastard ultra-righteously sat on the BONES of stolen children of defenceless poor people, including the African ancestors of the Mulatto Duchess of Sussex (43% Nigerian), and more BONES than the millions of skulls at the doorstep of Pol Pot (1925-1998), and JUDGED Sinners – **John 8:7, Matthew 7:1-6.** Only SAINTS have the Moral Right to Judge Sinners, direct descendants of THIEVES and owners of stolen and destroyed children of defenceless poor people do not have the Moral Right to Judge Sinners, especially when equitable, fair, and just REPARATION pends, and several centuries of unpaid interest accrue – **John 5:22.**

Karen Kwamboka: Psalm 53: No one is good, not even one. "Every saint has a past, and every sinner has a future" Wilde (1854-1900).

BEDFORD, ENGLAND: Based on cogent, irrefutable, and available evidence, Pure White Racist Senior District Judge Paul Robert Ayers, albeit Bedford's Class, unrelentingly LIED under oath and on record (Approved Judgement).

Facts are sacred: "The truth allows no choice." Dr Samuel Johnson (1709-1784).

Yinka Bamgbelu: Pure White Britons (predominantly but not exclusively pure white), not all, are bullies. President Trump, a genetic Briton, bullies BRITAIN because Britain is relatively economically and militarily impotent. **Leviticus 19:33-34:** Britons bully NIGERIANS because they know that Nigeria is economically and militarily impotent.

Karen Kwamboka: RACIST descendants of THIEVES and owners of stolen lives: Skin colour that they neither made nor chose is universally acknowledged to be irrefutably SUPERIOR, and their accent when speaking their own language is by far SUPERIOR than ours, but their intellects are not, are their indiscreetly crooked, vindictive, potently weaponised, unashamedly MEDIOCRE, and institutionally RACIST waste of money fish and chips Justice System is fundamentally designed to conceal that TRUTH – **Habakkuk 1:4.** Facts are sacred and cannot be overstated.

Yinka Bamgbelu: BEDFORD, ENGLAND: Senior District Judge Paul Robert Ayers, Sue Gregory (OBE), and Richard William Hill, Mason, fabricated reports, and/or lied under oath, including approved Judgements, and/or on record – **Habakkuk 1:4**. They were all PURE WHITE opportunist racist crooked bastards.

Karen Kwamboka: Matthew 12:27: Devils cannot cast out demons. Ignorant hereditary RACIST pure white bastards (predominantly but not exclusively pure white) are WORSE bullies than Trump. Opportunist RACIST pure white bastards (predominantly but not exclusively pure white) want us to defend ourselves against pure white RACIST crooked bastards before pure white Racist crooked bastard Freemason Judges – **Habakkuk 1:4.**

Yinka Bamgbelu: They hate us, and we know.

BEDFORD, ENGLAND: Pure White Senior District Judge Paul Robert Ayers, our brainless hereditary RACIST pure white bastard of our own Empire of STOLEN INHERITANCE - **Exodus 20:15, Habakkuk 2:6-9**. Unlike PUTIN'S SIBERIA, there are no gas fields in MASONS' Kempston, the land on which his mother and father were born yields only FOOD, he is verifiably a functional semi-illiterate, he is relatively very rich, and he dishonestly implied that he did not know that the pure white ancestors of his pure white father and mother were THIEVES and ultra-righteous Christian owners of stolen children of defenceless poor people, including the African ancestors of the Quasi-Mulatto (impure White/impure Black, < 43% Nigerian) grandniece and grandnephew of Major Andrew Mountbatten Windsor.

Karen Kwamboka: PURE WHITE RACIST KILLERS – **EXODUS 20:13**: Our own Nigerian Brother, Dr Richard Bamgboye, only 56, a General Medical Practitioner, and Indian, Dr Anand Kamath, only 42, a Dentist, came to Great Britain for Better Lives, but Evil RACIST BASTARDS sent them to infinite afterlife: Intolerant RACIST BASTARDS killed foreigners who disagreed with them, albeit hands-off – **Leviticus 19:33-34**; they must stay here because it is safer than NIGERIA. Anand and Richard were unlawfully KILLED, albeit hands-off. They did not deserve to die, and they did not want to die; They were overwhelmed with RACIST LIES, and Judges were in the loop.

"The white man is the devil." Elijah Mohammad (1897-1975).

Yinka Bamgbelu: "Those who have the power to do wrong with impunity seldom wait long for the will." Dr Samuel Johnson (1709-1784).

In a UNIPOLAR WORLD, the Yanks are free to steal whatever they want from wherever they choose. Pure White European Christians stole North America, Australia, and New Zealand - **Exodus 20:15.**

Karen Kwamboka: Maafa (1445-1888): Double Victimhood: Slavery decommissioned natural selection, reversed progressive evolution, and made it possible for millions of IMBECILES to retrogressively breed scores of millions of IMBECILES, and imbeciles oppress descendants of the robbed with yields of the robbery.

Yinka Bamgbelu: Trump has the POWER to bully Great Britain, but he will not, not only because he is a genetic Briton, but more out of pity, as a dying sheep cannot savage the dominant military and economic power on earth – Denis Healey (1917-2015) paraphrased.

"Canadians are growing increasingly concerned that they might face a future invasion by the United States. New polling revealed that a third of Canadians think Washington may attempt 'direct action' to take control of Canada." News

Karen Kwamboka: Exodus 20:15: Is stealing from others what others stole from others stealing? The Season of Armed Land Grab, **Ecclesiastes 3:1-8:** Britain and France stole CANADA from the Natives. There is nothing new under the GOD'S SUN. Britain and France do not have the Military and Economic Power to deter the YANKS from stealing CANADA and GREENLAND.

Yinka Bamgbelu: Very Dull Pure White Europeans, RACIST direct descendants of ultra-righteous CHRISTIAN THIEVES (**Exodus 20:15, Habakkuk 2: 6-9**) and owners of stolen children, including the African ancestors of the Duchess of Sussex, fought a Proxy War in Ukraine, with their HEARTS not their HEADS, and they are weaker and poorer.

Karen Kwamboka: "England: About thirty million, mostly fools." Thomas Carlyle (1795-1881).

IMBECILES, decorticate RACIST bastards, persecute our own people, self-educated Nigerians, from shit hole Africa, for the BLACKNESS that we neither made nor chose (Negurs did not choose BLACK).

Yinka Bamgbelu: "The supreme vice is shallowness." Wilde (1854-1900). Brainless hereditary RACIST shallow pure white bastards (predominantly but not exclusively pure white) see molecules, and they destroy all self-educated NIGERIANS, from shit hole Africa, who see quarks.

Karen Kwamboka: Ignorant one-dimensionally educated opportunist RACIST pure white FOOLS (predominantly but not exclusively pure white), ultra-righteous, very highly civilised, and super-enlightened descendants of PURE WHITE THIEVES and owners of stolen and destroyed lives – **Exodus 20:15, Habakkuk 2:6-9**. Crooked Racist Bastards Love their SUPERIOR SKIN COLOUR, but they hate freedom of expression because they don't want their own mentally gentler white children (OECD) and the pure white IMBECILES they shepherd (predominantly but not exclusively pure white) to know the truth, which is that only their universally acknowledged irrefutably superior skin colour and God Almighty, not Christ, are truly good. Facts are sacred and cannot be overstated.

Yinka Bamgbelu: Jeremiah 17:9: European Powers hate Trump, and he knows: Realism overrides absolute distaste.

THE RACIST TYRANNY OF PURE WHITE MAJORITY.

BEDFORD, ENGLAND: Pure White Senior District Judge Paul Ayers, Pure White Sue Gregory (OBE), and Pure White Mason, Richard Hill, fabricated reports and/or lied under oath and/or on record. Dark Black Constance Briscoe was JAILED for a lesser offence. Facts are sacred and cannot be overstated.

Karen Kwamboka: TRUMP'S POODLES. HEREDITARY RACIST PAPER TIGERS. PERCEPTION IS GRANDER THAN REALITY. A FIFTH RATE MILITARY POWER IMPERSONATES A SUPERPOWER: DELUSIONAL GRANDEUR OF THE STOLEN PAST - **EXODUS 20:15, HABAKKUK 2:6-9.**

Yinka Bamgbelu: Their hairs stand on end when they are challenged by self-educated NIGERIANS, from shit hole AFRICA. We and our type are the ones hereditary RACIST pure white bastards (predominantly but not exclusively pure white) would beat up without the support of the YANKS. If hereditary RACIST pure white bastards (predominantly but not exclusively pure white) are as ethical, and as brave, as they vulgarly brag, they must DIRECTLY, not through proxies, use extreme overwhelming violence to evict PUTIN from Crimea, he used extreme overwhelming violence to convert Bakhmut and Avdiivka from Bricks to RUBBLE and stole them – **Exodus 20:15.**

Karen Kwamboka: SLIMY HYPOCRISY: THE SERENGETI OF IMBECILES. RETROGRESSIVE EVOLUTION DRIVEN BY UNNATURAL SELECTION.

His superior pure white skin concealed his inferior dark black brain. His spinal cord is his highest centre. He is worthy only because he is pure white, and he is RICH only because the pure white ancestors of his pure white father and mother were THIEVES and owners of stolen lives – **Exodus 20:15, Habakkuk 2:6-9.**

Yinka Bamgbelu: Hereditary RACIST pure white bastards: Unearned and undeserved STOLEN POWERS (USURPED) mask hereditary intellectual impotence. No brain. Poor natural resources. Several centuries of stealing and SLAVERY preceded their huge stolen inheritance – **Exodus 20:15, Habakkuk 2:6-9.**

Karen Kwamboka: Facts are sacred and cannot be overstated: "The truth allows no choice." Dr Samuel Johnson.

BEDFORD, ENGLAND: GDC, Pure White Sue Gregory (OBE) our own Officer of the Most Excellent Order of our own Empire of Stolen Inheritance - **Exodus 20:15, Habakkuk 2:6-9**, unrelentingly lied under implied oath and on record – **Habakkuk 1:4.** The pure white ancestors of her pure white father and mother were incompetent RACIST liars too, they were THIEVES and owners of stolen children of defenceless poor people, including the AFRICAN ancestors of the Quasi-Mulatto, impure White/impure Black, <43% Nigerian, grandchildren of HRH King Charles.

Facts are sacred and cannot be overstated: "Find the truth and tell it." Harold Pinter (1930-2008).

Yinka Bamgbelu: Dark Black Quasi-Mulatto Former Judge (impure Black Briton) Constance Briscoe was JAILED for lying to liars.

Psalm 116: 11: "Lies are told all the time." Sir Michael Havers (1923-1992), QC, Attorney General 1980.

Pure White Mason Judges and Police Officers, not all, are LIARS.

Pure White Mark Fuhrman, a mere half-educated school dropout GED, was a RACIST liar.

Not all liars are RACIST, but all RACISTS are malicious liars.

"I have seen evil, and it has the face of Mark Fuhrman." Johnnie Cochran (1937-2005).

Karen Kwamboka: 2021 CENSUS: London's population is only 37% White British, and only a very small fraction of the 37% is PURE WHITE. By 2100, if Great Britain is not a lifeless NUCLEAR ASH, Pure White Britons will be EXTINCT.

Yinka Bamgbelu: Their Godforsaken Racist Hell Hole is SHIT, and they are worse than SHIT, and they know.

Facts are sacred and cannot be overstated: "The truth allows no choice." Dr Samuel Johnson (1709-1784).

"They may not have been well written from a grammatical point of view but I am confident I had not forgotten any of the facts." Geraint Evans, England's Welsh Postgraduate Tutor, Oxford

Karen Kwamboka: BEDFORD, ENGLAND: Pure White Poly-educated son of a relatively poor man, albeit England's Class Senior District Judge Paul Robert Ayers, alleged 33rd Degree Freemason (Scottish Rite), the archetypal pure white Englishman, and the Senior Vice President of the Association of Her Majesty's District Judges, it is not the TRUTH that daily dialogues with pure white IMBECILES (predominantly but not exclusively pure white) is a proper job that is worthwhile and manly.

Yinka Bamgbelu: BEDFORD, ENGLAND: Pure White Poly-educated son of a relatively poor man, albeit England's Class Senior District Judge Paul Robert Ayers, alleged 33rd Degree Freemason (Scottish Rite), the archetypal pure white Englishman, and the Senior Vice President of the Association of Her Majesty's District Judges, Our well respected unashamedly functional semi-illiterate and opportunist RACIST pure white bastard of our own Empire of Stolen Inheritance - **Exodus 20:15, Habakkuk 2:6-9**. Respect, Friendship, Integrity, and Charity of white supremacist WOLVES in sheep's Clothing.

What is the value of the RESPECT of pure white imbeciles (predominantly but not exclusively pure white)?

Karen Kwamboka: “We shall forge a colour-blind society based on merit.” President Trump.

Our own people’s (self-educated Nigerians) sole purpose is to win, and we believe we can. If hereditary RACIST pure white bastards (predominantly but not exclusively pure white) constructively SURRENDER in colour-blind and measurable OPEN COMPETITIONS – by resorting to RACIST CRIMINALITY, it is a compliment, as their SURRENDER corroborates our belief, which is that they are INFERIOR HUMAN BEINGS: Sincere immodesty is sincerer than insincere modesty.

Sincerity is the prime attribute of Jesus - **John 14:6.**

The motley assembly of exotic faiths associated with the 15 Holy Books in the House of Commons is SATANIC MUMBO JUMBO.

“Jesus is the bedrock of my faith.” HM (1926-2022), the Defender of our own FAITH – **John 14:6**

Yinka Bamgbelu: ASYMMETRIC INTERRACIAL MUTUAL HATE: They hate us, and they are very powerful, and we know; we hate them. They are very sad because apart from our INFERIOR SKIN COLOUR, which we neither made nor chose, and our more inferior accent when speaking an alien language, we are also properly created by Almighty God.

Karen Kwamboka: Ignorant descendants of RACIST THIEVES and owners of stolen lives wanted to do RACIST EVIL, but they were not smart enough to do it seamlessly.

Yinka Bamgbelu: The quality of human beings in their Godforsaken Racist Hell Hole Shit Country is very poor, so SHIT PEOPLE get the top.

BEDFORD, ENGLAND: Senior District Judge Paul Robert Ayers, Sue Gregory (OBE), Richard William Hill (Mason), fabricated reports, and/or lied under oath, and/or lied on record. They were all pure white. Dark Black Constance Briscoe was JAILED for a lesser offence: Apartheid by Stealth. Facts are sacred and cannot be overstated.

Karen Kwamboka: BEDFORD, ENGLAND: Pure White Senior District Judge Paul Robert Ayers, immodesty apart, sincere immodesty is sincerer than insincere modesty, the self-educated NIGERIAN, from shithole Africa, is overwhelmingly intellectually dominant, and he knows, and he will prove it by using cogent facts and irrefutable evidence to irreparably destroy you and your unashamedly MEDIOCRE, vindictive, indiscreetly crooked, potently weaponised, and institutionally RACIST was of money fish and chips Justice System. Facts are sacred and cannot be overstated.

Yinka Bamgbelu: BEDFORD, ENGLAND: Pure White Senior District Judge Paul Robert Ayers, you are FROTH: Perception is grander than reality, had you been Black and 100X as smart, you will not be a Senior District Judge in Great Britain (PURE WHITE PRIVILEGE). You have a grossly exaggerated sense of self-worth.

Karen Kwamboka: INTERRACIAL ENVY: Pure White Racist Scammers (predominantly but not exclusively pure white) are very sad because the HELPER (**John 14:26**) has uncovered the centuries-old unspoken myth that Christ-granted talent is related to the universally acknowledged irrefutably superior skin colour that the very fortunate wearer neither made nor chose.

Yinka Bamgbelu: 1976-2022: Having FAILED in practice, loads did, our HEREDITARY RACIST pure white bastard parked his liability at the public till, firstly as an apprentice Judge (Deputy District Judge), 1992-2000, because the RACIST was not trusted, so he kept repeating the same class.

Karen Kwamboka: Evil RACIST pure white bastards (disproportionately but not exclusively pure white) are worse, by far worse, than TRUMP'S ICE. ICE evicts foreigners, and kills only very few; Racist bastards kill only FOREIGNERS, albeit hands-off, with the mens rea hidden in the belly of the actus reus.

Yinka Bamgbelu: Only God Almighty is truly good - **Mark 10:18**; He will balance all the unbalanced.

Ecclesiastes 3:1-8: It is their time to kill foreigners. One day it will be the season of foreigners to kill their people. Nigerian, Dr Richard Bamgboye, only 56, was unlawfully killed, albeit hands-off.

Karen Kwamboka: To compete and win, on colour-blind level intellectual playing field, RACIST PURE WHITE BASTARDS (predominantly but not exclusively pure white) must resort to RACIST CRIMINALITY, secure in the knowledge that all Judges will be PURE WHITE, and their hope is that they would be hereditary RACIST pure white bastards too – **Habakkuk 1:4.**

Yinka Bamgbelu: They hate us, and we know. **Psalm 116:11**: Did Constance

Briscoe Lie to Racist Liars? The quality of human beings, including Judges, in their Godforsaken Racist Hell Hole SHIT COUNTRY is very poor, so a pure white IMBECILE was a Senior Judge.

Karen Kwamboka: "I emphasis the point." Pure White Racist Senior District Judge Paul Robert Ayers, albeit Bedford's Class, our own Senior Vice President of the Association of Her Majesty's District Judges.

A PURE WHITE IMBECILE: A PURE WHITE ADULT WITH THE BASIC SKILLS OF A CHILD. THE TRUTH IS HOLY, AND REPETITIVE HOLINESS IS HOLIER.

Our brainless hereditary RACIST poor pure white bastard of our own Empire of Stolen Inheritance – **Exodus 20:15, Habakkuk 2:6-9.**

Yinka Bamgbelu: BEDFORD, ENGLAND: Pure White Senior District Judge Paul Robert Ayers, the quality of human beings in your Country is generally very poor, so functional semi-illiterate pure white bastards reach the top.

"The best opportunity of developing academically and emotional." Pure White Senior District Judge Paul Robert Ayers.

A PURE WHITE IMBECILE: A PURE WHITE ADULT WITH THE BASIC SKILLS OF A CHILD. FACTS ARE SACRED AND CANNOT BE OVERSTATED.

Superior pure white skin colour, a huge stolen inheritance, and what else?

"They may not have been well written from a grammatical point of view but I am confident I had not forgotten any of the fact." Pure White Welshman, Geraint Evans, England's Class Senior Postgraduate Tutor, Oxford.

A PURE WHITE IMBECILE: A PURE WHITE ADULT WITH THE BASIC SKILLS OF A CHILD.

Facts are sacred and cannot be overstated.

Karen Kwamboka: NIGERIAN BABIES with huge oil wells and gas fields near their huts eat only 1.5/day in our own shithole Africa, a functional semi-illiterate pure white bastard whose pure white father and mother have never seen CRUDE OIL was our Senior District Judge, albeit Bedford's Class. Unlike PUTIN'S SIBERIA, there are no gas fields in bland, colourless, and almost lifeless Freemasons' Kempston.

Yinka Bamgbelu: BEDFORD, ENGLAND: GDC, Sue Gregory (OBE), Officer of the Most Excellent Order of our Empire of Stolen Inheritance - **Exodus 20:15, Habakkuk 2:6-9,** unrelentingly lied under implied oath and on record – **Habakkuk 1:4**. Impure Black, but Dark Black Constance Briscoe was JAILED for a lesser offence.

Karen Kwamboka: If Pure White Bedford's Senior District Judge Paul Robert Ayers read his approved Judgement, he was a FOOL, and if he did not, he lied as he implied that he did – **Habakkuk 1:4**. The pure white ancestors of his pure white mother and father were incompetent RACIST LIARS too, they were THIEVES and owners of stolen children of defenceless poor people, including the Quasi-Mulatto, impure White/impure Black, <43% Nigerian, grandniece and grandnephew of the Duke of Edinburgh.

Yinka Bamgbelu: INDUSTRIAL-SCALE INCESTUOUS BREEDING: INTELLECTUAL DEGRADATION AT THE VERY TOP: THE HEAD IS ROTTEN, SO THE BODY IS DEAD.

Their indiscreetly crooked, VINDICTIVE, unashamedly mediocre, potently weaponised, and institutionally RACIST Waste of Money Fish and Chips Justice System is FU*KED, irreparably FU*KED, as it has irreparably succumbed to INCEST, weakening of their common genetic pool, and associated mental and/or physical wonkiness (intellectual degradation), and hereditary white supremacist Freemason Judges, and others, who make loads of money from unashamed mediocrity and confusion prop shit up.

Karen Kwamboka: No brain. Poor natural resources. Several centuries of stealing and slavery preceded their huge stolen inheritance - **Habakkuk.**

Yinka Bamgbelu: Gigantic yields of several continuous centuries of ancestral theft – **Exodus 20:15, Habakkuk 2:6-9.**

INDISCREET CONFLICT OF INTEREST: "A government that robs Peter to pay Paul can always depend on the support of Paul." George Bernard Shaw (1856-1950).

Karen Kwamboka: Our own Pure White Freemason Senior District Judge Paul Robert Ayers of our own Empire of STOLEN INHERITANCE- **Exodus 20:15, Habakkuk 2:6-9.** Our brainless hereditary RACIST pure white bastard, a mere poly-educated former debt-collector Solicitor NORWICH. Unlike Putin's Siberia, there are no gas in Bedfordshire and where his pure white mother and father were born.

Yinka Bamgbelu: "They may not have been well written from a grammatical point of view but I am confident I had not forgotten any of the facts." Pure White Welsh Imbecile, Geraint Evans, albeit England's Class Senior Postgraduate Tutor, Oxford.

The quality of human beings in their Godforsaken Racist Hell Hole Shit Country is generally very poor, so a crooked, hereditary RACIST pure white Welsh Imbecile was their Senior Postgraduate Tutor, Oxford. Sheep unnaturally shepherd sheep. Shepherds know that sheep are MORONS, but sheep do not know that shepherds are MORONS too. Facts are sacred and cannot be overstated.

Karen Kwamboka: OYINBO OLE/ODE/BARAWO: A Racist descendant of THIEVES and owners of stolen lives – **Exodus 20:15, Habakkuk 2:6-9**. Poly-educated pure white son of a pure white plebeian hoe ultra-righteously sat on a very expensive highchair that his own pure white father and mother could not afford, which the pure white IMBECILES who sat before him (predominantly but not exclusively pure white) could not and did not buy, and the opportunist RACIST pure white bastard Judges SINNERS – **John 8:7, Matthew 7:1-6.**

Yinka Bamgbelu: Only He who has no sin has the MORAL RIGHT to Judge SINNERS - **John 5:22, Matthew 25:31-46, Revelation 3:21. Matthew 12:27**: RACIST descendants of THIEVES and owners of stolen lives do not have the MORAL RIGHT to Judge Sinners. Facts are sacred and cannot be overstated.

Karen Kwamboka: London is the natural resource of Great Britain. If one were to detach LONDON from Great Britain, she will instantly become the richest Third World Country (G20): The richest among the Second Class. The YANKS are NATO, and absolutely everything else is an auxiliary bluff, as without the YANKS, Europe, including Great Britain, is a sitting duck.

Yinka Bamgbelu: "The best opportunity of developing academically and emotional." Pure White Poly-educated son of a relatively poor man, albeit England's Class Senior District Judge Paul Robert Ayers, alleged 33rd Degree Freemason (Scottish Rite), the archetypal pure white Englishman, and the Senior Vice President of the Association of Her Majesty's District Judges.

A BRAINLESS PURE WHITE FOOL, ALBEIT ENGLAND'S CLASS SENIOR DISTRICT JUDGE: ONE OF THE GAINS OF SEVERAL CENTURIES OF STEALING, RACIST KILLING, AND SLAVERY IS THAT A FUNCTIONAL SEMI-ILLITERATE PURE WHITE BASTARD WAS A SENIOR DISTRICT JUDGE IN BEDFORD, GREAT BRITAIN. WHICH PART

OF SHIT IS GREAT? NO BRAIN. POOR NATURAL RESOURCES. SEVERAL CONTINUOUS CENTURIES OF STEALING AND SLAVERY PRECEDED THEIR HUGE STOLEN INHERITANCE - **EXODUS 20:15, HABAKKUK 2:6-9**. HE SHOULD FU*KING STAY HERE; IT IS SAFER THAN NIGERIA - **EXODUS 21:23-27.**

Poly-educated pure white SHIT, his pure white skin conceals his impure dark black brain. His spinal cord is his highest centre. Our very highly respected (by pure white imbeciles, predominantly but not exclusively pure white) unashamedly functional semi-illiterate poly-educated pure white bastard of our own Empire of STOLEN INHERITANCE - **Habakkuk 2:6-9, Exodus 20:15.**

Karen Kwamboka: Absolutely worthless, ignorant, one-dimensionally educated, and ultra-righteous descendants of THIEVES - **Exodus 20:15.** Hereditary RACIST pure white bastards propped up by gigantic yields of several continuous centuries of ancestral theft – **Habakkuk 2:6-9.**

OXFORD, ENGLAND: GDC, Mrs Helen Falcon, MBE, our Member of the Most Excellent Order of our own Empire of Stolen Inheritance – **Habakkuk 2:6-9, Exodus 20:15,** the archetypal MEDIOCRE GDC Committee Member, a mere dmf, the typical Postgraduate Dean, Oxford, the spouse of Mr Falcon, and a ROTARIAN (vulgarly charitable, hereditary white supremacist, and Antichrist Freemasonry Quasi-Religion without Voodoo and/or Occultists' RITUALS) unrelentingly lied under oath and on record – **Habakkuk 1:4.**

Yinka Bamgbelu: They hate us, and we know. PURE WHITE PRIVILEGE/ APARTHEID BY STEALTH: Dark Black Quasi-Mulatto (impure Black) Constance Briscoe was JAILED for a lesser offence. Police Officers, not all, are liars - **Psalm 116:11**. Had the dark black Quasi-African been pure white, male, Mason, and English, she would have 'WALKED'. All for one, and one for all: Integrity, friendship, respect, and charity. Their people are everywhere, and they control everything, including RACIAL HATRED AND FRAUD – **Habakkuk 1:4.**

Karen Kwamboka: European Paper Tigers: Perception is grander than reality. "All have taken what had other owners..." Dr Samuel Johnson (1709-1784). European Christians stole the land of Native Americans and Created a Super European Country in North America. The YANKS want to steal a very small part of Europe, and Europeans are powerless. Trump's Poodle: A 5th Rate Military Power Impersonates a SUPERPOWER: Delusional Grandeur of the Stolen Past.

If hereditary RACIST pure white bastards (predominantly but not exclusively pure white) are as brave as they vulgarly brag, they MUST DIRECTLY use GUNS to evict Putin from Crimea, he stole it with GUNS – **Exodus 20:15.**

Yinka Bamgbelu: THOROUGHLY SHIT PEOPLE: IGNORANT DESCENDANTS OF ULTRA-RIGHTEOUS PURE WHITE THIEVES – **EXODUS 20:15:** BARAWO. BEDFORD, ENGLAND: Pure White District Judge, Pure White Sue Gregory (OBE), Pure White Richard Hill (Mason) fabricated reports and/or lied under oath, including approved Judgements, and/or lied on record – **Habakkuk 1:4.** Dark Black Constance Briscoe was JAILED for a letter offence.

Karen Kwamboka: PROVERBS 9:10: COLLECTIVE SUPERFLUOUS SUPERIORITY: THE REFUGE OF THE INTELLECTUALLY DISFAVOURED – BY ALMIGHTY GOD.

Their Country is SHIT, and they are worse than SHIT, and they know. Skin colour that they neither made nor chose is universally acknowledged to be irrefutably SUPERIOR, but their intellect is not, and their indiscreetly crooked, VINDICTIVE, unashamedly mediocre, potently weaponised, and institutionally RACIST waste of money Fish and Chips Justice System is fundamentally designed to conceal that TRUTH – **Habakkuk 1:4.**

Yinka Bamgbelu: Our own NIGERIAN CHILDREN with gigantic oil wells and gas fields near their huts eat only 1.5/day in our own NIGERIA, a very bellyful hereditary RACIST pure white bastard whose pure white mother and father have never seen CRUDE OIL, and whose pure white ancestors, including the genetic Italian Jewish, Benjamin Disraeli (1804-1881), were fed like battery hens with huge yields of ancestral theft, yields of MERCILESS RACIST EVIL, Antichrist yields of millions of stolen children of defenceless poor people, including the AFRICAN ANCESTORS of the Quasi-Mulatto, impure White, impure Black, <43% Nigerian, grandchildren of the HRH King Charles.

Karen Kwamboka: UNBALANCED POWER, BUT MUTUAL RACE HATE

They hate us, and they are powerful. We hate them more, but we are powerless

"Sometimes people don't want to hear the truth because they don't want their illusions destroyed." Friedrich Nietzsche (1844-1900).

Yinka Bamgbelu: Pure White Poly-educated poor pure white man's son was granted the platform to display hereditary prejudice. Our own RACIST unashamedly functional semi-illiterate Freemason Senior Bedford's District Judge of our Empire of STOLEN INHERITANCE – **Exodus 20:15, Habakkuk 2:6-9**, a mere functional semi-illiterate former debt-collector Solicitor in NORWICH (5th Rate Partner). If the hereditary RACIST pure white bastard read his approved Judgement, he was a FOOL, and the opportunist RACIST pure white bastard did not, he lied as he implied that he did – **Habakkuk 1:4.** The pure white ancestors of his pure white mother and father were incompetent RACIST LIARS too, they were industrial-scale THIEVES and owners of stolen children of defenceless poor people, including the African ancestors of the impure Black/impure White QUASI-MULATTO (<43% Nigerian) niece and nephew of the PRINCE OF WALES. No brain. Poor natural resources. Several centuries of stealing and SLAVERY preceded their huge stolen inheritance (gigantic yields of several continuous centuries of ancestral theft – **Exodus 20:15, Habakkuk 2:6-9.** Facts are sacred and cannot be overstated.

"Affluence is not a birth right." Lord Cameron, Eton and Oxbridge-educated very rich man's son (**Mark 10:25).**

Karen Kwamboka: Our own NIGERIAN BABIES with gigantic gas fields near their huts eat only 1.5/day in our own NIGERIA, a very bellyful functional semi-illiterate pure white RACIST bastard whose pure white mother have never seen CRUDE OIL was our Senior District Judge in BEDFORD. Unlike PUTIN'S SIBERIA, there are no gas fields in bland, colourless, and almost lifeless NORFOLK/NORWICH (Coastal Dole/the Departure Lounge of life) and where the pure white mother and father of Bedford District Judge were born. An ignorant hereditary RACIST descendant of ultra-righteous pure white THIEVES – **Habakkuk 2:6-9, Exodus 20:15**. He is worthy only because he is pure white. He is rich only because the pure white ancestors of his pure white mother and father were ULTRA-RIGHTEOUS Pure White Thieves and owners of stolen lives.

Yinka Bamgbelu: OYINBO OLE/ODE/BARAWO: **Habakkuk 2:5**: Insatiably greedy hereditary RACIST pure white bastards (predominantly but not exclusively pure white) eat their own cakes, eat all ours, and have everything. They are greedier than the grave, and like death, they can never be satisfied. They love fighting, and AFRICANS are their preferred opponents: Flat track bullies

"How Europe underdeveloped Africa." Dr Walter Rodney (1942-1980).

Karen Kwamboka: Why should Black Africans sacrifice their lives by taking sides in a violent dispute between members of their brainlessly and baselessly

SELF-AWARDED SUPERIOR RACE, direct and/or indirect beneficiaries of SLAVERY?

Yinka Bamgbelu: BEDFORD, ENGLAND: District Judge, you are a lecherous pure white bastard. It is absolutely impossible for your Christ-granted talents and yields of the land on which your own pure white father and mother were born to sustain your very high standard of living. Your pure white ancestors were THIEVES – **Exodus 20:15, Habakkuk 2:6-9.**

Karen Kwamboka: Ecclesiastes 3:1-8: Now is the time for land and natural resources grab. Ija fara le wu: UNIPOLARITY: The YANKS should grab whatever they need, as in the very near future, the combined power of RUSSIA/ CHINA (MULTI POLARITY) will make it impossible for YANKS to steal whatever they need.

Yinka Bamgbelu: BEDFORD, ENGLAND: District Judge, the most important part of the matter is MONEY, and it not the yield of your Christ-granted talent, and unlike PUTIN'S SIBERIA, there are no gas fields in Robert Hibbert (1769-1849) and Tommy Robinson's LUTON and where your own pure white mother and father were born; it is absolutely impossible for you and your pure white type to COMPETE on a colour-blind level intellectual playing field without resorting to RACIST CRIMINALITY. Your Country is SHIT. You are worse than SHIT. Your ancestors were THIEVES and owners of stolen lives – **Exodus 20:15, Habakkuk 2:6-9.** Facts are sacred and cannot be overstated.

Karen Kwamboka: GDC/NHS: Sue Gregory (OBE) our own Officer of the Most Excellent Order of our own Empire of STOLEN INHERITANCE – **Habakkuk 2:6-9, Exodus 20:15,** unrelentingly lied under implied oath and on record – **Habakkuk 1:4.**

Giorgia Meloni, which should be CASTRATED, non-violent RAPISTS or non-violent paedophiles?

Brothers Jimmy Savile (1926-2011) and Rolf Harris (1930-2023): Not all Masons are paedophiles, but all functional semi-illiterate pure white MASON JUDGES are Racists.

Yinka Bamgbelu: APARTHEID BY STEALTH/WHITE PRIVILEGE: Brainless hereditary RACIST pure white bastards self-awarded SUPREME KNOWLEDGE, their brainless and baseless BIRTH RIGHT. When their own pure white kindred commit RACIST CRIMES against our own people, their pure white Judges who oversee the administration of their LAW criminally BURY RACIST EVIL – **Habakkuk 1:4**.

Karen Kwamboka: BEDFORD, ENGLAND: The Serengeti of Pure White IMBECILES (predominantly but not exclusively pure white): GDC/NHS: Pure White Mason, Brother Richard William Hill fabricated reports and unrelentingly lied under oath - **Habakkuk 1:4.** Dark Black Constance Briscoe was JAILED for a lesser offence. Facts are sacred and cannot be overstated. Their Country is SHIT, and they are worse than SHIT, and they know.

Yinka Bamgbelu: Lagos girls, nearly all, including Born-Again Christians, are glorified prostitutes and THIEVES; they all want men's MONEY: "The great question that has never been answered, and which I have not yet been able to answer, despite my thirty years of research into the feminine soul, is 'What does a woman want?'" Sigmund Freud (1856-1939).

Karen Kwamboka: Our own NIGERIA (oil/gas), Shell's docile cash cow since 1956(OLOIBIRI). GDC was established in 1956.

SLAVERY (Maafa, 1445-1888) rebuilt everything it succeeded and paid for everything it preceded.

Unlike PUTIN'S SIBERIA, there are no gas fields in Freemasons' KEMPSTON.

Yinka Bamgbelu: ENVY IS A THIEF: THEY HATE US, AND WE KNOW.

Ultra-righteous descendants of THIEVES and owners of stolen lives – **Habakkuk 2:6-9, Exodus 20:15.**

"Envy is weak." Yul Brynner (1920-1985).

If hereditary RACIST pure white bastards are as brave as they vulgarly brag, they MUST directly use guns to evict PUTIN from Crimea, he stole it with GUNS – **Exodus 20:15.**

Karen Kwamboka: Interracial envy is a thief. BEDFORD, ENGLAND: Pure White Senior District Judge Paul Robert Ayers, the pure white ancestors of your pure white mother and father were PROFESSIONAL THIEVES and owners of stolen lives.

Exodus 20:15, Habakkuk 2:6-9: Stealing is a very efficient way of making money, but it stifles natural selection, degrades the intellect, and reverses progressive evolution.

CHAPTER FIVE

Yinka Bamgbelu: Asymmetrical Mutual Race Hate: They hate us, and we know. We hate them more, but they don't know. They are very POWERFUL, and we are absolutely powerless, and to rub salt into our wounds, we have been robbed to penniless since their armed ancestors found our defenceless ancestors in the African bush, in the 15th Century (Maafa, 1445-1888). OYINBO OLE (THIEVES – **EXODUS 20:15**): Skin colour that they neither made nor chose is universally acknowledged to be irrefutably SUPERIOR, and their indiscreetly crooked, vindictive, unashamedly mediocre, potently weaponised, and institutionally RACIST waste of money fish and chips Justice System is fundamentally designed to conceal the TRUTH – **Habakkuk 1:4,** which is that their intellect is not.

Karen Kwamboka: BEDFORD, ENGLAND: Racist Pure White Senior District Judge Paul Robert Ayers, the Senior Vice President of the Association of Her Majesty's District Judges, the pure white ancestors of your pure white father and mother were THIEVES and owners of stolen lives - **Exodus 20:15**. An ignorant hereditary RACIST pure white FOOL. **Proverbs 20:15**: Skin colour is a great creation of Almighty God, but it is not the greatest.

Our own Mediocre, Physically Ill-Favoured, Mentally Wonky, Pure White Hereditary Racist, unashamedly functionally semi-illiterate, poly-educated poor man's son, a downmarket former debt-collector Solicitor in bland and colourless Norfolk/Norwich, (Coastal Dole/the Departure Lounge of Life), a mere lowlife 5th Rate Partner, and the Senior Vice President of the Association of Her Majesty's District Judges, Pure White Senior Bedford's District Judge Paul Robert Ayers, 3, St Paul's Square, MK 40 1SQ: You are a DUNCE. The brain that inherited from your pure white father and mother is good. Had you been BLACK. you will not be a Senior District Judge in BEDFORD. Our own MONEY, our own NIGERIA (oil/gas) is by far more relevant to the economic survival of all your mentally gentler white children (OECD), your pure white spouse, your pure white father, and your pure white mother than Robert Hibbert (1769-1849) and Tommy Robinson's LUTON.

Yinka Bamgbelu: APARTHEID BY STEALTH: Hereditary RACIST pure white bastards (predominantly but not exclusively pure white) prefer a world where SUBSTANCE (Christ granted talent) is subservient to superfluous.

Colourism: The universally acknowledged irrefutably SUPERIOR SKIN COLOUR that the very fortunate wearer neither made nor chose.

Karen Kwamboka: Like LUNATIC JIHADISTS (Terrorists), hereditary RACIST pure white bastards (predominantly but not exclusively pure white), ultra-righteous descendants of THIEVES and owners of stolen lives (**Habakkuk 2:6-9, Exodus 20:15),** trample on the law that their victims must obey, and they expect the law to protect them. They MUST stay here; it is safer than NIGERIA – **Exodus 21:23-27.**

Yinka Bamgbelu: They loved WARS, and Africans were their preferred opponents. They hate us, and we know. We hate them more, and they know. They are very powerful, and we know; we are powerless, and they know. Sincere immodesty is sincerer than insincere modesty. The mind that I did not choose is considerably FINER than yours, and I can easily prove it, but you will be destroyed in the process.

Karen Kwamboka: King's School and Oxbridge-educated Lord Justice Charles Anthony Haddon-Cave, KC, a RACIST first son of a very, very, very, very, very, very, RICH Tasmanian Colonialist Economic Cannibal (**Mark 10:25**), Tasmania and Oxbridge-educated very, very, very, rich man's son (**Mark 10:25**), Sir Charles Phillip Haddon-Cave (1925–1999), and a grandson of Francis Haddon-Cave, born in Hobart in early 20th-century Australian settlement; an impostor and an expert of deception (perception is grander than reality), and a closeted white supremacist descendant of DRUG LORDS (opium merchants of the Qing Dynasty), and a homie of Eton and Oxbridge-educated very, very, very, rich men's son, Archbishop Justin Welby (**Mark 10:25**), if it is the TRUTH that pure white people are superiorly created by Almighty God, why do you and your pure white kindred need RACIST CRIMINALITY to defeat a mere NIGERIAN, from shithole Africa, in an open debate?

Yinka Bamgbelu: King's School and Oxbridge-educated Lord Justice Charles Anthony Haddon-Cave, KC, a RACIST first son of a very, very, very, very, very, very, RICH Tasmanian Colonialist Economic Cannibal (**Mark 10:25**), Tasmania and Oxbridge-educated very, very, very, rich man's son (**Mark 10:25**), Sir Charles Phillip Haddon-Cave (1925–1999), and a grandson of Francis Haddon-Cave, born in Hobart in early 20th-century Australian settlement; an impostor and an expert of deception (perception is grander than reality), and a closeted white supremacist descendant of DRUG LORDS (opium merchants of the Qing Dynasty), and a homie of Eton and Oxbridge-educated very, very,

very, rich men's son, Archbishop Justin Welby (**Mark 10:25**), it is absolutely impossible for you and your Higher Upper-Class pure white type to use cogent facts and irrefutable evidence to disprove the TRUTH, which is that your pure white kindred, Senior District Judge Paul Robert Ayers, albeit Bedford's Class, unrelentingly lied under oath and on record – **Habakkuk 1:4.**

Karen Kwamboka: King's School and Oxbridge-educated Lord Justice Charles Anthony Haddon-Cave, KC, a RACIST first son of a very, very, very, very, very, very, RICH Tasmanian Colonialist Economic Cannibal (**Mark 10:25**), Tasmania and Oxbridge-educated very, very, very, rich man's son (**Mark 10:25**), Sir Charles Phillip Haddon-Cave (1925–1999), and a grandson of Francis Haddon-Cave, born in Hobart in early 20th-century Australian settlement; an impostor and an expert of deception (perception is grander than reality), and a closeted white supremacist descendant of DRUG LORDS (opium merchants of the Qing Dynasty), and a homie of Eton and Oxbridge-educated very, very, very, rich men's son, Archbishop Justin Welby (**Mark 10:25**), only your skin colour and God Almighty are truly good – **Mark 10:18**, and without it, you will be considerably diminished as a human being, and you know it. **Proverbs 20:15**: Colourism/ Apartheid by Stealth: Skin colour is a great creation of Almighty God, but it is not the greatest. Facts are sacred and cannot be overstated.

Yinka Bamgbelu: King's School and Oxbridge-educated Lord Justice Charles Anthony Haddon-Cave, KC, a RACIST first son of a very, very, very, very, very, very, RICH Tasmanian Colonialist Economic Cannibal (**Mark 10:25**), Tasmania and Oxbridge-educated very, very, very, rich man's son (**Mark 10:25**), Sir Charles Phillip Haddon-Cave (1925–1999), and a grandson of Francis Haddon-Cave, born in Hobart in early 20th-century Australian settlement; an impostor and an expert of deception (perception is grander than reality), and a closeted white supremacist descendant of DRUG LORDS (opium merchants of the Qing Dynasty), and a homie of Eton and Oxbridge-educated very, very, very, rich men's son, Archbishop Justin Welby (**Mark 10:25**), the brain that you inherited from your pure white mother, the source of your principal X Chromosome, is not good. The Y Chromosome from Sir Phillip Haddon-Cave (1925-1999) added very little genetic material. Had you been an impure Quasi-Mulatto, like Archie, <43% Nigerian, and 77X as smart as OBAMA (impure White/impure Black Mulatto), you would not be a Lord Justice in Great Britain.

Karen Kwamboka: BARAWO/OYINBO OLE/ODE: Closeted hereditary RACIST pure white bastards, half-educated school dropouts, and mere GED (predominantly but not exclusively pure white) see molecules, and they destroy self-educated NIGERIANS, from shit hole Africa, who see quarks. If you engage on a colour-blind level intellectual playing field, you will be uncovered and irreparably destroyed with cogent facts and irrefutable evidence.

Yinka Bamgbelu: Then, all Judges were pure white Freemasons, and most of them were THICKER than a gross of planks – **Proverbs 17:16**. Brothers Jimmy Savile (1926-2011), and Rolf Harris (1930-2023): It is not the TRUTH that all Masons are paedophiles, but all functional semi-illiterate pure white Mason Judges are RACIST BASTARDS.

Karen Kwamboka: BEDFORD, ENGLAND: Unbounded and unaccountable pure white supremacist Freemasons' unrelenting depravity. Pure White Brother Richard William Hill fabricated reports and unrelentingly lied under oath and on record – **Habakkuk 1:4**. Dark Black Constance Briscoe was JAILED for a lesser offence.

Yinka Bamgbelu: A hereditary RACIST pure white bastard could not COMPETE on a colour-blind level intellectual playing field, so he resorted to RACIST CRIMINALITY, secure in the knowledge that all Judges will be PURE WHITE, and his hope is that they would be hereditary RACIST pure white bastards too – **Habakkuk 1:4.**

Karen Kwamboka: An ignorant hereditary RACIST descendant of ultra-righteous pure white THIEVES and owners of stolen lives – **Exodus 20:15.**

Proverbs 19:14: BEDFORD, ENGLAND: Pure White Senior District Judge Paul Robert Ayers, a Moron Mason, if you do not control genetic mix, the quality of human beings produced will be very poor, and it will be possible for a crooked, RACIST, functional semi-illiterate pure white bastard to be a Senior District Judge, albeit Bedford's Class – **Habakkuk 1:4.**

Yinka Bamgbelu: Our own NIGERIAN BABIES with gigantic oil wells and gas fields near their huts eat ONLY 1.5/day in our own NIGERIA, a functional semi-illiterate pure white bastard whose pure white mother and father have never seen CRUDE OIL was our Senior District Judge in BEDFORD, Great Britain. Which part of our own shit hole AFRICA is great?

"How Europe underdeveloped Africa." Dr Walter Rodney (1942-1980).

Karen Kwamboka: A RACIST ultra-righteous descendant of pure white THIEVES and owners of stolen children of defenceless poor people – **Exodus 20:15**. No brain. Poor natural resources. Several centuries of stealing and slavery preceded their huge stolen inheritance - **Exodus 20:15, Habakkuk 2:6-9.**

Unlike PUTIN'S SIBERIA, there are no gas fields in Robert Hibbert (1769-1849) and Tommy Robinson's LUTON and where the pure white mother and father of Pure White Senior Bedford's District Judge Paul Robert Ayers were born.

Yinka Bamgbelu: They hate us, and we know. The Ne Plus Ultra of Slimy Hypocrisy: They are worse than indiscreetly white supremacist NICE AGENTS: Half-educated school dropouts and their type, mere GED; thoroughly wretched PURE WHITE SHIT PEOPLE (predominantly but not exclusively pure white), direct descendants of lowlife working-class pure white bastards who crossed the English Channel, not that long ago, without luggage or decent shoes.

Karen Kwamboka: INTELLECTUAL DEGRADATION AMONG THE SELF-AWARDED THINKING CLASS. STOLEN EXCEPTIONALISM: **EXODUS 20:15, HABAKKUK 2:6-9.**

"All have taken what had other owners, and all have had recourse to arms rather than quit the prey onto which they were fastened." Dr Samuel Johnson (1709-1784).

Yinka Bamgbelu: What did minor European Christians (working-class) take to America, and what did they find there that they did not steal? They stole the land, and stolen Africans worked it.

An opportunist RACIST pure white bastard was granted the platform to display hereditary prejudice.

Karen Kwamboka: King's School and Oxbridge-educated Lord Justice Charles Anthony Haddon-Cave, KC, a RACIST first son of a very, very, very, very, very, very, very, very, very, RICH Tasmanian Colonialist Economic Cannibal (**Mark 10:25**), Tasmania and Oxbridge-educated very, very, very, rich man's son (**Mark 10:25**), Sir Charles Phillip Haddon-Cave (1925–1999), and a grandson of Francis Haddon-Cave, born in Hobart in early 20th-century Australian settlement; an impostor and an expert of deception (perception is grander than reality), and a closeted white supremacist descendant of DRUG LORDS (opium merchants of the Qing Dynasty), and a homie of Eton and Oxbridge-educated very, very, very, rich men's son, Archbishop Justin Welby (**Mark 10:25**), you are VERY UGLY (physically ill-favoured) and mentally wonky. You owe everything to unearned privilege and undeserved patronage. You are SPECIAL only because you are pure white. You are RICH only because your pure white ancestors were THIEVES and owners of stolen lives – **Habakkuk 2:6-9, Exodus 20:15**. Facts are sacred and cannot be overstated.

Yinka Bamgbelu: They are BRAINLESS RACIST PURE WHITE SHIT PEOPLE (predominantly but not exclusively pure white), and they know, but they pretend that they don't. Their Country is SHIT, and they are worse than SHIT, and they destroy all self-educated NIGERIANS, from shit hole Africa, who know that they are brainless hereditary RACIST pure white bastards – **Proverbs 17:16.**

Karen Kwamboka: The Quality of Human Beings in their Godforsaken RACIST HELL HOLE Shit Country is very poor. If Lord Justice Haddon-Cave, KC, could disprove the TRUTH, which is that his own pure white kindred, Pure White Senior Bedford's District Judge Paul Robert Ayers, Sue Gregory (OBE), our own Officer of the Most Excellent Order of our own Empire of Stolen Inheritance – **Exodus 20:15, Habakkuk 2:6-9,** and Freemason, Brother Richard William Hill, fabricated reports and/or unrelentingly lied under oath and/or unrelentingly lied on record **– Habakkuk 1:4,** he would concomitantly disprove the belief of Peter Herbert, which is that the administration of English Law is a Negrophobic Charade.

Yinka Bamgbelu: OYINBO OLE/ODE/BARAWO: BEDFORD, ENGLAND: Pure White Senior District Judge Paul Robert Ayers, an ignorant hereditary RACIST pure white bastard, a mere former debt-collector Solicitor in Norfolk/ Norwich(Coastal Dole/the Departure Lounge of Life) brainlessly and baselessly self-awarded SUPREME KNOWLEDGE, and destroys all NIGERIANS, from shit hole Africa, who know that he is an impostor, an expert of deception, and an opportunist RACIST pure white bastard – **Habakkuk 1:4.**

Karen Kwamboka: PROVERBS 19:14: OYINBO OLE/ODE/BARAWO: BEDFORD, ENGLAND: Pure White Senior District Judge Paul Robert Ayers, bro', let me tell you, the quality of human beings in your Godforsaken Racist Hell hole Shit Country is very poor. If you do not control the genetic mix, you are recklessly throwing dice. The entire foundation of your civilisation is STEALING and sharing yields of Stealing. In 1833, insatiably greedy EVIL RACIST pure white bastards shared yields of millions of stolen children of defenceless poor people, including the African ancestors of the QUASI-MULATTO, impure White/impure Black, <43% Nigerian, grandchildren of HRH King Charles.

Yinka Bamgbelu: EXODUS 20:15: PURE WHITE EUROPEAN CHRISTIANS WERE THIEVES. THEY USED GUNS TO LOOT ALMOST EVERY SQUARE INCH OF THE ARMED WORLD. Insatiably greedy evil RACIST pure white bastards mercilessly slaughtered and dispossessed Natives in Australasia, Americas, West Indies, Africa, India, Etc. Their descendants will steal Greenland. If one's ancestors were armed land grabbers, it would be very naïve not to expect stealing to be part of one's genetic inheritances – **Habakkuk 2:6-9.**

Karen Kwamboka: A Quasi-Maharajah: A RACIST first son of a Quasi-Dalit, mere plebeian, lowlife, and lower working-class Scottish Wench, Mary Anne Macleod (1912-2000), who stowaway to America in 1930, without luggage or decent shoes; her son Lords it over European Kings and Queens.

Yinka Bamgbelu: They hate us, and we know. Our MISFORTUNES are intelligently designed by hereditary white supremacist Freemason Bastards: Half-educated School Dropouts and their SUPERIORS who have informal access to very powerful PURE WHITE FREEMASON JUDGES.

BEDFORD, ENGLAND: GDC, Pure White Freemason, Brother Richard William Hill fabricated reports and unrelentingly lied under oath - **Habakkuk 1:4.** Constance Briscoe was JAILED for a lesser offence. Reporting a PURE WHITE Racist Freemason Criminal to PURE WHITE Racist Mason Judges – is akin to reporting demons to devils, a barren exercise – **Matthew 12:27**. Facts are sacred and cannot be overstated. Dark Black Constance Briscoe (UGLY) was JAILED for a lesser offence.

"The white man is the devil." Elijah Mohammad (1897-1975).

Karen Kwamboka: BEDFORD, ENGLAND: Pure White Senior District Judge Paul Robert Ayers, the brain of your own pure white father did not sustain his standard of living. Your brain cannot sustain your standard of living. The brain of your pure white ancestors did not sustain their standard of living. Your land yields only FOOD. Your pure white ancestors were THIEVES and owners of stolen lives – **Habakkuk 2:6-9, Exodus 20:15.**

"Find the truth and tell it." Harold Pinter (1930-2008).

Yinka Bamgbelu: Brainlessly and baselessly self-awarded SUPERIORITY is their inviolable birthright, but only their SKIN COLOUR is superior, so they cheat.

BEDFORD, ENGLAND: Senior District Judge Paul Robert Ayers, Sue Gregory (OBE), Mason, Richard Hill, all pure white, lied under oath and/or on record. Constance Briscoe was JAILED for a lesser offence. Facts are sacred and cannot be overstated.

The quality of human beings in their Godforsaken Racist Hell Hole Shit Country is very poor because huge yields of slavery decommissioned natural selection and reversed progressive evolution and made it possible for scores of millions of pure white imbeciles (predominantly but not exclusively pure white) to breed more imbeciles.

"The blame is his who chooses. God is blameless." Plato

The mind that I didn't choose is finer than your SHIT. I do not believe in any part of your SHIT, as no part of your SHIT is good, not even one - **Psalm 53,** and I have the POWER to use cogent facts and irrefutable evidence to irreparably destroy you and your SHIT. Reasoning and vision do not have finite boundaries: The fellow is who He says He is - **John 14:6,** and the only sinless , exclusively appointed by God - **John 5:22,** will Judge all, including crooked white supremacist Freemason Judges, with the sword of TRUTH, not Jonathan Aitken's, but the Divine Sword of Transparent Truth – **Matthew 25:31-46, Revelation 3:21.**

1884: They have no cards. Direct descendants of very greedy evil RACIST pure white bastards - industrial-scale professional THIEVES are united only on paper, and they will never be able to defend themselves against the YANKS. THIEVES have UNITY of purpose in AFRICA.

Karen Kwamboka: Racist descendants of THIEVES and owners of stolen lives – **Exodus 20:15, Habakkuk 2:6-9**. Armed Land Grabbers: Indian Removal Act of 1830 and Trail of Tears, which displaced over 60,000 Native people. **Habakkuk 2:5**: Venezuela, Greenland Etcetera: Insatiably greedy European Christian bastards. They are greedier than the grave, and like death, they can never be satisfied. Wherever RACISTS slaughtered, they dispossessed, and whenever they robbed, they took possession – Black Wars of 1824-1832. Ignorant ultra-righteous hereditary RACIST descendants of merciless murderers – **Exodus 20:13,** and insatiable greedy bastards (THIEVES) – **Exodus 20:15.**

Yinka Bamgbelu: Hereditary RACIST pure white bastards, their hairs stand on end when they are challenged by self-educated Nigerians, from shit hole AFRICAN. Trump's Poodles. Paper Tigers. Flat track bullies of the third world type: Libya, Nigeria, Iraq, Iran, Afghanistan, Somalia, Yemen etcetera. If the YANKS are truly strong, they must use extreme overwhelming violence to evict PUTIN from Crimea, he used extreme overwhelming violence to convert Bakhmut and Avdiivka from bricks to rubble and stole them – **Exodus 20:15.**

"Bakhmut of our hearts." President Zelensky.

Karen Kwamboka: 'Putin is afraid of US but not Europe' President Trump

BRAINLESS NONSENSE.

If I have the POWER to blow up the world, who should I fear?

Extreme violence between RUSSIA and the USA will lead to the end of the world.

"I know not with what weapons World War III will be fought, but World War IV will be fought with sticks and stones." Albert Einstein (1879-1955).

World War IV will favour Africans: More proficient with sticks and stones.

"Stoning certainly teaches people a lesson." Ayatollah Sadegh Khalkhali (1926-2003).

Yinka Bamgbelu: "I would kidnap Putin." Healey.

BRAINLESS NONSENSE.

Delusional grandeur of the stolen past: A 5th Rate Military Power impersonates a SUPERPOWER.

A closeted RACIST descendant of kidnappers, carriers, and sellers of stolen African children, you fu*king can't kidnap KIM, but PUTIN can poison you. Without the support of the YANKS, your Country is a sitting duck.

Karen Kwamboka: 1976-2022: A brainless opportunist RACIST pure white bastard.1976-1992, he FAILED in practice, loads did, so he parked his liability at the public till (1992-2022). He was an apprentice Judge (Deputy District Judge) for too long, from 1992-2000, because he kept FAILING the promotion exam. 2000-2022: The hereditary RACIST pure white bastard sold unashamed mediocrity and confusion to the undiscerning in exchange for valuable consideration. A Quasi-Scammer. Quasi-Communism: Other people paid other people other people's money in exchange for CONFUSION.

Yinka Bamgbelu: Slavery decommissioned natural selection, reversed progressive evolution, and made it possible for scores of millions of pure white IMBECILES (predominantly but not exclusively pure white) to breed more millions of intellectually worthless IMBECILES. I am a NIGERIAN, from shit hole Africa. Immodesty apart, I am considerably more intelligent than you, and I shall prove it by using cogent facts and irrefutable evidence to irreparably destroy you and your Fish and Chips Justice System. Unlike PUTIN'S SIBERIA, there are no gas fields in John Foster's (1759-1832) Brickhill and hereditary white supremacist Freemasons' Kempston.

Karen Kwamboka: A brainless hereditary RACIST pure white bastard, having FAILED in practice (1976-1992), loads did, he was an apprentice Judge for close to a decade (1992-2000) because the poly-educated opportunist RACIST pure white son of pure white plebeian nobodies You are not intelligent, and that is why you did not do very well at school. You are very lucky that you are PURE WHITE, for had you been BLACK, you would be poor.

Yinka Bamgbelu: 1717, Quasi Voodoo Men Emerged: Prince Hall Freemason (1775): Segregationist, cultist, RACIST, and evil pure white Freemason bastards. Integrity, friendship, respect, and charity: All for one, and one for all. Hereditary white supremacist bastards, the EVIL RACIST CULT of ritualists emerged in the early 18th century - at a height of the barbarously RACIST, but extortionately profitable traffic in millions of stolen children of defenceless poor people, including the African ancestors of the QUASI-MULATTO (impure White/impure Black, <43% Nigeria) grandniece and grandnephew of Major Mountbatten Windsor.

Karen Kwamboka: King's School and Oxbridge-educated Lord Justice Charles Anthony Haddon-Cave, KC, a RACIST first son of a very, very, very, very, very, very, RICH Tasmanian Colonialist Economic Cannibal (**Mark 10:25**), Tasmania and Oxbridge-educated very, very, very, rich man's son (**Mark 10:25**), Sir Charles Phillip Haddon-Cave (1925–1999), and a grandson of Francis Haddon-Cave, born in Hobart in early 20th-century Australian settlement; an impostor and an expert of deception (perception is grander than reality), and a closeted white supremacist descendant of DRUG LORDS (opium merchants of the Qing Dynasty), and a homie of Eton and Oxbridge-educated very, very, very, rich men's son, Archbishop Justin Welby (**Mark 10:25**), Bro', let me tell you, your 'England is like a prostitute who, having sold her body all her life, decides to quit and close her business and then tells everybody that she wants to be chaste and protect her flesh as if it were jade – He Manzi (1919-2009).

Yinka Bamgbelu: "Sometimes people don't want to hear the truth because they don't want their illusions destroyed." Friedrich Nietzsche (1844-1900).

BARAWO/OYINBO OLE/ODE: TRUTHS disfavour hereditary RACIST

pure white bastards, so they resort to RACIST CRIMINALITY. Skin colour that they neither made nor chose is universally acknowledged to be irrefutably SUPERIOR, but their intellects are not, and their waste of money Fish and Chips Justice System is fundamentally designed to conceal that TRUTH – **Habakkuk 1:4.**

Karen Kwamboka: To deter the hereditary white supremacist oppressor, you must have UNSTOPPABLE NUKES. The RACIST oppressor is sane. Kim has NUKES, so neither the personal morality of a pure white son of a plebeian Scottish domestic servant nor international law can torch Kim.

Yinka Bamgbelu: BARAWO/OYINBO OLE/ODE: King's School and Oxbridge-educated Lord Justice Charles Anthony Haddon-Cave, KC, Royal Courts of Justice, Strand, WC2A 2LL, London, a Racist First Son of a very rich (**Mark 10:25**) Tasmanian Colonialist Economic Cannibal, Tasmania University and Oxbridge-educated, Sir Charles Phillip Haddon-Cave (1925–1999), a RACIST direct descendant of armed land grabbers, industrial-scale professional THIEVES—**Exodus 20:15, Habakkuk**, gun runners (firearm merchants), drug dealers (opium merchants of the Qing dynasty, opium wars of 1839–1842), and extremely nasty genocidal racist bastards, very crude and cruel sea wolves (Britannia rules the waves), exterminators of > 97% Native Tasmanians, absolutely unprovoked (Black wars 1824–1832) – **Exodus 20:13**, and in 1833, hereditary RACIST pure white bastards shared a tiny fraction of the Quadrillion they stole from our own Africa (Maafa, 1445–1888), and insatiably greedy RACIST pure white bastard replaced Slavery with colonisation—by partitioning Africa in 1884. Neo-colonialism is the New Slavery. Substitution is fraudulent emancipation.

"Moderation is a virtue only among those who are thought to have found alternatives." Dr Henry Kissinger (1923–2023).

Karen Kwamboka: Those who know the TRUTH obey the least.

"Those who know the least obey the best." George Farquhar (1677–1707).

I do not believe in any part of your FISH and CHIPS Justice System. Your Country is SHIT, and you are worse than SHIT. You are worthy only because you are pure white. You are RICH only because the pure white ancestors of your pure white mother and father were THIEVES and owners of stolen children of defenceless poor people, including the QUASI-MULATTO, impure White/ impure Black, <43% Nigerian, great grandchildren of HM (1926-2022).

Yinka Bamgbelu: They hate us, and we know. They fear untamed minds of self-educated Nigerians, from shit hole Africa, more than PUTIN'S POISONS. Facts are sacred and cannot be overstated.

OXFORD, ENGLAND: GDC, based on cogent, irrefutable, and available evidence, Pure White Mrs Helen Falcon (MBE), Member of the Most Excellent Order of our own Empire of Stolen Inheritance, gigantic yields of several continuous centuries of ancestral theft—**Exodus 20:15, Habakkuk**, a ROTARIAN (vulgarly charitable, hereditary white supremacist, and Antichrist Freemasonry Quasi-Religion without Voodoo or Occultists' Rituals), unrelentingly lied under oath and on record – **Habakkuk 1:4.** Dark Black Quasi-Mulatto (impure Black), Constance Briscoe, was JAILED for a lesser offence.

Karen Kwamboka: BARAWO/OYINBO OLE/ODE: They hate us, and we know. Our own Mrs Helen Falcon (OBE), a very dishonest typical pure white Englishwoman. A crooked closeted hereditary RACIST Member of the Most Excellent Order of our Empire of Stolen Inheritance – **Exodus 20:15, Habakkuk.**

Yinka Bamgbelu: "The English think incompetence is the same thing as sincerity." Quentin Crisp (1908-1999).

BARAWO/OYINBO OLE/ODE: If as the pure white kindred of King's School and Oxbridge-educated Lord Justice Charles Anthony Haddon-Cave, KC, a RACIST first son of a very, very, very, very, very, very, RICH Tasmanian Colonialist Economic Cannibal (**Mark 10:25**), Tasmania and Oxbridge-educated very, very, very, rich man's son (**Mark 10:25**), Sir Charles Phillip Haddon-Cave (1925–1999), and a grandson of Francis Haddon-Cave, born in Hobart in early 20th-century Australian settlement; an impostor and an expert of deception (perception is grander than reality), and a closeted white supremacist descendant of DRUG LORDS (opium merchants of the Qing Dynasty), and a homie of Eton and Oxbridge-educated very, very, very, rich men's son, Archbishop Justin Welby (**Mark 10:25**), implicitly vulgarly brag, they are truly intellectually superiorly created by Almighty God, what do hereditary RACIST pure white bastards need Blatant Racist Criminality for? No brain. Poor natural resources. Several centuries of stealing and SLAVERY preceded their huge STOLEN INHERITANCE (gigantic yields of several continuous centuries of ancestral theft, Maafa, 1445-1888). Ignorant descendants of THIEVES and owners of stolen lives - **Exodus 20:15, Habakkuk 2:6-9.**

Stifled free speech degrades originalism in independent thinking. Jesus was killed only because He spoke - **Matthew 27:32-56.**

"Jesus is the bedrock of my faith." HM (1926-2022).

Karen Kwamboka: They hate us, and we know. Ignorant opportunist RACIST descendants of ultra-righteous THIEVES and owners of stolen lives – **Habakkuk 2:6-9, Exodus 20:15.** Several centuries of stealing and slavery preceded their huge stolen inheritance (gigantic yields of several continuous centuries of ancestral theft, Maafa (1445-1888) – **Exodus 20:15, Habakkuk 2:6-9.** Facts are sacred and cannot be overstated.

Yinka Bamgbelu: Ignorant opportunist RACIST descendants of ultra-righteous pure white THIEVES and owners of stolen and destroyed lives. **Acts 2:17:** The Nigerian from shithole Africa is a FOETUS only because what he can vividly see is clearer than dreams, visions, and prophecies.

Karen Kwamboka: They are a properly organised gang of VERY POWERFUL PURE WHITE RACIST CRIMINALS; the pure white IMBECILES they shepherd (predominantly but not exclusively pure white) must not know that their shepherds are Wolves in Sheep's Clothing. If you trap EVIL RACIST CROOKED BASTARDS, you must leave them room to escape, if you don't, they will kill you, as their survival desires it – **Exodus 20:13.**

Yinka Bamgbelu: Asymmetric Mutual Race Hate: They hate us, and they are very powerful, and we know; we hate them more, but we are powerless, and they know. BEDFORD, ENGLAND: Pure White Senior District Judge Paul Robert Ayers, the most important part of the matter is MONEY, and it is not the yield of your Christ-granted talent, and unlike PUTIN'S SIBERIA, there are no GAS FIELDS in Bedfordshire and where your own pure white mother and father were born. Your pure white ancestors were THIEVES – **Exodus 20:15, Habakkuk 2:6-9.**

Karen Kwamboka: The head is intellectually degraded and the body is DEAD. The Quality of human beings in their Godforsaken Racist Hell Hole Shit Country is very poor – **Proverbs 17:16.**

OXFORD, ENGLAND: GDC, Pure White British Soldier, Stephanie Twidale (TD) unrelentingly lied under oath and on record – **Habakkuk 1:4.** Dark Black Constance Briscoe was JAILED for a lesser offence.

Yinka Bamgbelu: They hate us, and we know. Insatiably greedy pure white bastards (predominantly but not exclusively pure white) love only MONEY, our own MONEY. Our own NIGERIA, Shell's docile cash cow since 1956 (Oloibiri).

GDC was established in 1956.Slavery rebuilt everything it succeeded and paid for everything it preceded, including NHS (1948) and GDC (1956)

Unlike PUTIN'S SIBERIA, there are no gas fields in Tasmania, where Pure White Sir Charles Phillip Haddon-Cave (1925-1999), a RACIST Colonialist Economic Cannibal was born.

Karen Kwamboka: If for SECURITY reasons, the YANKS must buy Greenland, RUSSIANS must be allowed to buy smashed up UKRAINE, and significantly depopulated Ukraine should be considerably cheaper.

BARAWO/OYINBO OLE/ODE: They are PURE WHITE RACIST BASTARD CRIMINALS, including their Judges; in pursuant of self-preservation, it is safer to feign ignorance of their RACIST EVIL, as what they might do to bury UNCONTROLLABLE HEREDITARY MERCILESS RACIST HATRED could be worse the original evil.

"The cure must not be worse than the disease." Ibn Sina

Yinka Bamgbelu: Ignorant opportunist RACIST descendants of ultra-righteous PURE WHITE THIEVES – **Exodus 20:15, Habakkuk 2:6-9**. Facts are sacred and cannot be overstated.

Imagbon,1892.

Benin,1897.

"Ethical foreign policy." Robin Cook (1946-2005).

We and our type are the ones hereditary RACIST pure white bastards would beat up without the support of the YANKS. If opportunist RACIST pure white bastards are as ethical, and as brave as they vulgarly brag, they must, DIRECTLY, use GUNS to evict PUTIN from Crimea.

Karen Kwamboka: BARAWO/OYINBO OLE/ODE: BEDFORD, ENGLAND: Pure White Poly-educated son of a relatively poor man, albeit England's Class Senior District Judge Paul Robert Ayers, alleged 33rd Degree Freemason (Scottish Rite), the archetypal pure white Englishman, and the Senior Vice President of the Association of Her Majesty's District Judges, 'Bro', let me tell you, you are a leech because the pure white ancestors of your pure white mother and father were THIEVES and owners of stolen children of defenceless poor AFRICANS. You are worthy only because you are pure white, and you are RICH only because your ancestors were ULTRA-RIGHTEOUS RACIST THIEVES – **Exodus 20:15, Habakkuk 2:6-9.**

CHAPTER SIX

Yinka Bamgbelu: BEDFORD, ENGLAND: Pure White Poly-educated son of a relatively poor man, albeit England's Class Senior District Judge Paul Robert Ayers, alleged 33rd Degree Freemason (Scottish Rite), the archetypal pure white Englishman, and the Senior Vice President of the Association of Her Majesty's District Judges, 'Bro', let me tell you, if there are cogent and irrefutable evidence that the pure white ancestors of your pure white mother and father were THIEVES (**Exodus 20:15, Habakkuk 2:6-9**) and owners of stolen African children, including the African ancestors of our Mulatto Duchess of Sussex, impure Black/impure White (43% Nigerian), and if equitable, fair, and just REPARATION pends, what MORAL RIGHT do you have to Judge Sinners when there is proof that your ancestors were THIEVES – **Matthew 7:1-6, John 8:7.**

Karen Kwamboka: BARAWO/OYINBO OLE/ODE: King's School and Oxbridge-educated Lord Justice Charles Anthony Haddon-Cave, KC, Royal Courts of Justice, Strand, WC2A 2LL, London, a Racist First Son of a very rich (**Mark 10:25**) Tasmanian Colonialist Economic Cannibal, Tasmania University and Oxbridge-educated, Sir Charles Phillip Haddon-Cave (1925–1999), you are worthy only because you are pure white, and you are relatively very rich only because the pure white ancestors of your pure white mother and father were THIEVES – **Exodus 20:15.**

Yinka Bamgbelu: The pattern of Merciless Racist Evil is the same everywhere in their Godforsaken Racist Hell Hole Shit Country.

BARAWO/OYINBO OLE/ODE: The centuries-old unspoken myth that intellect is related to the universally acknowledged irrefutably superior skin colour that the very fortunate wearer neither made nor chose is the mother of all RACIST SCAMS.

Karen Kwamboka: IMMORTAL MENDACITY: BEDFORD, ENGLAND: GDC, Pure White Sue Gregory (OBE), Officer of the Most Excellent Order of our own Empire of Stolen Inheritance—**Habakkuk 2:6-9, Exodus 20:15,** unrelentingly lied under implied oath and on record – **Habakkuk 1:4.** Dark Black and 'UGLY', Constance Briscoe was JAILED for a lesser offence. Facts are sacred and cannot be overstated. Had the Quasi-Mulatto (impure Black) been pure White, male, English, and Freemason, she might have 'WALKED': All for one, and one for all: Integrity, friendship, respect, and charity – **Habakkuk 1:4.**

Yinka Bamgbelu: BARAWO/OYINBO OLE/ODE: Irreparable weakening of their common genetic pool: The quality of human beings in their Godforsaken Hell Hole Shit Country is very poor. Immortalised incompetent mendacity is the Ne plus ultra of STUPIDITY.

Karen Kwamboka: "People cry out against the sinner, yet it is not the sinful, but the stupid, who are our shame. There is no sin except stupidity.'" Wilde (1854-1900).

Exodus 20:15, Habakkuk 2:6-9: His Scottish ancestors were RACIST THIEVES and owners of stolen children of defenceless poor Africans. Stealing is part of his DNA, one of his Scottish genetic inheritances. What has changed? Pure White European Christians want everything in Europe, and the want everything that belongs to others, including all riches of Greenland and Venezuela.

Yinka Bamgbelu: BARAWO/OYINBO OLE/ODE: "All have taken what had other owners and all have had recourse to arms rather than quit the prey onto which they were fastened." Dr Samuel Johnson (1709-1784).

Then, the pure white Scottish ancestors of President Trump were industrial-scale professional thieves and owners of stolen children of defenceless poor people, including the African ancestors of the QUASI-MULATTO, impure White/impure Black, <43% Nigerian, grandniece and grandnephew of the Duke of Edinburgh.

"Time for Scots to say sorry for slavery.

Herald Scotland: Ian Bell, Columnist / Sunday 28 April 2013 / Opinion: According to the American founding father, the son of a Caithness Kirk minister had about him "an air of great simplicity and honesty'". The likes of James Boswell and Laurence Sterne also enjoyed the merchant's company.

To his contemporaries, he was, as the author Adam Hochschild has written, '"a wise, thoughtful man who embodied the Scottish virtues of frugality, sobriety, and hard work'". Oswald was a scholar of theology, philosophy, and history. He collected art, particularly Rubens and Rembrandt, and gave handsomely to charity. Oswald, who learned his trade in Glasgow, also represented Britain in negotiations with the Americans after their war of liberation. He was the cosmopolitan epitome of Enlightenment success. But when he wasn't busy with good works, Oswald waded in blood. The precise number of deaths that can be laid at his door is impossible to calculate. As the leading figure in Grant,

Oswald & Co, he had investments in each corner of the "'triangular trade'". In his own name, Oswald trafficked at least 13,000 Africans, although he never set foot on their continent. By the time he bought Auchincruive House and 100,000 acres in Ayrshire in 1764, he was worth £500,000. Writing in 2005, Hochschild thought this was ""roughly equivalent"" to $68 million (about £44m). This is conservative.

Oswald was remarkable, but not unique. Where Glasgow and its merchants in sugar, tobacco, and human life are concerned, there are plenty of names and no shortage of monuments: Dennistoun, Campbell, Glassford, Cochrane, Buchanan, Hamilton, Bogle, Ewing, Donald, Speirs, Dunlop. One way to understand what they wrought is simple: take pleasure in the city's architecture today and you are likely to be admiring the fruits of slavery.

Glasgow is not alone in that. London, Liverpool and Bristol also have their stories to tell. Edinburgh's once-great banks grew from foundations built on bones. The first Scottish venture into slavery set out from the capital in 1695. Montrose, Dumfries, Greenock and Port Glasgow each tried their hands. In the language of the present age, they were all in it together.

When commerce was coursing around the triangle, most of polite Scotland was implicated. The nobility (and country) rendered bankrupt in 1700 in the aftermath of the Darien Venture was by the mid-1760s contemplating big, elegant townhouses and 100,000-acre estates. You could call that a reversal of fortune. Contrary to the self-serving myth, it did not happen because of "'frugality, sobriety, and hard work".

Certain things need to be remembered about Scotland and slavery. One is that the mercantile class got stinking rich twice over: despite fortunes made from stolen lives, they were quick to demand compensation when slavery was ended in 1833. Britain's government decided that £20m, a staggering sum, could be raised. In his 2010 book, The Price of Emancipation, Nicholas Draper reckons Glasgow's mob got £400,000 – in modern terms, hundreds of millions.

Compensation cases also demonstrated that Scots were not merely following an English lead. According to Draper, a country with 10% of the British population accounted for at least 15% of absentee slavers. By another estimate, 30% of Jamaican plantations were run by Scots. For all the pride taken in the abolitionist societies of Glasgow and Edinburgh, the slaveholders did not suffer because of abolition. They were '"compensated'".

And that wasn't the worst of it. Thanks to Hollywood movies, the slave economy of the American South is still taken as barbarism's benchmark. Few realise that the behaviour of Scots busy getting rich in the slaveholders" empire was actually worse – routinely worse – than the worst of the cottonocracy. You need only count the corpses……………"

Karen Kwamboka: Then, all Judges were pure white Freemasons, and most of them were thicker than a gross of planks – **Proverbs 17:16.**

BARAWO/OYINBO OLE/ODE: BEDFORD, ENGLAND: Pure White, Crooked, and Hereditary RACIST Senior District Judge Paul Robert Ayers, a mere Poly-educated former debt collector Solicitor in Norwich (5th Rate Partner), albeit the Senior Vice President of the Association of Her Majesty's District Judges, and our own brainless hereditary RACIST pure white bastard of our own Empire of Stolen Inheritance, based on cogent, irrefutable, and available evidence, the pure white ancestors of your pure white father and mother were THIEVES - **Exodus 20:15,Habakkuk 2:6-9.**

Richard Oswald (1705-1784), the son of a Caithness Kirk minister, was a 33rd Degree Freemason (Scottish Rite).

Yinka Bamgbelu: BARAWO/OYINBO OLE/ODE: BEDFORD, ENGLAND: Pure White, Crooked, and Hereditary RACIST Senior District Judge Paul Robert Ayers, a mere Poly-educated former debt collector Solicitor in Norwich (5th Rate Partner), albeit the Senior Vice President of the Association of Her Majesty's District Judges, and our own brainless hereditary RACIST pure white bastard of our own Empire of Stolen Inheritance - **Exodus 20:15, Habakkuk 2:6-9,** let me tell you, your civilisation is based on STEALING and directly sharing yields of THEFT, including in 1833. Stealing is more efficient than hard work.

Karen Kwamboka: BEDFORD, ENGLAND: Poly-educated pure white son of a pure white plebeian hoe, a RACIST descendant of THIEVES and owners of stolen children of defenceless poor people, including the AFRICAN ANCESTORS of the Quasi-Mulatto, impure Black/impure White grandniece and grandnephew of the PRINCE OF WALES, an opportunist RACIST pure white bastard was granted the platform to display hereditary prejudice. Had he not been our Senior District Judge in BEDFORD, one wouldn't know him. What can a functional semi-illiterate pure white bastard, a mere former debt-collector Solicitor in Norwich have that one would voluntarily buy?

Yinka Bamgbelu: BARAWO/OYINBO OLE/ODE: Ignorant hereditary RACIST pure white bastards (predominantly but not exclusively pure white) see molecules, and they destroy self-educated NIGERIANS, from shithole AFRICA, who see quarks.

Karen Kwamboka: SIR KEIR STARMER: Why is it Evolutionary Progress, driven Natural Selection, to use NUCLEAR BOMBS to guard the continuing propagation of pure white IMBECILES (predominantly but not exclusively pure white); thoroughly shit people who natural selection would have deselected had it not been decommissioned?

"We have decommissioned natural selection." Dr E.O. Wilson (1929-2021).

"Natural selection will not remove ignorance from future generations." Dr Richard Dawkins.

Yinka Bamgbelu: Why didn't the Negro appeal?

Appeal to who?

Ignorant hereditary RACIST pure white bastards (predominantly but not exclusively pure white): Theirs is not an apple with a few worms; theirs is a ball of worms. Their Indiscreetly Racist Justice System is irreparably FU*KED. Reporting RACIST DEMONS to RACIST DEVILS is a barren exercise – **Matthew 12:27.**

Karen Kwamboka: "Blue-eyed devils." Elijah Mohammad (1897-1975).

"As hard hearted as a Scot of Scotland." An English saying

"I don't need international law. Only my morality can stop me." President Trump

The Scottish ancestors of Mary Anne Macleod (1912-2000) were Amoral Racist Pure White Bastards, Merchants of Stolen African children, including the AFRICAN ANCESTORS of the Quasi-Mulatto, impure White/impure Black (<43% Nigerian) grandniece and grandnephew of the DUKE OF EDINBURGH. Facts are sacred and cannot be overstated.

Yinka Bamgbelu: The MORALITY of a genetically Scottish RACIST pure white bastard.

"Many Scots masters were considered among the most brutal, with life expectancy on their plantations averaging a mere four years. We worked them to death then simply imported more to keep the sugar and thus the money flowing.

Unlike centuries of grief and murder, an apology cost nothing. So, what does Scotland have to say?" Herald Scotland: Ian Bell, Columnist, Sunday 28 April 2013

Karen Kwamboka: Delusional grandeur of the stolen past. Before Slavery, what? Then, there was only subsistence feudal agriculture.

"Agriculture not only gives riches to a nation, but the only one she can call her own." Dr Samuel Johnson (1709-1784).

Yinka Bamgbelu: Europe: Stagnated economies and tourists' museums built with yields of several centuries of ancestral theft." Matthew Whitaker paraphrased.

BEDFORD, ENGLAND: Pure White Senior District Judge Paul Robert Ayers, our own Senior Vice President of the Association of Her Majesty's District Judges, you are RICH only because your ancestors were THIEVES – **Habakkuk 2:6-9, Exodus 20:15.**

Karen Kwamboka: "Freedom of Expression is a basic right." Lady Hale

An unapologetic hereditary white supremacist pure white bastard, one-dimensionally educated historical IMBECILE, and a direct descendant of thoroughly wretched Scottish Crofters, low life abjectly poor plebeian nobodies.

Yinka Bamgbelu: "Someone must be trusted; let it be the Judges." Pure White Lord Denning (1899-1999), Oxbridge-educated unapologetic hereditary white supremacist Freemason. A very rich man's son (**Mark 10:25**).

Based on cogent, irrefutable, and available evidence, all functional semi-illiterate pure white Freemason Judges in Great Britain are RACISTS.

Karen Kwamboka: SLAVERY immeasurably transformed the standard of living of thoroughly wretched Barbarians, Rabbit hunters, and Agricultural Labourers who lived off the land, but the intellects of their direct descendants seem untouched.

Yinka Bamgbelu: "Jews, Scots, and Counterfeit money will be encountered all over the world." A German Saying

Thousands of Scots and Germans were merchants of stolen African children.

The ruler of our world is genetically Scottish German: Ani Ijebu ko da, Ijesha ko sunwon, iwo wa nje Ijebu-Jesha.

Karen Kwamboka: Based on several decades of very, very, proximate observations and direct experiences, a pure white woman is grossly overrated. Perception is grander than reality.

Psalm 39:5, Psalm 144:4: Ignorant hereditary RACIST pure white bastards (predominantly but not exclusively puree white), mere travellers passing through.

Yinka Bamgbelu: If everyone, not just Masons, at Bedfordshire Masonic Centre, the Keep, Kempston Road, Bedford, MK42 8AH, were asked to handwrite a short essay, most of them would not be able to write legibly, and of those who could write legibly, most of them would not be able to spell. Perception is grander than reality.

Our Premier, the Scholar from Fife, could not spell; in our Country of the blind, the partially sighted was our shepherd.

Our Prime Minister, the Oxbridge-educated homunculus Dalit, worships cows with milk, not bulls with no milk.

"Truth, Sir, is a cow which will yield such people no more milk, and so they are gone to milk the bull." Dr Samuel Johnson (1709-1784).

Karen Kwamboka: BEDFORD, ENGLAND: Pure White Senior District Judge Paul Robert Ayers, our poly-educated hereditary RACIST pure white RUBBISH. Our IMBECILE Freemason Senior Judge of our Empire of Stolen Inheritance – Exodus 20:15, Habakkuk 2:6-9. No brain. Poor natural resources. Several centuries of stealing and SLAVERY preceded their huge stolen inheritance (gigantic yields of several continuous centuries of ancestral theft – Maafa, 1445-1888).

Yinka Bamgbelu: Truths disfavour hereditary RACIST pure white bastards (predominantly but not exclusively pure white), so they subjugate them.

BEDFORD, ENGLAND: Pure White Senior District Judge Paul Robert Ayers, an ignorant RACIST descendant of pure white THIEVES and ultra-righteous owners of stolen children of defenceless poor people, including the African ancestors of the MULATTO (impure White/impure Black) Duchess of Sussex.

Karen Kwamboka: BEDFORD, ENGLAND: Pure White, Crooked, and Hereditary RACIST Senior District Judge Paul Robert Ayers, a mere Poly-educated former debt collector Solicitor in Norwich (5th Rate Partner), albeit the Senior Vice President of the Association of Her Majesty's District Judges, it is impossible, absolutely impossible, for you and your pure white type to compete on a colour-blind level intellectual playing field without resorting to RACIST CRIMINALITY; you are INFERIOR, certainly intellectually. Sincere immodesty is sincerer than insincere modesty. Sincerity is a prime attribute of Jesus.

Yinka Bamgbelu: Those who nearly passed or just passed the A/Level could become Judges within one of the dullest adult populations in the industrialised world (OECD), their indiscreet RACIST HELL HOLE SHIT COUNTRY. Intellectually worthless pure white RACIST SHIT.

Karen Kwamboka: BEDFORD, ENGLAND: Pure White Senior District Judge Paul Robert Ayers, it is not the TRUTH that daily dialogues with a pure white IMBECILE and his type - is a proper job that is worthwhile and manly.

Yinka Bamgbelu: "They may not have been well written from a grammatical point of view but I am confident I had not forgotten any of the facts. Geraint Evans, Pure White Welsh IMBECILE, England's Class Senior Postgraduate Tutor, Oxford.

A MORON CROOKED RACIST MASON.

Karen Kwamboka: "I emphasis the point." Pure White Senior Bedford's District Judge Paul Robert Ayers, our Senior Vice President of the Association of Her Majesty's District Judges.

A MORON STONEMASON: An ignorant RACIST descendant of THIEVES and owners of stolen lives – **Exodus 20:15, Habakkuk 2:6-9.**

"There is no sin except stupidity." Wilde (1854-1900).

President Trump, a genetic Briton, implied that Britons are excessively stupid.

Yinka Bamgbelu: Pure White Senior Bedford's District Judge Paul Robert Ayers: The hereditary RACIST pure white bastard will say that he made mistakes; of course, he did, and had he not made very many mistakes at school, the opportunist RACIST pure white bastard would not have settled for daily dialogues with pure white imbeciles (predominantly but not exclusively pure white) in a GRAND CATHEDRAL-LIKE COURT that was preceded by Slavery, future flats and absolutely inevitable distance future's NUCLEAR ASH.

29, Goldington Road, MK 40 3NN, is a block of flats.

Karen Kwamboka: President Trump, a genetic Briton, implied that Britain and Britons are STUPID SHIT.

OXFORD, ENGLAND: GDC, Pure White Opportunist Racist British Soldier, Stephanie Twidale (TD) unrelentingly LIED under oath and on record – Habakkuk 1:4. Dark Black 'UGLY' Constance Briscoe was JAILED for a lesser offence. Facts are sacred and cannot be overstated.

The YANKS are NATO, everything else is an auxiliary bluff.

Karen Kwamboka: OYINBO OLE/ODE: THE ONLY BLACK AFRICA THEY TRULY LOVE IS MONEY (NATURAL RESOURCES), AND ABSOLUTELY EVERYTHING ELSE IS DECEIT.

Urhobo children with gigantic oil wells and gas fields near their huts eat only 1.5/day in our own NIGERIA, a very bellyful unashamedly functional semi-illiterate hereditary RACIST pure white bastard, a mere poly-educated former debt-collector Solicitor in bland, colourless, and almost lifeless Norfolk/Norwich (Coastal Dole/the Departure Lounge of Life) whose pure white father and mother have never seen CRUDE OIL, and whose pure white ancestors, including John Bunyan (1628-1688) and John Foster (1759-1832) of BEDFORD, and Robert Hibbert (1769-1849) of LUTON, were fed like battery hens with gigantic yields of millions of stolen and destroyed children of defenceless poor people, including the African ancestors of the Quasi-Mulatto (impure White/impure Black) great grandchildren of the Duke of Edinburgh of Blessed Memory, Prince Phillip (1921-2021).

Philippians 1:21: Phillip was a 33rd Degree Freemason (Scottish Rite).

Facts are sacred: "The truth allows no choice." Dr Samuel Johnson (1709-1784).

Yinka Bamgbelu: BEDFORD, ENGLAND: Pure White Senior District Judge Paul Robert Ayers, our Senior Vice President of the Association of Her Majesty District Judges. Our Historical Imbecile of our own Empire of Stolen Inheritance – **Exodus 20:15, Habakkuk 2:6-9.**

"Study history, study history, in history lies all the secrets of statecraft." Sir Winston Churchill (1874-1965), unapologetic White Supremacist 33rd Degree Freemason (Scottish Rite).

Karen Kwamboka: BEDFORD, ENGLAND: Pure White Senior District Judge Paul Robert Ayers, our Senior Vice President of the Association of Her Majesty District Judges: An opportunist RACIST pure white bastard was granted the platform to display hereditary prejudice. No brain. Poor natural resources.

Several centuries of THIEVERY and SLAVERY preceded their huge stolen inheritance (gigantic yields of several continuous centuries of ancestral theft – Maafa, 1445-1888) – **Exodus 20:15, Habakkuk 2:6-9.**

Yinka Bamgbelu: If it is the TRUTH that hereditary RACIST pure white bastards are intellectually superiorly created by Almighty God, what do crooked pure white cretins need RACIST CRIMINALITY for?

OYINBO OLE/ODE/BARAWO: BEDFORD, ENGLAND: Senior District Judge Paul Robert Ayers lied under oath (approved Judgement). Sue Gregory (OBE) lied under implied oath and/or on record. Mason, Brother Richard Hill fabricated reports and lied under oath - **Habakkuk 1:4**. They were all pure white. Archie is impure, < 43% Nigerian. Dark Black 'UGLY' Constance Briscoe was JAILED for a lesser offence. Facts are sacred and cannot be overstated.

Karen Kwamboka: BEDFORD, ENGLAND: Pure White Senior District Judge Paul Robert Ayers, which part of Bedfordshire Masonic Centre, MK42 8AH, and Bedford County Court, MK40 1SQ, was not STOLEN, or which part did your own pure white mother and father buy, or which part preceded SLAVERY: The grand buildings or their chattels? One-dimensionally educated opportunist RACIST pure white bastard. A straight-faced descendant of THIEVES and owners of stolen lives – **Exodus 20:15, Habakkuk 2:6-9.**

Yinka Bamgbelu: Our ignorant hereditary RACIST pure white bastard of our own Empire of Stolen Inheritance – **Habakkuk 2:6-9**. Our ultra-righteous descendant of THIEVES - **Exodus 20:15**, and extremely nasty and merciless RACIST MURDERERS - **Exodus 20:13**, nastier than Yevgeny Prigozhin (1961-2023) and HITLER (1889-1945), and just by the by, several years of NAZI HOLOCAUST (1939-1945) was a mere storm in a teacup in comparison to BLACK HOLOCAUST (Maafa, 1445-1888).

CHAPTER SEVEN

Karen Kwamboka: "Vladimir Putin fears Donald Trump, but not Keir Starmer." President Trump paraphrased.

BEDFORD, ENGLAND: Pure White Senior District Judge Paul Robert Ayers, Pure White Sue Gregory (OBE), and Pure White Mason, Brother Richard Hill – fabricated reports and/or lied under oath, including approved Judgements, and/or lied on record – **Habakkuk 1:4.**

Crooked RACIST PURE WHITE BASTARDS: Their Country is SHIT, and they are worse than SHIT. Brainless hereditary RACIST pure white bastards. Grossly overrated pure white scatter-head crooked children of pure white plebeian nobodies. Everything, absolutely everything, is baselessly and brainlessly assumed in favour of the universally acknowledged irrefutably SUPERIOR SKIN COLOUR that very fortunate wearers neither made nor chose.

Yinka Bamgbelu: BEDFORD, ENGLAND: Pure White Senior District Judge Paul Robert Ayers, you are trapped. It is absolutely impossible to use cogent facts and irrefutable evidence to disprove the TRUTH, which is that you and your pure white type are INFERIOR HUMAN BEINGS, certainly intellectually. Sincere immodesty is sincerer than insincere modesty.

Ignorant hereditary RACIST pure white bastards (predominantly but not exclusively pure white). Ultra-righteous descendants of RACIST Pure White THIEVES – **Exodus 20:15.**

Perception is grander than reality: "The English think incompetence is the same thing as sincerity." Quentin Crisp (1908-1999).

Karen Kwamboka: Hereditary RACIST pure white bastards (predominantly but not exclusively pure white) do not deserve anyone's sympathy when a genetic Scottish Dalit, a RACIST son of a lowlife plebeian Scottish domestic servant (A MERE SERF), who became a Maharajah in North America, bullies them, because they are worse RACIST BULLIES.

Yinka Bambelu: BEDFORD, ENGLAND: Based on available evidence, Pure White Senior District Judge lied. Sue Gregory (OBE) lied. Mason, Richard Hill lied. They are all Pure White Crooked Racist Bastards. Constance Briscoe was

Karen Kwamboka: BEDFORD, ENGLAND: Pure White Senior District Judge Paul Robert Ayers, you are extremely lucky that you are PURE WHITE, a full member of your brainlessly and baselessly self-awarded SUPERIOR RACE, had you been an impure Quasi-Mulatto, impure Black/impure White, like Peter Herbert (OBE) or had the Judges been IMPURE BLACK like the Mother of our Duchess of Sussex, you would have been in DEEP SHIT - **Habakkuk**.

Yinka Bamgbelu: "Michael Jackson would have been found guilty if he'd been Black." Jo Brand.

Colourism-Psychosis: One of the enduring residues of several centuries of the extortionately profitable Pure White European Christians' Commerce in Millions of Stolen and DESTROYED LIVES.

Karen Kwamboka: I do not believe in any part of your FISH and CHIPS Justice System. You are RACIST CRIMINALS, and you are living a-lie. Your leverage is the certainty that all Judges will be PURE WHITE, and your hope is that they would be hereditary RACIST pure white bastards too – **Habakkuk 1:4.**

Yinka Bamgbelu: They were all pure white: Homogeneity in the administration of their law is an impregnable secure mask of MERCILESS RACIST EVIL, a very potent weapon of RACE WAR. Dark Black 'UGLY' Constance Briscoe was JAILED for a lesser offence. One rule for pure Whites, and a different rule for all others – **Habakkuk 1:4.**

Karen Kwamboka: Exodus 21:23-27: Hereditary RACIST pure white crooked bastards should come to Lagos and try RACIST SHIT, they would be summarily dealt with, but only LEGALLY, under our Native and Customary Laws, and Sir Keir Starmer cannot do anything about it. Like Vladimir Putin, in Nigeria, Nigerians fear Donald Trump, not Keir Starmer.

Yinka Bamgbelu: "We shall deal with the racist bastards when we get out of prison." Comrade Robert Mugabe (1924-2019).

They hate FOREIGNERS, and we know - **Leviticus 19:33-34**. They overwhelm our people with INCOMPETENT RACIST LIES and they kill foreigners, albeit hands-off, with the mens rea hidden in the belly of the actus reus.

Karen Kwamboka: Our own NIGERIAN BROTHER, Dr Richard Bamgboye, a General Medical Practitioner, only 56, and INDIAN DENTIST, Dr Anand Kamath, only 42, were unlawfully killed, albeit hands-off, with the mens rea hidden in the belly of the actus reus – **Exodus 20:13**. Based on several decades of very proximate observations and direct experiences, they are innately very wicked people.

Yinka Bamgbelu: Hereditary RACIST pure white bastards (predominantly but not exclusively pure white) have invented a perfectly legal method of killing foreigners: They start by criminally annulling yields of the Christ-granted talents of our own people (FORMAL EDUCATION), and they economically strangulate our own people, and they place insurmountable obstacles before our own people, and they sadistically irreparably destroy the minds of our own people, and they kill our own people, albeit hands-off. They hate us, and we know. They MUST stay here because it is safer than Nigeria – **Exodus 21:23-27.** It is not the TRUTH that their own people are the only ones who know how to kill people – **Exodus 20:13.**

Karen Kwamboka: Based on several decades of very proximate observations and direct experiences, the weapon of the pure white privileged dullard, the direct descendant of the Father of RACIST LIES - **John 8:44, John 10:10**, is the Mother of RACIST LIES, and her power is the certainty that all Judges will be PURE WHITE and her hope is that they would be hereditary RACIST pure white bastard too.

Yinka Bamgbelu: Our ignorant opportunist RACIST descendant of PROFESSIONAL THIEVES and owners of stolen lives. The ignorant one -dimensionally educated RACIST pure white bastard was our Senior District Judge in BEDFORD only because he FU*KING could not do anything else. Apart from debt-collection, what was in bland, colourless, and almost lifeless Norfolk/Norwich (Coastal Dole/the Departure Lounge of Life) for functional semi-illiterate opportunist RACIST Freemason Solicitors to do?

Karen Kwamboka: 1976-2022: Quasi-Communism: Our properly schooled impostor and an expert of deception, having FAILED in practice, loads did, the hereditary RACIST pure white bastard parked his liability at the public till and sold unashamed MEDIOCRITY and CONFUSION to the undiscerning in exchange for very valuable considerations.

Yinka Bamgbelu: 1976-2022: 46 Wasted Years. The opportunist RACIST pure white bastard will face the sword of truth, not Jonathan Aitken's, but the Divine Sword of the Transparent Truth of the only Judge that matters – **John 5:22.** Infinite sojourn in Al Jahannam is his inevitable destiny; he shall go to his RACIST ancestors, inside Dante's Inferno, for they shall never return to him – **2 Samuel Johnson 12:23**.

1976-1992: Our hereditary RACIST pure white bastard FAILED in practice, loads did.

1992-2000: For about a decade, our poly-educated pure white son of pure white plebeian nobodies was an apprentice Judge (Deputy District Judge); he FAILED promotion examinations, and kept repeating the class, hence almost one decade of apprenticeship.

Karen Kwamboka: "The best opportunity of developing academically and emotional." Pure White Senior Bedford's District Judge Paul Robert Ayers.

BRAINLESS PURE WHITE RACIST NONSENSE: OUR HIGHLY RESPECTED FUNCTIONAL SEMI-ILLITERATE HEREDITARY RACIST PURE WHITE BASTARD OF OUR EMPIRE OF STOLEN INHERITANCE - **EXODUS 20:15, HABAKKUK 2:6-9.**

"Yes, Sir, it does her honour, but it would do nobody else honour. I have indeed not read it all. But when I take up the end of a web, and find a packthread, I do not expect, by looking further, to find embroidery." Dr Samuel Johnson (1709-1784).

2000-2022: Our brainless hereditary RACIST pure white bastard of our own Empire of STOLEN INHERITANCE -**Exodus 20:15, Habakkuk 2:6-9.** Other people paid an opportunist RACIST unashamedly functional semi-illiterate pure white bastard other people's money in exchange for senseless CONFUSION: QUASI-COMMUNISM.

Yinka Bamgbelu: Sheep unnaturally shepherd sheep: Shepherds know that their sheep are morons, but sheep do not know that their shepherds are morons too. "Mediocrity weighing mediocrity in the balance, and incompetence applauding its brother………" Wilde (1854-1900).

Hereditary RACIST pure white bastards (disproportionately but not exclusively pure white) want all NIGERIANS, from shit hole Africa, in Great Britain, to be Born-Again Christians, who have been systematically BRAINWASHED to believe than MASONS are the New Truly Good God - **Mark 10:18**, and who pay Antichrist Ritualists Quasi-Protection Money (TITHE) through Churches of Christ.

Karen Kwamboka: If King's School and Oxbridge-educated very rich man's son (**Mark 10:25**), Lord Justice Charles Anthony Haddon-Cave, KC, a RACIST first son of a Tasmanian Colonialist Economic Cannibal, Sir Charles

Phillip Haddon-Cave (1925-1999), could disprove the TRUTH, which is that his own pure white kindred, Senior Bedford's District Judge Paul Robert Ayers, Sue Gregory (OBE), and Richard Hill (Mason) fabricated reports and/or unrelentingly lied under oath and/or on record, he will concomitantly disprove the implied belief of Senior Judge Peter Herbert (OBE), which is that the administration of English Law is a Negrophobic Charade.

Yinka Bamgbelu: Russia cannot win a War against the YANKS but may defeat the Europeans.

Hundreds of thousands of RUSSIANS have died. The probability that RUSSIA will avenge the death of her citizens - is 100%.

1940: Without the support of the YANKS, France surrendered within 6/52.

2026: In the same position as UKRAINE, but without the support of the YANKS, Great Britain would surrender within 6/7. What is great about that?

Karen Kwamboka: BEDFORD, ENGLAND: Pure White Senior District Judge Paul Robert Ayers, you are 'very poor'. You are RICH only because your pure white ancestors were THIEVES – **Exodus 20:15**. Before Slavery, what? Your land yields only FOOD. It is impossible, absolutely impossible, for your Christ-granted talent to sustain your very high standard. Unlike PUTIN'S SIBERIA, there are no gas fields in Freemasons' Kempston and where the pure white mother and father of Pure White Senior Bedford's District Judge Paul Robert Ayers, were born. An OPPORTUNIST RACIST descendant of ultra-righteous pure white THIEVES and owners of stolen lives – **Exodus 20:15, Habakkuk 2:6-9.**

Yinka Bamgbelu: OYINBO OLE/ODE/BARAWO: Pre-Slavery Agrarian economy was essentially subsistence.

Our own NIGERIA, Shell's docile cash cow since 1956 (OLOIBIRI). GDC was established in 1956.

Unlike PUTIN'S SIBERIA, there are no gas fields in Robert Hibbert (1769-1849) and Tommy Robinson's LUTON.

Karen Kwamboka: They hate us, and we know. We hate them more, and they know. They are very powerful. We are POWERLESS, and we have been robbed to penniless since their armed ancestors found our defenceless ancestors in the AFRICAN BUSH, in the 15th Century (Maafa, 1445-1888).

"How Europe underdeveloped Africa." Dr Walter Rodney (1942-1980).

Yinka Bamgbelu: They hate us, but not only because of our darker coat that we neither made nor chose. They FEAR untamed minds of self-educated NIGERIANS, from shit hole Africa, more than Putin's poisons.

Karen Kwamboka: Intellectual degradation of the Self-Awarded Thinking Class (Stolen, Unearned, and Undeserved Elitism): Ignorant Racist Descendants of THIEVES and owners of stolen lives – **Exodus 20:15, Habakkuk 2:6-9.**

Yinka Bamgbelu: They are RACIST CRIMINALS; we have evidence. GDC, Freemason, Brother Richard William Hill, Senior NHS Postgraduate Tutor, albeit Bedford's Class, fabricated reports and unrelentingly lied under oath and on record – Habakkuk 1:4. Quasi-Mulatto, impure Black, 'Ugly' Constance Briscoe was JAILED for a lesser offence: One rule for pure white, and another rule for all others – Archie is impure, <43% Nigerian.

Karen Kwamboka: A brainless opportunist RACIST pure white son of a pure white plebeian hoe: Perception is grander than REALITY. Their universally acknowledged irrefutably SUPERIOR PURE WHITE SKIN COLOUR, which they neither made nor chose, a huge stolen inheritance, and what else? Before SLAVERY, what?

Yinka Bamgbelu: Our brainless hereditary RACIST pure white bastard of our own Empire of STOLEN INHERITANCE – **Exodus 20:15, Habakkuk 2:6-9**, was granted the platform to display hereditary prejudice. What do you have? You do not have ANYTHING tangible that was not STOLEN or preceded SLAVERY (Maafa, 1445-1888).

Karen Kwamboka: A RACIST descendant of ultra-righteous PURE WHITE THIEVES and owners of stolen lives – **Exodus 20:15, Habakkuk 2:6-9**. The only evidence of his Higher IQ is the GIGANTIC STOLEN INHERITANCE that his thoroughly wretched pure white ancestors crossed the English Channel, not that long ago, without luggage or decent shoes – to latch onto.

Yinka Bamgbelu: Insincere modesty is DECEIT, and it is subservient to sincere immodesty. Sincerity is a prime attribute of Jesus.

BEDFORD, ENGLAND: Pure White Senior District Judge Paul Robert Ayers, immodesty apart, you are INFERIOR, certainly intellectually. Based on available evidence, it is absolutely impossible for you and your pure white type to compete on a colour-blind level intellectual playing field without resorting to RACIST CRIMINALITY – **Habakkuk 1:4.**

Karen Kwamboka: They were PROFESSIONAL THIEVES: Stealing was a very important part of their civilisation - **Exodus 20:15, Habakkuk 2:6-9.**

Then, Armed Sea Wolves, Industrial-Scale THIEVES, looted the defenceless world, brought yields of RACIST EVIL back to Britain, and made it possible for millions of pure white IMBECILES to thrive and breed more millions of pure white IMBECILES.

Yinka Bamgbelu: They are very special only because they are pure white and their ancestors were insatiably greedy RACIST THIEVES, apart from those, they are PURIFIED NOTHING. It is absolutely impossible for their Christ-granted talents and yields of their land to sustain their high standard of living.

Karen Kwamboka: BEDFORD, ENGLAND: Pure White Senior District Judge Paul Robert Ayers, you are RACIST LEECH because the pure white ancestors of your pure white mother and father were THIEVES and owners of STOLEN LIVES. You are worthy only because you are PURE WHITE. You are rich only because your ancestors were THIEVES – **Exodus 20:15, Habakkuk 2:6-9.**

Yinka Bamgbelu: OYINBO OLE/ODE/BARAWO: "He has refused to submit to a medical examination." Lord Justice Charles Anthony Haddon-Cave, KC.

BRAINLESS RACIST NONSENSE.

SHOCKING! "Why that is, because, dearest, you are a dunce." Dr Samuel Johnson (1709-1784).

Karen Kwamboka: OYINBO OLE/ODE: Lord Justice Charles Anthony Haddon-Cave, KC: Facts are sacred and cannot be overstated. If you engage on a colour-blind intellectual playing field, you shall be irreparably destroyed with cogent facts and irrefutable evidence. You are INFERIOR in every way that could be objectively measured. Sincere immodesty is sincerer than insincere modesty. Our brainless opportunist RACIST pure white bastard of our own Empire of stolen inheritance – **Exodus 20:15, Habakkuk**, saw molecules and he destroyed all self-educated Nigerians, from shithole Africa, who saw quarks; New Herod, **Matthew 2:16**.

Yinka Bamgbelu: Our pure white scatter-head hereditary RACIST pure white bastard (Alzheimer's disease or atypical dementia or something else), albeit England's Class Lord Justice; an ignorant direct descendant of pure white THIEVES and owners of stolen and destroyed lives – **Habakkuk.**

Karen Kwamboka: OYINBO OLE/ODE: They were all PURE WHITE. Homogeneity in the administration of their law is an impregnable very secure mask of merciless RACIST EVIL, and a very potent weapon of a raging, ASYMMETRIC, and PSYCHOLOGICAL RACE WAR.

Yinka Bamgbelu: Leviticus 19:33–34: They kill our people (NEGROES), and others, remotely. Nigerian, Dr Richard Bamgboye, only 56, a GP, and Indian, Dr Anand Kamath, only 42, Dentist, were unlawfully killed, albeit hands-off, with the mens rea hidden in the belly of the actus reus.

Karen Kwamboka: When their own people commit RACIST CRIMES against our people, their own people who oversee the administration of their own law, criminally bury RACIST EVIL, and their overwhelming leverage is the certainty that all Judges will be pure white, and their hope is that they would be hereditary RACIST pure white bastards too – **Habakkuk 1:4.**

Yinka Bamgbelu: OYINBO OLE/ODE/BARAWO: King's School and Oxbridge-educated very, very, rich man's son (**Mark 10:25**), Lord Justice Charles Anthony Haddon-Cave, KC, then in our own tribe in the AFRICA BUSH, your blue-eyed evil types (olojuu deru bomo) were treated with sticks and stones.

"Blue-eyed devils." Elijah Mohamad (1897-1975).

Karen Kwamboka: Pure White Briton, Dr Mungo Park (1771–1806) had guns (emphasis on the pleura), but the hereditary white supremacist bastard was treated with sticks and stones in the African bush.

"Stoning certainly teaches people a lesson." Ayatollah Sadegh Khalkhali (1926-2003).

Yinka Bamgbelu: YOUR COUNTRY IS SHIT. YOU ARE WORSE THAN SHIT.

Then, all Judges were pure white Freemasons, and most of them were thicker than a gross of planks.

BEDFORD, ENGLAND: Pure Senior District Judge Paul Robert Ayers, our own Senior Vice President of the Association of our own Majesty's District Judges, the mind that that the Nigerian, from shit hole Africa, did not choose is FINER than your Justice System. He does not believe in any part of SHIT, as no part of your SHIT is good, not even one – **Psalm 53**. He has the power to use cogent facts and irrefutable evidence to IRREPARABLY DESTROY you and every part of your SHIT Justice System – **Habakkuk 1:4.** BEDFORD: Sue Gregory (OBE), our Officer of the Most Excellent Order of our Empire of STOLEN INHERITANCE (**Exodus 20:15, Habakkuk 2:6-9)** unrelentingly lied and on record. Freemason, Brother Richard William Hill fabricated reports and unrelentingly lied under oath and on record. Senior Bedford's District Judge unrelentingly lied under oath (approved Judgement). They were all PURE WHITE. Racist bastards JAILED Impure Black (Quasi-Mulatto) Constance Briscoe for a lesser offence. Archie is impure Black, <43% Nigerian.

Karen Kwamboka: OYINBO OLE/ODE/BARAWO: Stolen Elitism: Baseless and Brainless Hereditary Advantages. Undeserved Privilege. Unearned Patronage. King's School and Oxbridge-educated Lord Justice Charles Anthony Haddon-Cave, KC, a Racist first son of a very, very, rich **(Mark 10:25**) and insatiably greedy (**Habakkuk 2:5**), Tasmanian Colonialist Economic Cannibal, I fell into a transient trance, and I saw Al Jahannam and in hell, I saw a very rich man's son, Tony Benn (1925-2014), Mrs Margaret Thatcher (1925-2013), Pol Pot (1925-1998), and your dad, Sir Charles Phillip Haddon Cave (1925-1999); you are a mere traveller passing through, and you shall absolutely inevitably reunite with your own father in Al Jahannam: You shall go to your Racist Economic Cannibal Father – in hell, for he will never return to you – **2 Samuel 12:23.**

Yinka Bamgbelu: "Britain can no longer count on the US for defence." Lord Sedwill

Without the direct support of the YANKS, Great Britain is a sitting duck.

OXFORD, ENGLAND: GDC, Pure White British Soldier, Stephanie Twidale (TD) unrelentingly lied under oath and on record – **Habakkuk 1:4**. Quasi-Mulatto (impure Black) 'Ugly' Constance Briscoe was Jailed for a lesser offence.

The YANKS are NATO, and absolutely everything else is an auxiliary bluff.

Karen Kwamboka: A brainless hereditary RACIST pure white bastard. What is special about you? Unlike PUTIN'S SIBERIA, there are no gas fields in Bedfordshire and where the pure white father and mother of Pure White Senior District Judge Paul Roberet Ayers were born, the land of which he was born yields only FOOD, he is verifiably a functional semi-illiterate, and he dishonestly implied that he did not know that the pure white ancestors of his pure white mother and father were THIEVES and owners of stolen lives, including the African ancestors of the Quasi-Mulatto (impure White/impure Black, <43% Nigerian) grand niece and grand nephew of Major Andrew Mountbatten Windsor. Facts are sacred and cannot be overstated.

Yinka Bamgbelu: An ignorant one-dimensionally educated hereditary RACIST descendant of insatiably greedy pure white bastards. Then, the basis of their RACIST EVIL CIVILISATION was stealing and sharing yields of stealing – **Exodus 20:15, Habakkuk 2:6-9.** In 1833, insatiably greedy RACIST PURE WHITE BASTARDS shared yields of stolen lives among scores of thousands of pure white RACIST economic cannibals, merchants of stolen and destroyed lives.

Karen Kwamboka: Hereditary RACIST pure white bastards love the gigantic yields of ancestral theft—**Exodus 20:15, Habakkuk,** firearm enforced involuntary mass migration of tens of millions of stolen African children, including the African ancestors of impure White/impure Black, Mulatto (43% Nigerian), Duchess of Sussex.

Yinka Bamgbelu: Ignorant descendants of THIEVES and owners of stolen lives do not want to pay equitable, fair, and just REPARATION and they do not want mass migration, so they want to eat all their own cakes, eat all the cakes of others, and have everything – **Habakkuk 2:5.**

Karen Kwamboka: OYINBO OLE/ODE: Prior to SLAVERY, there weren't very many proper houses in Tommy Robinson's LUTON: Slavery rebuilt everything it succeeded and paid for everything it preceded. Robert Hibbert (1769–1849), and tens of thousands of pure white crude and cruel merchants of stolen lives, demanded and accepted millions of pounds of the yields of millions of stolen and destroyed lives of children of defenceless poor people (AFRICANS) – **Habakkuk.**

Yinka Bamgbelu: "Ethical foreign policy." Robin Cook (1946-2005).

If hereditary RACIST pure white bastards (predominantly but not exclusively pure white) are as ethical, and as brave, as they vulgarly brag, they must use extreme overwhelming violence to evict PUTIN from CRIMEA, he used extreme overwhelming violence to convert Bakhmut and Avdiivka from bricks to rubble and stole them – **Exodus 20:15.**

Karen Kwamboka: "The white man was created a devil, to bring chaos upon the earth." Malcolm X (1925–1965)

Based on several decades of very proximate observations and direct experiences, ignorant one-dimensionally educated RACIST PURE WHITE BASTARDS are not only demons, but they are also THIEVES – **Exodus 20:15,** and if did not know those truths, it is proof that you could not see them as they truly are.

"I do not approve of anything that tampers with natural ignorance. Ignorance is like a delicate exotic fruit; touch it and the bloom is gone. The whole theory of modern education is radically unsound. Fortunately, in England, at any rate, education produces no effect whatsoever. If it did, it would prove a serious danger to the upper classes and probably lead to acts of violence in Grosvenor Square." Wilde (1854-1900).

Yinka Bamgbelu: "He is a typical Englishman, usually violent and always dull." Wilde (1854-1900)

BEDFORD, ENGLAND: GDC, Sue Gregory (OBE) unrelentingly lied under implied oath and on record - **Habakkuk 1:4**. They are NOT the only creation of Almighty God, and they are not immortal, and the universally acknowledged irrefutably SUPERIOR SKIN COLOUR that the very fortunate wearer neither made nor chose is not the only wonder of our world.

Proverbs 20:15: Their universally acknowledged irrefutably superior skin colour is a great creation of the Almighty, but it is not the greatest.

BEDFORD, ENGLAND: Pure White Senior District Judge Paul Robert Ayers, Poly-educated pure white son of pure white plebeian nobodies, and a mere former debt-collector Solicitor in Norwich (5th Rate Partner). The ignorant pure white bastard 5th Rate Senior District Judge, albeit within one of the dullest adult populations in the industrialised world (OECD), was granted the platform to display hereditary prejudice. He should fu*king stay here; it is safer than NIGERIA – **Exodus 21:23-27.**

"We shall deal with the racist bastards when we get out of prison." Comrade Robert Mugabe (1924-2019).

Our functional semi-illiterate pure white bastard of our own Empire of Stolen Inheritance – **Exodus 20:15, Habakkuk 2:6-9**. A properly schooled impostor and an expert of deception. Having FAILED in practice, loads did, the opportunist RACIST pure white bastard parked his liability at the public till and sold unashamed MEDIOCRITY and CONFUSION to the undiscerning, a QUASI-THIEF – **Exodus 20:15.**

CHAPTER EIGHT

Karen Kwamboka: Oxbridge-educated, Sir Charles Phillip Haddon-Cave (1925-1999), a Racist Colonialist Economic Cannibal, your direct ancestors were armed land, grabbers, insatiably greedy economic cannibals, racist genocidal bastard bullies, the decimators of Native Tasmanians, and industrial-scale professional thieves – **Exodus 20:15, Habakkuk 2: 6-9.**

President Trump is principally a genetic Briton because his principal X Chromosome is from his mother, a 100% genetic Briton.

Britons were bullies, and they are bullies, so they do not deserve Africans' sympathy when they are bullied and humiliated by Trump, a genetic Briton.

"Study history, study history, in history lies all the secrets of statecraft." Sir Winston Churchill (1874-1965), a hereditary bully.

Fake Special Relationship with a Colossus: GDP, USA, $31 trillion. GDP, UK, $4 trillion.

Guerrilla Warfare: Great Britain needs enemies, and special friends they have ready tools to destroy.

Bullies fear only those have the tools to kill them

"You have enemies? Good. That means you've stood up for something, sometime in your life." Sir Winston Churchill (1874-1965), unapologetic hereditary pure white supremacist thug, and 33rd Degree Ritualist Freemason (Scottish Rite).

Yinka Bamgbelu: Of course, they were. Where the fu*k did you think the insatiably greedy hereditary RACIST pure white bastards got all the money from?

"The English think incompetence is the same thing as sincerity." Quentin Crisp (1908-1999).

"The Rights of Man." Thomas Paine (1737-1809).

Ibn Sina: Deluded Hereditary RACIST Pure White Bastards (disproportionately but not exclusively pure white). What opportunist RACIST bastards have the

POWER to do to conceal RACIAL HATRED could be worse than RACIAL HATRED, so victims of Racist Evil should be wise to feign ignorance.

"The white man was created a devil, to bring chaos upon the earth." Malcolm X (1925-1965).

Galatians 6:7: Then, hereditary RACIST pure white bastards used yields of millions of stolen and destroyed lives to build Sacred Altars for Christ; ignorant evil racist bastards used yields of Merciless Racist Evil to build Churches and Cathedrals.

The Right Honourable John Foster (1759-1832), MP, and a very Wealthy Slave-Merchant, should confirm that prior to, Slavery, there weren't very many proper houses in Bedford. Slavery rebuilt everything it succeeded and paid for everything it preceded, including Brickhill Baptist Church.

Karen Kwamboka: They see a supposedly very highly respected Senior District Judge, albeit Bedford's Class. I see an opportunist RACIST pure white bastard who FAILED in practice, loads did, and the hereditary RACIST pure white bastard parked his LIABILITY at the public till. If they are not excessively STUPID, I must be MAD.

Hereditary RACIST Pure White Bastards, FREEMASONS: Based on several decades of very proximate observations and direct experiences, they are like RATS, and like RATS, they love to act without being seen, but like RATS, they are excessively stupid, so they defecate everywhere leaving tell-tale signs.

Yinka Bamgbelu: Freedom of expression is the most important right under God's free sun. So, if the pure white ancestors of one's pure white mother and father were THIEVES – **Exodus 20:15**, Merciless Racist Killers – **Exodus 20:13**, and owners of stolen children of defenceless poor people, including the African ancestors of the Quasi-Mulatto, impure White/impure Black (<43% Nigerian) grandniece and grandnephew of Major Andrew Mountbatten Windsor, and if one is verifiably a RACIST CROOK, it is plainly deductible that Freedom of Expression is not one of one's best friends.

"Freedom of Expression is a basic right." Lady Hale.

Karen Kwamboka: I feel you. Stealing is part of their DNA. We are all who we are, the inheritors of our inheritances, including the DNA of our individual ancestors. OYINBO OLE/ODE: One of the huge gains of several continuous centuries of merciless RACIST EVIL, stealing and slavery (Maafa, 1445-1888) is that an unashamedly functional semi-illiterate pure white bastard was our Senior District Judge, albeit Bedford's Class. No brain. Poor natural resources. Several centuries of stealing and slavery preceded their huge stolen inheritance (gigantic yields of several continuous centuries of ancestral theft – **Exodus 20:15, Habakkuk**).

Yinka Bamgbelu: It is a common belief in the African bush that stealing is hereditary**.** OYINBO OLE/ODE: Our own unashamedly functional semi-illiterate, verifiably indiscreetly crooked, and hereditary white supremacist pure white son of a pure white plebeian hoe was granted the platform to display hereditary prejudice. The universally acknowledged irrefutably superior skin colour that the very fortunate wearer neither made nor chose, a huge stolen inheritance, and what else?

Karen Kwamboka: Based on several decades of very proximate observations and direct experiences, they, not all, are SHIT PEOPLE, and only the universally acknowledged irrefutably superior skin colour that the very fortunate wearer neither made nor chose and Almighty God are truly good – Mark 10:18. OYINBO OLE/ODE: Perception is always grander than reality:

"Those who have robbed have also lied." Dr Samuel Johnson (1709-1784).

Ignorance is bliss: "Those who know the least obey the best." George Farquhar (1677-1707).

Facts are sacred and cannot be overstated.

Yinka Bamgbelu: Based on several decades of very proximate observations and direct experiences, they, nearly all, are thicker than a gross of planks. Then , all Judges were pure white FREEMASONS, and most of them were thicker than a tonne of concrete.

"I emphasis the point." Pure White Hereditary Racist, unashamedly functionally semi-illiterate, poly-educated poor man's son, a downmarket former debt-collector Solicitor in bland and colourless Norfolk/Norwich, (Coastal Dole the Departure Lounge of Life), a mere lowlife 5th Rate Partner, and the Senior Vice President of the Association of Her Majesty's District Judges, Bedford's District Judge Paul Robert Ayers, 3, St Paul's Square, MK 40 1SQ.

Brainless nonsense: His country is SHIT, and he his worse shit. He proof-read, approved, and immortalised what his functional semi-illiterate pure white mumsy spoke. Those who nearly passed or just passed the A/Level could do Law within one of the dullest adult populations in the industrialised world (OECD).

Karen Kwamboka: OYINBO OLE/ODE: Our own IMBECILE Freemason Senior District Judge, albeit Bedford's Class, of our own Empire of Stolen Inheritance – **Exodus 20:15, Habakkuk.**

"I don't want to talk grammar. I want to talk like a lady." George Bernard Shaw (1856-1950).

Yinka Bamgbelu: OYINBO OLE/ODE: His superior pure white skin concealed his inferior dark black brain. The spinal cord of the opportunist RACIST pure white bastard was his highest centre.

That they hate us, is certain, and they always look for new ways to injure us. The only Good Shepherd (John 10:11-18) shields us from Evil Racist Pure White Bastards. They love to do RACIST HATRED LEGALLY, but THICKO PLANKOS are too stupid to do Merciless Racial Hatred seamlessly – **Proverbs 17:16.**

Karen Kwamboka: OYINBO OLE/ODE: Nigerian children with gigantic oil wells and gas fields near their huts eat only 1.5/day in Nigeria, a very, very, very, very, bellyful functional semi-illiterate hereditary RACIST pure white bastard, a mere poly-educated (not Russell Group Inferior Class Alternative Education – **Proverbs 17:16**) for debt-collector Solicitor in bland, colourless, and almost lifeless Norfolk/Norwich (Coastal Dole/the Departure Lounge of Life) was our pure white Senior District Judge, albeit England's Class, in Bedford, Great Britain. Which part of our own shithole Africa is great?

OYINBO OLE/ODE: "How Europe underdeveloped Africa." Dr Walter Rodney (1942-1980).

Yinka Bamgbelu: 'Weakening of the common genetic pool, intellectual decline, and resultant cultural erasure.' President Trump paraphrased.

'Retrogressive cultural degradation impersonates progressive civilisation.' President Putin paraphrased.

Matthew 12:48-50: Why am I not richer than Elon Musk, if I am aware of the existence of the infinite reality, and he is not, and relative to the infinite reality that I am aware of, the finite reality he is aware of - is ZERO, Nothing?

GDC, Mrs Helen Falcon (MBE), our own Member of the Most Excellent Order of our own Empire of Stolen Inheritance – **Habakkuk 2:6-9, Exodus 20:15,** unrelentingly lied under oath and on record – **Habakkuk 1:4.** Constance Briscoe was JAILED for a lesser offence: Apartheid by stealth.

Karen Kwamboka: "Treating your adversary with respect is striking soft in a battle." Dr Samuel Johnson (1709-1784).

Ecclesiastes 3:1-8: "Now it is time to stand up and fight back...There are no good crackers, and if you find one, kill him before he changes." Brother Khalid Abdul Mohammad (1948- 2001), West Chester University, PA, February 17, 1992.

Yinka Bamgbelu: 'The Bro' who treated his irreconcilable enemy with insults instead of paying people to feed evil racist bastard bullets - invented civilisation.' Sigmund Freud (1856-1939) Paraphrased.

Karen Kwamboka: OYINBO OLE/ODE: Racist bastards love brainless and baseless skin colour SUPERIORITY, their inviolable self-awarded birthright, but they hate Freedom of Expression because they don't want their own mentally gentler white children (OECD) and the mentally wonkier pure white imbeciles they shepherd (predominantly but not exclusively pure white) to know the truth, which is that only the universally acknowledged irrefutably superior skin colour that the very fortunate wearer neither made nor chose and Almighty God are truly good – **Mark 10:18**.

Yinka Bamgbelu: OYINBO OLE/ODE: If our own hereditary RACIST pure white bastard of our own Empire of Stolen Inheritance – **Exodus 20:15, Habakkuk**, read his own approved Judgement, he was a PURE WHITE FOOL, and if our own opportunist RACIST pure white bastard did not, he lied as he implied that he did. Our brainless hereditary RACIST pure white bastard should stay here; it is safer than NIGERIA – **Exodus 21:23-27.** The pure white ancestors of his pure white mother and father were incompetent RACIST LIARS too, they were THIEVES and owners of stolen children of defenceless poor people, including the African ancestors of Quasi-Mulatto, impure White/impure Black (<43% Nigerian) great grandchildren of the Duke of Edinburgh of Blessed Memory, Prince Phillip (1921-2021).

Philippians 1:21: Phillip was a 33rd Freemason, Scottish Rite.

Karen Kwamboka: OYINBO OLE/ODE: Our own brainless hereditary RACIST pure white dunce of our own Empire of Stolen Inheritance - **Exodus 20:15, Habakkuk**. Had our own opportunist RACIST pure white bastard not made very, very, very, many mistakes at school, he would not have settled for daily dialogues with pure white IMBECILES (predominantly but not exclusively pure white) in their bland, colourless, and almost lifeless Market Town, near a

Major Motorway (M1): Based on cogent, irrefutable, and available evidence, the SERENGETI of hereditary RACIST pure white bastards (predominantly but not exclusively pure white. 1976-2022: Having FAILED in practice, loads did, the opportunist RACIST pure white bastard, a mere former debt-collector Solicitor in bland, colourless, and almost lifeless NORFOLK/NORWICH (Coastal Dole/ the Departure Lounge of Life), and a RACIST descendant of THIEVES, parked his liability at the public till, and the opportunist RACIST pure white bastard sold unashamed mediocrity and confusion to the undiscerning.

Yinka Bamgbelu: OYINBO OLE/ODE: Skin colour superiority: The collective refuge of the genetically intellectually impotent.

Based on cogent, irrefutable, and available evidence, hereditary RACIST pure white bastards (predominantly but not exclusively pure white) dressed up uncontrollable inter-racial intellectual envy and innate RACIAL HATRED and call them colour-blind and transparently impartial administration of the law. Based on available evidence, the administration of English Law is compatible with Antichrist Freemasonry Quasi-Religion, but incompatible with Christian belief. Sincere immodesty is sincerer than insincere modesty. Sincerity is one of the prime attributes of our own Messiah – **John 14:6**.

Karen Kwamboka: OYINBO OLE/ODE: BEDFORD, ENGLAND: GDC, Sue Gregory (OBE), Officer of the Most Excellent Order of our own Empire of Stolen Inheritance - **Exodus 20:15, Habakkuk**, unrelentingly lied under implied oath and record – **Habakkuk 1:4.** Constance Briscoe was JAILED for a lesser offence. Facts are sacred and cannot be overstated.

Yinka Bamgbelu: OYINBO OLE/ODE: APARTHEID LAW: One rule for pure whites, and another rule for all others – **Habakkuk 1:4.** Apartheid by stealth.

Karen Kwamboka: "Impure White/impure Black, Mulatto, Duchess of Sussex (43% Nigerian), was a victim of explicit and obnoxious RACIAL HATRED." John Bercow paraphrased.

Yinka Bamgbelu: OYINBO OLE/ODE: THEIR EMPIRE OF STOLEN LIVES. RACIST BULLIES: Racist descendants of THIEVES allowed their huge stolen advantages (Maafa, 1445-1888) to cloud their objective reasoning and judgement, and deluded by the grandeur of the stolen past, they brainlessly miscalculated and lost.

Karen Kwamboka: Two, only two, but two too many, brainless, shallow, and myopic Oxbridge-educated bastards.

1967: Oxbridge-educated Colonel Emeka Ojukwu (1933-2011) did not foresee that by 1970, several millions of NIGERIANS, including children would have died, and had he, he would have acted differently.

Yinka Bamgbelu: "The first class at Oxford, where I have examined, is an overrated mark." Hugh Redwald Trevor-Roper (1914-2003).

Had Oxbridge-educated Boris Johnson been smarter, he would have foreseen, in 2022, that by 2025, more than a million of his pure white kindred would be dead, and tens of millions of pure white people would have been displaced.

Karen Kwamboka: OYINBO OLE/ODE: Hereditary RACIST pure white bastards (predominantly but not exclusively pure white) know how to deal with self-educated NIGERIANS who disagree with them, but innately RACIST pure white bastards (predominantly but not exclusively pure white) do not know how to repair the scatter-heads of their own pure white kindred.

Yinka Bamgbelu: OYINBO OLE/ODE: Then, all Judges were pure white Freemasons, and most of them were thicker than a gross of planks, and pure white Freemason Judges who believed that daily dialogues with pure white IMBECILES (predominantly but not exclusively pure white) were worthwhile and manly, were scammers, and those who demanded and accepted very valuable considerations in exchange for daily dialogues with pure white imbeciles (predominantly but not exclusively pure white) were RACKETEERS (Quasi-Thieves – **Exodus 20:15).**

Karen Kwamboka: OYINBO OLE/ODE: Based on cogent and irrefutable evidence, those who were exposed to tortuous alternative education lacking rigour (**Proverbs 17:16**), and who nearly passed or just passed the A/Level - could become Judges and Police Officers within one of the dullest adult populations in the industrialised world (OECD).

Based on available evidence, Judges of the lowest courts, including District Judges, and Police Officers, are not recruited from the pool of the brightest people in any society.

Yinka Bamgbelu: "I have seen evil, and it has the face of Mark Fuhrman." Johnnie Cochran (1937-2005).

OYINBO OLE/ODE: Pure White Hereditary Racist, unashamedly functionally semi-illiterate, poly-educated poor man's son, a downmarket former debt-collector Solicitor in bland and colourless Norfolk/Norwich, (Coastal Dole/the

Departure Lounge of Life), a mere lowlife 5th Rate Partner, and the Senior Vice President of the Association of Her Majesty's District Judges, Bedford's District Judge Paul Robert Ayers, 3, St Paul's Square, MK 40 1SQ, a mere poly-educated (not Russell Group Lower-Class Alternative Education – **Proverbs 17:16**), verifiably crooked, unashamedly functional semi-illiterate, and opportunist RACIST bastard, and Mark Fuhrman (LAPD), a mere GED (Lower-Class Alternative Education – **Proverbs 17:16**) were pure white.

The grandniece and grandnephew of Major Andrew Mountbatten Windsor are impure White/impure Black (Quasi-Mulatto, <43% Nigerian).

"Find the truth and tell it." Harold Pinter (1930-2008).

Tasmania University and Oxbridge-educated very, rich man's son (Mark 10:25), Sir Charles Phillip Haddon-Cave (1925–1999), an innately white supremacist grandson of Francis Haddon-Cave, born in Hobart in early 20th-century Australian settlement; a properly schooled impostor and an expert of deception (perception is grander than reality), a direct descendant of genocidal insatiably greedy pure white bastards, the exterminators of Native Tasmanians, and a closeted white supremacist descendant of DRUG LORDS (opium merchants of the Qing Dynasty): Negroes, let me tell you, in my era, Judges were recruited only from the pool of Oxbridge-educated higher upper-class Britons, not from among poly-educated (not Russell Group Lower Class Alternative Education - **Proverbs 17:16**) functional semi-illiterate children of plebeian nobodies.

Karen Kwamboka: OYINBO OLE/ODE: Sir Keir Starmer, why is it desirable to use NUCLEAR BOMBS to guard the continuing propagation of pure white imbeciles (predominantly but not exclusively pure white adults with the basic skills of a child), those who natural selection would have deselected had it not been decommissioned?

"We have decommissioned natural selection......" Dr Edward Osborne Wilson (1929-2021).

"Natural selection will not remove ignorance from future generations." Dr Richard Dawkins.

OYINBO OLE/ODE: One of the gains of several continuous centuries of stealing and slavery (Maafa, 1445-1888) is that pure white imbeciles (predominantly but not exclusively pure white adults with the basic skills of a child) thrive in Great Britain - **Habakkuk.** Which part of our own shithole Africa is great?

OYINBO OLE/ODE: "How Europe underdeveloped Africa." Dr Walter Rodney (1942-1980).

Yinka Bamgbelu: OYINBO OLE/ODE: BEDFORD, ENGLAND: District Judge, based on cogent, irrefutable, and available evidence, it is absolutely impossible for you and your pure white type, including Richard Hill and Sue Gregory (OBE) - to compete on a colour-blind level intellectual playing field without resorting to RACIST CRIMINALITY.

Karen Kwamboka: OYINBO OLE/ODE: BEDFORD, ENGLAND: Pure White Hereditary Racist, unashamedly functionally semi-illiterate, poly-educated poor pure white man's son, a downmarket former debt-collector Solicitor in bland, colourless, and almost lifeless Norfolk/Norwich, (Coastal Dole/the Departure Lounge of Life), a mere lowlife 5th Rate Partner, and the Senior Vice President of the Association of Her Majesty's District Judges, Bedford's District Judge Paul Robert Ayers, 3, St Paul's Square, MK 40 1SQ, if you could disprove the truth, which is that your own pure white kindred, GDC, Richard William Hill, Senior NHS Postgraduate Tutor, albeit Bedfordshire Class, fabricated reports and unrelentingly lied under oath and on record – **Habakkuk 1:4**, and if you could disprove the truth which is that your own pure white kindred, GDC, Sue Gregory, OBE, Officer of the Most Excellent Order of our own Empire of Stolen Inheritance – **Exodus 20:15, Habakkuk**, unrelentingly lied under implied oath and on record – **Habakkuk 1:4**, you will concomitantly disprove the belief of some self-educated NIGERIANS, which is that some pure white people are grossly overrated, and you will also disprove the belief of Yinka Bamgbelu, which is that it is absolutely impossible for you and your pure white type, including Richard William Hill and Sue Gregory (OBE) to compete on a colour-blind level intellectual playing field without resorting to RACIST CRIMINALITY, and your overwhelming leverage being the certainty that all Judges will be pure white (homogeneity), and your hope being that they would all be hereditary RACIST pure white bastards too – **Habakkuk 1:4.** Your Country is SHIT, and you are worse than SHIT. Nigeria (oil/gas) is by far more relevant to the economic survival of all your mentally gentler white children (OECD) than Robert Hibbert (1769-1849) and Tommy Robinson's LUTON. No brain. Poor natural resources. Several centuries of stealing and slavery preceded their huge stolen inheritance (gigantic yields of several continuous centuries of ancestral theft – **Exodus 20:15, Habakkuk**). Facts are sacred and cannot be overstated.

Ignorant hereditary RACIST descendants of PURE WHITE THIEVES – **Exodus 20:15, Habakkuk**. Perception is grander than reality.

"Sometimes people don't want to hear the truth because they don't want their illusions destroyed." Friedrich Nietzsche (1844-1900).

Yinka Bamgbelu: OYINBO OLE/ODE/BARAWO: APARTHEID BY STEALTH/COLOURISM: A brainless hereditary RACIST pure white bastard was granted the platform to display hereditary prejudice.

Karen Kwamboka: OYINBO OLE/ODE: What they want is a world where substance is subservient to superfluous, and where Christ granted talent is subservient to skin colour.

Yinka Bamgbelu: OYINBO OLE/ODE: Our brainless hereditary RACIST pure white bastard of our Empire of stolen inheritance – **Exodus 20:15, Habakkuk**, was granted the platform to display hereditary prejudice. The 'Bro' FAILED in practice, loads did, parked his LIABILITY at the public till, and he DISHONESTLY sold unashamed mediocrity and confusion to the undiscerning – in exchange for very valuable considerations. Unlike PUTIN'S RUSSIA, there are no oil wells or gas fields in bland, colourless, and almost lifeless NORFOLK/NORWICH (Coastal Dole/the Departure Lounge of Life) and where the pure white mother and father of Pure White Hereditary Racist, unashamedly functionally semi-illiterate, poly-educated poor man's son, a downmarket former debt-collector Solicitor in Norwich, a mere lowlife 5th Rate Partner, and the Senior Vice President of the Association of Her Majesty's District Judges, Bedford's District Judge Paul Robert Ayers, 3, St Paul's Square, MK 40 1SQ, and the very highly luxuriant soil of Bishop's Stortford yields only FOOD. Bishop's Stortford's Cecil Rhodes (1853-1902) was a RACIST pure white bastard and a PROFESSIONAL THIEF – **Exodus 20:15, Habakkuk.**

OYINBO OLE/ODE: An ignorant one-dimensionally educated pure white bastard, and a very shallow opportunist RACIST descendant of PURE WHITE THIEVES – **Habakkuk, Exodus 20:15.**

"The supreme vice is shallowness." Wilde (1854-1900).

Karen Kwamboka: John 8:7, Matthew 7:1-6: OYINBO OLE/ODE: BEDFORD, ENGLAND: Our own Mediocre, Physically Ill-Favoured, and Mentally Wonky, Pure White, Hereditary Racist, unashamedly functional semi-illiterate, poly-educated, poor man's son, a downmarket former debt-collector

Solicitor in bland, colourless, and almost Norfolk/Norwich, (Coastal Dole/ the Departure Lounge of Life), a closeted white supremacist mere lowlife 5th Rate Partner, and the Senior Vice President of the Association of Her Majesty's District Judges, Bedford's District Judge Paul Robert Ayers, 3, St Paul's Square, MK 40 1SQ; our own brainless hereditary RACIST pure white bastard of our own Empire of stolen inheritance - **Exodus 20:15, Habakkuk**, ultra-righteously sat on a highchair that his pure white mother and father could not afford, which the pure white IMBECILES (predominantly but not exclusively pure white) who sat before him could not, and did not buy, in a Museum-Like Grand Court that was preceded by SLAVERY, future flats and absolutely inevitable distant future Nuclear Ash (29, Goldington Road, MK40 3NN is a block of flats), and Judged SINNERS. An ignorant hereditary RACIST descendant of ultra-righteous professional THIEVES: The Ne plus Ultra of Hypocrisy.

Yinka Bamgbelu: **John 5:22, Matthew 25:31-46, Revelation 3:21:** Only SAINTS have the moral right to Judge SINNERS. Racist descendants of THIEVES and owners of stolen children of defenceless poor people (AFRICANS) - do not have the moral right to Judge Sinners while sitting on the BONES of stolen lives, in Grand Courts preceded Slavery, and while equitable, fair, and just reparation pends, and several centuries of unpaid interest accrue: OYINBO OLE/ODE – **EXODUS 20:15, HABAKKUK.**

Karen Kwamboka: "Freedom of Expression is the cornerstone of our democracy." Lord Jacob Rees-Mogg, Eton and Oxbridge-educated closeted white supremacist very, very, very, rich man's son (**Mark 10:25).**

Yinka Bamgbelu: The report, by the OECD, warns that the UK needs to take significant action to boost the basic skills of the nation's young people. The 460-page study is based on the first-ever survey of the literacy, numeracy and problem-solving at work skills of 16 to 65-year-olds in 24 countries, with almost 9,000 people taking part in England and Northern Ireland to make up the UK results. The findings showed that England and Northern Ireland have some of the highest proportions of adults scoring no higher than Level 1 in literacy and numeracy - the lowest level on the OECD's scale. This suggests that their skills in the basics are no better than that of a 10-year-old.

AN IMBECILE: AN ADULT WITH THE BASIC SKILLS OF A CHILD.

Karen Kwamboka: BEDFORD, ENGLAND: OYINBO OLE/ODE: Our own Mediocre, Physically Ill-Favoured, and Mentally Wonky, Pure White,

Hereditary Racist, unashamedly functional semi-illiterate, poly-educated, poor man's son, a downmarket former debt-collector Solicitor in bland, colourless, and almost Norfolk/Norwich, (Coastal Dole/the Departure Lounge of Life), a closeted white supremacist mere lowlife 5th Rate Partner, and the Senior Vice President of the Association of Her Majesty's District Judges, Bedford's District Judge Paul Robert Ayers, 3, St Paul's Square, MK 40 1SQ, it is not the TRUTH that daily dialogues with pure white IMBECILES (predominantly but not exclusively pure white) is a proper job that is worthwhile and manly.

OYINBO OLE/ODE: OUR OPPORTUNIST RACIST DESCENDANT OF ULTRA-RIGHTEOUS PURE WHITE PROFESSIONAL THIEVES OF OUR EMPIRE OF STOLEN INHERITANCE (GIGANTIC YIELDS OF SEVERAL CONTINUOUS CENTURIES OF ANCESTRAL THEFT – **EXODUS 20:15, HABAKKUK.**

Yinka Bamgbelu: BEDFORD, ENGLAND: Our own Mediocre, Physically Ill-Favoured, and Mentally Wonky, Pure White, Hereditary Racist, unashamedly functional semi-illiterate, poly-educated, a poor man's son, a downmarket former debt-collector Solicitor in bland, colourless, and almost Norfolk/Norwich, (Coastal Dole/the Departure Lounge of Life), a closeted white supremacist mere lowlife 5th Rate Partner, and the Senior Vice President of the Association of Her Majesty's District Judges, Bedford's District Judge Paul Robert Ayers, 3, St Paul's Square, MK 40 1SQ, pure white skin, a huge stolen inheritance (gigantic yields of several continuous centuries of ancestral theft – **Exodus 20:15, Habakkuk**), and what else? Before Slavery, what? OYINBO OLE/ODE.

Accurate seers accurately foresaw that millions of Britons will be IMBECILES (adults with the basic skills of a child), so they looted AFRICA: Wherever they mercilessly slaughtered unarmed and defenceless poor people, including the African ancestors of the impure White/impure Black, Quasi-Mulatto (<43% Nigerian) niece and nephew of the Prince of Wales, they dispossessed them of their meagre possession, and whenever they robbed Africans of the meagre possession, they took possession – **Exodus 20:15, Habakkuk.**

OYINBO OLE/ODE: "Those who have robbed have also lied." Dr Samuel Johnson (1709-1784).

OYINBO OLE/ODE: "All have taken what had other owners and all have had recourse to arms rather than quit the prey onto which they were fastened." Dr Samuel Johnson (1709-1784).

Karen Kwamboka: Our own Mediocre, Physically Ill-Favoured, and Mentally Wonky, Pure White, Hereditary Racist, unashamedly functional semi-illiterate, poly-educated, a poor man's son, a downmarket former debt-collector Solicitor in bland, colourless, and almost Norfolk/Norwich, (Coastal Dole/the Departure Lounge of Life), a closeted white supremacist mere lowlife 5th Rate Partner, and the Senior Vice President of the Association of Her Majesty's District Judges, Bedford's District Judge Paul Robert Ayers, 3, St Paul's Square, MK 40 1SQ, a mere poly-educated (not Russell Group Lower-Class Alternative Education – **Proverbs 17:16**), verifiably crooked, unashamedly functional semi-illiterate, and opportunist RACIST bastard, you are verifiably physically and mentally wonky: Coarse, short (for a real man), dull, and generally ill-favoured. Based on cogent, irrefutable, and available evidence, then, in the African bush, during several centuries of highly civilised and ultra-righteous European Christians' carrying trade, your physically and/or mentally wonky people like you were REJECTED – **Habakkuk.**

Yinka Bamgbelu: OYINBO OLE/ODE: BEDFORD, ENGLAND: Our own Mediocre, Physically Ill-Favoured, and Mentally Wonky, Pure White, Hereditary Racist, unashamedly functional semi-illiterate, poly-educated, a poor man's son, a downmarket former debt-collector Solicitor in bland, colourless, and almost Norfolk/Norwich, (Coastal Dole/the Departure Lounge of Life), a closeted white supremacist mere lowlife 5th Rate Partner, and the Senior Vice President of the Association of Her Majesty's District Judges, Bedford's District Judge Paul Robert Ayers, 3, St Paul's Square, MK 40 1SQ, it is plainly deductible that the pure white ancestors of your own pure white mother and father were extremely nasty RACIST MURDERERS – **Exodus 20:13**, nastier than Yevgeny Prigozhin (1961-2023) and the tall dwarf, Corporal Adolf Hitler (1889-1945), and just by the by, several years of NAZI HOLOCAUST (1939-1945) was a mere storm in a teacup in comparison to Maafa, BLACK HOLOCAUST (1445-1888), and they were insatiably greedy industrial scale Professional THIEVES – **Exodus 20:15,** Armed Robbers, Armed Land Grabbers, Gun Runners (Firearm Merchants), DRUG DEALERS (Opium Merchants of the Qing Dynasty), and owners of stolen and destroyed lives of the children of defenceless poor Africans - **Habakkuk**.

CHAPTER NINE

Karen Kwamboka: They hate us, and we know, but they don't know that we know that they do. BEDFORD, ENGLAND: OYINBO OLE/ODE: Our own Mediocre, Physically Ill-Favoured, and Mentally Wonky, Pure White, Hereditary Racist, unashamedly functional semi-illiterate, poly-educated, a poor man's son, a downmarket former debt-collector Solicitor in bland, colourless, and almost Norfolk/Norwich, (Coastal Dole/the Departure Lounge of Life), a closeted white supremacist mere lowlife 5th Rate Partner, and the Senior Vice President of the Association of Her Majesty's District Judges, Bedford's District Judge Paul Robert Ayers, 3, St Paul's Square, MK 40 1SQ, let me tell you, the most important part of the matter is MONEY, and it was stolen with GUNS – **Exodus 20:15**. Prior to SLAVERY, there was only subsistence feudal agriculture. You are not genetically an aboriginal Briton. Your thoroughly wretched pure white ancestors crossed the English Channel, not that long ago, without luggage or decent shoes, solely, to latch onto yields of millions of stolen and destroyed lives of the children of defenceless poor people, including the African ancestors of the impure White/impure Black, Mulatto, Duchess of Sussex (43% Nigerian). You are verifiably a closeted RACIST descendant of ULTRA-RIGHTEOUS PURE WHITE THIEVES – **Exodus 20:15, Habakkuk**, your pure white European ancestors, including Humphrey Morice (1671-1731), were PURE WHITE PROFESSIONAL THIEVES.

Yinka Bamgbelu: OYINBO OLE/ODE: Racist descendants of ultra-righteous pure white armed robbers, armed land grabbers, gun runners (firearm merchants), drug dealers (opium merchants of the Qing Dynasty), and owners of stolen children of defenceless poor people - oppress AFRICAN descendants of the robbed with yields of the robbery – **Exodus 20:15, Habakkuk.** In 1833, pure white descendants of pure white robbers shared part of the huge yields of millions of stolen children of defenceless poor people (AFRICANS) – among tens of thousands of merchants of stolen and destroyed lives – **Habakkuk.**

Karen Kwamboka: OYINBO OLE/ODE: "England is like a prostitute who, having sold her body all her life, decides to quit and close her business and then tells everybody that she wants to be chaste and protect her flesh as if it were jade." He Manzi (1919-2009).

Yinka Bamgbelu: OYINBO OLE/ODE: "Humphrey Morice (1771-1831). the Governor of the Bank of England, died only two years before very greedy pure white bastards shared stolen money (1833) - Exodus **20:15.** He was an engaged merchant and shipowner. He made it his business to learn the details of the trade, which he expressed in careful instructions to his team of captains. He explained how trading practices varied from one African port to the next. He knew that staying on the coast too long gathering cargo risked higher mortality, so he worked out cooperative practices among his ships to evacuate the slaves quickly. He instructed his captains to slaves between the ages of twelve and twenty-five, two males to a female: Good and healthy, and not blind, lame or blemished. He no doubt followed the advice of his Jamaican factors about the defects to be carefully avoided: Dwarfish and gigantick size wch are equaly disagreeable, ugly faces, long tripeish breasts wch ye Spaniards mortally hate, yellowish skins, livid spots in ye skin wch turns to an incurable evil. Films in ye eyes. Loss of fingers, toes, or teeth, navels sticking out, ruptures wch ye Gambia slaves are very subject to, bandy legs, sharp shins, lunaticks, idiots, lethargicks." The Slave Ship: A Human History by Marcus Rediker paraphrased.

Then, insatiably greedy Racist Bastards did not carry ugly idiots.

Those who know the truth obey the least.

"Those who know the least obey the best." George Farquhar (1677-1707).

Karen Kwamboka: Hardened Evil RACIST Pure White Bastards (predominantly but not exclusively pure white) CRIMINALLY WEAPONISED their Justice System, and used it to kill foreigners – **Leviticus 19:33-34;** they want to kill me too - **Exodus 20:13.** The mind that I did not choose is finer than their indiscreetly crooked, VINDICTIVE, unashamedly mediocre, potently weaponised, and institutionally RACIST Fish and Chips Justice System, and I do not believe in any part of SHIT, as no part of SHIT is good, not even one – **Psalm 53**, and I have the POWER to use cogent facts and irrefutable evidence to irreparably destroy you and SHIT – **Habakkuk 1:4.** Facts are sacred and cannot be overstated.

Yinka Bamgbelu: OYINBO OLE/ODE: Racist descendants of ultra-righteous pure white THIEVES. Pure white Freemason Judges who Judge SINNERS, of all shades, are crooked incompetently mendacious RACIST bastards too: The Ne Plus Ultra of Hypocrisy. Demons cannot cast out demons - **Matthew 12:27.**

BEDFORD, ENGLAND: Based on cogent, irrefutable, and available evidence, our own Mediocre, Physically Ill-Favoured, and Mentally Wonky, Pure White, Hereditary Racist, unashamedly functional semi-illiterate, poly-educated, a poor man's son, a downmarket former debt-collector Solicitor in bland, colourless, and almost Norfolk/Norwich, (Coastal Dole/the Departure Lounge of Life), a closeted white supremacist mere lowlife 5th Rate Partner, and the Senior Vice President of the Association of Her Majesty's District Judges, Bedford's District Judge Paul Robert Ayers, 3, St Paul's Square, MK 40 1SQ, unrelentingly lied under oath and on record (approved judgement) -**Habakkuk 1:4.** Had he been Black, the crooked, opportunist RACIST, and unashamedly poly-educated functional semi-illiterate pure white bastard would have been deterred.

Karen Kwamboka: OYINBO OLE/ODE: APARTHEID LAW BY STEALTH: Constance Briscoe was JAILED for a lesser offence. One rule for Pure Whites, and another rule for all others. Had she been pure White, English, Male, and Freemason, all for one, and one for all might have FREED HER – **Habakkuk 1:4.**

Yinka Bamgbelu: OYINBO OLE/ODE: BEDFORD, ENGLAND: Our own Mediocre, Physically Ill-Favoured, and Mentally Wonky, Pure White, Hereditary Racist, unashamedly functional semi-illiterate, poly-educated, a poor man's son, a downmarket former debt-collector Solicitor in bland, colourless, and almost Norfolk/Norwich, (Coastal Dole/the Departure Lounge of Life), a closeted white supremacist mere lowlife 5th Rate Partner, and the Senior Vice President of the Association of Her Majesty's District Judges, Bedford's District Judge Paul Robert Ayers, 3, St Paul's Square, MK 40 1SQ, your country is SHIT, and you are worse than SHIT. Your brain is not good. Sincere immodesty is sincerer than insincere modesty. It is impossible for you and your pure white type to COMPETE on a level colour-blind intellectual playing field without resorting to RACIST CRIMINALITY – **Habakkuk 1:4.**

Karen Kwamboka: OYINBO OLE/ODE: A Racist son of Anne Mary Macleod (1912-2000) - a mere working class plebeian Scottish domestic servant treated the British Premier, a Knight of the Most Excellent Order of our Empire of Stolen Inheritance - **Exodus 20:15, Habakkuk**, like a domestic servant.

"Could you take on the Russians by yourselves." President Trump

Yinka Bamgbelu: OYINBO OLE/ODE: A 5th Rate Military Power impersonates a SUPERPOWER.

The YANKS are NATO, and absolutely everything else is an auxiliary bluff If hereditary RACIST pure white bastards (predominantly but not exclusively pure white) are as brave as they ostensibly brag, they must directly, not indirectly (proxy war) – use GUNS to evict PUTIN FROM CRIMEA, he stole it with GUNS – **Exodus 20:15.**

OXFORD, ENGLAND: GDC, British Soldier, Stephanie Twidale (TD) unrelentingly lied under oath and on record – **Habakkuk 1:4**. Had she been Black, she would have been in trouble. Constance Briscoe was JAILED for a lesser offence. Facts are sacred and cannot be overstated.

Freedom of expression is the inviolable cornerstone of European civilisation.

Christ was killed only because He spoke – **Matthew 27:32-56**. He was not punished for speaking but was KILLED solely to prevent Him from speaking.

"Freedom of expression is a basic right." Lady Hale.

Karen Kwamboka: OYINBO OLE/ODE: BEDFORD, ENGLAND, District Judge, our brainless hereditary RACIST pure white bastard of our own Empire of Stolen Inheritance – **Exodus 20:15, Habakkuk**, what do you have that is tangible and was not STOLEN or preceded SLAVERY? You are FROTH. You are worthy only because you are pure white. You are rich only because your ancestors were PROFESSIONAL THIEVES. Our own money, NIGERIA (oil/gas), is by far more relevant to the economic survival of all your own mentally gentler white children (OECD), your pure white mother, your pure white father, and your pure white spouse than Freemasons' Kempston. You are a leech. The pure white ancestors of your pure white mother and father were PROFESSIONAL THIEVES and owners of stolen children of defenceless poor people (AFRICANS). Unlike PUTIN'S RUSSIA, there are no oil wells or gas fields in bland, colourless, and almost lifeless John Bunyan's Bedford and where your own pure white mother and father were born.

"The truth allows no choice." Dr Samuel Johnson (1709-1784).

Yinka Bamgbelu: OYINBO OLE/ODE: "The first human who hurled an insult instead of a spear/stone was the founder of civilisation." Sigmund Freud (1856-1939).

Our ignorant hereditary RACIST pure white son of a pure white plebeian hoe of our own Empire of Stolen Inheritance – **Exodus 20:15, Habakkuk**, ultra-righteously sat on the BONES of stolen children of defenceless poor people (AFRICANS), more BONES than the millions of skulls at the doorstep of Pol Pot (1925-1998), and Judged SINNERS.

Karen Kwamboka: OYINBO OLE/ODE: "Every Saint has a past, and every sinner has a future." Wilde (1854-1900).

Equitable, fair, and just reparation pends, and several centuries of unpaid interest accrue.

John 5:22, Matthew 25:31-46: Only SAINTS have the moral right to Judge SINNERS.

Yinka Bamgbelu: OYINBO OLE/ODE: Racist descendants of ultra-righteous industrial-scale PROFESSIONAL THIEVES do not have the moral right to Judge SINNERS - **John 8:7, Matthew 7:1-6**, as demons cannot cast out demons - **Matthew 12:27**. Facts are sacred and cannot be overstated.

Karen Kwamboka: OYINBO OLE/ODE: They hate us, and we know. Ignorant hereditary RACIST pure white bastards (predominantly but not exclusively pure white), and ultra-righteous descendants of THIEVES love SKIN COLOUR SUPERIORITY (Colourism/Apartheid by stealth), their brainlessly and baselessly self-awarded birthright, but they hate Freedom of Expression.

Yinka Bamgbelu: OYINBO OLE/ODE: They are greedier than the grave, and like death, insatiably greedy pure white bastards (predominantly but not exclusively pure white) can never be satisfied, so they eat their own cakes, eat ours, and have everything – **Habakkuk 2:5**.

Karen Kwamboka: Then, their direct ancestors carried and sold millions of stolen children of defenceless poor people, now they steal natural resources. European Christians will always steal from Africa, but what evil greedy bastards steal will vary from generation to generation.

Yinka Bamgbelu: OYINBO OLE/ODE: They are Innate Thieves. There is no law in their Godforsaken RACIST HELL HOLE; their law is what Freemasons want. We are all who we are, the inheritors of our individual inheritances, the genes of our individual ancestors. If one's ancestors were PROFESSIONAL THIEVES and owners of stolen children of defenceless poor Africans, it would be very naïve not to expect RACIAL HATRED complicated by incompetent mendacity to be part of one's genetic inheritances: Persecutory Negrophobia guarded by Negrophobic Perjury – **Habakkuk 1:4**.

CHAPTER TEN

Karen Kwamboka: OYINBO OLE/ODE: "Civilisation erasure in Europe." J.D. Vance

A direct descendant of Minor Europeans (Working Class) who stowaway to North America without passports, Visas, luggage, and decent shoes.

Yinka Bamgbelu: OYINBO OLE/ODE: Based on cogent, irrefutable, and available evidence, the entire foundation of European civilisation is Maafa (1445-1888): Several continuous centuries of carrying and selling millions of stolen children of defenceless poor people, including the African ancestors of the impure White/impure Black Quasi-Mulatto (<43% Nigerian) – grandniece and grandnephew of Major Andrew Mount-Batten Windsor.

Karen Kwamboka: OYINBO OLE/ODE: Their Museum like Grand Court that was preceded by SLAVERY, and evidently built with yields of Merciless Racist Evil: Stolen Lives – **Exodus 20:15, Habakkuk.**

BEDFORD, ENGLAND: OYINBO OLE/ODE: Our own Mediocre, Physically Ill-Favoured, and Mentally Wonky, Pure White Hereditary Racist, unashamedly functionally semi-illiterate, poly-educated poor man's son, a downmarket former debt-collector Solicitor in bland and colourless Norfolk/Norwich, (Coastal Dole/ the Departure Lounge of Life), a mere lowlife 5th Rate Partner, and the Senior Vice President of the Association of Her Majesty's District Judges, Bedford's District Judge Paul Robert Ayers, 3, St Paul's Square, MK 40 1SQ, which part of Bedford County Court, MK40 1SQ, and Bedfordshire's Freemasons' Temple, the Keep, MK42 8AH, was not STOLEN - **Exodus 20:15**, or which part did your own pure white mother and father buy, or which part preceded slavery: The grand buildings or their very expensive chattels.

Yinka Bamgbelu: OYINBO OLE/ODE: It is absolutely impossible for a pure white woman, a Member of the Most Excellent Order of our own Empire of Stolen Inheritance - **Exodus 20:15, Habakkuk,** to be a RACIST CRIMINAL because pure white people, nearly all, are SAINTS:

Certum est quia impossibile est.

BRAINLESS RACIST NONSENSE!

Karen Kwamboka: Oxford, November 25, 2009: Based on very proximate contacts, our own very ugly, physically ill-favoured, and mentally wonky homunculus hereditary RACIST pure white bastard cougar, with an asymmetric muscular ass, like those of a professional javelin thrower (FATIMA WHITBREAD), stank.

Yinka Bamgbelu: Based on a very proximate contact, Mrs Helen Falcon, a crooked closeted hereditary RACIST Member of the Most Excellent Order of our own Empire of Stolen Inheritance – **Exodus 20:15, Habakkuk**, a ROTARIAN (vulgarly charitable, Antichrist, and hereditary white supremacist Freemasonry Quasi-Religion without Voodoo or Occultists' Rituals) a typical pure white Englishwoman had a very, very, distinct body odour, the pure white cougar stank.

"The truth allows no choice." Dr Samuel Johnson (1709-1784).

Karen Kwamboka: "Britons stank." W.S.

Wole Soyinka, not William Shakespeare (1564-1616), should know, as at least one of his wives and some of his concubines were Britons.

Yinka Bamgbelu: OYINBO OLE/ODE: Hereditary RACIST pure white bastards (predominantly but not exclusively pure white) dressed up inter-racial intellectual envy and hereditary RACIAL HATRED and called it impartial colour-blind administration of the law. Trump's poodles. Flat track bullies. Deluded paper tigers. Fake superpowers. Their hairs stand on end when they are challenged by self-educated NIGERIANS; if hereditary RACIST pure white bastards (predominantly but not exclusively pure white) are as brave as they vulgarly brag, they must directly use GUNS to evict PUTIN from Crimea, he stole it with GUNS – **Exodus 20:15**. Facts are sacred and cannot be overstated.

Karen Kwamboka: OXFORD, ENGLAND: GDC, Mrs Helen Falcon, MBE, unrelentingly lied under oath and on record - **Habakkuk 1:4.** The pure white ancestors of her pure white father and mother were incompetent RACIST LIARS too, they were PROFESSIONAL THIEVES – **Exodus 20:15**, extremely nasty RACIST KILLERS – **Exodus 20:13,** and owners of stolen children of defenceless poor people, including the impure Black/impure White (<43% Nigerian) grandniece and grandnephew of Pure White Major Andrew Mountbatten Windsor.

Yinka Bamgbelu: OYINBO OLE/ODE: BEDFORD, ENGLAND: District Judge Paul Robert Ayers, A brainless hereditary RACIST pure white bastard, what do you own that is the yield of transparent virtue, or was not directly or indirectly stolen, or preceded SLAVERY? Unlike PUTIN'S SIBERIA, there are no gas fields in Tommy Robinson's LUTON and where your own pure white father and mother were born. An ignorant hereditary RACIST descendant of THIEVES: No brain. Poor natural resources. Several centuries of stealing and slavery preceded their huge stolen inheritance (gigantic yields of several continuous centuries of ancestral theft – **Exodus 20:15, Habakkuk**). Facts are sacred and cannot be overstated.

Karen Kwamboka: OYINBO OLE/ODE: GDC, Mrs Helen Falcon (MBE), our incompetently mendacious Member of the Most Excellent Order of our own Empire of Stolen Inheritance – **Exodus 20:15, Habakkuk.** Constance Briscoe was jailed for a lesser offence. Facts are sacred and cannot be overstated.

Yinka Bamgbelu: OYINBO OLE/ODE: Properly rehearsed ultra-righteousness and deceptively schooled civilised decorum were preceded by several continuous centuries of MERCILESS RACIST EVIL (Maafa, 1445-1888). Facts are sacred and cannot be overstated.

Their armed direct pure white ancestors were direct and indirect professional thieves – **Exodus 20:15.**

Karen Kwamboka: OYINBO OLE/ODE: Then, in the African bush, armed, civilised, European, and ultra-righteous Christian hunters of children of defenceless poor people (AFRICANS), hereditary RACIST pure white bastards, and those they armed, stalked African children like prey, and the evil bastards hunted in packs.

"There is no hunting like the hunting of man, and those who have hunted armed men long enough and liked it, never care for anything else thereafter." Ernest Hemingway (1899-1961).

Yinka Bamgbelu: OYINBO OLE/ODE: Hereditary RACIST pure white bastards (predominantly but not exclusively pure white) seek to conceal hereditary RACIAL HATRED by adorning it with a cloak of deceit (homogeneity in the administration of their law is a potent weapon of RACE WAR), and when RACIST EVIL unravelled, they always declared that they diligently performed their duties. OYINBO ODE/OLE: Ignorant descendants of THIEVES – **Habakkuk, Exodus 20:15.**

"When a stupid man is doing something, he is ashamed of, he always declares that it is his duty." George Bernard Shaw (1856-1950).

Karen Kwamboka: OYINBO OLE/ODE: "The white man is the devil." Elijah Mohammad (1897-1975).

If you did not know that truth, it is proof that you could not see him as he truly is.

Clarence Thomas, Negro Lynching: "As a black American, as far as I am concerned, it is high tech lynching for uppity who in any way dared to think for themselves, to do for themselves, to have different ideas, and it is a message that unless you kowtow to an old order – that is what would happen to you; you will be lynched, destroyed, caricatured by a Committee of the US Senate rather than hung from a tree."

Yinka Bamgbelu: OYINBO OLE/ODE: They are SHIT PEOPLE and they know, but they don't know that we know too. BEDFORD, ENGLAND: GDC, Freemason, Brother Richard William Hill fabricated reports and unrelentingly lied under oath – **Habakkuk 1:4.** Constance Briscoe was JAILED for a lesser offence: Apartheid Law by Stealth. Facts are sacred and cannot be overstated.

Karen Kwamboka: OYINBO OLE/ODE: COLOURISM: If as our own hereditary RACIST crooked pure white bastard of our own Empire of Stolen Inheritance – **Exodus 20:15, Habakkuk**, implicitly vulgarly bragged, he is superiorly created (brainless and baseless skin colour superiority) by Almighty God, what did our own hereditary RACIST pure white bastard need RACIST CRIMINALITY for? An ultra-righteous descendant of industrial-scale professional THIEVES – **Habakkuk, Exodus 20:15.**

Yinka Bamgbelu: OYINBO OLE/ODE: Lord Justice Haddon-Cave, KC, based on cogent, irrefutable, and available evidence, the pure white ancestors of your own pure white father, Sir Charles Phillip Haddon-Cave (1925-1999), a RACIST Tasmanian Colonialist Economic Cannibal, were THIEVES – **Exodus 20:15.**

"The blame is his who chooses. God is blameless." Plato.

The mind that the Nigerian, from shithole Africa, did not choose is finer than your Justice System, and I shall use cogent facts and irrefutable evidence to irreparably destroy you and SHIT – **Habakkuk 1:4.**

Karen Kwamboka: OYINBO OLE/ODE: When hereditary RACIST pure white bastards (predominantly but not exclusively pure white) FU*KED, which was very often, GENIUS JEWS, their Jim Will Fix It, were their GO-TO-PEOPLE.

"Jews are intelligent and creative, Chinese are intelligent but not creative, Indian are servile, and Africans are morons." Professor James Watson, DNA (1928-2025).

OYINBO ODE: One-dimensionally educated genetic Scottish RACIST pure white bastard.

Yinka Bamgbelu: OYINBO ODE: One-dimensionally educated pure white dunce: "Societies that live closer to the equator are warmer. Why are they also poorer?" Tomas Pueyo.

Because they were ROBBED during several centuries of merciless RACIST EVIL: The greediest economic cannibalism, and the evilest RACIST TERRORISM the world will ever know – Maafa (1445-1888).

Karen Kwamboka: OYINBO OLE/ODE: "The white man, not the Jew, is the devil." Khalid Abdul Mohammad (1948-2001).

Millions of Jews are pure white, but Archie is impure, <43% Nigerian (Quasi-Mulatto).

"The white man is not only practicing Racism and Zionism, and with the prostitution ring, the so-called Jew man with the Jew woman all over the world to make a few dollars, he is also practicing sexism. He's a racist, he's a Zionist, an imperialist. He's a no-good bastard. He's not a devil; the white man is the Devil." Khalid Abdul Mohammad (1948–2001), San Francisco State University, May 21, 1997

Yinka Bamgbelu: OYINBO OLE/ODE: Flat track bullies: If hereditary RACIST pure white bastards (predominantly but not exclusively pure white) are truly brave, as they ostensibly brag, they must directly use GUNS to evict PUTIN from CRIMEA, he stole it with guns - **Exodus 20:15**.

Karen Kwamboka: OYINBO OLE/ODE: Ignorant hereditary RACIST pure white bastards, ultra-righteous descendants of industrial-scale professional THIEVES; their creator, evidently hates them, so He cursed them with dark-black brains, and blessed them, above all others, with the universally acknowledged irrefutably superior skin colour that the very fortunate wearer neither made nor chose.

Yinka Bamgbelu: OYINBO OLE/ODE: BEDFORD, ENGLAND: District Judge, your Country is SHIT, and you are worse than SHIT. It is not the TRUTH that daily dialogues with pure white imbeciles (predominantly but not exclusively pure white), but including Geraint Evans (Welsh Dunce the Younger), is a proper Job that is worthwhile and manly.

"They best opportunity of developing academically and emotional." Our own Mediocre, Physically Ill-Favoured, and Mentally Wonky, Pure White Hereditary Racist, unashamedly functionally semi-illiterate, poly-educated poor man's son, a downmarket former debt-collector Solicitor in bland and colourless Norfolk/ Norwich, (Coastal Dole/the Departure Lounge of Life), a mere lowlife 5th Rate Partner, and the Senior Vice President of the Association of Her Majesty's District Judges, Bedford's District Judge Paul Robert Ayers, 3, St Paul's Square, MK 40 1SQ.

BRAINLESS NONSENSE: HIS LANGUAGE, NOT ANY OF OURS.

Omo ale ti ko gbo ede baba re.

Karen Kwamboka: The yield of his very elementary mind. His pure white skin concealed his impure dark black brain. His spinal cord is his highest centre.

The hereditary RACIST pure white bastard approved and immortalised what his pure white mother and father spoke, which is poly-educated pure white supervisors in LUTON approved and authorised. They hate us, and we know. The administration of their law is a very potent weapon of RACE WAR – **Habakkuk 1:4.**

Yinka Bamgbelu: OYINBO OLE/ODE: A brainless hereditary RACIST pure white bastard. The pure white ancestors of your pure white mother and father were THIEVES and owners of stolen children of defenceless poor people (Africans). The mind that the NIGERIAN, from shithole Africa, did not choose is FINER than your indiscreetly crooked, VINDICTIVE, unashamedly mediocre, potently weaponised, and institutionally RACIST Fish and Chips Justice System, and he does not believe in any part of your SHIT, as no part of your SHIT is good, not even one – **Psalm 53,** as he has the power to use cogent facts and irrefutable evidence to irreparably destroy you and every part of your MEDIOCRE SHIT – **Habakkuk 1:4.**

Karen Kwamboka: OYINBO OLE/ODE: "They may not have been well written from a grammatical point of view." Geraint Evans, England's Class Senior Postgraduate Tutor, Oxford.

OYINBO OLE/ODE: OUR OWN MONEY. OUR OWN NIGERIA, SHELL'S DOCILE CASH COW SINCE 1956 (OLOIBIRI). GDC WAS ESTABLISHED IN 1956.

Unlike Putin's Russia, there are no oil wells or gas in Freemasons' KEMPSTON and where the pure white mother and father of Bedford's District Judge Paul Robert Ayers were born – **Exodus 20:15, Habakkuk.**

Yinka Bamgbelu: OYINBO OLE/ODE: They don't want their own mentally gentler white children (OECD) and the pure white imbeciles they shepherd (predominantly but not exclusively pure white) to know the TRUTH, which is that apart from our own darker coat, which we neither made nor chose, and our more INFERIOR ACCENT when speaking an alien language, we are also properly created by Almighty God, and to conceal this Divine TRUTH, and to save face, members of their brainlessly and baselessly self-awarded SUPERIOR RACE resort to RACIST CRIMINALITY, and they steal yields of our people's Christ-granted talents, secure in the knowledge that all Judges will be pure white and their hope is that they would be pure white Freemason bastards too – **Habakkuk 1:4**.

Karen Kwamboka: OYINBO OLE/ODE: Envy is a thief: Persecutory Negrophobia guarded by Negrophobic Perjury.

"Envy is weak." Yul Brynner (1920-1985).

When envy and RACIAL HATRED copulate, insanity is their offspring.

Pure white, RACIST, and powerful, but brainless crooked bastards – **Habakkuk 1:4.**

Yinka Bamgbelu: OYINBO OLE/ODE: Our own Mediocre, Physically Ill-Favoured, and Mentally Wonky, Pure White Hereditary Racist, unashamedly functionally semi-illiterate, poly-educated poor man's son, a downmarket former debt-collector Solicitor in bland and colourless Norfolk/Norwich, (Coastal Dole/the Departure Lounge of Life), a mere lowlife 5th Rate Partner, and the Senior Vice President of the Association of Her Majesty's District Judges, Bedford's District Judge Paul Robert Ayers, 3, St Paul's Square, MK 40 1SQ. Our IMBECILE Freemason Senior District Judge of our own Empire of Stolen Inheritance was granted the platform to display hereditary prejudice. No brain. Poor natural resources. Several continuous centuries of stealing and slavery preceded their huge stolen inheritance – **Exodus 20:15, Habakkuk.** Our people's misfortunes, nearly all, are intelligently designed by hereditary white supremacist Freemasons, and they think that we do not know, but we do.

Then, all Judges were pure white FREEMASONS, and most of them were thicker than a gross of planks.

OXFORD, ENGLAND: GDC, British Soldier, Stephanie Twidale (TD) unrelentingly lied under oath and on record – **Habakkuk 1:4**. Had she not been a member of their PURE WHITE brainlessly and baselessly self-awarded superior race, she would have been punished or deterred. Impure White/Impure Black Constance Briscoe was JAILED for a lesser offence: Judicial Apartheid by Stealth: One rule for pure Whites, and another rule for all others.

Karen Kwamboka: OYINBO OLE/ODE: Facts are sacred and cannot be overstated: "Find the truth and tell it." Harold Pinter (1930-2008).

Our Duchess of Sussex is a MULATTO, impure White/impure Black (43% Nigerian). Had she been pure White, Britons would have loved her.

OYINBO OLE/ODE: "Racial hatred is rife throughout most organisations across Britain." Sir Sadiq Khan, Knight of the Most Excellent Order of our Empire of Stolen Inheritance – **Exodus 20:15, Habakkuk,** the Mayor of London.

Some Members of the Royal Family are victims of Racial Hatred.

"Meghan Markle was the victim of explicit racial hatred." John Bercow, a former speaker.

Yinka Bamgbelu: EUROPEAN POWERS: Pure white hereditary RACIST descendants of THIEVES and owners of stolen children of defenceless poor people, including the AFRICAN ancestors of the impure White/impure Black (Quasi-Mulatto) niece and nephew of the Prince of Wales.

Karen Kwamboka: Delusional grandeur of the stolen past.

OYINBO OLE/ODE: EUROPEAN POWERS (DELUDED PAPER TIGERS) ARE IRREPARABLY DISCREDITED: THE YANKS ARE NATO, AND ABSOLUTELY EVERYTHING ELSE IS AN AUXILIARY BLUFF.

Had the YANKS not been part of NATO, there would not have been a very destructive war between cousins (genetically very similar people), in Eastern Europe.

Yinka Bamgbelu: OYINBO OLE/ODE: Had the YANKS not been part of NATO, Sweden and Finland would not have joined NATO.

African descendants of Slaves shouldn't be very sad when European Powers, direct descendants of PURE WHITE RACIST THIEVES and owners of stolen children of defenceless poor people (AFRICANS), directly/indirectly engage in a very destructive war against their own pure white kindred:

Gambari pa Fulani, Hausa ni Hausa nje.

CHAPTER ELEVEN

Karen Kwamboka: OYINBO OLE/ODE: Very highly civilised, super-enlightened, and ultra-righteous descendant of THIEVES and owners of stolen children of defenceless poor people (AFRICANS) – **Exodus 20:15, Habakkuk.**

Proverbs 16:33: "God does not play dice." Albert Einstein

If in 2022, hereditary RACIST pure white bastards, direct descendants of THIEVES and owners of stolen children of defenceless poor people, including the African ancestors of the Quasi Mulatto, impure Black/impure White (43% Nigerian) grandniece and grandnephew of Major Andrew Mountbatten Windsor, foresaw 2025, would they have stood shoulder to shoulder with a tall dwarf and rattled the cage of a bear?

NATO: "Barking at the gates of Russia" Pope Francis (1936-2025).

Yinka Bamgbelu: OYINBO OLE/ODE: BEDFORD, ENGLAND: Based on cogent, irrefutable, and available evidence, Our own Mediocre, Physically Ill-Favoured, and Mentally Wonky, Pure White, Hereditary Racist, unashamedly functionally semi-illiterate, poly-educated poor man's son, a downmarket former debt-collector Solicitor in bland and colourless Norfolk/Norwich, (Coastal Dole/ the Departure Lounge of Life), a mere lowlife 5th Rate Partner, and the Senior Vice President of the Association of Her Majesty's District Judges, Bedford's District Judge Paul Robert Ayers, 3, St Paul's Square, MK 40 1SQ unrelentingly lied under oath (approved Judgement) and on record – **Habakkuk 1:4**. A brainless hereditary RACIST pure white bastard, the pure white ancestors of his pure white mother and father were incompetent RACIST LIARS too, they were THIEVES and owners of stolen children of defenceless poor people (Africans) – **Exodus 20:15, Habakkuk.**

Karen Kwamboka: OYINBO OLE/ODE: BEDFORD, ENGLAND: Senior District Judge Paul Robert Ayers, let me tell you, your RACIST CIVILISATION is intellectually flawed. Your Country is SHIT, and you are worse than SHIT. You are worthy only because you are pure white. You are rich only because the pure ancestors of your pure white mother and father were THIEVES - **Exodus 20:15, Habakkuk,** extremely nasty RACIST MURDERERS – **Exodus 20:13,** and owners of stolen children of defenceless poor people, including the

Africa ancestors of our impure Black/impure White (43% Nigerian), Mulatto Duchess of Sussex. Facts are sacred and cannot be overstated.

Yinka Bamgbelu: OYINBO OLE/ODE: BEDFORD, ENGLAND: Our own Senior District Judge Paul Robert Ayers of our own Empire of Stolen Inheritance – **Habakkuk, Exodus 20:15**, a RACIST descendant of ultra-righteous professional THIEVES, let me tell you, reasoning and vision do not have finite boundaries. The fellow is who He says He is, and He told the TRUTH when He disclosed pictures His unbounded mind painted, before Jews and Gentiles, in the COUNCIL - **John 14:6.**

Karen Kwamboka: OYINBO OLE/ODE: You are SHIT. Had you been Black and 10X as smart, you would not have been our Senior District Judge in Bedford, Great Britain. You were our Senior District Judge only because you FU*KING couldn't do anything else. Apart from debt-collection, what was in bland, colourless, and almost lifeless Norfolk/Norwich (Coastal Dole/the Departure Lounge of Life) for verifiably functional semi-illiterate Freemason Solicitors to do? When pure white Solicitors and Barristers (predominantly but not exclusively pure white) FAIL in practice (loads do), if they were Freemasons, they became Judges or something else, and if they were not, they became Politicians or something else.

A RACIST PURE WHITE FREEMASON JUDGE OF OUR OWN EMPIRE OF STOLEN INHERITANCE – **EXODUS 20:15, HABAKKUK.**

Karen Kwamboka: Our indiscreetly RACIST unashamedly functional semi-illiterate pure white Senior District Judge of our Empire of Stolen Inheritance – **Exodus 20:15, Habakkuk**, albeit Bedford's Class, was granted the platform, by retrogressive Freemasons' patronage rather than progressive colour-blind merit, to display hereditary prejudice. Superior pure white skin colour, a huge stolen inheritance (gigantic yields of several continuous centuries of ancestral theft – **Exodus 20:15, Habakkuk**), and what else? OYINBO OLE/ODE: Before slavery, what? Then, there was only subsistence feudal agriculture.

OYINBO OLE/ODE: "Agriculture not only gives riches to a nation but the only one she can call her own." Dr Samuel Johnson (1709-1784).

Yinka Bamgbelu: OYINBO OLE/ODE: BEDFORD, ENGLAND: Senior District Judge Paul Robert Ayers, our verifiable functional semi-illiterate, crooked, and white supremacist Freemason of our own Empire of Stolen Inheritance, based on available evidence, your brain is not good. Only your superior skin colour and Almighty God are truly good - **Mark 10:18.**

Hereditary RACIST pure white bastards (predominantly but not exclusively pure white) love brainless and baseless skin colour superiority, but they hate FREEDOM OF EXPRESSION because they don't want their own mentally gentler white children (OECD) and the pure white IMBECILES they shepherd to know the TRUTH, which is that they are properly packaged FROTH: Properly schooled impostors and experts of deception: One-dimensionally educated pure white rubbish: Perception is always grander than reality. Based on several decades of very proximate observations and direct experiences, the pure white man is grossly overrated.

Karen Kwamboka: OYINBO OLE/ODE: Straight-faced hereditary RACIST descendants of THIEVES and owners of stolen children of defenceless poor people – **Exodus 20:15, Habakkuk.**

If we aren't very smart, why are we very rich (the sixth largest economy on earth)?

Yinka Bamgbelu: OYINBO OLE/ODE: Shepherds did not bring stolen African children back home to Great Britain, extremely nasty and insatiably greedy Economic Cannibals carried their cargo of stolen African children to their stolen New World, which was not new to those they found there, and sold stolen children of defenceless poor Africans to European Christian owners of stolen plantations, and after several centuries of merciless RACIST EVIL, ignorant descendants of THIEVES and owners of stolen children of defenceless poor people became ultra-righteous, very highly civilised, super-enlightened, and Christian: OYINBO OLE: **Exodus 2015:** The ancestors of Eton and Oxbridge-educated Archbishop Justin Welby were slave merchants - **Habakkuk.**

Karen Kwamboka: Maafa (1445-1888) rebuilt everything it succeeded and paid for everything it preceded, including Cambridge University (1209), and Eton College (1440).

Yinka Bamgbelu: OYINBO OLE/ODE: Lord Justice Charles Anthony Haddon-Cave, KC, you are worthy only because you are pure white. You are rich only because your pure white ancestors were THIEVES - **Exodus 20:15, Habakkuk**. Unlike PUTIN'S SIBERIA, there are no gas fields in Tasmania, where your own pure white father, Sir Charles Phillip Haddon-Cave (1925-1999), was born. You are a LEECH, and your pure white direct ancestors were armed land grabbers and colonialist economic cannibals (THIEVES – **Exodus 20:15, Habakkuk**).

Karen Kwamboka: OYINBO OLE/ODE: Prior to SLAVERY, there weren't very many proper houses in the BEDFORD of John Foster (1759-1832), and there were fewer proper houses in the LUTON of Robert Hibbert (1769-1849) and Tommy Robinson.

Yinka Bamgbelu: OYINBO OLE/ODE: Hereditary RACIST pure white bastards are more familiar with BLACKS of Afro-Caribbean extraction, such Diane Abbott, David Lammy, and their type: Direct descendants of stolen African children who were unnaturally selected, genetically reversed, artificially paired up, deliberately bred for hard labour, and reared like cattle on stolen plantations – in the their stolen new world, which was not new to the Natives.

Karen Kwamboka: OYINBO OLE/ODE: BEDFORD, ENGLAND: Pure White Senior District Judge Paul Robert Ayers, based on cogent, irrefutable, and available evidence, the pure white ancestors of your pure white mother and father were THIEVES – **Habakkuk, Exodus 20:15**, RACIST MURDERERS – **Exodus 20:13**, and owners of stolen children of defenceless poor people, including the AFRICAN ANCESTORS of the impure Black/impure White – Quasi-Mulatto (<43% Nigerian) grandniece and grandnephew of Major Andrew Mountbatten Windsor. Facts are sacred and cannot be overstated.

Yinka Bamgbelu: Truths disfavour hereditary RACIST pure white bastards, so they steal POWER, and use it to subjugate it.

Karen Kwamboka: BEDFORD, ENGLAND: OYINBO OLE/ODE: Pure White Senior District Judge Paul Robert Ayers, it is not the TRUTH that daily dialogues with pure white imbeciles, predominantly but not exclusively pure white, including Pure White Geraint Evans, is not a proper job that is worthwhile and manly.

Yinka Bamgbelu: OYINBO OLE/ODE: BEDFORD, ENGLAND: Pure White Senior District Judge Paul Robert Ayers, our own brainless hereditary RACIST pure white bastard of our own Empire of Stolen Inheritance – **Exodus 20:15, Habakkuk:** The most important part of the matter is MONEY, and it is not the yield of your brainless and baseless self-awarded higher IQ, and unlike PUTIN'S SIBERIA, there are no gas fields in Freemasons' Kempston and where your own pure white mother and father were born. Your ancestors were THIEVES. Our own MONEY, Nigeria(oil/gas) is by far more relevant to the economic survival of all your own mentally gentler white children (OECD), your pure white mother, your pure white father, and your pure white spouse than John Bunyan's BEDFORD.

Karen Kwamboka: OYINBO OLE/ODE: "They may not have been well written from a grammatical point of view but I am confident I had not forgotten any of the facts." Pure White Geraint Evans, England's Class Welsh Postgraduate Tutor, OXFORD.

OYINBO OLE/ODE: One of the gains of several centuries of stealing and slavery is that a functional semi-illiterate, crooked, and hereditary RACIST pure white Welsh bastard was our Senior Postgraduate Tutor, Oxford.

Yinka Bamgbelu: OYINBO OLE/ODE: No brain. Poor natural resources. Several centuries of stealing and slavery (gigantic yields of several continuous centuries of stolen inheritance – **Exodus 20:15, Habakkuk**) – preceded their huge stolen trust fund. Facts are sacred and cannot be overstated.

Karen Kwamboka: OYINBO OLE/ODE: Insatiably greedy hereditary RACIST pure white bastards (predominantly but not exclusively pure white); ignorant descendants of extremely nasty and EVIL RACIST KILLERS, thieves, and owners of stolen children of defenceless poor Africans. The evil RACIST pure white bastards are no longer here, but it would be very naïve not to expect their sadistic genes of savagery, RACISM, and crude cruelty to continue to flow through the veins of their pure white direct descendants who remain here.

OYINBO OLE/ODE- **EXODUS 20:15, HABAKKUK**: "I know of no evil that has ever existed, nor can imagine any evil to exist, worse than the tearing of eighty thousand persons annually from their native land, by a combination of the most civilised nations inhabiting the most enlightened part of the globe, but more especially under the sanction of the laws of that Nation which calls herself the most free and the most happy of them all." Prime Minister William Pitt the Younger

Yinka Bamgbelu: OYINBO OLE/ODE: It is the TRUTH that Pure White European Christian Slave-Merchants were very bellyful, happy, and free, and more so after the very greedy economic cannibals shared part of the loot of MERCILESS RACIST EVIL, in 1833, but it is not the TRUTH that evil RACIST pure white bastards who, inhumanely, buried other people's stolen children in the bellies of SLAVE-SHIPS.

Karen Kwamboka: Their RACIST CIVILISATION is Fu*ked, and irreparably Fu*ked, because it is akin to Malignant Melanoma: Excision is impossible, and palliation is SUICIDE, albeit a slow one. They are genetically irreparably damaged. SLAVERY decommissioned natural selection and reversed progressive evolution. Gigantic yields of millions of stolen children of defenceless poor people (AFRICANS) made it possible for millions of pure white IMBECILES (predominantly but not exclusively pure white) to breed more millions of PURE IMBECILES – of all shades.

Yinka Bamgbelu: OYINBO OLE/ODE: BEDFORD, ENGLAND: Pure White Senior District Judge Paul Robert Ayers, based on cogent, irrefutable, and available evidence, your Country is SHIT, a grossly overrated SHIT, and you are worse than SHIT. Without the support of the YANKS, your Country is a sitting duck.

"Could you face the Russians by yourselves?" President Trump.

Karen Kwamboka: OYINBO OLE/ODE: We and our type are the ones hereditary RACIST bastards would beat up without the support of the YANKS. Facts are sacred and cannot be overstated.

Yinka Bamgbelu: OYINBO OLE/ODE: BEDFORD, ENGLAND: Pure White Senior

District Judge Paul Robert Ayers, you are verifiably a functional semi-illiterate, indiscreetly RACIST, and crooked, and the ancestors of your pure white mother and father were PROFESSIONAL THIEVES and owners of stolen African children - **Exodus 20:15, Habakkuk**, so you do not have the MORAL RIGHT to Judge Sinners – **John 8:7, Matthew 7:1-6**. Only SAINTS should Judge SINNERS – **John 5:22, Matthew 25:31-46, Revelation 3:21**; you are not a SAINT, and you know it. An ignorant one-dimensionally educated hereditary pure white bastard. An ultra-righteous descendant of Pure White THIEVES – **Exodus 20:15, Habakkuk**. Equitable, fair, and just REPARATION pends, and several continuous centuries of unpaid interest accrue.

Karen Kwamboka: OYINBO OLE/ODE: BEDFORD, ENGLAND: Pure White Senior District Judge Paul Robert Ayers, let me tell you, based on cogent, irrefutable, and available evidence, your indiscreetly crooked, VINDICTIVE, potently weaponised, unashamedly mediocre, and institutionally RACIST Fish and Chips Justice System is FU*KED, irreparably FU*KED, as it has foreseeably succumbed to INCEST, weakening of the common genetic pool, and associated physical and/or mental wonkiness, and hereditary white supremacist Freemason Judges, and others, who make loads of money from unashamed mediocrity and confusion prop SHIT UP:

Conflict of Interest: "A government that robs Peter to pay Paul can always depend on the support of Paul." George Bernard Shaw (1856-1950).

Yinka Bamgbelu: OYINBO OLE/ODE: Intellectually ungifted pure white bastards (predominantly but not exclusively pure white) do not want their own mentally white children (OECD) and the pure white imbeciles they shepherd (predominantly but not exclusively pure white) to know the TRUTH, which is that apart from our own INFERIOR SKIN COLOUR, which we neither made nor chose, and our more inferior accent when speaking an alien language, we are also properly created by Almighty God, and to conceal this TRUTH, and to save face, members of their brainlessly and baselessly self-awarded SUPERIOR RACE resort to Racist Criminality, and they steal yields of our own people's (self-educated Nigerians) Christ-granted, and their overwhelming leverage is the certainty that all Judges will be pure white, and the hope of the opportunist RACIST pure white bastards (predominantly but not exclusive pure white) is that they would be hereditary RACIST pure white bastards too – **Habakkuk 1:4.** Superior pure white skin, a huge stolen inheritance, and what else? Before Slavery, what? OYINBO OLE/ODE: An ignorant, one-dimensionally educated, opportunist RACIST, and ultra-righteous descendant of PURE WHITE PROFESSIONAL THIEVES – **Habakkuk, Exodus 20:15**. Your pure white ancestors were THIEVES; if your pure white mother and father did not tell you that TRUTH, they lied to you.

"Those who have robbed have also lied." Dr Samuel Johnson (1709-1784).

Karen Kwamboka: "Sometimes people don't want to hear the truth because they don't want their illusions destroyed." Friedrich Nietzsche (1844-1900).

BEDFORD, ENGLAND: Pure White Sue Gregory (OBE), our own Officer of the Most Excellent Order of our own Empire of Stolen Inheritance – **Exodus 20:15, Habakkuk,** unrelentingly lied under implied oath and on record – **Habakkuk 1:4.**

Their Apartheid Law: Had she been Black like Constance Briscoe, or a Mulatto (impure White/impure Black) like the Duchess of Sussex, she would have been deterred.

OYINBO OLE/ODE: "Michael Jackson would have been found guilty if he'd been Black." Jo Brand.

Yinka Bamgbelu: OYINBO OLE/ODE: "British Justice is RACIST and should not be trusted by ethnic minorities." Quasi-Mulatto, impure White/impure Black, Peter Herbert, OBE, our Officer of the Most Excellent Order of our own Empire of Stolen Inheritance – **Exodus 20:15, Habakkuk,** and a very Senior

Expert of their indiscreetly crooked, VINDICTIVE, unashamedly mediocre, potently weaponised, institutionally RACIST, and waste of money fish and chips FAKE LAW – **Luke 11:52.**

"Study history, study history, in history lies all the secrets of statecraft." Sir Winston (1874-1965), unapologetic hereditary white supremacist 33rd Degree FREEMASON, Scottish Rite. Facts are sacred and cannot be overstated.

"I want to say that I believe unequivocally that Meghan has been the victim of explicit and obnoxious racism. I am crystal clear about that". John Bercow, a former speaker.

Karen Kwamboka: Based on cogent, irrefutable, and available evidence, Constance Briscoe was Jailed for a lesser offence: Had she been pure white, well-born, very rich, English, male, and Freemason, she might have 'WALKED': Integrity, friendship, respect, and charity: All for one, and one for all – **Habakkuk 1:4.**

Yinka Bamgbelu: OYINBO OLE/ODE: "The highest reach of injustice is to be deemed just when you are not." Plato.

Karen Kwamboka: If intellect is a function of their universally acknowledged irrefutably SUPERIOR SKIN COLOUR, what do hereditary RACIST pure white bastards need Blatant Racist Criminality for?

Yinka Bamgbelu: OYINBO OLE/ODE: Hereditary RACIST pure white bastards expect our own people, self-educated NIGERIANS, to defend ourselves against hereditary RACIST pure white bastards - before hereditary RACIST pure white bastard Freemason Judges - inside Grand Museum-like Courts preceded by SLAVERY.

Reductio ad absurdum!

OYINBO OLE/ODE: OUR OWN NIGERIA, SHELL'S DOCILE CASH COW SINCE 1956 (OLOIBIRI). GDC WAS ESTABLISHED IN 1956.

Karen Kwamboka: OYINBO OLE/ODE: Unlike PUTIN'S SIBERIA, there are no gas fields in Bedfordshire and where the pure white mother and father of Bedford's District Judge Paul Robert Ayers - were born.

Yinka Bamgbelu: OYINBO OLE/ODE: Our own Nigerian children with huge oil wells and gas fields near their huts eat only 1.5/day in our own

NIGERIA, a very, very, very, bellyful hereditary RACIST pure white bastard, a mere poly-educated functional semi-illiterate former debt-collector Solicitor (5th Rate Partner) in bland, colourless, and almost lifeless Norfolk/Norwich (Coastal Dole/Departure Lounge of Life) – whose pure white mother and father have never seen CRUDE OIL, and whose pure white ancestors, including JOHN FOSTER (1759-1832), were fed like battery hens with huge yields of millions of stolen and destroyed children of defenceless poor people, including the AFRICAN ANCESTORS of the Quasi-Mulatto, impure White, impure Black (<43% Nigerian) grandniece and grandnephew of Major Andrew Mountbatten Windsor, was our Senior District Judge, albeit Bedford's Class.

Karen Kwamboka: OYINBO OLE/ODE: CROOKED RACIST PURE WHITE BASTARDS (PREDOMINANTLY BUT NOT EXCLUSIVELY PURE WHITE) SHOULD STAY HERE; IT IS SAFER THAN NIGERIA - **EXODUS 21:23-327.**

OYINBO OLE/ODE (THIEVES - **HABAKKUK, EXODUS 20:15**): Then, insatiably greedy pure white Racist Bastards carried and sold millions of stolen AFRICAN CHILDREN, now THIEVES steal our own natural resources from our own AFRICA: Substitution is fraudulent emancipation. Facts are sacred and cannot be overstated.

Yinka Bamgbelu: OYINBO OLE/ODE: OXFORD, ENGLAND: GDC: Stephanie Twidale (TD) unrelentingly lied under oath and on record - **Habakkuk 1:4.** The pure white ancestors of her pure white father and mother were incompetent RACIST LIARS too, they were THIEVES – **Exodus 20:15, Habakkuk.** Facts are sacred and cannot be overstated. Constance Briscoe was JAILED for a lesser offence – **Habakkuk 1:4.** Their indiscreetly crooked and unashamedly mediocre waste of money fish and chips Justice System that is overseen by hereditary white supremacist Freemason Judges for the benefit of their own pure white kindred (predominantly but not exclusively pure white). Based on several decades of very proximate observations and direct experiences, the pure white man is grossly overrated. Perception is grander than reality.

Karen Kwamboka: OYINBO OLE/ODE: BEDFORD, ENGLAND: Pure White District Judge Paul Robert Ayers, if you could disprove the TRUTH, which is that your own pure white kindred, OXFORD, ENGLAND: GDC: Stephanie Twidale (TD) unrelentingly lied under oath and on record - **Habakkuk 1:4**, you will concomitantly confirm the TRUTH, which is that your own Country, Great Britain is not GREAT SHIT, and you are not worse than SHIT.

Yinka Bamgbelu: Our own direct ancestors were never CARRIED – during the pure white European Christians' Carrying Trade. Hereditary RACIST pure white bastards are more familiar with Negroes of Afro- Caribbean extraction, such as David Lammy and Diane Abbott, direct descendants of stolen African children who were unnaturally selected, genetically reversed, unnaturally selected, paired up, and deliberately bred for very hard labour – by highly civilised, super-enlightened, and ultra-righteous European Christians, on stolen land, in their stolen New World – **Exodus 20:15, Habakkuk.**

Karen Kwamboka: OYINBO OLE/ODE: If I were President PUTIN, I would NUKE the bastards, but only if the YANKS would look away. Hereditary RACIST direct descendants of European Christians who enslaved AFRICANS (Maafa, 1445-1888), shared stolen money in 1833, and in 1884, partitioned Africa and looted her.

"How Europe underdeveloped Africa." Dr Walter Rodney (1942-1980).

Yinka Bamgbelu: OYINBO OLE/ODE: BEDFORD, ENGLAND: Pure White Senior District Judge Paul Robert Ayers, you are FROTH. You are worthy only because you are pure white, and you are rich only because the pure white ancestors of your pure white father and mother were THIEVES. It is absolutely impossible for your Christ-granted talent and yields of the land on which your own pure white father and mother were born to sustain your high standard of living. It is plainly deductible that SLAVERY rebuilt everything it succeeded and paid for everything it preceded, including Bedfordshire Masonic Centre, the Keep, MK42 8AH, Bedford County Court, MK40 1SQ, Etcetera. Immodesty apart, based on cogent, irrefutable, and available evidence, I am intellectually dominant: Sincere immodesty is sincerer than insincere modesty. I am aware of the existence of the supernatural. The mind that I did not choose is FINER than your indiscreetly crooked, VINDICTIVE, unashamedly mediocre, potently weaponised, and waste of money Fish and Chips Justice System, and I do not believe in any part of SHIT, as no part of SHIT is good, not even one – **Psalm 53**, I have the POWER to use cogent facts and irrefutable evidence to irreparably destroy you and SHIT– **Habakkuk 1:4.**

Karen Kwamboka: 1976-2022: Our Poly-educated (not Russell Group Lower-Class Alternative Education - **Proverbs 17:16**), was born in 1952, and the opportunist RACIST pure white bastard might have not read a book unrelated to LAW - since 1970. Had the closeted white supremacist pure white bastard been Black, and 10X as smart, he would not be a Senior Judge in Great Britain:

Homogeneity in the administration of their law is an impregnable secure mask of Merciless Racist Evil, a very potent weapon of RACE WAR – **Habakkuk 1:4.**

Yinka Bamgbelu: Blame everything on SLAVERY (Maaf, 1445-1888): OYINBO OLE/ODE: Gigantic yields of millions of stolen children of defenceless poor people, including the AFRICAN ANCESTORS of the Quasi-Mulatto, impure White/impure Black (<43% Nigerian) niece and nephew of the PRINCE OF WALES, decommissioned natural selection, and reversed progressive evolution, and made it possible for millions of pure white IMBECILES (predominantly but not exclusively pure white) – to breed more millions of pure white IMBECILES (predominantly but not exclusively pure white). One, only one of thousands, of the evidence of stagnation, weakness, and decline is that a scatter-head, crooked, and hereditary RACIST pure white bastard was our Senior NHS Postgraduate Tutor, albeit Bedfordshire's Class.

Karen Kwamboka: OYINBO OLE/ODE: What was left when our Senior District Judge of our own Empire of Stolen Inheritance – **Habakkuk, Exodus 20:15,** was a crooked hereditary RACIST pure white bastard?

Yinka Bamgbelu: BEDFORD, ENGLAND: GDC, our Pure White Sue Gregory (OBE), Officer of the Most Excellent Order of our own Empire of Stolen Inheritance – **Exodus 20:15, Habakkuk,** unrelentingly lied under implied oath and on record – **Habakkuk 1:4.** Constance Briscoe was JAILED for a lesser offence. Facts are sacred and cannot be overstated.

Karen Kwamboka: BEDFORD, ENGLAND: OYINBO OLE/ODE: Based on cogent, irrefutable, and available evidence, Pure White Senior District Judge Paul Robert Ayers unrelentingly lied under oath and on record – **Habakkuk 1:4**. Constance Briscoe was JAILED for a lesser offence.

"The truth allows no choice." Dr Samuel Johnson (1709-1784).

Yinka Bamgbelu: BEDFORD, ENGLAND: GDC, Pure White Freemason, Brother Richard William Hill fabricated reports and unrelentingly lied under oath and on record – **Habakkuk 1:4.**

Constance Briscoe was JAILED for a lesser offence.

"Find the truth and tell it." Harold Pinter (1930 – 2008)

Karen Kwamboka: It is plainly deductible that our misfortunes, nearly all, are intelligently designed by members of the Antichrist Freemasonry Quasi-

Religion: Hereditary RACIST pure white bastards (predominantly but not exclusively pure white) are not deterred by His Justice – **John 5:22**, because evil crooked white supremacist bastards do not believe in His exceptionalism – **John 14:6.**

Based on several decades of very proximate observations and direct experiences, their Country is SHIT, and they are verifiably worse than SHIT.

Yinka Bamgbelu: OYINBO OLE/ODE: BEDFORD, ENGLAND: Pure White Senior District Judge Paul Robert Ayers, our own brainless hereditary RACIST pure white bastard of our own Empire of Stolen Inheritance – **Exodus 20:15, Habakkuk**. Our ultra-righteous waste of money FAKE JUDGE. If you engage on a colour-blind level intellectual playing field, you will be destroyed with cogent facts supported by irrefutable evidence; you are INFERIOR. Your ancestors were THIEVES – Exodus 20:15. Sincere immodesty (**Psalm 51:6**) is sincerer than insincere modesty (**Romans 12:2**).

Sincerity is a prime attribute of our own Messiah.

You are very lucky that you are pure white. Had you been BLACK and 10X as smart, you would not have been a Senior District Judge even within one of the least literate and least numerate adult populations in the industrialised world (OECD).

CHAPTER TWELVE

Karen Kwamboka: OYINBO OLE/ODE: If all the Master Builders (33rd Degree Freemasons, Scottish Rite) at Bedfordshire Masonic Temple, the Keep, Bedford Road, Kempston, MK42 8AH, could disprove the TRUTH, which is that their own pure white kindred, Freemason, Brother Richard William Hill, fabricated reports and unrelentingly lied under oath and on record – **Habakkuk 1:4**, they will concomitantly disprove the implied expressed experiences of our Quasi-Mulatto (impure White/impure Black) expert of their Law – **Luke 11:52**, Peter Herbert (OBE), Officer of the Most Excellent Order of our own Empire of Stolen Inheritance – **Exodus 20:15, Habakkuk**, which is that English Law is equal for Pure Whites and Blacks, but its administration is not, and the administration of any law is MEAT – **Habakkuk 1:4.**

"Rightful liberty is unobstructed action according to our will within limits drawn around us by the equal rights of others. I do not add 'within the limits of the law' because law is often but the tyrant's will, and always so when it violates the rights of the individual." President **Thomas Jefferson (1743-1826).**

Yinka Bamgbelu: Leviticus 19:33-34: They are RACIST CRIMINALS, and to tie loose ends, they destroy foreigners who know, and their leverage is the certainty that all Judges will be pure white, and their hope is that they would be hereditary RACIST pure white bastards too - **Habakkuk.**

Karen Kwamboka: OYINBO OLE/ODE: Killing and Stealing are HEREDITARY. If there are cogent and irrefutable evidence that the pure white ancestors of one's pure white mother and father were THIEVES – **Exodus 20:15**, Racist Killers – **Exodus 20:13**, and owners of stolen lives - **Habakkuk**, Stealing and Killing must be part of one's genetic inheritances. We are all who we are, the inheritors of our inheritances, genes of our own individual ancestors.

Yinka Bamgbelu: OYINBO OLE/ODE: Then, evil, and insatiably greedy RACIST pure white bastards carried and sold millions of stolen children of defenceless poor people from our own AFRICA, and now THIEVES steal our own natural resources from our own AFRICA.

Substitution is fraudulent emancipation: Grand Racist Deceit.

OYINBO OLE/ODE: Slavery (Maafa,1445-1888) preceded Partition and Colonisation (1884). Neo-Colonialism is the new SLAVERY – **Habakkuk.**

"Moderation is a virtue, but only among those who are thought to have found alternatives." Dr Henry Kissinger (1923-2023)

Karen Kwamboka: It is BLATANT DISHONESTY that Blacks and Whites are measured with the same yardstick by pure white supremacist Freemason Judges (disproportionately but not exclusively pure white).

Yinka Bamgbelu: They hate us, and we know, but they don't know that we know that they do. The only BLACK they truly love is our own MONEY, and absolutely everything else is DECEIT. Their type, hereditary RACIST pure white bastards (predominantly but not exclusively pure white) killed the Nigerian Medical Practitioner, Dr Richard Bamgboye, only 56, and the Indian Dentist, Dr Anand Kamath, only 42, albeit hands-off, with the mens rea hidden in the belly of the actus reus.

Karen Kwamboka: OYINBO OLE/ODE: COLOURISM/WHITE PRIVILEGE/APARTHEID BY STEALTH/HEREDITARY RACIAL HATRED: They are not the only creation of Almighty God, and they are not immortal, and the universally acknowledged irrefutably SUPERIOR SKIN COLOUR that they very fortunate wearer neither made nor chose is not the only wonder of the world.

Proverbs 20:15: Skin colour is a great creation of Almighty God, but it is not the greatest.

Yinka Bamgbelu: SERENGETI: THE NEW WORLD ORDER. If Denmark refuses the annexation of Greenland, what can Denmark's Army do if President Trump orders the US Army to kidnap the King and Queen of Denmark, bring them back to the USA, and place them under house arrest in Washington?

Karen Kwamboka: "The white man is the devil." Elijah Mohammad (1897-1975).

Based on cogent, irrefutable, and available evidence, he is not only a devil, but he is also an incompetent RACIST LIAR, and a THIEF – **Exodus 20:15.**

Yinka Bamgbelu: Based on cogent, irrefutable, and available evidence, a pure white man is not only a devil, but he is also an insatiably greedy bastard, a RACIST murderer, albeit hands-off, and a THIEF. Prior to SLAVERY, what? Then, there was only subsistence feudal agriculture.

"Agriculture not only gives riches to a nation, but the only one she can call her own." Dr Samuel Johnson (1709-1784).

"The most potent weapon in the hands of the oppressor is the mind of the oppressed." Steve Biko (1946-1977).

Karen Kwamboka: Their indiscreetly RACIST, unashamedly mediocre, and VULGARLY CORRUPT Justice System that is overseen by MASONS for the benefit of Masons

Yinka Bamgbelu: OYINBO OLE/ODE: BEDFORD, ENGLAND: Pure White Senior District Judge Paul Robert Ayers, our opportunist RACIST descendant of ultra-righteous pure white THIEVES, a parasitic bastard with all the characteristics of the archetypal Scottish leech. They hate us, and we know

"The impudence of an Irishman is the impudence of a fly, that buzzes about you, and you put it away, but it returns, flutters, and teases you. The impudence of a Scotsman is the impudence of a leech that fixes and sucks your blood." Dr Samuel Johnson (1709-1784).

Karen Kwamboka: In the future, multi-trillionaire American Oligarchs will be richer than some Countries, including European Countries, and they will trample on them.

Yinka Bamgbelu: OYINBO OLE/ODE: Pure White European Christians were THIEVES **- Exodus 20:15, Habakkuk.**1445-1888, Maafa: They carried and sold millions of stolen children of defenceless poor people (Africans). 1833: They shared stolen money – **Exodus 20:15, Habakkuk 2:6-9.** 1884: They partitioned Africa and looted her. Now Neo-Colonialism is the New Slavery.

Karen Kwamboka: If King's School and Oxbridge-educated Lord Justice Haddon-Cave, KC, a closeted white supremacist pure white son of a very rich (**Mark 10:25**), pure white Tasmanian Colonialist Economic Cannibal, could disprove the TRUTH, which is that his own pure white kindred, Pure White, Senior Bedford's District Judge Paul Robert Ayers, unrelentingly LIED under oath and on record (approved Judgement) – **Habakkuk 1:4**, Pure White Sue Gregory (OBE), our own Officer of the Most Excellent Order of our own Empire of Stolen Inheritance – **Exodus 20:15**, Habakkuk, unrelentingly lied under implied oath and on record – **Habakkuk 1:4**, Pure White Freemason, Brother Richard Hill, fabricated reports and unrelentingly lied under oath and on record – **Habakkuk 1:4**, British Soldier, Stephanie Twidale (TD), unrelentingly lied under oath and on record – **Habakkuk 1:4,** and Mrs Helen Falcon(MBE), our own Member of the Most Excellent Order of our own Empire of Stolen Inheritance (gigantic yields of several continuous centuries of ancestral theft: OYINBO OLE/ODE

– **Exodus 20:15, Habakkuk,** and a very high ranking ROTARIAN (vulgarly charitable, Antichrist, and hereditary white supremacist Freemasonry Quasi-Religion without voodoo or occultists' rituals), unrelentingly lied under oath and on record - Habakkuk, he would concomitantly disprove the verifiable TRUTH, which is that Great Britain is a RACIST HELL HOLE, and the administration of English Law is a Negrophobic charade – **Habakkuk 1:4.**

Yinka Bamgbelu: Habakkuk 2: 6-9: King's School and Oxbridge-educated Lord Justice Haddon-Cave, KC, a closeted white supremacist pure white son of a very rich (**Mark 10:25**), Oxbridge-educated pure white Tasmanian Colonialist Economic Cannibal, the pure white ancestors of your own pure white father and mother were THIEVES and owners of stolen children of defenceless poor people, including the Quasi-Mulatto, impure White/impure Black (<43% Nigerian) great grandchildren of the Duke of Edinburgh of Blessed Memory, Prince Phillip (1921-2021).

Philippians 1:21: Phillip was 33rd Degree Freemason, Scottish Rite.

Karen Kwamboka: OYINBO OLE/ODE: King's School and Oxbridge-educated Pure White Lord Justice Charles Anthony Haddon-Cave, KC, a closeted RACIST first son of a very rich (Mark 10:25) insatiably greedy Tasmanian Colonialist Economic Cannibal, let me tell you, the SUPERNATURAL EXISTS and it is consistently accessible to those who stand where it can come - **John 14:26**. Immodesty apart, and solely in terms of PURIFIED TRUTH, I am superiorly created by Almighty God, certainly intellectually. Sincerity, not modesty, is a prime attribute of our own Messiah. There is nothing modest about **John 14:6**. Sincere immodesty is sincerer than insincere modesty.

Yinka Bamgbelu: OYINBO OLE/ODE: King's School and Oxbridge-educated Lord Justice Haddon-Cave, KC, a closeted white supremacist pure white son of a very rich (**Mark 10:25**), Oxbridge-educated pure white Tasmanian Colonialist Economic Cannibal, Sir Charles Phillip Haddon-Cave (1925-1999), let me tell you, reasoning and vision do not have finite boundaries, and the fellow is who He says He is - **John 14:6.** You Country is SHIT, and you are worse than SHIT, but you did not know because all those above you are like you, and those below you are worse.

Karen Kwamboka: OYINBO OLE/ODE: King's School and Oxbridge-educated Lord Justice Haddon-Cave, KC, a closeted white supremacist pure white son of a very rich (**Mark 10:25**), Oxbridge-educated pure white Tasmanian

Colonialist Economic Cannibal, I do not believe in any part of your indiscreetly crooked, VINDICTIVE, potently weaponised, unashamedly mediocre, and institutionally RACIST Fish and Chips Justice System, as no part of SHIT is good, not even one – **Psalm 53**, and I shall use cogent facts and irrefutable evidence to irreparably destroy you and your waste of money Racist Shit – **Habakkuk1 :4.** Skin colour that the very fortunate wearer neither made nor chose is universally acknowledged to be irrefutably SUPERIOR, but his intellect is not, and their CONFUSED JUSTICE SYSTEM is fundamentally designed to conceal that that TRUTH. BULLIES should evict Putin from Crimea, he stole it – **Exodus 20:15.** We and our type are the ones hereditary RACIST pure white bastards (predominantly but not exclusively pure white) would beat up without the support of the YANKS. A 5th Rate Military Power impersonates a SUPERPOWER: Delusional grandeur of the stolen past – **Habakkuk 2:6-9.** Facts are sacred and cannot be overstated.

Yinka Bamgbelu: "The truth allows no choice." Dr Samuel Johnson (1709-1784).

OYINBO OLE/ODE: Based on several decades of very proximate observations and direct experiences, their indiscreetly crooked, VINDICTIVE, unashamedly mediocre, potently weaponised, and institutionally RACIST Waste of Money Fish and Chips Justice System is FU*KED, irreparably FU*KED, as it has foreseeably succumbed to INCEST, weakening of the common genetic pool, and the associated physical and/or mental wonkiness, and hereditary white supremacist Freemason Judges, and others, who make loads of money from unashamed mediocrity and confusion prop shit up.

CONFLICT OF INTEREST: "A government that robs Peter to pay Paul can always depend on the support of Paul." George Bernard Shaw (1856-1950).

Karen Kwamboka: "Envy is weak." Yul Brynner (1920-1985).

OYINBO OLE/ODE: Envy is a thief. An ignorant opportunist RACIST pure white bastard dressed up uncontrollable toxic envy and hereditary RACIAL HATRED and called them something else (colour-blind and transparently impartial administration of their law). If they are not RACISTS, what do they need RACIST CRIMINALITY for? Oxford, England: GDC, Pure White Senior British Soldier, Stephanie Twidale (TD) unrelentingly lied under oath and on record – **Habakkuk 1:4.** The pure white ancestors of her pure white father and mother were incompetent RACIST LIARS too, they were industrial-scale professional THIEVES – **Exodus 20:15, Habakkuk 2:6-9,** extremely nasty and merciless RACIST KILLERS, nastier than Yevgeny Prigozhin (1961-2023) and Adolf Hitler (1889-1945), and just by the by, several years of NAZI HOLOCAUST (1939-1945) was a mere storm in a teacup in comparison to several centuries of BLACK HOLOCAUST (Maafa, 1445-1888), and they were also very proficient armed robbers and looters, gun runners, drug dealers (opium merchants of the Qing Dynasty), and owners of stolen children of defenceless poor people, including the AFRICAN ancestors of the impure Black/impure white Quasi-Mulatto (<43% Nigerian) grand niece and nephew of Major Andrew Mountbatten Windsor.

Yinka Bamgbelu: OYINBO OLE/ODE: BEDFORD, ENGLAND: District Judge Paul Robert Ayers, what do you own that is the yield of transparent virtue? You do not have anything. Your pure white ancestors were THIEVES. The HUGE STOLEN INHERITANCE - **Exodus 20:15, Habakkuk 2:6-9** - that you brag about is not the yield of your Christ-granted talent, and unlike PUTIN'S SIBERIA, there are no gas fields in bland, colourless, and almost lifeless John Bunyan's Bedford and where your own pure white father and mother were born.

Those who know the TRUTH obey the least: "Those who know the least obey the best." George Farquhar (1677-1707).

Karen Kwamboka: When it became apparent to Jews and Gentiles that the fellow was intellectually unplayable, He was kidnapped and killed - **Matthew 27:32-56,** solely to prevent Him from speaking.

"Freedom of Expression is the cornerstone of our democracy." Eton and Oxbridge-educated rich man's son (**Mark 10:25**), Lord Jacob Rees-Mogg.

Yinka Bamgbelu: ONLY SAINTS HAVE THE MORAL RIGHT TO JUDGE SINNERS – **John 5:22.**

"Every Saint has a past, and every Sinner has a future." Wilde (1854-1900).

Matthew 7:1-6, John 8:7: RACIST descendants of pure white THIEVES and owners of stolen children of defenceless poor people do not have the MORAL RIGHT to Judge SINNERS.

Karen Kwamboka: "I have seen evil, and it has the face of Mark Fuhrman." Johnnie Cochran (1937-2005).

Unqualified RACIST pure white bastards climb to the position of POWER solely based on the universally acknowledged irrefutably SUPERIOR SKIN COLOUR that they neither made nor chose.

Like Mark Fuhrman, a mere GED, albeit USA's Class Senior Police Officer, Senior Bedford's District Judge Paul Robert Ayers, a mere poly-educated former debt-collector Solicitor in NORFOLK/NORWICH, is also a RACIST pure white bastard.

Yinka Bamgbelu: "British Justice is Racist and should not be trusted by ethnic minorities." Peter Herbert (OBE)

Why should ethnic minority Britons fight and die for the continuing propagation of as RACIST JUDICIAL PHILOSOPHY that holds one race superior, and another inferior?

Karen Kwamboka: "Europe cannot defend itself without the support of NATO and the YANKS are NATO, and absolutely everything else is an auxiliary bluff. Europeans are afraid of Putin, but Ukrainians are not." President Zelensky paraphrased.

I/5 of Ukraine has been converted to rubble.

Yinka Bamgbelu: Their overpromoted hereditary RACIST poly-educated pure white bastard should FU*KING FU*K OFF. He should stay here; it is safer than NIGERIA - **Exodus 21:23-27**. No brain. Poor natural resources. Several centuries of stealing and slavery preceded their HUGE STOLEN INHERITANCE (gigantic yields of several continuous centuries of ancestral theft – Maafa (1445-1888) – **Exodus 20:15, Habakkuk 2:6-9.**

Karen Kwamboka: ASYMMETRIC MUTUAL RACE HATE:

RACISTS hate us, and we know. We hate the hereditary RACIST pure white bastards more (predominantly but not exclusively pure white), but they did not know. They are very powerful, and we are powerless and have been ROBBED to, penniless – since their armed ancestors found our defenceless ancestors in the AFRICAN BUSH in the 15th Century (Maafa, 1445-1888).

"How Europe underdeveloped Africa." Dr Walter Rodney (1942-1980).

Ignorant descendants of THIEVES and owners of stolen lives – **Exodus 20:15, Habakkuk 2:6-9**.

Yinka Bamgbelu: Hundreds of thousands of Russians have died. The probability that Russia will retaliate against those who directly or indirectly caused the death of her citizens - is 100%.

OXFORD, ENGLAND: GDC, Pure White Senior British Soldier, Stephanie (TD) unrelentingly lied under oath and on record – **Habakkuk 1:4.** Dark Black and 'UGLY', Constance Briscoe was JAILED for a lesser offence. Their Country, a Racist Hell Hole, is SHIT, and they are worse than SHIT, but they don't know.

Karen Kwamboka: TRUMP'S POODLES: DELUSIONAL GRANDEUR OF THE STOLEN PAST.

Hereditary RACIST pure white bastards (predominantly but not exclusively pure white) loved fighting and defenceless AFRICANS were their preferred opponents of Flat Track Racist Bullies:

Imagbon, 1892.

Benin, 1897.

Extremely nasty vicious bastards. If hereditary RACIST pure white bastards (predominantly but not exclusively pure white) are as BRAVE as they vulgarly brag, they must DIRECTLY, not through myopic and gullible proxies, use extreme overwhelming violence to evict PUTIN from Crimea, he used extreme overwhelming violence to convert Avdiivka and Bakhmut from bricks to rubble and stole them – **Exodus 20:15.**

Yinka Bamgbelu: BEDFORD, ENGAND: Pure White Senior District Judge Paul Robert Ayers, the most important part of the matter is MONEY, and unlike PUTIN'S SIBERIA, there are no gas fields in bland, colourless, and almost lifeless NORFOLK/NORWICH (Coastal Dole/the Departure Lounge of Life) and where your own pure white mother and father were born. You are not a SAINT because your ancestors were THIEVES – **Exodus 20:15, Habakkuk 2:6-9.**

Karen Kwamboka: Hereditary RACIST pure white bastards (predominantly but not exclusively pure white) became super-enlightened, highly civilised, and ultra-righteous, but only after several continuous centuries of MERCILESS RACIST EVIL (Maafa, 1445-1888).

"Blue-eyed devils." Elijah Mohammad (1897-1975).

Matthew 12:27: Blue-eyed devils cannot cast out green-eyed demons.

Yinka Bamgbelu: Then, insatiably greedy crooked bastards won in crooked courts before crooked Judges, but in the WAR when the Corporal flipped, the only sinless Judge looked away, and insatiably greedy crooked bastards lost everything and more – **John 5:22.**

Karen Kwamboka: Opportunist RACIST pure white bastards (predominantly but not exclusively pure white) dress up UNCONTROLLABLE HEREDITARY RACIAL HATRED and call it something else. They hate us, and we know.

BEDFORD, ENGLAND: GDC, Pure White Richard William Hill fabricated reports and unrelentingly lied under oath and on record – Habakkuk 1:4. Dark Black and 'UGLY', Constance Briscoe was JAILED for a lesser offence.

Yinka Bamgbelu: They don't want their own mentally gentler white children (OECD) and the pure white IMBECILES they shepherd (predominantly but not exclusively pure white) to know the TRUTH, which is that the universally acknowledged BLACK INFERIORITY is limited to our darker skin colour and our more inferior accent when speaking a foreign language, and apart from those, we are human beings too, and we are also properly created by Almighty God, and to conceal this DIVINE TRUTH, they criminally steal yields of our own people's Christ-granted talents, and their leverage is the certainty that all Judges will be their own PURE WHITE KINDRED, and their hope is that they would be hereditary RACIST pure white bastards too – **Habakkuk 1:4.**

Karen Kwamboka: Facts are sacred and cannot be overstated. Opportunist RACIST pure white bastards (predominantly but not exclusively pure white) dress up uncontrollable INNATE RACIAL HATRED and call it something else.

BEDFORD, ENGLAND: GDC, Sue Gregory, OBE, our own Officer of the Most Excellent Order of our own Empire of Stolen Inheritance – **Exodus 20:15, Habakkuk 2: 6-9**, unrelentingly lied under implied oath and on record – **Habakkuk 1:4**. Quasi-Mulatto, impure Black, Constance Briscoe was JAILED for a lesser offence.

Psalm 116:11: Why is lying to liars to a crime?

Yinka Bamgbelu: BEDFORD, ENGLAND: Pure White Senior District Judge Paul Robert Ayers, let me tell you, the mind that I did not choose is FINER than yours. I am intellectually dominant, and I know, and I shall use cogent facts and irrefutable evidence to irreparably DESTROY you and your indiscreetly crooked, VINDICTIVE, unashamedly mediocre, potently weaponised, and institutionally RACIST waste of money fish and chips FAKE LAW – **Habakkuk 1:4.**

Karen Kwamboka: "The cure must not be worse than the disease." Ibn Sina

BEDFORD, ENGLAND: Pure White Senior District Judge Paul Robert Ayers, your Country is SHIT, and you are worse than SHIT. They are all PURE

WHITE, and they are a gang of RACIST CRIMINALS, including their Judges, and in pursuant of self-preservation, we, their irreconcilable enemies, must conceal this TRUTH from them, as what they might do to conceal RACIST EVIL might be worse than the ORIGINAL SIN – **Habakkuk 1:4.**

Yinka Bamgbelu: There is nothing new under God's sun

2026: The Yanks kidnapped the President of a Country with no Nuclear Bombs. It would be absolutely impossible to similarly kidnap Kim from Pyongyang.

Karen Kwamboka: 1884-1885: Following the partition of Africa by Insatiably Greedy Economically Cannibalistic Pure White European Christians, in 1892, armed Pure White British Christian Bastards evicted Awujale Olasimbo Tunwase of Ijebu land from his palace, converted it to their Military Garrison, and from 1893 onwards scores of Mulattos were born by Ijebu girls.

Yinka Bamgbelu: Opportunist RACIST pure white bastards (predominantly but not exclusively pure white) dress up uncontrollable hereditary RACIAL HATRED and call it competent, colour-blind, and impartial administration of English Law.

BEDFORD, ENGLAND: Senior District Judge Paul Robert Ayers, Sue Gregory (OBE), and Mason, Richard Hill fabricated reports, and/or unrelentingly lied under oath, including approved Judgements, and/or unrelentingly lied on record – Habakkuk 1:4. Impure Black (Quasi-Mulatto), 'Ugly' Constance Briscoe was JAILED for a lesser offence. Facts are sacred and cannot be overstated.

Karen Kwamboka: BARAWO/OYINBO OMO OLE/ODE: They hate us, and we know. Modesty and sincerity are among the prime attributes of Christ-John **14:6,** but insincere modesty is subservient to sincere immodesty. Our brainless hereditary RACIST pure white bastards were granted the platform to display hereditary prejudice. The openly disclosure of what I know about you will be absolutely unacceptable to you, and you have unbounded, unaccountable, and illegal power to do an undo.

Yinka Bamgbelu: BEDFORD, ENGLAND: Pure White Senior District Judge Paul Robert Ayers, if you could disprove the TRUTH, which is that you, and some of your own pure white kindred, including Sue Gregory(OBE),Helen Falcon (MBE), a Quasi-Freemason, albeit without voodoo and/or occultists' rituals (Rotarian), Stephanie Twidale (TD), and Richard Hill (Mason), unrelentingly lied under oath, you will concomitantly disprove the implied belief of Peter Herbert (OBE), which is that some Pure White Judges are indiscreetly RACIST.

Karen Kwamboka: "The cure must not be worse than the disease." Ibn Sina.

Their Country is SHIT, and they are worse than SHIT. They are all PURE WHITE, and they are a gang of RACIST CRIMINALS, including their Judges, and in pursuant of self-preservation, one must conceal these TRUTHS from them, as what they might do, in desperation, to conceal RACIST EVIL could be worse than RACIAL HATRED. Facts are sacred and cannot be overstated.

Yinka Bamgbelu: King's School and Oxbridge-educated rich man's son (**Mark 10:25**), Lord Justice Charles Anthony Haddon-Cave, KC, a RACIST first son of Oxbridge-educated, insatiably greedy, and indiscreetly white supremacist Tasmanian Colonialist Economic Cannibal, if you could disprove the TRUTH, which is that your own pure white kindred, Bedford's District Judge Paul Robert Ayers, Mrs Helen Falcon, MBE, Sue Gregory, OBE, and British Soldier, Stephanie Twidale (TD) Etcetera, unrelentingly lied under oath and/or on record – **Habakkuk 1:4**, you will confirm that the NEGRO is mental.

Certum est quia impossibile est.

CHAPTER THIRTEEN

Karen Kwamboka: "He has refused to submit to a medical examination." King's School and Oxbridge-educated rich man's son (**Mark 10:25**), Lord Justice Charles Anthony Haddon-Cave, KC, a RACIST first son of Oxbridge-educated, insatiably greedy, and indiscreetly white supremacist Tasmanian Colonialist Economic Cannibal.

Yinka Bamgbelu: OYINBO OLE/ODE/OLODO: Brainless Nonsense: An ignorant hereditary RACIST descendant of THIEVES and owners of stolen children of poor people, including the AFRICAN ANCESTORS of the Quasi-Mulatto, impure White/impure Black, <43% Nigerian, great grandchildren of the Duke of Edinburgh of Blessed Memory, Prince Phillip (1921-2021).

Philippians 1:21: Phillip was a 33rd Degree Freemason (Scottish Rite).

Karen Kwamboka: Hereditary RACIST Pure White Bastards (predominantly but not exclusively pure white) trample on their own law and do whatever RACIST EVIL they like to us and use their Fish and Chips Justice System to bar us from defending ourselves against their HEREDITARY RACIAL HATRED – **Habakkuk 1:4.**

Yinka Bamgbelu: King's School and Oxbridge-educated rich man's son (**Mark 10:25**), Lord Justice Charles Anthony Haddon-Cave, KC, a RACIST first son of Oxbridge-educated, insatiably greedy, and indiscreetly white supremacist Tasmanian Colonialist Economic Cannibal, apart from creating very cushy salaried job for pure white Barristers and Solicitors (disproportionately but not exclusively pure white), what do pure white IMBECILES (predominantly but not exclusively pure white) need expensive administration of English Law for – **Habakkuk 1:4**?

Karen Kwamboka: ICE: ENFORCERS OF IMMIGRATION LAWS. Hereditary RACIST descendants of working-class Pure White UNDOCUMENTED CAUCASIAN REFUGEES from Europe, on stolen Native Americans' Land, half-educated school dropout GED and their type, dress up interracial intellectual envy and call RACIST EVIL a different name.

Yinka Bamgbelu: New Herod, **Matthew 2:16**: They deceive their own mentally gentler white children (OECD) and the pure white imbeciles they shepherd (predominantly but not exclusively pure white) that they are very highly civilised, super-enlightened, and ultra-righteous GENIUSES who do everything above board and LEGALLY: Rules-based procedures, precedent, statute etcetera, including RACIAL HATRED and FRAUD, and they destroy all self-educated NIGERIANS, from shit hole Africa, who know that they are not.

Karen Kwamboka: RACIST descendants of THIEVES and owners of kidnapped and sold children of defenceless poor people, including the African ancestors of QUASI-MULATTO, <43% Nigerian, impure White/impure Black grandniece and grandnephew of the Duke of Edinburgh, do not want their mentally gentler pure white children (OECD) and the pure white imbeciles they shepherd (predominantly but not exclusively pure white) to know the TRUTH, which is that apart from our INFERIOR SKIN COLOUR and our more inferior accent when speaking a foreign language, we are human beings too, and we are also properly created by God Almighty, and to conceal DIVINE TRUTHS, members of their brainlessly and baselessly self-awarded SUPERIOR RACE resort to Racist Criminality, and they criminally steal yields of Christ-granted talents of Self-educated NIGERIANS, from shit hole, secure in the knowledge that all Judges will be PURE WHITE, and their hope is that they would be hereditary RACIST pure white bastards too – **Habakkuk 1:4.** Facts are sacred and cannot be overstated.

Yinka Bamgbelu: OXFORD, ENGLAND: GDC, Pure White British Soldier, Stephanie Twidale (TD) unrelentingly lied under oath and on record – **Habakkuk 1:4**. Impure Black, 'Ugly' Constance Briscoe (Quasi-Mulatto) was JAILED for a lesser offence. Facts are sacred and cannot be overstated.

Karen Kwamboka: BEDFORD, ENGLAND: Pure White Senior District Judge Paul Robert Ayers, 46 Wasted Years (1976-2022: Having FAILED in practice, loads did, our own opportunist RACIST pure white bastard, an impostor, and an expert of deception parked his LIABILITY at the public till and the ignorant descendant of THIEVES and owners of stolen children of defenceless poor people, including the African ancestors of the impure White/impure Black, <43% Nigerian, Quasi-Mulatto, niece and nephew of the Prince of Wales.

Yinka Bamgbelu: "There is not a truth existing which I fear or would wish unknown to the whole world." President Thomas Jefferson (1743-1826).

TRUTHS disfavour hereditary RACIST pure white bastards (predominantly but not exclusively pure white) so they stifle them.

Karen Kwamboka: If skin colour that one neither made nor chose is universally acknowledged to be irrefutably superior, but if one's intellect is not, and if there are cogent and irrefutable evidence that one's pure white ancestors were THIEVES and owners of stolen lives, it is plainly deductible that Freedom of Expression is not one's friend.

Yinka Bamgbelu: Dr Samuel Johnson's Theory on Self-Preservation is not UNIVERSAL. Stephen Lawrence (1974-1993): If a mob of PURE WHITE RACIST BASTARDS, with very sharp knives in their hands, corners a Negro, in a peach black alley, the Negro must run, and run very fast for dear life.

"Why, Sir; to be sure when you wish a man to have that belief which you think is of infinite advantage, you wish well to him; but your primary consideration is your own quiet. If a madman were to come into this room with a GUN in his hand, no doubt we should pity the state of his mind; but our primary consideration would be to take care of ourselves. We should knock him down first, and pity him afterwards." Dr Samuel Johnson (1709-1784).

Karen Kwamboka: Pure White Skin, a Huge Stolen Inheritance, and What Else. Before Slavery, what? A Racist pure white bastard. An ignorant descendant of THIEVES and owners of Stolen Lives – **Exodus 20:15, Habakkuk 2:6-9.**

"The best opportunity of developing academically and emotional." Pure White Senior Bedford's District Judge Paul Robert Ayers.

BRAINLESS NONSENSE: A RACIST MORON MASON.

Our own RACIST PURE WHITE IMBECILE Freemason Senior District Judge of our own Empire of Stolen Inheritance; a RACIST descendant of THIEVES and owners of stolen lives ultra-righteously sat on the BONES of stolen children of defenceless poor people and Judged SINNERS – **Matthew 7:1-6, John 8:7.**

Yinka Bamgbelu: When bullies bully bullies, the weaker bullies do not deserve anyone's sympathy.

TRUMP BULLIES THEM: "Could you face the Russians by yourselves." President Trump

Karen Kwamboka: If Pure White Presidents or Rulers oppress members of other races to a great degree, they will map out the basis of their powers, rise, and decapitate them, and if need be, including KAMIKAZE. There is a remedy in human nature against tyranny, that will keep us safe under all forms of Government.' Dr Samuel Johnson (1709-1784) paraphrased.

Yinka Bamgbelu: CULTURAL ERASURE: CIVILISATION DEGRADATION.

"Pardon him Theodotus: He is a barbarian and thinks that the customs of his tribe and Island are the laws of nature." George Bernard Shaw (1856-1950).

Karen Kwamboka: "I want to say that I believe unequivocally that Meghan has been the victim of explicit and obnoxious racism. I am crystal clear about that." John Bercow.

"All sections of UK society are institutionally racist." Sir Bernard Hogan-Howe.

"Racism is rife throughout most organisations across Britain." Sir Sadiq Khan.

"White supremacy is real, and it needs to be shattered." Dr Cornel West.

Facts are sacred and cannot be overstated: "Find the truth and tell it." Harold Pinter (1930-2008).

Yinka Bamgbelu: It is me hereditary RACIST pure white bastards want, but it is my daughter they got.

Based on several decades of very proximate observations and direct experiences, their Country is SHIT, and they are worse than SHIT. There is no law in their SHIT COUNTRY, what Freemasons want is their law – **Habakkuk 1:4.**

Karen Kwamboka: You are a CRIMINAL RACIST JUDGE that patronage rather than merit granted a platform to display hereditary prejudice. We shall uncover and irreparably destroy you, and we are prepared to perish in the process. No brain. Poor natural resources. Several centuries of stealing and slavery preceded their huge stolen inheritance -**Exodus 20:15, Habakkuk 2:6-9.**

Yinka Bamgbelu: If the hereditary RACIST pure white bastard could disprove the TRUTH, which is that he, Pure White Senior Bedford's District Judge Paul Robert Ayers, unrelentingly lied under oath (approved Judgement) and on record – **Habakkuk 1:4,** and if he could disprove the TRUTH, which is that his own pure white kindred, Sue Gregory (OBE), our own Officer of the Most Excellent Order of our own Empire of Stolen Inheritance – **Exodus 20:15, Habakkuk 2:6-9**, unrelentingly lied under implied oath and on record – **Habakkuk 1:4,**

and if he could disprove the TRUTH, which is that his own pure white kindred, Freemason, Brother Richard William Hill fabricated reports and unrelentingly lied under oath and/or on record – **Habakkuk 1:4**, he would concomitantly disprove the TRUTH, which is that he is an opportunist RACIST pure white bastard, and a straight-faced CRIMINAL RACIST SENIOR DISTRICT JUDGE, albeit Bedford's Class, that patronage rather than merit granted a platform to display hereditary prejudice: OYINBO OLE/ODE. No brain. Poor natural resources. Several centuries of stealing and slavery preceded their huge stolen inheritance.

Karen Kwamboka: King's School and Oxbridge-educated very rich man's son (**Mark 10:25**), Lord Justice Charles Anthony Haddon-Cave, KC, which part of the Old Bailey (1907), and the Royal Courts of Justice (1882) was not STOLEN, or which part did your own pure white father and mother buy, or which part preceded SLAVERY: The grand buildings or their chattels? Maafa, 1445-1888, rebuilt everything it succeeded and paid for everything it preceded.

Yinka Bamgbelu: If King's School and Oxbridge-educated pure white RACIST son of a very rich Tasmanian Colonialist Economic Cannibal (**Mark 10:25**), Lord Justice Charles Anthony Haddon-Cave, KC, and Comprehensive School and Poly-educated pure white son of poorer nobodies, Bedford's Senior District Judge Paul Robert Ayers, could disprove the TRUTH, which is that their own pure white kindred, GDC, Mrs Helen Falcon (MBE), our own Member of the Most Excellent Order of our own Empire of Stolen Inheritance – **Exodus 20:15, Habakkuk**, unrelentingly lied under oath and on record – **Habakkuk 1:4,** and if they could also disprove the TRUTH that their own pure white kindred, GDC, British Soldier, Stephanie Twidale (TD), unrelentingly lied under oath and on record – **Habakkuk 1:4**, and if they could also disprove the TRUTH, which is that their own pure white kindred, Sue Gregory (OBE), our own Officer of the Most Excellent Order of our own Empire of Stolen Inheritance – **Habakkuk 2:6-9, Exodus 20:15**, an ignorant, hereditary RACIST descendant of PURE WHITE PROFESSIONAL THIEVES and owners of stolen children of defenceless poor people, including the AFRICAN ANCESTORS of the impure White/impure Black (Quasi-Mulatto, <43% Nigerian) grandniece and grandnephew of Major Andrew Mountbatten Windsor, unrelentingly lied under implied oath and record – **Habakkuk 1:4**, they will concomitantly disprove the TRUTH, which is that In disputes between pure white people, pure white Freemason Judges wear only one hat - that of an impartial Judge, but in disputes between pure white people and Negroes, pure white Freemason Judges wear the hats of the Counsels to their pure white kindred, and they Judge only Negroes.

Karen Kwamboka: OYINBO OLE/ODE/BARAWO: Falsus in uno, falsus in omnibus.

Those who know the TRUTH obey the least: "Those who know the least obey the best." George Farquhar (1677-1707).

Yinka Bamgbelu: PERCEPTION IS GRANDER THAN REALITY: Our brainless hereditary RACIST pure white bastard. Unlike PUTIN'S SIBERIA, there are no gas fields in John Foster's Brickhill, Freemasons' Kempston, and where the pure white mother and father of Pure White Senior Bedford's District Judge Paul Robert Ayers were born. The highly luxuriant soil of Tommy Robinson's LUTON yields only FOOD, and Luton's Robert Hibbert (1769-1849) was a RACIST pure white bastard Briton, and an insatiably greedy merchant of stolen lives. Bedford, England, Pure White Senior District Judge Paul Robert Ayers, your Pure White ancestors were Professional THIEVES – **Habakkuk 2:6-9, Exodus 20:15.** Facts are sacred and cannot be overstated**.**

Karen Kwamboka: Poly-educated pure white RUBBISH gave the game away when he approved what his pure white mother and father spoke.

Like his mentally gentler white children (OECD), the pure white IMBECILES (predominantly but not exclusively pure white) who sat before the RACIST pure white bastard did not know that his nomination and constructive appointment by dementing or demented hereditary white supremacist Freemason Lords – was not based on progressive, colour-blind, and measurable objectivity, and the last time the opportunist RACIST pure white bastard passed through a filter of measurable objectivity was when he studied 5th Rate Law at Poly, and it showed.

Yinka Bamgbelu: BEDFORD, ENGLAND: Pure White Senior District Judge Paul Robert Ayers, based on available evidence, you are a RACIST and a liar. Retrogressive Masonry patronage rather than progressive, colour-blind, and measurable objectivity granted an opportunist RACIST pure white bastard the platform to display hereditary prejudice. He should stay here; it is safer than NIGERIA – **Exodus 21:23-27.**

Karen Kwamboka: BEDFORD, ENGLAND: Pure White Senior District Judge Paul Robert Ayers, if you and your pure white type engage on a colour-blind level intellectual playing field, you will be uncovered and irreparably DESTROYED; you are INFERIOR. Sincere immodesty is sincerer than insincere modesty

BEDFORD, ENGLAND: Pure White Senior District Judge Paul Robert Ayers unrelentingly lied under oath (approved Judgement) and on record – **Habakkuk 1:4.**

Karen Kwamboka: Our own Nigeria, Shell's Docile Cash Cow since 1956 (OLOIBIRI). GDC was established in 1956.

Unlike PUTIN'S SIBERIA, there are no gas fields in Bedfordshire and where the pure white mother and father of Bedford's District Judge were born

Our own NIGERIAN BABIES with gigantic oil wells and gas fields near their huts eat only 1.5/day in our own NIGERIA, a very bellyful poly-educated pure white bastard, a mere former debt-collector Solicitor in bland, colourless, and almost lifeless Norfolk/Norwich (Coastal Dole/the Departure Lounge of Life) whose pure white father and mother have never seen CRUDE OIL, and whose pure white ancestors, including the pure white Jewish ancestors of Benjamin Disraeli (1804-1881) were fed like battery hens with huge yields of millions of stolen and destroyed children of defenceless poor people, including the African ancestors of our impure White/impure Black, 43% Nigerian, Mulatto Duchess of Sussex, was our District Judge in BEDFORD, England.

Yinka Bamgbelu: BEDFORD, ENGLAND: Pure White Senior District Judge Paul Robert Ayers, the pure white ancestors of your pure white mother and father were THIEVES - **Exodus 20:15, Habakkuk 2:6-9.**

If we aren't very smart, why are we very RICH, the sixth largest economy on earth?

Karen Kwamboka: Shepherds didn't bring any of the millions of stolen African children to GREAT BRITAIN, they carried stolen children of poor people to their stolen New World (not new to the Natives), and they LIED to their IMBECILE SHEEP that they were paragons of wisdom and virtue who, like Mother Teresa of Calcutta did only very, very, good charitable works in Africa.

OYINBO OLE (THIEVES) – **Exodus 20:15, Habakkuk 2:6-9:** "How Europe underdeveloped Africa." Dr Walter Rodney (1942-1980).

Yinka Bamgbelu: BEDFORD, ENGLAND: Pure White Senior District Judge Paul Robert Ayers, you are a LEECH. You are worthy only because you are PURE WHITE. You are RICH only because your pure white ancestors were THIEVES – **Exodus 20:15, Habakkuk 2:6-9.**

Karen Kwamboka: Habakkuk 2:5. Closeted RACIST beneficiaries of gigantic yields of involuntary mass migration, at gunpoint, Maafa,1445-1888, do not want to pay equitable, fair, and just REPARATION, and they do not want voluntary mass migration; insatiably greedy bastards are greedier than the grave, and like death, they will never be satisfied.

OYINBO OLE/ODE/BARAWO: Insatiably greedy pure white bastards (predominantly but not exclusively pure white), eat all their own cakes, eat all our own cakes, and have everything. Slavery preceded Colonisation, and Neo-Colonialism is the New SLAVERY – **Exodus 20:15, Habakkuk 2:6-9.**

Yinka Bamgbelu: Hereditary RACIST pure white bastards tell lies all the time, but they lie that they don't lie - **Psalm 144, Psalm 116:11.**

"Lies are told all the time." Oxbridge-educated pure white son of a very rich man, Sir Robert Michael Havers, QC, Attorney General (1980)

Karen Kwamboka: RACIST descendants ultra-righteous PURE WHITE THIEVES (**Exodus 20:15, Habakkuk**), predominantly but not exclusively pure white) hate us, and we know, but they pretend that they do not know that we know that they do. OYINBO OLE/ODE:

"It is incumbent upon the court and all those professionals involved to conclude court proceedings as quickly as possible. This hopefully ensures that a child has stability, love and affection and the parents working together to ensure that he has the best opportunity of developing academically and emotional." Pure White Hereditary Racist, unashamedly functionally semi-illiterate, poly-educated poor pure white man's son, a downmarket former debt-collector Solicitor in bland, colourless, and almost lifeless Norfolk/Norwich, (Coastal Dole/the Departure Lounge of Life), a mere lowlife 5th Rate Partner, and the Senior Vice President of the Association of Her Majesty's District Judges, Bedford's District Judge Paul Robert Ayers, 3, St Paul's Square, MK 40 1SQ – proof-read and approved judgement.

BRAINLESS PURE WHITE RACIST NONSENSE: PURIFIED PURE WHITE SHIT.

"Yes, Sir, it does her honour, but it would do nobody else honour. I have indeed not read it all. But when I take up the end of a web, and find a packthread, I do not expect, by looking further, to find embroidery." Dr Samuel Johnson (1709-1784).

Yinka Bamgbelu: OYINBO OLE/ODE: The yield of a very elementary mind, evidently, lacking rigour: Our unashamedly functional semi-illiterate, indiscreetly crooked, and hereditary RACIST pure white son of poor pure white plebeian nobodies probably studied law at poly (not Russell Group Second-Class Alternative Education – **Proverbs 17:16**) and it showed.

Karen Kwamboka: OYINBO OLE/ODE: Our own MONEY. Our own NIGERIAN CHILDREN with gigantic oil wells and gas fields near their huts eat only 1.5/day in our own NIGERIA, a very bellyful opportunist RACIST pure white bastard whose pure white mother and father have never seen CRUDE OIL, and whose pure white ancestors, including ultra-righteous John Bunyan (1628-1688), were fed like battery hens with gigantic yields of millions of stolen and destroyed lives of the children of defenceless poor people (AFRICANS), was our Senior District Judge in Bedford, Great Britain. Which part of indiscreet crookedness, unashamed mediocrity, and confusion is great?

Yinka Bamgbelu: It is not the truth that Kamala Harris stated that Trump's administration packed courts with mediocre pure white Judges, but homogeneity in the administration of the law is the impregnable secure mask of MERCILESS RACIST EVIL, a very potent weapon of a latent but RAGING asymmetrical RACE WAR: Power imbalance.

"Those who have the power to do wrong with impunity seldom wait long for the will." Dr Samuel Johnson (1709-1784).

It is obvious that Russia hates Great Britain more than Ukraine, and if the YANKS were to look away, Russia would declare war against Great Britain.

The YANKS, not NATO, are the defenders of Great Britain. Without the YANKS, Great Britain is a sitting duck.

"England will fight to the last American." An American saying.

"Could you face the Russians by yourselves." President Trump

Karen Kwamboka: OYINBO OLE/ODE: Our opportunist RACIST pure white bastard was granted the platform to display hereditary prejudice, and the indiscreetly crooked hereditary RACIST pure white bastard treated the Judiciary as if it were his pure white father's private enterprise.

"Treating your adversaries with respect is striking soft in a battle." Dr Samuel Johnson (1709-1784).

1976-2022: After FAILING in practice, loads did, the ignorant hereditary RACIST pure white bastard parked his liability at the public till and the indiscreetly crooked, unashamedly functional semi-illiterate, and hereditary RACIST pure white bastard sold unashamed mediocrity, incompetent mendacity, and confusion to the undiscerning. Facts are sacred and cannot be overstated. The hereditary RACIST pure white bastard should stay here; it is safer than NIGERIA – **Exodus 21: 23-27.**

"We shall deal with the racist bastards when we get out of prison." Robert Mugabe (1924-2019).

Yinka Bamgbelu: Our ignorant brainless hereditary RACIST pure white bastard of our own Empire of Stolen Inheritance – **Exodus 20:15, Habakkuk**, approved and immortalised what his pure white mother and father spoke, the type of STORIES his pure white father used to tell when he returned home from his regular pub crawl, Nag's Head, Greene King, Queen Victoria Etcetera, at very odd hours, thoroughly stoned, hungry, angry, and very RANDY, and which his poly-educated pure white superiors and supervisors authorised and approved – **Habakkuk 1:4.**

Karen Kwamboka: BEDFORD, ENGLAND: Pure White Hereditary Racist, unashamedly functionally semi-illiterate, poly-educated poor pure white man's son, a downmarket former debt-collector Solicitor in bland, colourless, and almost lifeless Norfolk/Norwich, (Coastal Dole/the Departure Lounge of Life), a mere lowlife 5th Rate Partner, and the Senior Vice President of the Association of Her Majesty's District Judges, Bedford's District Judge Paul Robert Ayers, 3, St Paul's Square, MK 40 1SQ, the most important part of the matter is MONEY, and our own MONEY, Nigeria (oil/gas), is by far more relevant to the economic survival of all your own mentally gentler white children (OECD), your pure white mother, your pure white father, and your pure white spouse than bland, colourless, and almost lifeless pure white Tommy Robinson and Robert Hibbert's LUTON. Ignorant hereditary RACIST pure white bastards, and ultra-righteous descendants of THIEVES – **Exodus 20:15, Habakkuk 2:6-9.**

CHAPTER FOURTEEN

Yinka Bamgbelu: Based on cogent, irrefutable, and available evidence, HHJ Perusko studied law at Poly: Not Russell Group, glorified GED, Lower-Class Alternative Education – **Proverbs 17:16**. Those who nearly passed or just passed the A/Level could become Judges within one of the dullest adult populations in the industrialised world (OECD).

Just as it was in Professor Stephen Hawking's School, then, at our own University of Lagos, the brightest students did mathematics, physics, and chemistry, and did not attend lectures at the Faculty of Law.

"In my school, the brightest boys did math and physics, the less bright did physics and chemistry, and the least bright did biology. I wanted to do math and physics, but my father made me do chemistry because he thought there would be no jobs for mathematicians." Dr Stephen Hawking (1942-2018).

Karen Kwamboka: OYINBO OLE/ODE: Based on several decades of very proximate observations and direct experiences, theirs is a grossly overrated, overhyped, overpopulated, and MEDIOCRE TRADE that is dying slowly and imperceptibly, and is overseen by members of the Vulgarly Charitable, Hereditary White Supremacist, and Antichrist Racist Freemasonry Quasi-Religion (Mediocre Mafia, Spiritually Ignorant New Pharisees – **Mark 10:27-32**, Experts of their indiscreetly crooked, VINDICTIVE, unashamedly mediocre, potently weaponised, and institutionally RACIST Justice System - **Luke 11:52**, New Good Samaritan – **Luke 10:25-37**, New Good Shepherd, **John 10:11-18**, and the self-awarded New Truly Good God – **Mark 10:18**.

Yinka Bamgbelu: OYINBO OLE/ODE: Pure White Hereditary Racist, unashamedly functionally semi-illiterate, poly-educated poor pure white man's son, a downmarket former debt-collector Solicitor in bland, colourless, and almost lifeless Norfolk/Norwich, (Coastal Dole/the Departure Lounge of Life), a mere lowlife 5th Rate Partner, and the Senior Vice President of the Association of Her Majesty's District Judges, Bedford's District Judge Paul Robert Ayers, 3, St Paul's Square, MK 40 1SQ, our brainless hereditary RACIST pure white former debt-collector Solicitor in NORWICH. You were not a Judge because you were intellectually exceptional. You were a Senior District Judge in BEDFORD only because you are PURE WHITE and Mason – **Habakkuk 1:4.**

Karen Kwamboka: If sincerity is a prime attribute of our own Messiah, immodesty should be subservient to sincerity, as sincere immodesty is sincerer than insincere modesty.

Reasoning and vision do not have finite boundaries. The fellow is who He says He is - **John 14:6**. The mind that I did not choose is finer than your indiscreetly crooked, VINDICTIVE, unashamedly mediocre, potently weaponised, and institutionally RACIST Fish and Chips Justice System, and I do not believe in any part of your SHIT, as no part of your SHIT is good, not even one – **Psalm 53**, and I have the power to use cogent facts and irrefutable evidence to irreparably destroy you and your SHIT: OYINBO OLE/ODE – **EXODUS 20:15, HABAKKUK.**

Yinka Bamgbelu: "All sections of UK society are institutionally racist." Sir Bernard Hogan-Howe

The JUDICIARY is part of UK society.

'British Justice is untrustworthy, verifiably RACIST, and should not be trusted by ethnic minorities." Peter Herbert (OBE) paraphrased.

Karen Kwamboka: King's School and Oxbridge-educated Lord Justice Charles Anthony Haddon-Cave, KC, a RACIST first son of a very, very, very, very, very, very, RICH Tasmanian Colonialist Economic Cannibal (**Mark 10:25**), Tasmania and Oxbridge-educated very, very, very, rich man's son (**Mark 10:25**), Sir Charles Phillip Haddon-Cave (1925–1999), and a grandson of Francis Haddon-Cave, born in Hobart in early 20th-century Australian settlement; an impostor and an expert of deception (perception is grander than reality), and a closeted white supremacist descendant of DRUG LORDS (opium merchants of the Qing Dynasty), and a homie of Eton and Oxbridge-educated very, very, very, rich men's son, Archbishop Justin Welby (**Mark 10:25**), based on cogent, irrefutable, and available evidence, let me tell you what you may know or mayn't know, your unashamedly mediocre, VINDICTIVE, indiscreetly crooked, potently weaponised, and institutionally RACIST Fish and Chips Justice is FU*KED, irreparably FU*KED, as it has foreseeably succumbed to INCEST, weakening of the common genetic pool, and associated physical and mental wonkiness, and hereditary white supremacist Freemason Judges, and others, who make loads of money from unashamed mediocrity and confusion prop shit up: Conflict of interest.

"A government that robs Peter to pay Paul can always depend on the support of Paul." George Bernard Shaw (1856-1950).

Yinka Bamgbelu: OYINBO OLE/ODE: What they want is a retrogressive world where everything is subservient to the universally acknowledged irrefutably superior skin colour that very fortunate wearers neither made nor chose (APARTHEID BY STEALTH). Their skin colour is superior, but their intellects are not, and their indiscreetly RACIST Justice System is fundamentally designed to conceal that TRUTH – **Habakkuk 1:4.**

"British Justice is Racist and should not be trusted by ethnic minorities." Peter Herbert (OBE), an expert of their law – **Luke 11:52.**

The Ne plus ultra of evil is injustice motivated by the dark coat that the wearer neither made nor chose:

"The highest reach of injustice is to be deemed just when you are not." Plato

Karen Kwamboka: OYINBO OLE/ODE: BEDFORD, ENGLAND: District Judge, based on cogent, irrefutable, and available evidence, yours is a Racist Hell Hole that is overseen by hereditary white supremacist Freemason Judges for the benefit of pure white imbeciles (predominantly but not exclusively pure white) – **Habakkuk 1:4.**

Yinka Bamgbelu: Without the direct support of the YANKS, Great Britain is a sitting duck.

"Could you face the Russians by yourselves?" President Trump

Karen Kwamboka: OXFORD, ENGLAND: GDC, Pure White British Soldier, Stephanie Twidale (TD) unrelentingly lied under oath and on record - **Habakkuk 1:4**. 'Ugly', dark black Constance Briscoe, impure Black (Quasi-Mulatto) was JAILED for a lesser offence.

Yinka Bamgbelu: 1976-2022: An opportunist RACIST pure white bastard, a mere poly-educated former debt-collector Solicitor in bland, colourless, and almost lifeless NORFOLK/NORWICH (Coastal Dole/the Departure Lounge of Life) who FAILED in practice, loads did, and parked his LIABILITY at the public till was granted the platform to display hereditary prejudice.

What RACIST BASTARDS want is intellectual superiority, but He hates them, so He gave them superior skin colour, and in protest, they steal what He gave to self-educated NIGERIANS, from shit hole Africa

BEDFORD, ENGLAND: Senior District Judge Paul Robert Ayers, Sue Gregory (OBE), our own Officer of the Most Excellent Order of our own Empire of STOLEN INHERITANCE – **Exodus 20:15, Habakkuk 2:6-9,** and Freemason, Brother Richard William Hill, they were all PURE WHITE, and they all LIED on record. Impure Black (Quasi-Mulatto) Constance Briscoe was JAILED for a lesser offence – **Habakkuk 1:4**. Facts are sacred and cannot be overstated.

Karen Kwamboka: 2025 SURVEY: 95% of legal professionals corroborated Peter Herbert (OBE) and Confirmed RACIAL HATRED is very common in the administration of English Law.

Yinka Bamgbelu: In Great Britain, 13% of inmates are BLACKS despite being only 3% of the population. Which part of indiscreet RACIAL HATRED is great?

"The white man is the devil." Elijah Mohammed (1897-1975).

Based on several decades of very proximate observations and direct experiences, he is not only a devil, but he is also a THIEF, and if you did not know that TRUTH, it is proof that you could not see him as he truly is – **Habakkuk 1:4.**

Karen Kwamboka: OYINBO OLE/ODE: Pure White Mediocre Rubbish. When pure white (predominantly but not exclusively pure white) Solicitors and Barristers FAILED in practice, loads did, if they were Freemasons, they became Judges or something else, and if not, they became Politicians or something else – **Habakkuk 1:4.**

Yinka Bamgbelu: OYINBO OLE/ODE: Hereditary RACIST pure white bastards (predominantly but not exclusively pure white) are not deterred by His Justice - **John 5:22,** because they do not believe in His exceptionalism - **John 14:6.**

Karen Kwamboka: OYINBO OLE/ODE: A manager at GDC, 37, Wimpole Street, London, W1G 8DQ, Jonathan Martin, indiscreetly crooked, unapologetically white supremacist, and poly-educated pure white rubbish (not Russell Group Lower-Class Inferior Alternative Education -**Proverbs 17:16**) unrelentingly lied under oath and/or on record – **Habakkuk 1:4**. The pure white ancestors of his pure white mother and father were incompetent RACIST LIARS too, they were THIEVES – **Exodus 20:15,** extremely nasty and mercilessly evil RACIST KILLERS – **Exodus 20:13**, and owners of stolen children of defenceless poor people, including the AFRICAN ancestors of the impure White/impure Black, Mulatto (43% Nigerian) Duchess of Sussex. Jonathan looked 100% White.

Yinka Bamgbelu: OYINBO OLE/ODE. OUR OWN MONEY. OUR OWN NIGERIA, SHELL'S DOCILE CASH COW SINCE 1956 (OLOIBIRI), GDC WAS ESTABLISHED IN 1956.

A manager at GDC, 37, Wimpole Street, London, W1G 8DQ, Jonathan Martin, dishonestly implied that he did not know that SLAVERY rebuilt everything it succeeded and paid for everything it preceded, including Dame Margaret Seward's (1935-2021) GDC, established in 1956, and in same year, Shell discovered a huge reserve of commercially viable oil in Oloibiri.

"Coincidence is God's way of remaining anonymous." Albert Einstein (1879-1955).

Karen Kwamboka: They kill foreigners - Leviticus **19:33-34.** BEDFORD, ENGLAND: GDC, Sue Gregory (OBE) our Officer of the Most Excellent Order of our own Empire of Stolen Inheritance - **Exodus 20:15, Habakkuk**, unrelentingly lied under implied oath and on record – **Habakkuk 1:4**. Her type 'KILLED' the Nigerian, Dr Richard Bamgboye, GP, only 56, and the Indian, Dr Anand Kamath, Dentist, only 42, albeit hands-off, with the mens rea hidden in the belly of the actus reus.

Yinka Bamgbelu: OYINBO OLE/ODE: They hate us, and we know, but they dishonestly imply that they don't, and they pretend that they do not know that we know that they do. King's School and Oxbridge-educated Lord Justice Charles Anthony Haddon-Cave, KC, a RACIST first son of a very, very, very, very, very, very, RICH Tasmanian Colonialist Economic Cannibal (**Mark 10:25**), Tasmania and Oxbridge-educated very, very, very, rich man's son (**Mark 10:25**), Sir Charles Phillip Haddon-Cave (1925–1999), and a grandson of Francis Haddon-Cave, born in Hobart in early 20th-century Australian settlement; an impostor and an expert of deception (perception is grander than reality), and a closeted white supremacist descendant of DRUG LORDS (opium merchants of the Qing Dynasty), and a homie of Eton and Oxbridge-educated very, very, very, rich men's son, Archbishop Justin Welby (**Mark 10:25**),, which part of the Old Bailey and the Royal Courts of Justice was not STOLEN, or which part did your own pure white mother and father buy, or which part preceded SLAVERY? Our brainless opportunist RACIST pure white bastard, an ignorant descendant of THIEVES and owners of stolen children of defenceless poor people (AFRICANS). The pure white skin of the opportunist RACIST pure white bastard concealed his impure dark black brain. His spinal cord is his highest centre. He dishonestly implied that he did not know that the pure white ancestors of his pure white mother and father were THIEVES, and he further dishonestly implied that he did not know that SLAVERY rebuilt everything it succeeded and paid for everything it preceded, including the Royal College of Surgeons (1880), the Royal Courts of Justice (1882), the Old Bailey (1907), the NHS (1948), the GDC (1956) Etcetera...Ignorant hereditary RACIST descendants of ultra-righteous pure white THIEVES – **Exodus 20:15, Habakkuk.**

Karen Kwamboka: OYINBO OLEW/ODE: BEDFORD, ENGLAND: District Judge, the most important part of everything is MONEY, and unlike PUTIN'S RUSSIA, there are no oil wells or gas fields in Tommy Robinson's LUTON and where your own pure white mother and father were born. Our own MONEY, Nigeria (oil/gas), is by far more relevant to the economic survival of all your own mentally gentler white children (OECD), your pure white mother, your pure white father, and your pure white spouse than bland, colourless, and almost lifeless Freemasons' Kempston.

Yinka Bamgbelu: OYINBO OLE/ODE: Hereditary RACIST pure white bastards love WARS: Black War/Native Tasmanian Genocidal Massacre (1827-1832), Ijebu Kingdom, Imagbon Massacre (1892), Benin Kingdom, Benin Massacre (1897) Etcetera. We and our type are ones RACIST BASTARDS would beat up without the support of the YANKS.

Karen Kwamboka: OYINBO OLE/ODE: **Psalm 118:22, Luke 20:17:** There were Antichrist Freemasons and Antichrist Freemasons' Temples in Bakhmut and Avdiivka. If hereditary RACIST pure white bastards (predominantly but not exclusively pure white) are as BRAVE as the vulgarly brag, they must DIRECTLY use extreme overwhelming violence to evict PUTIN from Crimea, he used extreme overwhelming violence to convert Bakhmut and Avdiivka from bricks to rubble and stole them – **Exodus 20:15**.

"Bakhmut of our hearts." President Zelensky.

Yinka Bamgbelu: Based on several decades of very proximate observations and direct experiences, hereditary RACIST pure white bastards (predominantly but not exclusively pure white) fear the untamed minds of self-educated NIGERIANS more than PUTIN'S POISONS. Brainless and baseless SUPERIORITY is their birth right, so they must always win, but only skin colour that they neither made nor chose and Almighty God are truly good – **Mark 10:18.**

Karen Kwamboka: OYINBO OLE/ODE: Based on several decades of very proximate observations and direct experiences, hereditary RACIST pure white bastards (predominantly but not exclusively pure white) are psychologically and intellectually insecure, and they are more impervious to other views than LUNATIC JIHADISTS; unipolar ignorant RACIST pure white bastards (predominantly but not exclusively pure white), who like Trump, Xi, Putin, Kim, MBS, Ayatollah Ali Khamenei, Babies Etcetera – expect everyone to love them unconditionally, and ignorant one-dimensionally educated hereditary RACIST pure white bastards (predominantly but not exclusively pure white) expect everyone to see the world with the unipolar lens of their brainlessly and baselessly self-awarded hegemony, and unearned and deserved stolen advantages, and they expect everyone to FEAR them, and say and/or write only what they love to hear: The tyranny of the pure white majority (predominantly but not exclusively pure white): Creeping DPRK.

Yinka Bamgbelu: OYINBO OLE/ODE: Our brainless hereditary RACIST pure white bastard of our own Empire of Stolen Inheritance – Exodus **20:15, Habakkuk**, sat on a very expensive highchair that his pure white mother and father could not afford, and which the pure white imbeciles (predominantly but not exclusively pure white) who sat before him could not and did not buy, and he Judged sinners – **Matthew 7:1-6, John 8:7**: The Ne Plus Ultra of Hypocrisy.

Karen Kwamboka: OYINBO OLE/ODE: BEDFORD, ENGLAND: Pure White Senior District Judge Paul Robert Ayers, our own opportunist RACIST pure white bastard of our own Empire of Stolen Inheritance – **Exodus 20:15, Habakkuk,** was granted the platform to display hereditary prejudice. He should stay here; it is safer than NIGERIA – **Exodus 21:23-27. John 8:7, Matthew 7:1-6:** Only He who has no sin (**John 5:22, Matthew 25:31-46**) has the MORAL RIGHT to Judge Sinners, a RACIST pure white bastard, and an ultra-righteous descendant of PURE WHITE THIEVES, does not have the moral right to Judge sinners. No brain, Poor natural resources. Several centuries of stealing and slavery preceded their huge stolen inheritance (gigantic yields of several centuries of ancestral theft – **Exodus 20:15, Habakkuk**). Facts are sacred and cannot be overstated.

Yinka Bamgbelu: Museum like Courts built with yields of millions of stolen and destroyed lives, the foundation of BONES, more bones than the millions of skulls at the doorstep of POL POT (1925-1998).

BEDFORD, ENGLAND: Pure White Senior District Judge Paul Robert Ayers, which part of Bedford County Court, MK40 1SQ, and Bedfordshire Masonic

Centre, MK42 8AH, was not STOLEN, or which part did your own pure white mother and father buy, or which part preceded SLAVERY: The grand buildings or their chattels?

OYINBO OLE/ODE/BARAWO: Those who know the TRUTH obey the least. "Those who know the least obey the best." George Farquhar (1677-1707).

Karen Kwamboka: BEDFORD, ENGLAND: Pure White Senior District Judge Paul Robert Ayers, your Country is SHIT, and you are worse than SHIT. The most important part of the matter is MONEY, and it is not the yield of your land or talent. Unlike PUTIN'S RUSSIA, there are no oil wells or gas fields in Freemasons' Kempston and where your own pure white mother and father were born. You are a properly schooled impostor and an expert of deception - with all the characteristics of the SCOTTISH LEECH. You are worthy only because you are pure white, and you are rich only because your ancestors were THIEVES – **Exodus 20:15, Habakkuk.**

"The impudence of an Irishman is the impudence of a fly, that buzzes about you, and you put it away, but it returns, flutters, and teases you. The impudence of a Scotsman is the impudence of a leech, that fixes and sucks your blood." Dr Samuel Johnson (1709-1784).

Yinka Bamgbelu: Homogeneity in the administration of English Law is a very potent weapon of RACE WAR.

Their people are everywhere in their Godforsaken Racist Hell Hole, and they control almost everything, including RACIAL HATRED and FRAUD - **Habakkuk 1:4**. Integrity, friendship, respect, and charity: All for one, and one for all.

Karen Kwamboka: Vulgarly charitable (New Pharisees), Antichrist, and Hereditary White Supremacist Freemasonry Quasi-Religion (Mediocre Mafia, Experts of the Law (**Luke 11:52**), New Good Samaritans, **Luke 10:25-37**, New Good Shepherd (**John 10:11-18**), brainlessly and baselessly self-awarded New Truly Good God, Dissenters of the Faith – **John 14:6**, and Defenders of Faiths. No brain. Poor natural resources. Several centuries of stealing and slavery preceded their huge stolen inheritance (gigantic yields of several continuous centuries of ancestral theft – Maafa, 1445-1888).

Yinka Bamgbelu: BEDFORD, ENGLAND: Pure White Senior District Judge Paul Robert Ayers, our own Senior Vice President of the Association of

Her Majesty's District Judges, Pure White Sue Gregory (OBE), our own Officer of the Most Excellent Order of our own Empire of Stolen Inheritance - **Exodus 20:15, Habakkuk 2:6-9,** Pure White Freemason, Brother Richard William Hill, Senior NHS Postgraduate Tutor, albeit Bedfordshire's Class, fabricated reports, and/or unrelentingly lied under oath, including approved Judgements, and/or lied on record – **Habakkuk 1:4.** 'Ugly' Quasi-Mulatto, impure Black Constance Briscoe was JAILED for a lesser offence.

Karen Kwamboka: Their Fish and Chips Justice System is FU*KED, irreparably FU*KED – **Habakkuk 1:4.** Ignorant descendants of THIEVES – **Exodus 20:15, Habakkuk 2:6-9.**

"The legal system lies at the heart of any society, protecting rights, imposing duties, and establishing a framework for the conduct of almost every social, political, and economic activity. Some argue that the law is in its death throes while others postulate a contrary prognosis that discerns numerous signs of law's enduring strength. Which is it?" Professor Raymond Wacks, Emeritus Professor of Law, Hong Kong

Facts are sacred.

Yinka Bamgbelu: When their people commit racist crimes against our people, closeted white supremacist bastards who oversee the administration of their law criminally bury RACIAL HATRED – **Habakkuk 1:4.** Freemason, Brother Richard William Hill fabricated reports and unrelentingly lied under oath and on record. Had the Racist Bastard been Black, or had the Judges been Black, he would have been in trouble. Dark Black Constance Briscoe was JAILED for a lesser offence: Apartheid by stealth.

Karen Kwamboka: An opportunist RACIST pure white bastard was granted the platform to display hereditary prejudice. 1976-2022: After FAILING in practice, loads did, the ignorant hereditary RACIST pure white bastard parked his liability at the public till and the ignorant hereditary RACIST descendant of THIEVES and owners of stolen children of defenceless poor people, including the AFRICAN ANCESTORS of the Quasi-Mulatto, impure White, impure Black, <43% Nigerian, grandniece and grandnephew of Major Andrew Mountbatten Windsor, sold unashamed mediocrity and confusion to the undiscerning, in exchange for very valuable considerations. The most important part of the matter is MONEY, and unlike PUTIN'S SIBERIA, there are no gas fields in John Foster's (1759-1832) Brickhill, Freemasons' Kempston, and where the pure white mother and father of our pure white Senior District Judge Paul Robert Ayers, our Senior Vice President of the Association of Her Majesty's District Judges, were born.

Yinka Bamgbelu: Our Brainless OPPORTUNIST RACIST pure white bastard, his hair stands on end when he is challenged by self-educated Nigerians, from shit hole AFRICA. We and our type are the ones hereditary RACIST pure white bastards (predominantly but not exclusively pure white) would beat up without the support of the YANKS.

"England will fight to the last American." An American saying.

CHAPTER FIFTEEN

Karen Kwamboka: "Ethical foreign policy." Robin Cook (1946-2005). A 5th Rate Military Power impersonates a SUPERPOWER. They will not defeat Pakistan.

If one-dimensionally educated self-awarded highly ethical hereditary RACIST pure white bastards (predominantly but not exclusively pure white) are as brave as they vulgarly brag, they must DIRECTLY use overwhelming extreme violence to evict PUTIN from Crimea, he used extreme overwhelming violence to convert Bakhmut and Avdiivka from bricks to rubble and stole them – **Exodus 20:15**. Facts are sacred and cannot be overstated.

Yinka Bamgbelu: A brainless pure white bastard. An ignorant hereditary RACIST descendant of THIEVES - **Exodus 20:15**, RACIST KILLERS - **Exodus 20:13**, and owners of stolen children of defenceless poor people (AFRICANS) with a GED BRAIN was our Senior District Judge, albeit within one of the dullest adult populations in the industrialised world.

Karen Kwamboka: OYINBO OLE/ODE: They are SHIT PEOPLE and they know that we know. His Country is SHIT, and he is verifiably worse than SHIT.

"When a stupid man is doing something, he is ashamed of, he always declares that it is his duty." George Bernard Shaw (1856-1950).

Yinka Bamgbelu: OYINBO OLE/ODE: ENVY IS A THIEF: Had the opportunist RACIST pure white bastard been BLACK and 10X as smart, he would not have been our Senior District Judge in BEDFORD. He was a properly schooled impostor and an expert of deception. Everything, absolutely everything, is baselessly and brainlessly assumed in favour of the universally acknowledged irrefutably SUPERIOR SKIN COLOUR that the very fortunate wearer neither made nor chose – **Habakkuk 1:4.**

Karen Kwamboka: OYINBO OLE/ODE: OUR OWN MONEY.OUR OWN NIGERIA, SHELL'S DOCILE CASH COW SINCE 1956, OLOIBIRI. GDC WAS ESTABLISHED IN 1956.

OYINBO OLE/ODE: Unlike Putin's Russia, there are no oil wells or gas fields in bland, colourless, and almost lifeless Tommy Robinson and Robert

Hibbert's (1769-1849) LUTON, and the very highly luxuriant soil of Bishop's Stortford yields only FOOD. Bishop's Stortford's Cecil Rhodes (1853-1902) was a RACIST pure white bastard and a THIEF – **Exodus 20:15, Habakkuk.**

Yinka Bamgbelu: They are demigods, but they are not our God - **Exodus 20:5.** They are not the only creation of Almighty God, and they are not immortal, and the universally acknowledged irrefutably superior skin colour that the very fortunate wearer neither made nor chose is not the only wonder of our world.

Karen Kwamboka: Proverbs 20:15: They hate us, and they know that we know. Skin colour is a great creation of Almighty God, but it is not the greatest.

Tasmania University and Oxbridge-educated very, rich man's son (Mark 10:25), Sir Charles Phillip Haddon-Cave (1925–1999), and an innately white supremacist grandson of Francis Haddon-Cave, born in Hobart in early 20th-century Australian settlement; a properly schooled impostor and an expert of deception (perception is grander than reality), and a closeted white supremacist descendant of DRUG LORDS (opium merchants of the Qing Dynasty): Yinka Bamgbelu, are you are RACIST?

Yinka Bamgbelu: OYINBO OLE/ODE: Brainless Nonsense. Tasmania University and Oxbridge-educated very, rich man's son (**Mark 10:25**), Sir Charles Phillip Haddon-Cave (1925–1999), and an innately white supremacist grandson of Francis Haddon-Cave, born in Hobart in early 20th-century Australian settlement; a properly schooled impostor and an expert of deception (perception is grander than reality), and a closeted white supremacist descendant of DRUG LORDS (opium merchants of the Qing Dynasty), you were not only a RACIST BASTARD, but you were also a thief – **Exodus 20:15, Habakkuk.** Our own NIGERIAN CHILDREN with gigantic oil wells and gas fields near their huts eat only 1.5/day in our own NIGERIA, a very bellyful, unashamedly functional semi-illiterate, indiscreetly crooked, vindictive, and opportunist RACIST pure white bastard, a mere poly-educated former debt-collector Solicitor in bland, colourless, and almost lifeless NORFOLK/NORWICH (Coastal dole/the departure lounge of life), and our lowlife 5th Rate Partner, albeit within one of the dullest adult populations in the industrialised world (OECD), whose pure white mother and father have never seen CRUDE OIL, and whose pure white ancestors, including John Foster (1759-1832) of Brickhill, Bedford, were fed like battery hens with gigantic yields of millions of stolen children of defenceless poor people, including the AFRICAN ancestors of the impure White/ impure Black (QUASI-MULATTO, <43% NIGERIAN) great grandchildren of the

Duke of Edinburgh of Blessed Memory, Prince Phillip (1921-2021), thrives in Great Britain. Which part of our own shithole Africa is great?

Karen Kwamboka: OYINBO OLE/ODE: "How Europe underdeveloped Africa." Dr Walter Rodney (!942-1980).

Then, and only then, all Judges were pure white Freemasons, and most of them were thicker than a gross of planks. Then, the pure white man was grossly overrated.

Philippians 1:21: Phillip was a 33rd Degree Freemason, Scottish Rite (Mediocre Mafia) – **Habakkuk 1:4.**

Yinka Bamgbelu: OYINBO OLE/ODE: Facts are sacred and cannot be overstated: "The truth allows no choice." Dr Samuel Johnson (1709-1784).

Degraded, depraved, erased, and deluded little piglets: Delusional Grandeur of the stolen past - **Exodus 20:15, Habakkuk**. Before Slavery, what? Then, there was only subsistence feudal agriculture.

"Agriculture not only gives riches to a nation, but the only one she can call her own." Dr Samuel Johnson (1709-1784).

Karen Kwamboka: OYINBO OLE/ODE. They hate us, and they know that we know. They should stay here; it is safer than NIGERIA – **Exodus 21:23-27**. Ignorant one-dimensionally educated direct descendants of the father of incompetent Racist Lies - **John 8:44, John 10:10** (THIEVES - **Exodus 20:15, Habakkuk**): Superiority is their brainless and baseless self-awarded birth right. Anyone, particularly mere NEGROES, from shithole Africa, who disagree with SUPERIOR PURE WHITE PEOPLE – is certainly a lunatic:

Certum est quia impossibile est.

Yinka Bamgbelu: OYINBO OLE/ODE: Part of the enduring residues of the Original Sin: Maafa (1445-1888). Colonisation replaced SLAVERY. Neo-colonialism is the NEW SLAVERY.

Karen Kwamboka: Substitution is fraudulent emancipation.

"Moderation is a virtue only among those who are thought to have found alternatives." Dr Henry Kissinger (1923-2023).

Yinka Bamgbelu: Our BRAINLESS hereditary Racist pure white bastard of our own Empire of Stolen Inheritance - **Exodus 20:15, Habakkuk**. No brain. Poor natural resources. Several centuries of stealing and slavery preceded their gigantic stolen inheritance (huge yields of several continuous centuries of ancestral theft).

Those who know the truth obey the least.

"Those who know the least obey the best." George Farquhar (1677-1707).

Facts are sacred and cannot be overstated.

OYINBO OLE/ODE: The land on which his pure white father and mother were born yields only FOOD, he is a mere poly-educated former debt-collector Solicitor in Norfolk/Norwich (Coastal Dole/the Departure Lounge of Life), an ignorant lowlife 5th Rate Partner, unlike Putin's Russia, there are no oil wells or gas fields in Freemasons' Kempston and where his pure white mother and father were born, he is rich, and he dishonestly implied that he did not know that the pure white ancestors of his pure white mother and father were industrial-scale Professional THIEVES – **Exodus 20:15, Habakkuk**, extremely nasty and merciless RACIST KILLERS – **Exodus 20:13**, and owners of stolen children of defenceless poor people, including the AFRICAN ancestors of the Quasi-Mulatto (impure White/impure Black, < 43% Nigerian) grandniece and grandnephew of Mr Andrew Mountbatten Windsor.

Karen Kwamboka: OYINBO OLE/ODE: They hate us, and they know that we know. The only BLACK hereditary RACIST pure white bastards (predominantly but not exclusively pure white) truly love is our own MONEY; absolutely everything else is deceit - **Exodus 20:15, Habakkuk.**

Yinka Bamgbelu: Tasmania University and Oxbridge-educated very, rich man's son (Mark 10:25), Sir Charles Phillip Haddon-Cave (1925–1999), and an innately white supremacist grandson of Francis Haddon-Cave, born in Hobart in early 20th-century Australian settlement; a properly schooled impostor and an expert of deception (perception is grander than reality), and a closeted white supremacist descendant of DRUG LORDS (opium merchants of the Qing Dynasty), let me tell you, **i**n 1833, very greedy RACIST pure white bastards shared a very small fraction of yields of millions of stolen and destroyed lives of the children of poor people, including the AFRICAN ancestors of impure White/impure Black, 43% Nigerian Mulatto Duchess of Sussex. Their pure white ancestors loved millions of stolen African children, Maafa (1445-1888).

Karen Kwamboka: Tasmania University and Oxbridge-educated very, rich man's son (**Mark 10:25**), Sir Charles Phillip Haddon-Cave (1925–1999), and an innately white supremacist grandson of Francis Haddon-Cave, born in Hobart in early 20th-century Australian settlement; a properly schooled impostor and an expert of deception (perception is grander than reality), and a closeted white supremacist descendant of DRUG LORDS (opium merchants of the Qing Dynasty), let me tell you, in 1884, greedy RACIST pure white European Christian Bastards, including your own pure white ancestors, partitioned AFRICA and looted her. OYINBO OLE/ODE – **EXODUS 20:15, HABAKKUK.**

"The colonialists care nothing for Africa for her own sake. They are attracted by African riches, and their actions are guided by the desire to preserve their interests in Africa against the wishes of the African people. For the colonialists all means are good if they help them to possess these riches" Patrice Lumumba (1925-1961): Assassinated, fed European Christians made bullets spat out by European made guns.

Yinka Bamgbelu: "The white man was created a devil, to bring chaos upon, the earth." Malcolm X (1925-1965).

If you did not know that truth, it is proof that you couldn't see the innately evil RACIST bastard as he truly is. Innately evil RACIST BASTARDS should stay here; it is safer than NIGERIA – **Exodus 21:23-27.**

Dr Mungo Park (1771-1806) had Birmingham made guns, but the illegal alien was killed with sticks and stones.

"Stoning certainly teaches people a lesson." Ayatollah Khalkhali (1926-2011).

Karen Kwamboka: Our brainless opportunist RACIST pure white bastard was granted the platform to display hereditary prejudice. The hereditary RACIST pure white bastard treated the JUDICIARY as if it were his pure white father's private enterprise.

BEDFORD, ENGLAND: Pure White Senior District Judge Paul Robert Ayers, our Senior Vice President of the Association of Her Majesty's District Judges, what do you have that is the yield of transparent virtue? You do not have anything. Your Country is SHIT, and you are worse than SHIT. You are worthy only because you are pure white, and you are relative rich only because the pure white ancestors of your pure white mother and father were THIEVES – **Exodus 20:15, Habakkuk.**

Yinka Bamgbelu: "Negro is a stage in the slow evolution from monkeys to man." Dr Frantz Fanon (1925-1961).

"We are no longer your monkeys." Patrice Lumumba (1925-1961).

Karen Kwamboka: Our own MONEY. Our own NIGERIAN CHILDREN with huge oil wells and gas fields near their huts eat only 1.5/day in our own NIGERIA, a very bellyful poly-educated pure white son of a pure white plebeian hoe. A RACIST direct descendant of pure white THIEVES and owners of stolen children of defenceless poor people was our Senior District Judge. OYINBO OLE/ODE – **EXODUS 20:15, HABAKKUK.**

Facts are sacred and cannot be overstated. 1940: Without the support of the YANKS, France surrendered within 6/52.

Yinka Bamgbelu: 2025: In terms of geographic size, Great Britain is a small fraction of UKRAINE. In the same position as UKRAINE, but without the support of the YANKS, Great Britain will surrender within 6/7.

Delusional grandeur of the stolen past – **Exodus 20:15, Habakkuk**. 5th Rate Military Power impersonates SUPERPOWERS.

Karen Kwamboka: "British Justice is racist and should not be trusted by ethnic minorities." Peter Herbert (OBE), Officer of the Most Excellent Order of our Empire of Stolen Inheritance. A Quasi-Mulatto (impure White/impure Black) expert of our Law - **Luke 11:52.**

Yinka Bamgbelu: OYINBO OLE/ODE: Judicial Apartheid is the Ne plus Ultra of RACIAL HATRED, and it desires homogeneity in the administration of their law – **Habakkuk 1:4.**

"Trump's administration packed courts with white Judges." Kamala Harris.

Only very stupid AFRICANS expect descendants of Slave-owners to voluntarily relinquish several centuries-old STOLEN advantageous positions – in exchange for NOTHING. OYINBO OLE/ODE: **EXODUS 20:15, HABAKKUK.**

Karen Kwamboka: "We shall forge a colour-blind society based on merit." President Trump. Real progress desires the promotion of colour-blind, transparent, and measurable objectivity. "The 99% of the meetings I go to, I am the only non-white person in the room. But why are we so surprised when most of the senior positions in Scotland are filled exclusively by people who are White. Take my Portfolio alone, the Lord President, White. The Lord Justice Clerk, White. Every High Court Judge, White. The Lord Advocate, White. The Solicitor General,

White. The Chief Constable, White. Every Deputy Chief Constable, White. Every Assistant Chief Constable, White. The head of the Law Society, White. The head of the faculty of advocates, White. Every Prison Governor, White. Not just Justice, the Chief Medical Officer, White. The Chief Nursing Officer, White. The Chief Veterinary Officer, White. The Chief Social Work Adviser, White. Almost every trade union in this country is headed by people who are White. In the Scottish Government, every director general is White, and every chair of every public body is White." A former Scottish First Minister.

Yinka Bamgbelu: Tasmania University and Oxbridge-educated very, rich man's son (**Mark 10:25**), Sir Charles Phillip Haddon-Cave (1925–1999), and an innately white supremacist grandson of Francis Haddon-Cave, born in Hobart in early 20th-century Australian settlement; a properly schooled impostor and an expert of deception (perception is grander than reality), and a closeted white supremacist descendant of DRUG LORDS (opium merchants of the Qing Dynasty, let me tell you, if brainless and baseless SELF-AWARDED SUPERIORITY is the birth right of your descendants, and if as pure white RACIST BASTARDS (Colourism) - (predominantly but not exclusively pure white) vulgarly brag, they are SUPERIORLY Created by Almighty God, why do hereditary pure white bastards (predominantly but not exclusively pure white) need RACIST CRIMINALITY to defeat self-educated NIGERIANS – in open debates?

Tasmania University and Oxbridge-educated very, rich man's son (Mark 10:25), Sir Charles Phillip Haddon-Cave (1925–1999), and an innately white supremacist grandson of Francis Haddon-Cave, born in Hobart in early 20th-century Australian settlement; a properly schooled impostor and an expert of deception (perception is grander than reality), and a closeted white supremacist descendant of DRUG LORDS (opium merchants of the Qing Dynasty: Negroes, if you have cogent and irrefutable evidence that pure white British Soldier, Stephanie Twidale (TD) unrelentingly lied under oath and on record - **Habakkuk 1:4**, why didn't you seek legal redress? You did not because you did not have cogent and irrefutable evidence to support your allegation of RACIST CRIME.

Yinka Bamgbelu: BRAINLESS NONSENSE! Tasmania University and Oxbridge-educated very, rich man's son (**Mark 10:25**), Sir Charles Phillip Haddon-Cave (1925–1999), and an innately white supremacist grandson of Francis Haddon-Cave, born in Hobart in early 20th-century Australian settlement; a properly schooled impostor and an expert of deception (perception is grander than reality), and a closeted white supremacist descendant of DRUG

LORDS (opium merchants of the Qing Dynasty), let me tell you, you were a DISHONEST indiscreetly hereditary white supremacist bastard, as you implied that you did not know that reporting demons to demons (**Matthew 12:27**) - is a baren exercise, an exercise in futility, and motivated by uncontrollable INNATE RACIAL HATRED, you dishonestly implied that you did not know that the actions evil RACIST pure white bastards (predominantly but not exclusively pure white) are bound to take to conceal Merciless RACIST EVIL, are likely to be worse than their original sin, and in pursuant of SELF-PRESERVATION, self-educated Nigerians, victims of Merciless Racist Evil, accept frying pan instead of fire: The best of the Merciless Racist Evil.

Karen Kwamboka: OYINBO OLE/ODE: When one is BLACK, one is dirty, physically, morally, and spiritually. Colourism, the refuge of the intellectually ungifted pure white bastards (predominantly but not exclusively pure white). Indiscreet RACIAL HATRED is the cure for dirty black coats that the wearers neither made nor chose.

Yinka Bamgbelu: RUSSIA hates Britain more than Ukraine. If Russia believes that Britain has directly and/or indirectly caused the death of tens of thousands of her citizens, the probability that RUSSIA will retaliate is 100%. We are at war.

Karen Kwamboka: Peter Herbert (OBE), impure White/impure Black (a Quasi-Mulatto), our Officer of the Most Excellent Order of our Empire of Stolen Inheritance – **Exodus 20:15, Habakkuk,** and an expert of our law, **Luke 11:52**, explicitly warned Africans that the administration of English Law is untrustworthy, and reasonably implied that Africans who join the British Armed Forces, propagate RACIAL HATRED.

Yinka Bamgbelu: Our own MONEY. Our own Nigerian Babies with gigantic oil wells and gas fields near their huts eat only 1.5/day in our Nigeria, a very bellyful verifiably functional semi-illiterate pure white bastard, a mere poly-educated former debt-collector Solicitor in Norwich (lowlife 5th Rate Partner) whose pure white mother and father have never seen CRUDE OIL, and whose pure white ancestors including John Bunyan (1628-1688) and John Foster (1759-1832) were fed like battery hens with huge yields of millions of stolen children of defenceless poor people, including the Quasi-Mulatto, impure White/impure Black, <43% Nigerian, grandchildren of HRH King Charles, was our Senior District Judge in BEDFORD, Great Britain. Which part of our own shit hole Africa is great?

“How Europe underdeveloped Africa.” Dr Walter Rodney (1942-1980).

Karen Kwamboka: Superiority is their brainless and baseless birth right. They must win, but they are BRAINLESS, so they steal power and use it to gain what their brains cannot.

BEDFORD, ENGLAND: Pure White Senior District Judge Paul Robert Ayers, Pure White Sue Gregory (OBE), our own Officer of the Most Excellent Order of our own Empire of Stolen Inheritance – **Habakkuk 2:6-9, Exodus 20:15**, and Pure White Freemason, Brother Richard William Hill lied fabricated reports and/or unrelentingly lied under oath, including approved Judgements, and/or unrelentingly lied on record – **Habakkuk 1:4**. Had they been BLACK, the indiscreetly crooked RACIST pure white bastards would have been in trouble.

“Michael Jackson would have been found guilty if he’d been Black.” Jo Brand

OYINBO OLE/ODE/BARAWO: Dark Black and ‘UGLY’, Quasi-Mulatto (impure Black) Constance Briscoe was JAILED for a lesser offence.

Yinka Bamgbelu: OYINBO OLE/ODE: Hereditary RACIST pure white bastards fear the untamed minds of self-educated NIGERIANS than Putin’s poisons. The centuries-old unspoken myth that Christ-granted talents are related to the universally acknowledged irrefutably SUPERIOR SKIN COLOUR that very fortunate wearers neither made nor chose, and the principal beneficiaries of STOLEN ADVANTAGES brainlessly and baselessly associated with colourism – are scared because their centuries-old myth is unravelling.

Karen Kwamboka: Hereditary white supremacist pure white bastards (predominantly but not exclusively pure white) want all NIGERIANS to be Born-Again Christians, who have been systematically brainwashed to believe that MASONS are the New Truly Good God - **Mark 10:18**, and who pay Antichrist Freemasons Quasi-Protection Money (Tithe) through Churches of Christ.

CHAPTER SIXTEEN

Yinka Bamgbelu: Ignorant descendants of THIEVES and owners of stolen children of defenceless poor people. They love fighting, and Africans are their preferred opponents.

Their ancestors were the World Champions at using GUNS to mercilessly slaughter unarmed AFRICANS.

Looters and Racist Murderers:

Imagbon, 1892. Benin, 1897.

If hereditary RACIST pure white bastards (predominantly but not exclusively pure white) are truly brave, as they vulgarly brag, they must DIRECTLY use guns to evict Putin from Mariupol, he stole it with guns – **Exodus 20:15.**

Karen Kwamboka: Their Country is SHIT, and they are worse than SHIT. Their SHIT Country where a poly-educated functional semi-illiterate pure white son of plebeian nobodies was a Senior District Judge.

BEDFORD, ENGLAND: Pure White Senior District Judge Paul Robert Ayers, it is not the TRUTH that daily dialogues with pure white IMBECILES (predominantly but not exclusively pure white) is a proper job that is worthwhile and manly.

"They may not have been well written from a grammatical point of view but I am confident I had not forgotten any of facts." Pure White Welshman, Geraint Evans, England's Class Senior Postgraduate Tutor, Oxford. OYINBO ODE.

Yinka Bamgbelu: One of the gains of several continuous centuries of stealing and SLAVERY is that a pure white Welsh IMBECILE was a Senior Postgraduate Tutor, Oxford. No brain. Poor natural resources. Several centuries of STEALING and SLAVERY preceded their huge stolen inheritance (gigantic yields of several continuous centuries of ancestral theft – **Habakkuk 2:6-9, Exodus 20:15)**. Facts are sacred and cannot be overstated.

Karen Kwamboka: Psalm 39:5, Psalm 144:4: They are innately extremely wicked bastards, and had they been immortal, it would have been sound logic to destroy them, including KAMIKAZE, but they are not, and will face the sword of TRUTH, not Jonathan Aitken's, but the Divine Sword of Transparent Truth – **John 5:22.**

Yinka Bamgbelu: They hate us, and they know that we know; He hates them more, so He blessed them with the universally acknowledged irrefutably SUPERIOR SKIN COLOUR and cursed them with dark black brains.

Karen Kwamboka: Those who nearly passed or just passed the A/LEVEL could become Judges and Police Officers - in their indiscreet RACIST HELL HOLE, one of the dullest adult populations in the industrialised world (OECD). There is no law in their country; their law is what vulgarly charitable, Antichrist, and hereditary white Supremacist Freemasons want. Then, all Judges were pure white, and most of them were thicker than a gross of planks – **Habakkuk 1:4.**

Yinka Bamgbelu: OYINBO OLE/ODE: Our pure white IMBECILE Freemason Senior District Judge of our Empire of Stolen Inheritance – **Exodus 20:15, Habakkuk**. A little piglet, a 5th Rate Military Power Impersonates a SUPERPOWER. Delusional Grandeur of the Stolen Past. No brain. Poor natural resources. Several centuries of STEALING and SLAVERY preceded their huge STOLEN INHERITANCE (gigantic yields of several continuous centuries of ancestral theft – **Habakkuk, Exodus 20:15**).

Karen Kwamboka: “The blame is his who chooses. God is blameless.” Plato

BEDFORD, ENGLAND: Pure White Senior District Judge Paul Robert Ayers, our own Senior Vice President of the Association of Her Majesty’s District Judges, let me tell you, the mind that I did not choose is FINER than your indiscreetly crooked, vindictive, potently weaponised, unashamedly mediocre, and institutionally RACIST waste of money fish and chips Justice System, and I do not believe in any part of your SHIT, as no part of your SHIT is good, not even one – **Psalm 53**, and I have the POWER to use cogent facts and irrefutable evidence to irreparably destroy you and every part of SHIT – **Habakkuk 1:4.**

Yinka Bamgbelu: Hereditary RACIST pure white bastards (predominantly but not exclusively pure white) are WORSE BULLIES, so they do not deserve anyone’s sympathy when they are bullied by their own kindred, President Trump, a genetic Briton

They dress up interracial intellectual envy and call it colour-blind impartial administration of the law.

Karen Kwamboka: Three, only three, but three too many, opportunist RACIST pure white bastards, were granted the platform to display hereditary RACIST pure white bastards were granted the platform to display hereditary prejudice. They hate us, and we know. If as hereditary RACIST pure white bastards (predominantly but not exclusively pure white) vulgarly brag, they are Superior Creations of Almighty God, why do they need RACIST CRIMINALITY to defeat mere NIGERIANS, from shit hole Africa?

Yinka Bamgbelu: BEDFORD, ENGLAND: Pure White Senior District Judge Paul Robert Ayers, it is absolutely impossible for you and your pure white type to COMPETE on a colour-blind level intellectual playing field without resorting to RACIST CRIMINALITY. You are INFERIOR. Sincere immodesty is sincerer than insincere modesty.

Karen Kwamboka: Unlike PUTIN'S SIBERIA, there are no gas fields in bland, colourless, and almost lifeless Freemasons' Kempston and where the pure white father and mother of Pure White Senior Bedford's District Judge Paul Robert Ayers, were born. Our own MONEY. Our own NIGERIA, Shell's docile cash cow since 1956 (OLOIBIRI). GDC was established in 1956. Our own NIGERIAN BABIES with gigantic oil wells and gas fields near their huts eat only 1.5/day in our own NIGERIA, a very bellyful functional semi-illiterate pure white bastard, whose pure white mother and father have never seen CRUDE OIL was our Senior District Judge in Bedford. Then, insatiably greedy RACIST pure white bastards, and very aggressive PROFESSIONAL THIEVES, carried and sold millions of stolen children of defenceless poor AFRICANS, now THIEVES steal our own natural resources from our own AFRICA. Slavery preceded Colonisation. Neo-Colonialism is the New SLAVERY. Facts are sacred and cannot be overstated.

"Moderation is a virtue only among those who are thought to have found alternatives." Dr Henry Kissinger (1923-2023).

"The white man is the devil." Elijah Mohammad (1897-1975).

Substitution is fraudulent emancipation.

Yinka Bamgbelu: OYINBO OLE/ODE/BEDFORD, ENGLAND: Pure White Freemason, Brother Richard William Hill, England Class Senior NHS Postgraduate Tutor, Bedfordshire fabricated reports and unrelentingly lied under oath - **Habakkuk 1:4.** Pure White Senior District Judge Paul Robert Ayers, our own Senior Vice President of the Association of Her Majesty's District Judges, unrelentingly lied under oath and on record – **Habakkuk 1:4,** Pure White Sue Gregory, our own Officer of the Most Excellent Order of the Most Excellent Order of our Empire of Stolen Inheritance – **Exodus 20:15, Habakkuk 2:6-9.**

Karen Kwamboka: When the adversary is the JUDGE, a very hardened HEREDITARY RACIST pure white bastard who wore the MASK of a colour-blind impartial Judge as a cloak of DECEIT. He should stay here; it is safer. Evil Crooked Judges do not live long in NIGERIA

"We shall deal with the racist bastards when we get out of prison." Comrade Robert Mugabe (1924-2019).

Yinka Bamgbelu: They are a GANG of Pure White RACIST CRIMINALS

"Their Justice System is a properly organised RACIST CRIME SYNDICATE that impersonates colour-blind impartial administration of the law." Peter Herbert (OBE) paraphrased.

Karen Kwamboka: The pattern of merciless RACIST EVIL is the same everywhere in their Godforsaken RACIST HELL HOLE – **Habakkuk 1:4.**

BEDFORD, ENGLAND: GDC, Pure White Freemason, Brother Richard William Hill fabricated reports and unrelentingly lied under oath and on record – **Habakkuk 1:4**. They were all PURE WHITE. Their overwhelming leverage is the certainty that all JUDGES will be pure white, and the hope of opportunist RACIST pure white bastard (disproportionately but not exclusively pure white) is that they would be hereditary RACIST pure white bastards too**.** Ignorant straight-faced Racist descendants of ultra-righteous pure white THIEVES – **Exodus 20:15, Habakkuk 2:6-9.**

Yinka Bamgbelu: Genetic THIEVES: If there are cogent and irrefutable evidence that the pure white ancestors of one's pure white mother and father were THIEVES and owners of stolen lives, it would be very naïve not to expect STEALING guarded by incompetent mendacity to be part of one's genetic inheritances: Persecutory Negrophobia guarded by Negrophobic Perjury.

Karen Kwamboka: A Crooked Racist Soldier, albeit England's Class.

OXFORD, ENGLAND: Pure White British Soldier, Stephanie Twidale (TD) unrelentingly lied under oath and on record – **Habakkuk 1:4**. Dark Black, 'Ugly', and impure Black Quasi-Mulatto, Constance Briscoe was JAILED for a lesser offence. Apartheid by stealth. Facts are sacred and cannot be overstated.

Yinka Bamgbelu: Cowardice Ne Plus Ultra: A very hardened opportunist RACIST pure white bastard wore the mask of a colour-blind impartial Judge. He should fu*king stay here; it is safer than NIGERIA

BEDFORD, ENGLAND: Pure White Senior District Judge Paul Robert Ayers unrelentingly lied under oath (approved Judgement) and on record – **Habakkuk 1:4.**

Wales, GDP, <£85 billion, a mere Quasi-Province of London, GDP Greater London, >£500 billion: GDC/NHS: Pure White Welshman, Geraint Evans, England's Class Senior Postgraduate Tutor, Oxford, unrelentingly lied under implied oath and on record - **Habakkuk 1:4.** Impure Black, Quasi-Mulatto, Constance Briscoe was JAILED for a lesser offence. Apartheid by stealth. Facts are sacred and cannot be overstated.

https://www.youtube.com/watch?v=BlpH4hG7m1A&feature=youtu.be

"They may not have been well written from a grammatical point of view, but I am confident I had not forgotten any of the facts." Dr Geraint Evans, Postgraduate Tutor, Oxford

https://youtu.be/rayVcfyu9Tw

Karen Kwamboka: OYINBO OLE/ODE: BEDFORD, ENGLAND: District Judge, it is not the TRUTH that daily dialogues with pure white IMBECILES (predominantly but not exclusively pure white) is a proper job that is worthwhile and manly.

Their hairs stand on end when they are challenged by self-educated NIGERIANS; we and our type are the ones hereditary RACIST pure white bastards (predominantly but not exclusively pure white) would beat up without the support of the YANKS.

Yinka Bamgbelu: Psalm 118:22, Luke 20:17: Their people are everywhere and they control almost everything in their Godforsaken Racist Hell Hole, including RACIAL HATRED and FRAUD – **Habakkuk 1:4**. Integrity, friendship, respect, and charity: All for one, and one for all (Mediocre Mafia)..

Karen Kwamboka: A FAKE SUPERPOWER: DELUSIONAL GRADEUR OF THE STOLEN PAST – HABAKKUK 2:6-9, EXODUS 20:15. IGNORANT DESCENDANTS OF THIEVES AND OWNERS OF STOLEN LIVES. TRUMP'S POODLES. FLAT TRACK BULLIES.

"England will fight to the last American." An American saying

"Could you take on the Russians by yourselves." President Trump

Yinka Bamgbelu: If hereditary RACIST pure white bastards are as brave as they vulgarly brag, they MUST directly use overwhelming extreme violence to evict PUTIN from Crimea, he used extreme overwhelming violence to convert Bakhmut and Avdiivka from bricks to rubble and stole them – **Exodus 20:15.**

Hereditary RACIST pure white bastards (predominantly but exclusively pure white) want all NIGERIANS to be scatter-head and gullible Born-Again Christians who pay Antichrist Freemasons Protection Money (TITHE)inside Churches of Christ. If you did not know that MASONS. Then, all Judges were pure white Freemasons, and most of them were thicker than a gross of planks.

Karen Kwamboka: OYINBO OLE/ODE. They hate us, and they know that we know. King's School and Oxbridge-educated Lord Justice Charles Anthony Haddon-Cave, KC, a RACIST first son of a very, very, very, very, very, very, RICH Tasmanian Colonialist Economic Cannibal (**Mark 10:25**), Tasmania University and Oxbridge-educated very, very, very, rich man's son (**Mark 10:25**), Sir Charles Phillip Haddon-Cave (1925–1999), and a grandson of Francis Haddon-Cave, born in Hobart in early 20th-century Australian settlement; an impostor and an expert of deception (perception is grander than reality), and a closeted white supremacist descendant of DRUG LORDS (opium merchants of the Qing Dynasty), and a homie of Eton and Oxbridge-educated very, very, very, rich men's son, Archbishop Justin Welby (**Mark 10:25**),It is absolutely impossible to use cogent facts and irrefutable evidence to disprove the TRUTH, which is that your own pure white kindred, Sue Gregory, OBE, Officer of the Most Excellent Order of our Empire of Stolen Inheritance, and Freemason, Brother Richard William Hill are very hardened Racist Crooks. Let me tell you, yours is a degraded, indiscreetly crooked, unashamedly mediocre, and institutionally RACIST culture that impersonates high civilisation. Based on cogent, irrefutable, and available evidence, they are a properly organised gang of RACIST CRIMINALS, and they know that we know – **Habakkuk 1:4.**

"Pardon him Theodotus: He is a barbarian and thinks that the culture of his tribe and Island are laws of nature." George Bernard Shaw (1856-1950).

Yinka Bamgbelu. They are THIEVES, and their ancestors were insatiably greedy ARMED PROFESSIONAL THIEVES – **Exodus 20:15, Habakkuk**; Russian Stolen Money should be used to equitably, fairly, and justly repay several continuous centuries of ancestral theft (REPARATION), including the money that evil, greedy, crooked, and RACIST pure white bastards shared in 1833

Based on several decades of very proximate observations and direct experiences, there is no LAW **(Habakkuk 1:4)** in their Godforsaken Racist Hell Hole; what vulgarly charitable, hereditary white supremacist, and Antichrist FREEMASONS (Mediocre Mafia) want is their law, and absolutely everything else is deceit.

OYINBO OLE/ODE: AN IGNORANT HEREDITARY RACIST DESCENDANT OF ULTRA-RIGHTEOUS PURE WHITE THIEVES AND OWNERS OF STOLEN CHILDREN OF DEFENCELESS POOR PEOPLE (AFRICANS) – **EXODUS 20:15, HABAKKUK**.

OYINBO OLE/ODE: "How Europe underdeveloped Africa." Dr Walter Rodney (1942-1980).

Karen Kwamboka: BEDFORD, ENGLAND: GDC, Freemason, Brother Richard William Hill, Senior NHS Postgraduate Tutor, albeit Bedfordshire Class, fabricated reports and unrelentingly lied under oath and on record - **Habakkuk 1:4**. Had he been BLACK or had the Judges been Black, he would have been deterred. The pure white ancestors of his pure white father and mother were incompetent RACIST LIARS too, they were THIEVES and owners of stolen children of defenceless poor people, including the AFRICAN ancestors of impure White/impure Black, QUASI-MULATTO (<43% Nigerian) grandniece and grandnephew of Mr Andrew Mountbatten Windsor.

IGNORANT DESCENDANTS OF THIEVES – **EXODUS 20:15, HABAKKUK**: "Those who have robbed have also lied." Dr Samuel Johnson (1709-1784).

Yinka Bamgbelu: If as they vulgarly brag, it is the TRUTH that they are superiorly created by Almighty God, why do hereditary RACIST pure white bastards (predominantly but not exclusively pure white) need BLATANT RACIST CRIMINALITY to defeat our own people, self-educated NIGERIANS – on a colour-blind level intellectual playing field?

Karen Kwamboka: For their indiscreetly crooked, VINDICTIVE, unashamedly mediocre, potently weaponised, and institutionally RACIST Fish and Chips Justice System to work as designed, they must have SUPREME KNOWLEDGE, but they don't, so they destroy all self-educated NIGERIANS who know that they are brainless hereditary RACIST pure white bastards (predominantly but not exclusively pure white): New Herod, **Matthew 2:16.**

Yinka Bamgbelu: Their indiscreetly corrupt fish and chips Justice System that is overseen by the FREEMASONS for the benefit of pure white IMBECILES (predominantly but not exclusively pure white). They don't want their own mentally gentler white children (OECD) and the pure white imbeciles they shepherd (predominantly but not exclusively pure white), including Tommy Robinson and his pure white troops, to know the TRUTH, which is that apart from our INFERIOR SKIN COLOUR, which we neither made nor chose, and our more INFERIOR accent when speaking an alien language, we are also properly created by Almighty God, and to conceal this TRUTH and to save face, hereditary RACIST pure white bastards (predominantly but not exclusively pure white), brainlessly and baselessly SELF-WARD SUPERIOR KNOWLEDGE, and opportunist RACIST evil pure white bastards (predominantly but not exclusively pure white) steal yields of our own people's Christ-granted talents (self-educated Nigerians), and their unplayable overwhelming leverage is the certainty that all JUDGES will be pure white, and their hope is that they would be hereditary RACIST pure white bastards too. No brain. Poor natural resources. Several centuries of stealing and slavery preceded their huge stolen inheritance (gigantic yields of several continuous centuries of ancestral theft – **Exodus 20:15, Habakkuk**).

Karen Kwamboka: Ignorant hereditary RACIST pure white bastards (predominantly but not exclusively pure white) lied to their own mentally gentler white children (OECD) and the pure white imbeciles they shepherd (predominantly but not exclusively pure white) that they are ULTRA-RIGHTEOUS GENIUSES, very highly civilised, and super-enlightened – who do everything LEGALLY: Rules-based procedures, precedent, and statute, including RACIAL HATRED and FRAUD – **Habakkuk 1:4.**

Yinka Bamgbelu: Based on cogent, irrefutable, and available evidence, their own indiscreetly crooked, VINDICTIVE, potently weaponised, unashamedly mediocre, and institutionally RACIST Fish and Chips Justice System is FU*KED, irreparably FU*KED, as it has foreseeably succumbed to INCEST, weakening of their common genetic pool, and associated physical and mental wonkiness, and hereditary white supremacist Freemason Judges, and others, who make loads of MONEY from unashamed mediocrity and confusion PROP SHIT UP – **Habakkuk.**

Karen Kwamboka: CONFLICT OF INTEREST: "A government that robs Peter to pay Paul can always depend on the support of Paul." George Bernard Shaw (1856-1950).

Their Country is SHIT, and they are worse than SHIT, and they know. Culturally degraded poor white bastards, little piglets deceive the undiscerning that they are culturally advanced and ultra-righteous.

Yinka Bamgbelu: We need only food, shelter and Freedom of Expression, and we shall use cogent facts and irrefutable evidence to irreparably destroy RACIST Pure White Bastards.

Opportunist RACIST pure white bastards (predominantly but not exclusively pure white) have absolute POWER over our lives and all those things inferior to life, including our livelihood and material possessions, but hereditary RACIST pure white bastards do not have any power of our minds while we breathe God's free air. They have the power to directly destroy the body, and indirectly destroy the mind that it housed, but evil RACIST pure white bastards (predominantly but not exclusively pure white) do not have the power to directly destroy the mind and spare the body where it dwells.

Karen Kwamboka: "The white man is the devil." Elijah Mohammed (1897-1975).

If you did not know that TRUTH, it is the proof that you are a gullible FOOL who could not see the innately evil RACIST bastards as they truly are.

Yinka Bamgbelu: It is absolutely impossible for King's School and Oxbridge-educated very rich man's son (**Mark 10:25**), a inheritor of Stolen Elitism, Unearned Privileges, and Undeserved Patronage, Pure White Lord Justice Charles Anthony Haddon-Cave, KC, a RACIST first son of a Tasmanian Colonialist Economic Cannibal, to disprove the TRUTH, which is that his fellow Senior Judge, albeit England's Class, Pure White Senior Bedford's District Judge Paul Robert Ayers, is a HARDENED RACIST pure white criminal who unrelentingly lied under oath (approved Judgement) and on record – **Habakkuk 1:4**. Facts are sacred. They are SHIT, and they cretins who sat before them are worse than SHIT; all descendants of THIEVES or direct or indirect beneficiaries of gigantic yields of several continuous centuries of ORGANISED STEALING – **Exodus 20:15, Habakkuk 2:6-9.**

Karen Kwamboka: Hereditary RACIST pure white bastards (predominantly but not exclusively pure white) are more familiar with BLACKS of Afro-Caribbean extraction such as David Lammy and Diane Abbott, direct descendants of stolen children of defenceless poor people, who were unnaturally selected, genetically reversed, paired up and deliberately bred for hard labour – by very highly civilised, super-enlightened, and ultra-righteous European Christians – on Stolen Lands of Aborigines (Native Americans Etcetera).

Yinka Bamgbelu: They are not the only creation of Almighty God, and they are not immortal. Did Constance Briscoe lie to liars? **Psalm 116:11**: "Lies are told all the time." Sir Robert Michael Havers (1923-1992), QC. Constance Briscoe was JAILED for a lesser offence: One rule for pure WHITES, and another rule for all others: JUDICIAL APARTHEID BY STEALTH. Had she been pure white, English, male, Oxbridge-educated, and Freemason, she might have 'WALKED': Integrity, friendship, respect, and charity: All for one, and one for all (Mediocre Mafia).

"British Prime Minister attacks racial bias in Universities and the Justice System. 'David Cameron has persuaded a leading labour MP to 'defect' by launching a government investigation into why black people make up such a high proportion of the prison population. Mr Cameron said Mr Lammy would examine why blacks and ethnic minorities make up nearly a quarter of Crown Court defendants – compared to 14 percent of the population. He added: 'If you are black, you are more likely to be in a prison cell than studying in a university. And if you are black, it seems you're more likely to be sentenced to custody for a crime than if you are white. 'We should investigate why this is and how we can end this possible discrimination. That's why I have asked David Lammy to lead a review. Mr Lammy, who is a qualified barrister, said: 'I am pleased to accept the Prime Minister's invitation." Mr Paul Dacre, 2016.

Karen Kwamboka: If as hereditary RACIST pure white bastards (predominantly but not exclusively pure white) immodestly imply, they are truly superiorly created by Almighty God, why do PURE WHITE RACIST CRETINS (predominantly but not exclusively pure white) need Racist Criminality, guarded by pure white closeted RACIST JUDGES, to defeat mere self-educated Nigerians, from shit hole Africa.

OXFORD, ENGLAND: Pure White Mrs Helen Falcon, MBE, our own Member of the Most Excellent Order of our own Empire of Stolen Inheritance - **Exodus 20:15, Habakkuk 2:6-9**, the typical pure white Englishwoman, the archetypal Member of GDC Committee, a ROTARIAN (vulgarly charitable, hereditary RACIST, and Antichrist Freemasonry Quasi-Religion – without Voodoo or Occultists' Rituals), and the typical Postgraduate Dean, Oxford, unrelentingly lied under oath and on record – **Habakkuk 1:4.** Constance Briscoe was JAILED for a lesser offence. Apartheid by stealth. Facts are sacred and cannot be overstated.

CHAPTER SEVENTEEN

Yinka Bamgbelu: OYINBO OLE/ODE/BARAWO: BEDFORD, ENGLAND: Pure White Senior District Judge Paul Robert Ayers, you are worthy only because you are PURE WHITE, but you are not special because you are pure white, there are pure white people in ALBANIA, GDP, <$30 billion; you are special only because England is very rich, the sixth largest economy on earth, GDP, >$4 trillion.

"Affluence is not a birth right." Lord Cameron.

Karen Kwamboka: Prior to SLAVERY, there was only subsistence feudal agriculture.

Maafa (1445-1888) rebuilt everything it succeeded and paid for everything it preceded.

"Agriculture not only gives riches to a nation, but the only one she can call her own." Dr Samuel Johnson (1709-1784).

Karen Kwamboka: They are properly schooled impostors and experts of deception, and if you did not know those TRUTHS, it is proof that you couldn't see the innately evil pure white bastards (predominantly but not exclusively pure white).

Those who know TRUTHS obey the least.

"Those who know the least obey the best." George Farquhar (1677-1707).

Yinka Bamgbelu: 'Judiciary in England and Wales 'institutionally racist', says https://www.theguardian.com › law › oct › judiciary-[i...18 Oct 2022—Exclusive: more than half of legal professionals in survey said they saw a judge acting in a racially biased way.

If all Pure White Legal Professionals in Great Britain were excluded from the Guardian Survey, 50% will become 100%.

Karen Kwamboka: Judges are human beings; some Judges are INDISCREET RACIST BASTARDS.

"Someone must be trusted, let it be the Judges." Lord Denning (1899-1999), an indiscreetly hereditary white supremacist pure white bastard, and alleged FREEMASON.

BEDFORD, ENGLAND: Pure White Hereditary Racist, unashamedly functionally semi-illiterate, poly-educated poor man's son, a downmarket former debt-collector Solicitor in bland, colourless, and almost lifeless Norfolk/Norwich, (Coastal Dole/the Departure Lounge of Life), a mere lowlife 5th Rate Partner, and the Senior Vice President of the Association of Her Majesty's District Judges, Bedford's District Judge Paul Robert Ayers, 3, St Paul's Square, MK 40 1SQ, based on cogent, irrefutable, and available evidence, your pure white ancestors were THIEVES – **Exodus 20:15,** Racist Murderers – **Exodus 20:13,** and owners of stolen children of defenceless poor people (AFRICANS) - **Habakkuk,** including the AFRICAN ancestors of the impure White/impure Black (Quasi-Mulatto, <43% Nigerian) great grandchildren of the Duke of Edinburgh of Blessed Memory, Prince Phillip (1921-2021).

"The truth allows no choice." Dr Samuel Johnson (1709-1784).

Philippians 1:21: Based on cogent, irrefutable, and available evidence, Phillip was a 33rd Degree FREEMASON (Scottish Rite).

Yinka Bamgbelu: Then, only then, all Judges were pure white FREEMASONS, and most of them were thicker than a gross of planks, and then verdicts were prior agreed inside SATANIC FREEMASONS' TEMPLES, and in open courtrooms incompetent art always incompetently imitated life – **Habakkuk 1:4.**

Karen Kwamboka: BEDFORD, ENGLAND: Pure White Hereditary Racist, unashamedly functionally semi-illiterate, poly-educated poor man's son, a downmarket former debt-collector Solicitor in bland, colourless, and almost lifeless Norfolk/Norwich, (Coastal Dole/the Departure Lounge of Life), a mere lowlife 5th Rate Partner, and the Senior Vice President of the Association of Her Majesty's District Judges, Bedford's District Judge Paul Robert Ayers, 3, St Paul's Square, MK 40 1SQ, which part of Bedford County Court, MK40 1SQ, and Bedfordshire Masonic Centre, MK42 8AH, was not STOLEN, or which part did your own pure white mother and father buy, or which part preceded SLAVERY: The grand buildings or their chattels? Ignorance is bliss. "The supreme vice is shallowness." Wilde (1854-1900). No brain. Poor natural resources. Several centuries of STEALING and SLAVERY preceded their huge stolen inheritance (gigantic yields of several centuries of ancestral theft – **Exodus 20:15, Habakkuk**). Facts are sacred and cannot be overstated.

Yinka Bamgbelu: Based on cogent, irrefutable, and available evidence, they are a properly organised gang of RACIST pure white criminals, and hereditary pure white supremacist Freemason Judges are in the loop of MERCILESS RACIST EVIL – **Habakkuk 1:4.**

Matthew 12:27: Reporting pure white RACIST Freemason Criminals to hereditary pure white supremacist Freemason Criminal Judges – is akin to reporting Devils to Demons.

"Blue-eyed demons." Elijah Mohammed (1897-1975).

BEDFORD, ENGLAND: 'Richard William Hill: A Hereditary RACIST, crooked, degraded, depraved, decayed, deluded, vindictive, and pure white little piglet criminal: Negrophobic Perjurer and Negrophobic Persecutor.' President Putin Paraphrased: GDC, Freemason, Brother Richard William Hill, England's Class Senior NHS Postgraduate Tutor, Bedfordshire fabricated reports and unrelentingly lied under oath and on record – **Habakkuk 1:4.** Constance Briscoe was JAILED for a lesser offence. Opportunist RACIST pure white bastards will investigate allegations of RACIST EVIL against their own pure white kindred, and when they find that they are based on TRUTHS, to save face, they will criminally bury RACIAL HATRED.

Karen Kwamboka: BEDFORD, ENGLAND: 'Paul Robert Ayers, Senior District Judge, albeit England's Class: An indiscreetly OPPORTUNIST RACIST, crooked, and pure white little piglet.' President Putin Paraphrased:

Hereditary Racist, indiscreetly crooked, unashamedly functionally semi-illiterate, poly-educated poor man's son, a downmarket former debt-collector Solicitor in bland, colourless, and almost lifeless Norfolk/Norwich, (Coastal Dole/the Departure Lounge of Life), a mere lowlife 5th Rate Partner, and the Senior Vice President of the Association of Her Majesty's District Judges, Bedford's District Judge Paul Robert Ayers, 3, St Paul's Square, MK 40 1SQ, the BRAIN that you inherited from your pure white father and mother is not good. Your country is shit; you are worse than shit. Everything, absolutely everything, is brainlessly and baselessly assumed in favour of the universally acknowledged irrefutably superior skin colour that the very fortunate wearer neither made nor chose. Their hairs stand on end when they are challenged by NIGERIANS; we and our type are the ones hereditary RACIST pure white bastards (predominantly but not exclusively pure white) would beat up without the support of the YANKS. If hereditary RACIST pure white bastards (predominantly but not exclusively pure white) are as BRAVE as they vulgarly brag, they must directly use GUNS to evict Putin from Crimea, he stole it with GUNS – **Exodus 20:15.** A 5th Rate Military Power impersonates a SUPERPOWER: Delusional grandeur of the stolen past – **Habakkuk.**

Yinka Bamgbelu: Our own MONEY, our own NIGERIAN CHILDREN with gigantic oil wells and gas fields near their huts eat only 1.5/day in our own NIGERIA, a very bellyful, functional semi-illiterate, and opportunist RACIST pure white bastard whose pure white father and mother have never seen CRUDE OIL was our Senior District Judge, in our very bland, colourless, and almost lifeless Market Town – near a Major Motorway (M1).

Karen Kwamboka: Accurate seers accurately foresaw that an unashamedly functional semi-illiterate, crooked, and hereditary RACIST pure white bastard will be our own Senior District Judge in our own Bedford, in our own Godforsaken RACIST HELL HOLE - Great Britain, so they embarked on armed robbery and dispossession raids in almost every square inch of the unarmed and defenceless world: Wherever hereditary RACIST pure white bastards merciless used guns to slaughter AFRICANS, they took possession, and whenever insatiably greedy RACIST pure white bastards robbed unarmed and defenceless Natives, they took possession, and EVIL RACIST pure white bastards used gigantic yields of several continuous centuries industrial -scale professional stealing - **Exodus 20:15**, to create SOCIALIST ELDORADO for scores of millions of pure white IMBECILES, and they decommissioned natural selection, and reversed progressive evolution, and made it possible for scores of millions of PURE WHITE IMBECILES (predominantly but not exclusively pure white) to retrogressively breed more scores of millions of pure white imbeciles (predominantly but not exclusively pure white).

"The white man is the devil." Elijah Mohammed (1897-1975).

Yinka Bamgbelu: "Trump's administration packed courts with white Judges." Kamala Harris

Based on cogent, irrefutable, and available evidence, homogeneity in the administration of their law is an intelligently designed impregnable secure mask of MERCILESS RACIST EVIL, a very potent weapon of war, AN UNDECLARED ASYMMETRIC RACE WAR – **Habakkuk 1:4.**

JUDICIAL DIVERSITY: ACCELERATING CHANGE. "The near absence of women and Black, Asian and minority ethnic judges in the senior judiciary, is no longer tolerable. It undermines the democratic legitimacy of our legal system; it demonstrates a denial of fair and equal opportunities to members of underrepresented groups, and the diversity deficit weakens the quality of justice." Sir Geoffrey Bindman, KC and Karon Monaghan, KC.

Karen Kwamboka: Their retrogressive civilisation that subjugates progressive colour-blind objectivity, individual development, and overall growth is evidently backwards.

Hypocritical Racist Pure White Bastards (Predominantly but not exclusively pure white): They hate us, and we know. Racist little bastard pure white piglets: "I am very fond of my pigs, but that does not stop me from eating them." Archbishop Runcie (1921-2000).

Yinka Bamgbelu: Proverbs 9:10: They begged Him for intellectual superiority, but He hates them, so He gave them superior skin colour, and blessed them with a more superior accent when speaking their own language, and in protest, they CRIMINALLY steal yields of self-educated NIGERIANS Christ-granted talents, secure in the knowledge that all Judges will be pure white and their hope is that they would be hereditary RACIST pure white bastards too – **Habakkuk 1:4.**

Karen Kwamboka: OXFORD, ENGLAND: 'Stephanie Twidale (Territorial Defence Soldier, albeit Britain's Class): 'A RACIST, crooked, and pure white little piglet.' President Putin Paraphrased. GDC, British Soldier, Stephanie Twidale (TD) unrelentingly lied under oath and on record – **Habakkuk 1:4.** The pure white ancestors of her pure white father and mother were incompetent RACIST LIARS too, they were THIEVES – **Exodus 20:15, Habakkuk,** Merciless Racist Killers – **Exodus 20:13**, and owners of stolen children of defenceless poor people, including the AFRICANS ancestors of impure White/impure Black, 43% Nigerian, Mulatto Duchess of Sussex**.** Had Stephanie Twidale (TD) been BLACK or had the Judges been BLACK, she would have been deterred: White Privilege (Apartheid by stealth). Constance Briscoe was JAILED for a lesser offence. The pure white ancestors of Stephanie Twidale's pure white father and mother were incompetent RACIST LIARS too, they were THIEVES – **Exodus 20:15**, RACIST MURDERERS – **Exodus 20:13**, and owners of stolen children of defence poor people, including the AFRICAN ancestors of the impure White/impure Black (< 43% Nigerian) niece and nephew of the PRINCE OF WALES.

Yinka Bamgbelu: Racist descendants of THIEVES – **Exodus 20:15**, extremely nasty RACIST MURDERERS – **Exodus 20:13**, and owners of stolen children of defenceless poor people (AFRICANS) – **Habakkuk**, seem to believe that the destruction of self-educated Nigerians is the cure for the degradation, decline, decay, and erasure that President Putin and President Trump lamented.

"Cultural erasure." President Trump.

A RACIST PURE WHITE BASTARD: **Matthew 7:1-6, John 8:7**: Stolen Indian Land - **Exodus 20:15**, where incestuously conceived decorticate imbecilic bastards, including children of plebeian nobodies, are armed and prepared to die, but not alone.

Karen Kwamboka: "There is no civilisation there, only complete degradation." President Putin

"We shall forge a colour-blind society based on merit." President Trump

Yinka Bamgbelu: Hereditary pure white supremacist bastards expect self-educated NIGERIANS to believe that President Trump, an unapologetic pure white supremacist bastard, is capable of progressive colour-blind and measurable objectivity. Their ancestors used guns to grab Indians' land, and stolen Africans worked stolen land.

Karen Kwamboka: When hereditary RACIST pure white bastards know what verifiably irrefutably intellectually dominant self-educated NIGERIANS (sincere immodesty is sincerer than insincere modesty), truly feel, they will BAN FREEDOM OF EXPRESSION FOR NIGERIANS, if they don't, they will be ruthlessly uncovered and irreparably destroyed. They must do their worst, and we shall do ours.

Yinka Bamgbelu: If skin colour that one neither made nor chose is universally acknowledged to be irrefutably SUPERIOR, but if one's intellect is not, and if there are cogent and irrefutable evidence that the pure what ancestors of one's pure white father and mother were THIEVES – **Exodus 20:15**, Merciless Racist Killers – Exodus 20:13, and owners of stolen children of defenceless poor people - **Habakkuk,** including the AFRICAN ANCESTORS of the Quasi-Mulatto, impure White/impure Black (<43% Nigerian) niece and nephew of Mr Andrew Mountbatten Windsor, it will be very naïve not to expect RACIAL HATRED complicated by incompetent mendacity to be part of one's genetic inheritances: Persecutory Negrophobia guarded by Negrophobic Perjury – **Habakkuk**.

Karen Kwamboka: "The blame is his who chooses. God is blameless." Plato

RACIAL HATRED COULD BE HEREDITARY.

We are all who we are, the inheritors of our inheritances, genes of our individual ancestors. It is inequitable, unjust, and unfair to punish RACIST PURE WHITE BASTARDS (predominantly but not exclusively pure white) for genetic characteristics they neither made nor chose.

Yinka Bamgbelu: "Freedom of Expression is a basic right." Lady Hale.

King's School and Oxbridge-educated Lord Justice Charles Anthony Haddon-Cave, KC, a RACIST first son of a very, very, very, very, very, very, RICH Tasmanian Colonialist Economic Cannibal (**Mark 10:25**), Tasmania and Oxbridge-educated very, very, very, rich man's son (**Mark 10:25**), Sir Charles Phillip Haddon-Cave (1925–1999), and a grandson of Francis Haddon-Cave, born in Hobart in early 20th-century Australian settlement; an impostor and an expert of deception (perception is grander than reality), and a closeted white supremacist descendant of DRUG LORDS (opium merchants of the Qing Dynasty), and a homie of Eton and Oxbridge-educated very, very, very, rich men's son, Archbishop Justin Welby (**Mark 10:25**)**:** I do not believe in any part of your INDISCREETLY RACIST CIVILISATION: 'Retrogressive degradation impersonates progressive civilisation.' President Putin paraphrased. Yours is not an apple with a few worms, yours is a ball of worms; no part of your SHIT is good, not even one - Psalm 53, and I have overwhelming power to use cogent facts and irrefutable evidence to irreparably destroy you and your SHIT Justice System – **Habakkuk 1:4.**

Karen Kwamboka: One-dimensionally educated ignorant RACIST PURE WHITE BASTARDS (predominantly but not exclusively pure white), ultra-righteous descendants of THIEVES – **Exodus 20:15**, Racist Murderers – **Exodus 20:13**, and owners of stolen children of defenceless poor people (AFRICANS) - **Habakkuk**. The entire foundations of their Museum like Satanic Temples to Baal, are BONES, the BONES of stolen BLACK AFRICAN CHILDREN, and more BONES than the millions of skulls at the doorstep of Pol Pot (1925-1998).

Yinka Bamgbelu: Exodus 21:23-27: He should stay here; it is safer than NIGERIA. A brainless opportunist RACIST pure white bastard was granted the platform to display hereditary prejudice. No brain. Poor natural resources. Several centuries of stealing and slavery preceded their huge stolen inheritance (gigantic yields of several continuous centuries of ancestral theft – **Exodus 20:15, Habakkuk).**

Karen Kwamboka: It is not the TRUTH that in civilised countries, or in countries aspiring to be civilised, or in countries pretending to be civilised, pure white people have the RIGHT to commit Racist Crimes (Negrophobic Perjury) before crooked pure white supremacist Mason Judges – **Habakkuk 1:4.**

Yinka Bamgbelu: "England would fight to the last American." An American saying

"Could you face the Russians by yourselves." President Trump.

Karen Kwamboka: Trump's Poodles: A deluded 5th Rate Military Power impersonates a SUPERPOWER. Deluded grandeur of the stolen past. Ignorant racist pure white bastards. Direct descendants of THIEVES and owners of stolen children of defenceless poor people (AFRICANS). He should stay here; it is safer than NIGERIA – **Exodus 21:23-27**. Their hairs stand on end when they are challenged by NIGERIANS, we and our type are the ones hereditary RACIST pure white bastards would beat up without the support of the YANKS.

Yinka Bamgbelu: Perception is grander than reality. If hereditary RACIST pure white bastards (predominantly but not exclusively pure white) are as brave as they vulgarly brag, they must DIRECTLY use extreme overwhelming violence to evict PUTIN from CRIMEA, he used extreme overwhelming violence to convert BAKHMUT and AVDIIVKA from bricks to rubble and stole them – **Exodus 20:15.**

Karen Kwamboka: Police Officers and Judges of the Lowest Courts, including District Judges, are not recruited from the pool of the brightest people in any society.

"Trump's administration packed courts with mediocre pure white Judges." Kamala Harris Paraphrased.

Yinka Bamgbelu: President Trump: Migration is the least of the problems on STOLEN INDIAN LAND: Maggots thrive on rotten cadavers. Your problem is absolutely irreparable. Rotten Cadavers where Maggots thrive may hear His Voice - **John 5:25**, but they will never be RESURRECTED.

Karen Kwamboka: Based on several decades of very proximate observations and direct experiences, the pure white man is grossly overrated. Perception is grander than reality.

Matthew 27:32-56: The fellow was kidnapped, lynched like Gadhafi (1942-2011), and crucified, not because He a mendacious lunatic, He was killed solely to prevent Him from speaking TRUTHS to power.

CHAPTER EIGHTEEN

Yinka Bamgbelu: Racist pure bastards love yields of several continuous centuries of enforced mass migration of millions of stolen children of defenceless poor people, at GUNPOINT, but insatiably greedy racist bastards do not want to pay equitable, fair, and just REPARATION, and they don't want mass migration. Insatiably Greedy Racist thieves eat all their own cakes, eat all ours, and they continue to have everything. They are greedier than the grave, and like death, evil RACIST pure white bastards (predominantly but not exclusively pure white) can never be satisfied – **Habakkuk 2:5.**

Karen Kwamboka: A brainless hereditary RACIST pure white bastard. Had he not been our Senior District Judge in BEDFORD, one wouldn't know him. What was in NORFOLK/NORWICH for a functional semi-illiterate, indiscreetly crooked, and opportunist RACIST Freemason Solicitors to do

Yinka Bamgbelu: An ignorant opportunist RACIST descendant of THIEVES and owners of stolen lives – **Habakkuk 2:6-9, Exodus 20:15**. A mere Polytechnic-educated (not elite and lacked rigour) pure white son of a pure white plebeian hoe sat on the BONES of stolen children of defenceless poor people, including the African ancestors of Meghan Markle, 43% Nigerian, the Duchess of Sussex, and more BONES than the millions of skulls at the doorstep of Pol Pot (1925-1998), in a Grand Museum Court that was preceded by SLAVERY, and the ignorant one-dimensionally educated bastard RACIST pure white bastard Judged SINNERS – **Matthew 7:1-6, John 8:7.**

Karen Kwamboka: They hate us, and we know. We hate them more, but they don't know. They are very, very, very, POWERFUL, and we are powerless, and we have been ROBBED to penniless since their ancestors found ours in the African bush in the 15th Century: Asymmetric Mutual Race Hate

Yinka Bamgbelu: Ina njo, ogiri ko sa

"Racism is alive and well and living in Tower Hamlets, in Westminster and, yes, sometimes in the judiciary." Judge Peter Herbert, Quasi-Mulatto (impure White/impure Black) Officer of the Most Excellent Order of our own Empire (OBE) of Stolen Inheritance - **Exodus 20:15, Habakkuk.**

OYINBO OLE/ODE: It is plainly deductible that SLAVERY rebuilt everything is succeeded and paid for everything it preceded, including the Royal College of Surgeons, 1880, the Royal Courts of Justice, 1882, the Old Bailey, 1907, the NHS, 1948, the GDC, 1956, and absolutely everything else.

"Sometimes people don't want to hear the truth because they don't want their illusions destroyed." Friedrich Nietzsche (1844-1900).

Karen Kwamboka: Our positions are absolutely hopeless because those we are supposed the report BLATANT RACIST CRIMINALITY to (Pure White Freemason Police Officers and Judges) are the Racist criminals that we have compelling evidence against, and reporting demons to demons is an

Yinka Bamgbelu: "The white man was created a devil, to bring chaos upon the earth." Malcolm X (1925-1965).

He is not only a devil, but he is also a THIEF - **Exodus 20:15**.

Apart from creating cushy salaried jobs for pure white Imbecile Freemason Solicitors and Barristers (predominantly but not exclusively pure white) who FAILED in practice (loads did), what do pure white IMBECILES (predominantly but not exclusively pure white) nee

Karen Kwamboka: Kamala Harris did not say that Trump's administration packed courts with mediocre pure white Judges.

It is not the TRUTH that daily dialogues with pure white IMBECILES (predominantly but not exclusively pure white) is a proper job that is worthwhile and mainly.

Yinka Bamgbelu: GDC: England's Class Senior NHS Nurse, Ms Rachael Bishop, unrelentingly lied under oath and on record - **Habakkuk 1:4.**

A libidinous looking (in season and in heat) indiscreetly crooked and opportunist racist typical pure white Englishwoman.

"She is a typical Englishwoman, usually violent and always dull." Wilde (1854-1900) paraphrased.

"A complaints such as Mrs Bishop's could trigger an enquiry." Pure White Stephen Henderson, LLM, BDS, England's Class Head at Scottish MDDUS.

BRAINLESS RACIST NONSENSE: THE BRAIN THAT HE INHERITED FROM HIS PURE WHITE MOTHER AND FATHER IS NOT GOOD.

"I don't want to talk grammar. I want to talk like a lady." George Bernard Shaw (1856-1950).

"He is a typical Englishman, usually violent and always dull." Wilde (1854-1900).

Opportunist RACIST pure white bastards were granted the platform to display hereditary prejudice.

Quasi-Mulatto, impure Black, a direct descendant of Cane Plantation Negroes, Dark Black and 'UGLY': Constance Briscoe was JAILED for a lesser offence: Apartheid by stealth.

Did Constance Briscoe lie to liars?

Why is it a crime, under English law, to lie to very hardened RACIST liars?

Psalm 116:11: "Lies are told all the time." Sir Robert Michael Havers (1923-1992), QC.

Based on several decades of very proximate observations and direct experiences, the quality of human beings in their Godforsaken RACIST HELL HOLE is very poor (OECD).

Facts are sacred and cannot be overstated: "The truth allows no choice." Dr Samuel Johnson (1709-1784).

Karen Kwamboka: New Herod, **Matthew 2:16:** Hereditary Racist Pure White Bastards (predominantly but not exclusively pure white) brainlessly and baselessly self-awarded intellectual ceiling, and they destroy all independent thought above their arbitrary ceiling.

Euroclear Bank, 1 Boulevard du Roi Albert II, 1210 Brussels, Belgium.

Belgium, 1884/1885, European Economic Cannibalistic Christians partitioned our own Africa and looted her.

"How Europe underdeveloped Africa." Dr Walter Rodney (1942-1980).

Yinka Bamgbelu: Equitable, fair, and just REPARATION pends, and several centuries of unpaid interest accrue – **Exodus 20:15, Habakkuk 2:6-9.** Their ancestors were THIEVES and owners of stolen lives. SLAVERY rebuilt everything it succeeded and paid for everything it preceded, including Euroclear Bank, 1 Boulevard du Roi Albert II, 1210 Brussels, Belgium.

Karen Kwamboka: Pure White European Christians, including King Leopold II (1835-1909), were industrial-scale THIEVES – **Exodus 20:15**, extremely nasty RACIST MURDERERS – **Exodus 20:13**, and owners of stolen children of defenceless poor people (AFRICANS) - **Habakkuk**. Racist bastards should use stolen Russian money to pay REPARATION.

Yinka Bamgbelu: Their pure white ancestors were THIEVES - **Exodus 20:15**, Racist Murderers – **Exodus 20:13**, insatiably greedy pure white bastards, and owners of stolen lives – **Habakkuk 2:6-9.**

"I have seen evil, and it has the face of Mark Fuhrman." Johnnie Cochran (1937-2005).

Karen Kwamboka: Sir Keir Starmer, KBE, using Nuclear Bombs to preserve the continuing propagation of PURE WHITE IMBECILES (predominantly but not exclusively pure white) is SATANIC, as it is Anti God's creations, Natural Selection and Progressive Evolution.

Yinka Bamgbelu: BEDFORD, ENGLAND: Pure White Senior District Judge Paul Robert Ayers, our own Senior Vice President of the Association of Her Majesty's District Judges, based on several decades of very proximate observations and direct experiences, the Quality of human beings in your Country is very poor (OECD). It is ABSOLUTELY IMPOSSIBLE for you and your pure white type to compete on a colour-blind level intellectual playing field without resorting to RACIST CRIMINALITY – **Habakkuk 1:4**.

Based on cogent, irrefutable, and available evidence, Pure White Senior Bedford's District Judge Paul Robert Ayers, our own Senior Vice President of the Association of Her Majesty's District Judges unrelentingly lied under oath (approved Judgement) and on record – **Habakkuk 1:4.**

Based on cogent, irrefutable, and available evidence, Pure White Sue Gregory (OBE), our own Officer of the Most Excellent Order of our own Empire of Stolen Inheritance – **Exodus 2015, Habakkuk 2:6-9**, unrelentingly lied under implied oath and on record – **Habakkuk 1:4.**

Based on cogent, irrefutable, and available evidence,

Pure White Freemason, Brother Richard William Hil, Senior NHS Postgraduate Tutor, albeit Bedfordshire's Class, fabricated reports and unrelentingly lied under oath and on record – **Habakkuk 1:4.**

Karen Kwamboka: 'UGLY', Dark Black Quasi-Mulatto (impure Black), Constance Briscoe was JAILED for a lesser offence: Apartheid by stealth.

Truths are Holy, and Holiness cannot be overstated: "Find the truth and tell it." Harold Pinter (1930-2008).

Yinka Bamgbelu: Based on cogent, irrefutable, and available evidence, PURE WHITE BELGIAN CHRISTIANS were participants in the barbarous traffic in millions of stolen children of defenceless poor people (AFRICANS), and Slavery rebuilt everything it succeeded and paid for everything it preceded.

Karen Kwamboka: Leviticus 19:33-34: The

Quality of Human Beings in their Godforsaken Racist Hell Hole is very poor (OECD). Hereditary RACIST pure white bastards (predominantly but not exclusively pure white) have INVENTED a perfectly legal method of 'KILLING' irrefutably intellectually dominant self-educated NIGERIANS, from shit hole Africa (sincere immodesty is sincerer than insincere modesty). A Nigerian, from shit hole Africa, Dr Richard Bamgboye, a General Medical Practitioner, only 56, and Indian, Dr Anand Kamath, a Dentist, only 42, were unlawfully KILLED, albeit hands-off, with the mens rea hidden in the belly of the actus reus. They hate us, and we know.

Yinka Bamgbelu: King Leopold II (1835-1909), the owner of stolen Congo, was an insatiably greedy Racist Pure White Bastard, a Crude and Cruel Negrophobic Murderer – **Exodus 20:13**, and THIEF - **Exodus 20:15**; he stole Congo, and looted her, and millions of Africans were worked to death.

Karen Kwamboka: John 8:44, John 10:10: Based on several decades of proximate observations and direct experiences, the pure white man is not your friend, and if you did not know that TRUTH, it is proof that you cannot see him as he truly is. Direct descendants of the father of lies.

Yinka Bamgbelu: BEDFORD, ENGLAND: Paul Robert Ayers, the Senior Vice President of the Association of Her Majesty's District Judges, a closeted RACIST functional semi-illiterate crooked pure white imbecile, albeit our Senior District Judge in Bedford, let me tell you, the mind that the NIGERIAN, from shit hole Africa, did not choose is FINER than your unashamedly MEDIOCRE, vindictive, potently weaponised, indiscreetly crooked, and institutionally RACIST Fish and Chips Justice System, and he does not believe in any part of SHIT, as no part of SHIT is good, not even one – **Psalm 53,** and he has the POWER to use cogent facts and irrefutable evidence to irreparably destroy you and every part of SHIT. An ignorant hereditary RACIST ultra-righteous descendant of pure white THIEVES and owners of stolen children of defenceless poor people (AFRICANS). Facts are sacred and cannot be overstated.

Karen Kwamboka: CULTURALLY DECAYED, DEPRAVED, AND ERASED HEREDITARY WHITE SUPREMACIST BASTARDS ARE CONSUMED BY INTERRACIAL INTELLECTUAL ENVY AND INNATE RACE HATE.

Sincere immodesty is sincerer than insincere modesty.

Envy is a thief.

“Envy is weak.” Yul Brynner (1920-1985).

Yinka Bamgbelu: Hereditary RACIST pure white bastards (predominantly but not exclusively pure white) have allowed unintelligent and uneducated prejudice to cloud objective reasoning and Judgement.

Karen Kwamboka: They love brainless and baseless SKIN COLOUR SUPERIORITY, but they hate Freedom of Expression because they don’t want their mentally gentler white children (OECD) and the pure white imbeciles they shepherd (predominantly but not exclusively pure white) to know the TRUTH, which is that only the universally acknowledged irrefutably superior skin colour that they neither made nor chose and Almighty God are truly good – **Mark 10:18**.

Yinka Bamgbelu: If it is the TRUTH that they are superior creations of Almighty God, why do hereditary RACIST pure white bastards (predominantly but not exclusively pure white) need RACIST CRIMINALITY to defeat our people, NIGERIANS, from shit hole Africa - in open debates?

Karen Kwamboka: Hereditary RACIST pure white bastards (predominantly but not exclusively pure white) know how to destroy NIGERIANS who disagree with them, but they do not know how to repair the crooked scatter heads of their own pure white kindred: Apartheid by stealth. Pure white skin conceals an impure dark black brain: Archie is impure, <43% Nigerian. Their spinal cord is their highest centre.

Yinka Bamgbelu: BEDFORD, ENGLAND: Paul Robert Ayers, the Senior Vice President of the Association of Her Majesty’s District Judges, a closeted RACIST functional semi-illiterate crooked pure white imbecile, albeit our Senior District Judge in Bedford, the most important part of the matter is MONEY: Your land yields only FOOD. Your ancestors were THIEVES, Racist Murderers, and owners of stolen children of poor people (AFRICANS). What else? Before Slavery, what? Unlike PUTIN’S RUSSIA, there are no oil wells or gas fields in bland, colourless, and almost lifeless Freemasons’ KEMPSTON and where your own pure white father and mother were born. Facts are sacred.

"Find the truth and tell it." Harold Pinter (1930-2008).

Karen Kwaboka: 1976-2022: Our brainless hereditary RACIST pure white bastard of our Empire of Stolen Inheritance – **Exodus 20:15, Habakkuk**; the brain that he inherited from his pure white father and mother is not good. Having FAILED in practice, loads did, the poly-educated functional semi-illiterate opportunist RACIST pure white bastard parked his liability at the public till and sold unashamed mediocrity to the undiscerning.

PERCEPTION IS GRANDER THAN REALITY.

Yinka Bamgbelu: "European Countries, nearly all, are irreparably decayed" President Trump paraphrased.

"One of the all marks of moral and intellectual decay is that OXFORD, ENGLAND: GDC, Pure White Mrs Helen Falcon (MBE), Member of the Most Excellent Order of our Empire of Stolen Inheritance - **Habakkuk, Exodus 20:15**, a ROTARIAN (vulgarly charitable Freemasonry Quasi-Religion without VOODOO or occultists' rituals) unrelentingly lied under oath and on record - **Habakkuk 1:4.** The pure white ancestors of her pure white father and mother were incompetent RACIST LIARS too, and like the direct ancestors of the former Archbishop of Canterbury, Justin Welby, a closeted white supremacist Eton and Oxbridge-educated rich men's son(**Mark 10:25**), they were THIEVES - **Exodus 20:15**, extremely nasty Racist Murderers (**Exodus 20:13**), and owners of stolen children of defenceless poor people, including the AFRICAN ancestors of the impure White (57%)/impure Black (43%) Duchess of Sussex.

Karen Kwamboka: Black woman, Constance Briscoe was JAILED for a lesser offence. Had Mrs Helen Falcon, MBE, a ROTARIAN (vulgarly charitable Masonry Quasi-Religion without VOODOO or occultists' rituals) been BLACK or had the Judges been BLACK, she would have been deterred. Facts are sacred and cannot be overstated.

Yinka Bamgbelu: Why should Black Britons join the British Army and fight RUSSIANS in pursuant of the continuing propagation of a RACIST PHILOSOPHY that treats Pure White People SUPERIORLY, and all others inferiorly – Bob Marley (1945-1981)? Had Constance Briscoe been PURE WHITE, male, English, Oxbridge-educated, and Freemason, she might have 'WALKED'.

Karen Kwaboka: If King's School and Oxbridge-educated Lord Justice Charles Anthony Haddon-Cave, KC, a RACIST first son of a very, very, very,

very, very, very, RICH Tasmanian Colonialist Economic Cannibal (**Mark 10:25**), Tasmania and Oxbridge-educated very, very, very, rich man's son (**Mark 10:25**), Sir Charles Phillip Haddon-Cave (1925–1999), and a grandson of Francis Haddon-Cave, born in Hobart in early 20th-century Australian settlement; an impostor and an expert of deception (perception is grander than reality), and a closeted white supremacist descendant of DRUG LORDS (opium merchants of the Qing Dynasty), and a homie of Eton and Oxbridge-educated very, very, very, rich men's son, Archbishop Justin Welby (**Mark 10:25**), could disprove the TRUTH which is that his own pure white kindred, OXFORD, ENGLAND: GDC, Pure White Mrs Helen Falcon (MBE), Member of the Most Excellent Order of our Empire of Stolen Inheritance **- Habakkuk, Exodus 20:15,** unrelentingly lied under oath and on record – **Habakkuk 1:4,** he will concomitantly disprove President Trump's implied belief that European Countries, nearly all, are irreparably decayed.

Yinka Bamgbelu: TRUTHS disfavour hereditary RACIST pure white bastards (predominantly but not exclusively pure white), so they steal power and use it to subjugate them.

It is absolutely impossible for Paul Robert Ayers, the Senior Vice President of the Association of Her Majesty's District Judges, a closeted RACIST functional semi-illiterate crooked pure white imbecile, albeit our Senior District Judge in Bedford, to disprove the TRUTH, which is that he, his own pure white kindred OXFORD, ENGLAND: GDC, Pure White Mrs Helen Falcon (MBE), Member of the Most Excellent Order of our Empire of Stolen Inheritance - **Habakkuk, Exodus 20:15,** and their pure white kindred – to disprove the TRUTH which is that it is absolutely impossible for they and their pure white type to compete on a colour-blind level intellectual playing field without resorting to RACIST CRIMINALITY (Persecutory Negrophobia guarded by Negrophobic Perjury) - **Habakkuk 1:4.** Sincere immodesty is sincerer than insincere modesty. Sincerity is the prime attribute of our own MESSIAH.

Karen Kwamboka: Abuse of temporary power is the fullest definition of evil.

"Those who have the power to do wrong with impunity seldom wait long for the will." Dr Samuel Johnson (1708-1784).

Yinka Bamgbelu: Hereditary RACIST pure white bastards (predominantly but not exclusively pure white) deceive their own mentally gentler white children (OECD) and the pure white IMBECILES they shepherd (predominantly but not exclusively pure white) that they are very highly civilised and super-enlightened ULTRA-RIGHTEOUS GENIUSES who do everything above board and LEGALLY: Rules-based procedures, precedent, statute etcetera, including RACIAL HATRED and FRAUD – **Habakkuk 1:4.**

Karen Kwamboka: BEDFORD, ENGLAND: Paul Robert Ayers, the Senior Vice President of the Association of Her Majesty's District Judges, a closeted RACIST functional semi-illiterate crooked pure white imbecile, albeit our Senior District Judge in Bedford, based on cogent, irrefutable, and available evidence, your pure white ancestors were THIEVES – **Habakkuk, Exodus 20:15,** extremely nasty and merciless racist murderers – **Exodus 20:13**, nastier than Yevgeny Prigozhin (1961-2023), and Hitler (1889-1945), and just by the by, several years of NAZI HOLOCAUST (1939-1945) was a mere storm in a teacup in comparison to MAAFA (1445-1888), and owners of stolen children of defenceless poor people (AFRICANS), and it is absolutely impossible for your Christ-granted talents to sustain your high standard of living. Based on cogent, irrefutable, and available evidence, sexed up legal transcripts are not uncommon in the administration of English Law. Constance Briscoe was JAILED for a lesser offence.

Yinka Bamgbelu: President Trump implied that Europeans and European Countries, nearly all, are SHIT (irreparably decayed and erased pure white rubbish (predominantly but not exclusively pure white).

BEDFORD ENGLAND: Paul Robert Ayers, the Senior Vice President of the Association of Her Majesty's District Judges, a closeted RACIST functional semi-illiterate crooked pure white imbecile, albeit our Senior District Judge in Bedford, you are worthy only because you are pure white, and you are RICH only because the pure white ancestors of your pure white mother and father were THIEVES – **Exodus 20:15, Habakkuk**. Our own MONEY, our own NIGERIA (oil/gas) is by far more relevant to the economic survival of all your mentally gentler white children than bland, colourless, and almost lifeless TOMMY ROBINSONS' LUTON. You are a leech, and the pure white ancestors of your pure white father and mother were THIEVES and owners of stolen children of defenceless poor people including the AFRICAN ancestors of the impure Black/ impure WHITE, 43% Nigerian, Duchess of Sussex. Had you been Black and 10X you would not be a Senior District Judge in Great Britain.

CHAPTER NINETEEN

Karen Kwamboka: Hereditary RACT pure white bastards (predominantly but not exclusively pure white) should FU*K OFF and stay here because it is safer than NIGERIA – **Exodus 21:23-27**. No brain. Poor natural resources. Several centuries of STEALING and SLAVERY preceded their huge STOLEN INHERITANCE (gigantic yields of several centuries of ancestral theft – **Habakkuk**).

"I was thrown under the bus." Mohammed Salah.

Trump throws decayed, depraved, and erased Europeans and Europe under the bus.

The YANKS are NATO, and absolutely everything else is an auxiliary bluff.

China/GDP, $20 trillion. US/GDP, $30 trillion. EU/GDP, $20 trillion.

1940: Without the support of the YANKS, France surrendered within 6/52.

The YANKS and the English Channel are the true territorial defenders of England, not STEPHANIE TWIDALE and her type. Based on cogent, irrefutable, and available evidence, GDC, British Soldier, Stephanie Twidale (TD) unrelentingly lied under oath and on record – **Habakkuk 1:4.** Had she been BLACK, the crooked pure white bastard opportunist British Soldier (Territorial Defence) would have been in trouble). Constance Briscoe was JAILED for a lesser offence. Facts are sacred and cannot be overstated. A corrupt Justice System that is overseen by MASONS essentially for the benefit of pure white people. Based on cogent, irrefutable, and available evidence, it is not the TRUTH that Blacks are equal to pure white people under English Law. Only STUPID Negroes expect direct descendants of PROFESSIONAL THIEVES – **Exodus 20:15**, Racist Murderers – **Exodus 20:13**, and owners of stolen children of defenceless poor people (AFRICANS), to voluntarily relinquish several centuries-old stolen advantageous positions in exchange for NOTHING.

"Michael Jackson would have been found guilty if he'd been black" Jo Brand

Yinka Bamgbelu: Hereditary RACIST pure white bastards (predominantly but not exclusively pure white) expect us to defend ourselves against pure white racist criminal bastards before pure white RACIST CRIMINAL bastard Judges – **Habakkuk 1:4,** a logical fallacy: Reductio ad absurdum.

Karen Kwamboka: If King's School and Oxbridge-educated Lord Justice Charles Anthony Haddon-Cave, KC, a RACIST first son of a very, very, very, very, very, very, RICH Tasmanian Colonialist Economic Cannibal (**Mark 10:25**), Tasmania and Oxbridge-educated very, very, very, rich man's son (**Mark 10:25**), Sir Charles Phillip Haddon-Cave (1925–1999), and a grandson of Francis Haddon-Cave, born in Hobart in early 20th-century Australian settlement; an impostor and an expert of deception (perception is grander than reality), and a closeted white supremacist descendant of DRUG LORDS (opium merchants of the Qing Dynasty), and a homie of Eton and Oxbridge-educated very, very, very, rich men's son, Archbishop Justin Welby (**Mark 10:25**, could disprove the TRUTH, which is that his own pure white kindred, GDC, Pure White Mrs Helen Falcon (MBE), Member of the Most Excellent Order of our Empire of Stolen Inheritance - **Habakkuk, Exodus 20:15,** unrelentingly lied under oath and on record - **Habakkuk 1:4,** he will concomitantly disprove the implied belief of Peter Herbert (OBE), which is that the administration of English Law is unashamedly mediocre, indiscreetly institutionally RACIST, and a crooked Negrophobic charade.

"Britain's justice system is racist and should not be trusted by ethnic minorities." Peter Herbert (OBE), our Officer of the Most Excellent Order of our own Empire of Stolen Inheritance. **Luke 11:52**: A Quasi-Mulatto (impure Black/ impure White) expert of their indiscreetly crooked, vindictive, potently weaponised, unashamedly mediocre, and institutionally RACIST Fish and Chips Justice System – **Habakkuk 1:4.** No brain. Poor natural resources. Several centuries of stealing and slavery preceded their huge stolen inheritance – **Exodus 20:15, Habakkuk.**

Yinka Bamgbelu: Certum est quia impossibile est: It is absolutely impossible for GDC, Pure White Mrs Helen Falcon (MBE), Member of the Most Excellent Order of our Empire of Stolen Inheritance - **Habakkuk, Exodus 20:15**, to be a RACIST CRIMINAL, so the NIGERIAN, from shit hole Africa, is a LUNATIC.

Karen Kwamboka: Brainless Racist Nonsense.

Yinka Bamgbelu: WE DISAGREE!

"To disagree with three-fourths of the British public on all points is one of the first requisites of sanity, one of the deepest consolations in all moments of spiritual doubt." Wilde (1854-1900), London-Irish.

Gigantic yields of millions of stolen children of defenceless poor people (AFRICANS), not feudal agriculture, lured Irish people, including George Bernard Shaw (1856-1950), to Great Britain.

Karen Kwamboka: SLAVERY immeasurably transformed the standard of living of thoroughly wretched Barbarians, Rabbit Hunters, and agricultural labourers who lived off the land, but the intellects of their direct descendants seem untouched.

Then, there was only subsistence feudal agriculture.

"Agriculture not only gives riches to a nation, but the only one she can call her own." Dr Samuel Johnson (1709-1784).

Yinka Bamgbelu: Tommy Robinson, the education that you and your own pure white kindred, including GDC, Mrs Helen Falcon (MBE), Member of the Most Excellent Order of our Empire of Stolen Inheritance - **Habakkuk, Exodus 20:15,** were exposed to within one of the dullest adult populations in the industrialised world (OECD) was MEDIOCRE SHIT, as it lacked rigour, and it showed.

Karen Kwamboka: Tommy Robinson, let me tell you, economic growth requires cheap labour (Skilled Mass Immigration), just as civilisation requires SLAVES (selective forced mass emigration).

"The fact is, that civilisation requires slaves. The Greeks were quite right there. Unless there are slaves to do the ugly, horrible, uninteresting work, culture and contemplation become almost impossible." Wilde (1854-1900).

Paul Robert Ayers, the Senior Vice President of the Association of Her Majesty's District Judges, a closeted RACIST functional semi-illiterate crooked pure white imbecile, albeit our Senior District Judge in Bedford: The only evidence of his HIGHER IQ is the huge stolen inheritance that his thoroughly wretched pure white ancestors crossed the English Channel, not that long ago, without luggage or decent shoes, to latch onto.

Yinka Bamgbelu: Sincere immodesty is sincerer than insincere modesty. Sincerity is a prime attribute of our own MESSIAH. Tommy Robinson, it is absolutely impossible for your own pure white kindred, including GDC, Pure White Mrs Helen Falcon (MBE), Member of the Most Excellent Order of our Empire of Stolen Inheritance - Habakkuk, Exodus 20:15, to COMPETE on a colour-blind intellectually level playing field without resorting to RACIST CRIMINALITY – **Habakkuk 1:4.**

Karen Kwamboka: They don't want their own mentally gentler white children (OECD) and the pure white IMBECILES (predominantly but not exclusively pure white) to know the TRUTH, which is that apart from our INFERIOR SKIN COLOUR, which we neither made nor chose, and our more INFERIOR ACCENT when speaking an alien language, we are also properly created by Almighty God, and to conceal this TRUTH and to save face, members of their brainlessly and baselessly self-awarded SUPERIOR RACE – resort to Racist Criminality, secure in the knowledge that all Judges will be PURE WHITE, and their hope is that they would be hereditary RACIST pure white bastards too – **Habakkuk 1:4.**

Yinka Bamgbelu: If Tommy Robinson could disprove the TRUTH, which is that his pure white kindred, GDC, Pure White Mrs Helen Falcon (MBE), Member of the Most Excellent Order of our Empire of Stolen Inheritance - **Habakkuk, Exodus 20:15,** unrelentingly lied under oath and on record - **Habakkuk 1:4,** he will concomitantly confirm the belief of scores of millions of Britons, which is that Antichrist Islam, Antichrist Judaism, Antichrist Freemasonry Quasi-Religion (Mediocre Mafia), and all other motley assemblies of exotic religions and faiths associated with the 15 Holy Books in the House of Commons, are not intellectually flawed SATANIC MUMBO JUMBO – **John 14:6.**

Karen Kwamboka: One of the reasons why the GDP of the USA is 8-10X bigger than that of the UK. $>3<4 trillion: $>30 trillion, is because a crooked and hereditary RACIST pure white cougar, a mere dmf, was paid the salary of the Postgraduate Dean, Oxford. The education that the mere dmf was exposed to within one of the dullest adult populations in the industrialised world lacked rigour, and it showed.

Yinka Bamgbelu: Tommy Robinson, let me tell you, your ancestors were THIEVES and owners of stolen children of defenceless poor people, including the African ancestors of the IMPURE (<43% Nigerians) niece and nephew of the Prince of Wales. You are worthy only because you are pure white, and you are rich only because the pure white ancestors of your pure white ancestors were THIEVES – **Exodus 20:15, Habakkuk.**

Karen Kwamboka: Tommy Robinson, you should go to the graveyard in your hometown, LUTON, and invoke the spirit of Robert Hibbert (1769-1849), he should confess that prior SLAVERY, there weren't very many proper houses in LUTON.

Yinka Bamgbelu: If we aren't very smart, why are we very RICH, the sixth largest economy on earth?

OYINBO OLE/ODE: Shepherds did not bring stolen AFRICAN CHILDREN back home to Great Britain, they lied to their moron sheep that they were paragons of wisdom and virtue who, like TARZAN of Africa and Mother Teresa of Calcutta, did only very good works in AFRICA.

TRUMP'S POODLES: FLAT TRACK BULLIES.

BEDFORD, ENGLAND: Paul Robert Ayers, the Senior Vice President of the Association of Her Majesty's District Judges, a closeted RACIST functional semi-illiterate crooked pure white imbecile, albeit our Senior District Judge in Bedford, your pure white ancestors were THIEVES - **Exodus 20:15.**

BEDFORD, ENGLAND: GDC, Sue Gregory (OBE), Officer of the Most Excellent Order of our Empire of Stolen Inheritance – **Exodus 20:15, Habakkuk**, unrelentingly lied under implied oath and on record – **Habakkuk 1:4.** Had she been BLACK or had the Judges been BLACK, she would have been deterred. Constance Briscoe was JAILED for a lesser offence.

Karen Kwamboka: It is not the TRUTH that former Judge, Constance Briscoe is the only incompetently dishonest BRITON.

Psalm 116:11: "Lies are told all the time." Sir Robert Michael Havers (1923-1992)

BEDFORD, ENGLAND: Paul Robert Ayers, the Senior Vice President of the Association of Her Majesty's District Judges, a closeted RACIST functional semi-illiterate crooked pure white imbecile, albeit our Senior District Judge in Bedford, , the pure white ancestors of your pure white mother and father were LIARS, thieves, and owners of stolen children of defenceless poor people (AFRICANS) – Habakkuk.

"Those who have robbed have also lied." Dr Samuel Johnson (1709-1784).

Yinka Bamgbelu: Their RACIST MUSEUMS built on foundations of BONES of millions of Stolen and Destroyed lives, more BONES than the millions of skulls at the doorstep of POL POT (1925-1998). Ignorant descendants of RIGHTEOUS THIEVES. Theirs are relics of the stolen past.

Karen Kwamboka: They looted the world and used huge yields of stealing and slavery to create a LAVISH SOCIALIST ELDORADO for millions of imbeciles, and they decommissioned colour-blind natural selection, and they reversed progressive evolution, and made it possible for millions of imbeciles to, unsustainably, breed more millions of imbeciles - **Habakkuk.**

OYINBO OLE/ODE: "How Europe underdeveloped Africa." Dr Walter Rodney (1942-1980).

Yinka Bamgbelu: HEREDITARY RACIAL HATRED GUARDED BY INCOMPETENT RACIST LIES.

Karen Kwamboka: One of the hallmarks of European moral and intellectual decay, as implied by President Trump, is that BEDFORD, ENGLAND: GDC, Freemason, Brother Richard William Hill, Senior NHS Postgraduate Tutor, Bedfordshire, albeit England's Class, fabricated reports and unrelentingly lied under oath and on record – **Habakkuk 1:4.**

Yinka Bamgbelu: Hereditary RACIST pure white bastards will investigate allegations of RACIST EVIL against their own pure white kindred, and when they find that RACIST EVILS are based on TRUTHS, they will criminally bury RACIAL HATRED, secure in the knowledge that all Judges will be PURE WHITE and their hope is that they would be hereditary RACIST pure white bastards too; they are not deterred by His Justice (**John 5:22**) because they do not believe in His exceptionalism – **John 14:6.**

Karen Kwamboka: Had former Judge Constance Briscoe been pure white, English, male, and Freemason, she might have 'WALKED'. Facts are sacred and cannot be overstated.

OYINBO OLE/ODE: Defenders of FAITHS are dissenters of THE FAITH - **John 14:6**. Integrity, friendship, respect, and charity: All for one, and one for all.

Yinka Bamgbelu: Not all Pure White Freemasons are Pure White Paedophiles like Pure White Brothers Jimmy Savile (1926-2011) and Rolf Harris (1930-2023), but all functional semi-illiterate and/or dishonest pure white Freemason Judges in Great Britain are RACISTS. Their people are everywhere, and they control almost everything in their Godforsaken RACIST HELL HOLE – **Habakkuk 1:4.**

Karen Kwamboka: Ignorant opportunist RACIST descendants of THIEVES and owners of stolen children of defenceless poor people (AFRICANS) kill foreigners, albeit hands-off, with the mens rea hidden belly of the actus reus - **Leviticus 19:33-34**. Mrs Helen Falcon's type killed the NIGERIAN, Dr Richard Bamgboye, a General Medical Practitioner, only 56, and the INDIAN, Dr Anand Kamath, a Dentist, only 42, albeit hands-off.

Yinka Bamgbelu: King's School and Oxbridge-educated Lord Justice Charles Anthony Haddon-Cave, KC, a RACIST first son of a very, very, very,

very, very, very, RICH Tasmanian Colonialist Economic Cannibal (**Mark 10:25**), Tasmania and Oxbridge-educated very, very, very, rich man's son (**Mark 10:25**), Sir Charles Phillip Haddon-Cave (1925–1999), and a grandson of Francis Haddon-Cave, born in Hobart in early 20th-century Australian settlement; an impostor and an expert of deception (perception is grander than reality), and a closeted white supremacist descendant of DRUG LORDS (opium merchants of the Qing Dynasty), and a homie of Eton and Oxbridge-educated very, very, very, rich men's son, Archbishop Justin Welby (**Mark 10:25**), did you know that the combined GDP of the European Union is about $20 trillion, which is about 10X bigger than that of Russia, $2.1 trillion?

OUR OWN NIGERIA: SHELL'S DOCILE CASH COW SINCE 1956 (OLOIBIRI). GDC WAS ESTABLISHED IN 1956.

Unlike PUTIN'S RUSSIA, there are no oil wells or gas fields in bland, colourless, and almost lifeless NORFOLK/NORWICH (Coastal Dole/the Departure Lounge of life) and where the pure white father and mother of Paul Robert Ayers, the Senior Vice President of the Association of Her Majesty's District Judges, a closeted RACIST functional semi-illiterate crooked pure white imbecile, albeit our Senior District Judge in Bedford, were born. Perception is grander than reality.

Karen Kwamboka: Psalm 118:22, Luke 20:17: If hereditary white supremacist bastards, defenders of FAITHS, and dissenters of the FAITH - **John 14:6,** are truly brave, they must DIRECTLY use extreme overwhelming violence to evict PUTIN from CRIMEA, he used extreme overwhelming violence to convert Bakhmut and Avdiivka from bricks to rubble and stole them – **Exodus 20:15.**

"Bakhmut of our hearts." Brother President Zelensky.

There were 33rd Degree Freemasons and Masonic Temples in Bakhmut: Integrity, friendship, respect, and charity: All for one, and one for all.

"Ethical foreign policy." Robin Cook (1946-2005).

Yinka Bamgbelu: Their hairs stand on end when they are challenged by our people (NIGERIANS); we and our type are the ones hereditary RACIST pure white bastards (predominantly but not exclusively pure white) would beat up without the support of the YANKS.

"Could you face the Russians by yourselves?" President Trump

Karen Kwamboka: Russians have not injured us in any way; Hereditary White Supremacist Pure White Freemason Bastards are our enemies, and there a period for everything, and whenever it becomes legal to defend ourselves, we shall deal with EVIL RACIST PURE WHITE BASTARDS (predominantly but not exclusively pure white)- **Ecclesiastes 3:1-8.**

"We shall deal with racist bastards when we get out of prison." Comrade Robert Mugabe (1924-2019).

Yinka Bamgbelu: RETROGRESSIVE INTELLECTUAL AND CULTURAL DECLINE/ERASURE: They are pure white RACIST CRIMINALS and they are very powerful; if you are STUPID and do not know that TRUTH or pretend you don't that they are excessively stupid, you are safe, and should thrive in their Godforsaken RACIST HELL HOLE, but if you know that they are brainless morons, properly schooled impostors, and experts of deception, hereditary RACIST pure white bastards (predominantly but not exclusively pure white) will destroy you.

Karen Kwamboka: Their skin colour is SUPERIOR, but their intellects are not. It is absolutely impossible for hereditary RACIST pure white bastards (predominantly but not exclusively pure white) to compete on a colour-blind level intellectual playing field without resorting to INCOMPETENT RACIST LIES and RACIST CRIMINALITY.

Yinka Bamgbelu: Gigantic yields of millions of stolen and destroyed lives, including those of the African Ancestors of ARCHIE, <43% Nigerian (Impure Black/Impure White), not feudal agriculture, lured Mary Anne Macleod (1912-2000) to AMERICA.

Karen Kwamboka: They loved yields of forced mass emigration of millions of stolen children of defenceless poor people (AFRICANS), they hate equitable, fair, and just REPARATION, and they hate mass economic migration.

Yinka Bamgbelu: Greedy RACIST pure white bastards (predominantly but not exclusively pure white) eat their own cakes, eat ours, and want everything. **Habakkuk 2:5**: They are greedier than the grave, and like death, insatiably greedy hereditary white supremacist bastards can never be satisfied.

Karen Kwamboka: RETROGRESSIVE CULTURAL ERASURE: He hates them, so He blessed them with the universally acknowledged irrefutable SUPERIOR SKIN COLOUR, and He cursed them with dark black brains, and in protest, they criminally steal yields of NIGERIANS Christ-granted talents, secure in the knowledge that all Judges will be pure white and their hope is that they would be hereditary RACIST pure white bastards too – **Habakkuk 1:4.**

Yinka Bamgbelu: BLATANT RACIST CRIMINALITY CONCEALS HEREDITARY INTELLECTUAL IMPOTENCE: When their own people commit RACIST CRIMES against our own people, their own people who oversee the administration of their Law criminally bury HEREDITARY RACIAL HATRED – **Habakkuk 1:4.**

Karen Kwamboka: INDISCREET RACIAL EVIL JUSTICE SYSTEM INCOMPETENTLY IMPERSONATES THE COMPETENT AND IMPARTIAL ADMINISTRATION OF THEIR INSTITUTIONALLY RACIST MEDIOCRE LAW _ **HABAKKUK 1:4:** No brain. Poor natural resources. Several centuries of stealing and SLAVERY preceded their huge stolen inheritance (yields of several centuries of ancestral theft – **Exodus 20:15, Habakkuk**). Facts are sacred and cannot be overstated.

Yinka Bamgbelu: SUPERIORITY is the birth right of Members of their brainlessly and baselessly self-awarded SUPERIOR RACE, and anyone, particularly mere Negroes, who refuse to accept that they are SUPERIORLY CREATED by Almighty God, will be destroyed with incompetent RACIST LIES – **Habakkuk 1:4.**

New Herod, **Matthew 2:16, Matthew 14:** Hereditary RACIST pure white bastards (predominantly but not exclusively pure white) are psychologically and intellectually INSECURE, and they are more impervious to independent thinking than DOGMATIC LUNATIC JIHADISTS, and like Trump, Xi, Putin, Kim, MBS, and BABIES, they expect everyone to love them unconditionally, and they expect everyone to see the world only from their perspective (UNIPOLARITY), and they expect everyone to say and/or write only what they love to hear: Ignorant evil bastards.

CHAPTER TWENTY

Karen Kwamboka: The Yellow ancestors of Kim did not kidnap and imprison a whole people (body and soul) overnight, they did gradually, and the basic rights to disclose pictures painted by independent free minds - were the first to be withdrawn.

"Freedom of Expression is a basic right." Lady Hale.

Yinka Bamgbelu: One of the hallmarks of European moral and intellectual decay, as implied by President Trump is that OXFORD, ENGLAND: GDC, British Soldier (TD, a 5th Rate Military Power/ A Fake Superpower), Stephanie Twidale, unrelentingly LIED under oath and on record - **Habakkuk 1:4**. Everything is brainlessly and baselessly assumed in favour of the universally acknowledged irrefutably SUPERIOR SKIN COLOUR that the very fortunate wearer neither made nor chose. A crooked racist pure white bastard, her country is SHIT, and she is worse than SHIT. She is worthy only because she is PURE WHITE, and she is rich only because the pure white ancestors of her pure white father and mother were PROFESSIONAL THIEVES – **Exodus 20:15, Habakkuk**, extremely nasty and merciless RACIST KILLERS – **Exodus 20:13**, and owners of stolen children of defenceless poor people, including the AFRICA ancestors of our Duchess of Sussex (Impure White. 57%/Impure Black, 43%).

Her type killed the NIGERIAN, Dr Richard Bamgboye, a General Medical Practitioner, only 56, and the INDIAN, Dr Anand Kamath, a Dentist, only 42, albeit hands-off.

Karen Kwamboka: It is me extremely nasty RACIST pure white bastards want, but it is the daughter they got; they should stay here because it is safer than AFRICA – **Exodus 21:23-27.**

"Sometimes people don't want to hear the truth because they don't want their illusions destroyed." Friedrich Nietzsche (1844-1900).

Yinka Bamgbelu: One of the gains of several continuous centuries of STEALING and SLAVERY is that a scatter head pure white bastard was a British Soldier, GDC, British Soldier (TD, a 5th Rate Military Power/ A Fake Superpower), Stephanie Twidale. Without the YANKS, NATO is froth.

Karen Kwamboka: 'Elon Musk mocked after saying children should be 'proud' that the 'whites in the West' ended slavery.'

BRAINLESS NONSENSE!

Yinka Bamgbelu: MAAFA (1445-1888): Why did it take greedy PURE WHITE RACIST economic cannibals several centuries to understand **Exodus 20:13, Exodus 20:15?**

Karen Kwamboka: Paul Robert Ayers, the Senior Vice President of the Association of Her Majesty's District Judges, a closeted RACIST functional semi-illiterate crooked pure white imbecile, albeit our Senior District Judge in Bedford, your SKIN COLOUR is superior and your accent when speaking your own language is more superior, but your intellect is not, and VINDICTIVE, unashamedly mediocre, potently weaponised, indiscreetly DISHONEST, and institutionally RACIST Fish and Chips Justice System is fundamentally designed to conceal that TRUTH.

Yinka Bamgbelu: Paul Robert Ayers, the Senior Vice President of the Association of Her Majesty's District Judges, a closeted RACIST functional semi-illiterate crooked pure white imbecile, albeit our Senior District Judge in Bedford, MONEY IS MEAT: Unlike PUTIN'S RUSSIA, there are no oil wells or gas fields in TOMMY ROBINSON'S Luton, and our own NIGERIA is by far more relevant to the economic survival of all your own white children, your pure white mother, your pure white father, and your own pure white spouse than bland, colourless, and almost lifeless NORFOLK/NORWICH (Coastal Dole/the Departure Lounge of Life). No brain. Poor natural resources. Several centuries of stealing and slavery preceded their huge stolen inheritance. Gigantic yields of several continuous centuries of ANCESTRAL THEFT have distorted the realities of hereditary RACIST pure white bastards (predominantly but not exclusively pure white) – **Exodus 20:15, Habakkuk.**

Those who the TRUTH obey the least.

"Those who know the least obey the best." George Farquhar (1677-1707).

Karen Kwamboka: A white supremacist son of a Scottish Domestic Servant treated the British Premier, a Knight of the Most Excellent Order of our Empire, like a domestic servant.

"We have many trump cards in our hands." President Macron

"You have no cards." President Trump

1940: Without the support of the YANKS, France surrendered within 6/52.

Yinka Bamgbelu: If RACIST descendants of THIEVES and owners of stolen children of poor people (AFRICANS) have GOOD CARDS, they must evict the YANKS from NATO, admit UKRAINE, invoke ARTICLE 5, and use extreme overwhelming violence to EVICT PUTIN from CRIMEA, he used extreme overwhelming violence to convert Bakhmut and Avdiivka from bricks to rubble and stole them – **Exodus 20:15.**

Karen Kwamboka: "Patriotism is the last refuge of a scoundrel." Dr Samuel Johnson (1709-1784).

"My recommendation is that patriotic young Brits should keep their political opinions to themselves and join the Army Reserve. That way, they get genuine military training perfectly legally and are even paid while doing so." Nick Griffin

Yinka Bamgbelu: BRAINLESS NONSENSE: AN IGNORANT HEREDITARY RACIST PURE WHITE FANTASIST. ARCHIE IS IMPURE, <43% NIGERIAN.

England is the natural resource of Nick Griffin's Wales. If Wales is detached from England at the River Severn, in Monmouthshire, and other boundary regions, her GDP will remain higher than that of ALBANIA, and DPRK, but lower than that of Lagos State Nigeria, and UKRAINE.

Karen Kwamboka: Sheep unnaturally shepherd sheep. Shepherds know that sheep are MORONS, but sheep do not know that shepherds are MORONS too.

"Mediocrity weighing mediocrity in the balance, and incompetence applauding its brother........" Wilde (1854-1900).

Yinka Bamgbelu: CULTURAL ERASURE: The culture of their ancestors was based on stealing and sharing STOLEN MONEY. In 1833, they shared loads of the yields of millions of stolen children of defenceless poor people (AFRICANS).

OYINBO OLE/ODE: There is CULTURAL ERASURE when civilisations built with yields of millions of stolen and destroyed children of defenceless poor people (AFRICANS) cannot be sustained with yields of transparent virtue - **Habakkuk.**

Karen Kwamboka: RACIST inheritors of huge yields of ancestral theft dishonestly implied that they did not know the difference between vice and virtue, and that vice is more profitable than virtue because Stealing is more efficient than hard work.

"Why, Sir, if the fellow does not think as he speaks, he is lying; and I see not what honour he can propose to himself from having the character of a liar. But if he does really think that there is no distinction between virtue and vice, why, Sir, when he leaves our houses let us count our spoons." Dr Samuel Johnson (1709-1784).

Yinka Bamgbelu: Pakistanis who FAILED Norman Tebbit's (1931-2025) Cricket Test do not believe that Britain is worth dying for. Why should AFRICANS die for CORRUPT AND RACIST UKRAINE?

Karen Kwamboka: Why should AFRICAN descendants of SLAVES be concerned when pure white European Christians, descendants of pure white SLAVE-OWNERS, use their own pure white kindred to fight a proxy war against their pure white kindred, when the destruction of all of descendants of THIEVES and owners of stolen children of defenceless poor people (AFRICANS) - favours AFRICA and AFRICANS?

Yinka Bamgbelu: A brainless hereditary RACIST pure white bastard, albeit England's Class Senior District Judge; skin colour that he neither made nor chose is SUPERIOR, but his intellect is not, and he would kill to conceal that TRUTH.

Karen Kwamboka: Hereditary RACIST pure white bastards (predominantly but not exclusively pure white) see self-educated NIGERIANS as existential threats.

Yinka Bamgbelu: Rightly so.

Karen Kwamboka: Yinka Bamgbelu, what do you mean by – 'rightly so'?

Yinka Bamgbelu: Karen Kwamboka, you should ask King's School and Oxbridge-educated rich man's son (**Mark 10:25**), albeit England's Class Lord Justice, KC, to tell you which part of the Royal Courts of Justice, WC2A 2LL, was not STOLEN, or which part his pure white father and mother buy, or which part preceded SLAVERY; if he is not as DISHONEST as the pure white ancestors of his pure white mother and father, the opportunist white supremacist bastard should confirm the TRUTH, which that SLAVERY rebuilt everything it succeeded and paid for everything it preceded, including GDC (1956), NHS (1948), Old Bailey (1907), Royal Courts of Justice (1882), Royal College of Surgeons (1880), Industrial Revolution, Etcetera. Then, almost everything was actively and deliberately stolen with GUNS – **Exodus 20:15, Habakkuk**.

"All have taken what had other owners, and all have had recourse to arms rather than quit the prey onto which they were fastened." Dr Samuel Johnson (1709-1784)

Yinka Bamgbelu: Poly-educated hereditary RACIST pure white son of a pure white plebeian hoe ultra-righteously sat on the BONES of stolen children of defenceless poor people (AFRICANS), more BONES than the millions of skulls at the doorstep of Pol Pot (1925-1998), and the opportunist RACIST pure white bastard Judged SINNERS – **John 8:7, Matthew 7:1-6:** Slimy Hypocrisy, the Ne plus Ultra of Hypocrisy.

Karen Kwamboka: "Hypocrisy is the homage vice pays to virtue." Francois de La Rochefoucauld (1613-1680).

BEDFORD, ENGLAND: Paul Robert Ayers, the Senior Vice President of the Association of Her Majesty's District Judges, a closeted RACIST functional semi-illiterate crooked pure white imbecile, albeit our Senior District Judge in Bedford, a crooked hereditary RACIST pure white bastard, an ultra-righteous descendant of pure white THIEVES Judged SINNERS. Only He who has no sin and was directly appointed by the sole creator has the MORAL RIGHT to Judge SINNERS – **John 5:22.**

Yinka Bamgbelu: FLAT TRACK BULLIES. TRUMP'S POODLES.

Their hairs stand on end when they are challenged by AFRICANS; we and our type are the ones hereditary RACIST pure white bastards (predominantly but not exclusively pure white) would be up without the support of the YANKS. If opportunist RACIST pure white bastards (predominantly but not exclusively pure white) are as brave as they vulgarly brag, they must use VIOLENCE to evict PUTIN from Crimea.

Karen Kwamboka: BEDFORD, ENGLAND: Paul Robert Ayers, the Senior Vice President of the Association of Her Majesty's District Judges, a closeted RACIST functional semi-illiterate crooked pure white imbecile, albeit our Senior District Judge in Bedford, a crooked hereditary RACIST pure white bastard, a RACIST pure white bastard was granted the platform to display hereditary prejudice. Those they spin, and on whose behalf, they spin others, are among the dullest adults in the industrialised world (OECD). No brain. Poor natural resources. Several centuries of STEALING and SLAVERY preceded their huge STOLEN INHERITANCE (yields of several centuries of ancestral theft – **Exodus 20:15, Habakkuk).**

Yinka Bamgbelu: BEDFORD, ENGLAND: Paul Robert Ayers, the Senior Vice President of the Association of Her Majesty's District Judges, a closeted RACIST functional semi-illiterate crooked pure white imbecile, albeit our Senior

District Judge in Bedford, a crooked hereditary RACIST pure white bastard, you and your pure white type are INFERIOR creations of Almighty God. Sincere immodesty is sincerer than insincere modesty. Intellectual superiority should be concealed only if it does not interfere with sincerity.

Sincerity is a prime attribute of our own MESSIAH – **John 14:6.**

Karen Kwamboka: BEDFORD, ENGLAND: Paul Robert Ayers, the Senior Vice President of the Association of Her Majesty's District Judges, a closeted RACIST functional semi-illiterate crooked pure white imbecile, albeit our Senior District Judge in Bedford, a crooked hereditary RACIST pure white bastard, it is absolutely impossible for you and your pure white type to compete on a level intellectual playing field without resorting to RACIST CRIMINALITY- **Habakkuk 1:4.**

Yinka Bamgbelu: BEDFORD, ENGLAND: GDC, Sue Gregory (OBE), Officer of the Most Excellent Order of our Empire of STOLEN INHERITANCE – **Exodus 20:15, Habakkuk,** unrelentingly lied under implied oath and on record – **Habakkuk 1:4.** Constance Briscoe was JAILED for a lesser offence. Facts are sacred and cannot be overstated.

"The height of cleverness is to be able to conceal it." Francois de La Rochefoucauld (1613-1680).

"The English think incompetence is the same thing as sincerity." Quentin Crisp (1908-1999).

Karen Kwamboka: BEDFORD, ENGLAND: Paul Robert Ayers, the Senior Vice President of the Association of Her Majesty's District Judges, a closeted RACIST functional semi-illiterate crooked pure white imbecile, albeit our Senior District Judge in Bedford, a crooked hereditary RACIST pure white bastard, you are an opportunist RACIST DUNCE. You are RICH only because the pure white ancestors of your pure white mother and father were THIEVES, and you are worthy only because you are pure white. The universally acknowledged irrefutably SUPERIOR SKIN COLOUR that the fortunate wearer neither made nor chose, yields of several continuous centuries of ancestral theft (Maafa, 1445-1888), and what else? Before Slavery, what? Then, there was only subsistence feudal agriculture.

OYINBO OLE/ODE: "Agriculture not only gives riches to a nation, but the only one she can call her own." Dr Samuel Johnson (1709-1784),

The PURE WHITE BASTARD should fu*king fu*k off, and he should stay here because it is safer than NIGERIA, as there, we shall extract a revenge, but only under the Law, God's Law – **Exodus 21:23-27**.

"We shall deal with the racist bastards when we get out of prison." Comrade Robert Mugabe (1924-2019).

Yinka Bamgbelu: 'Cultural Erasure.' – President Trump: Yields of millions of stolen lives paid brainless pure white bastards (predominantly but not exclusively pure white) the top dollar - in exchange for retrogressive CONFUSION but yields of transparent virtue cannot, so CULTURAL ERASURE preceded by cultural decay is progressive because it seeks to reverse several centuries of free-loading (Stealing and Slavery – **Habakkuk, Exodus 20:15**).

Karen Kwamboka: Their ancestors were PROFESSIONAL THIEVES – **Exodus 20:15, Habakkuk**. Slavery preceded Colonisation. Neo-Colonialism is the New Slavery.

SUBSTITUTION IS FRAUDULENT EMANCIPATION.

"Moderation is a virtue only among those who are thought to have found alternatives." Dr Henry Kissinger (1923-2023).

Yinka Bamgbelu: Poly-educated pure white son of a pure white plebeian hoe artificially created an intellectual ceiling, and the hereditary RACIST pure white bastard brainlessly and baselessly SELF-AWARDED SUPREME KNOWLEDGE, and the opportunist RACIST pure white bastard, albeit Bedford's Class Senior District Judge, destroys all NIGERIANS who know that he is a brainless pure white bastard; a properly schooled impostor and an expert of deception should stay here because in NIGERIA, we shall fight back, and we shall avulse a tooth for a tooth – **Exodus 21:23-27.**

Karen Kwamboka: Would Sweden and Finland have joined NATO if the YANKS were not part of NATO or if they foresaw that the YANKS would leave NATO if it were in their best interest to do so?

Paul Robert Ayers, the Senior Vice President of the Association of Her Majesty's District Judges, a closeted RACIST functional semi-illiterate crooked pure white imbecile, albeit our Senior District Judge in Bedford, a crooked hereditary RACIST pure white bastard, the pure white ancestors of your pure white mum and dad were RACIST THIEVES – **Exodus 20:15, Habakkuk.** You are relevant only because you are pure white, and you are rich only because the pure white ancestors of your pure white mother and father were THIEVES and owners of stolen children of defenceless poor people, including the AFRICAN ancestors of the impure White/impure Black, <43% Nigerian, niece and nephew of the PRINCE OF WALES, and apart from those, you are absolutely worthless: PURIFIED FROTH.

Yinka Bamgbelu: 1884: After Maafa (1445-1888), European Christians partitioned AFRICA and looted her. Greedy economic cannibals should pay equitable, fair, and just reparation, and settle several centuries of accruing interest: OYINBO OLE/ODE. **Habakkuk 2:5**: Based on several decades of very proximate observations and direct experiences, they are greedier than the grave, and like death, insatiably greedy RACIST pure white bastards can never be satisfied.

"The colonialists care nothing for Africa for her own sake. They are attracted by African riches, and their actions are guided by the desire to preserve their interests in Africa against the wishes of the African people. For the colonialists all means are good if they help them to possess these riches." Patrice Lumumba, 1925-1961, fed European made bullets spat out by European made guns because he disagreed with RACIST Colonialist Economic Cannibals.

Karen Kwamboka: 1976-2022: A brainless hereditary RACIST pure white rubbish FAILED in practice, loads did, and the opportunist RACIST pure white bastard parked his liability at the public till and sold unashamed mediocrity and confusion to the undiscerning. His Country is SHIT and he is worse than SHIT.

Yinka Bamgbelu: CULTURAL DECAY PRECEDED CULTURAL ERASURE: Our hereditary RACIST pure white bastard is an ignorant descendant of THIEVES; the closeted white supremacist thug was granted the platform to display hereditary prejudice

Brainless and baseless SUPERIORITY is their birthright. They are pure white, brainless, crooked, RACIST, but very powerful.

BEDFORD, ENGLAND: GDC, Sue Gregory (OBE), Officer of the Most Excellent Order of our Empire of Stolen Inheritance – **Exodus 20:15, Habakkuk**, unrelentingly lied under implied oath and on record – **Habakkuk 1:4.** Constance Briscoe was JAILED for a lesser offence.

"He is a typical Englishman, usually violent and always dull." Wilde (1854-1900).

BEDFORD,ENGLAND: GDC, Freemason, Brother Richard William Hill, England's Class Senior Postgraduate Tutor, Bedfordshire, fabricated reports and unrelentingly lied under oath - **Habakkuk 1:4.** The pure white ancestors of his pure white mother and father were incompetent RACIST liars too, like the pure white Tasmanian-settler ancestors of Sir Charles Phillip Haddon-Cave (1925-1999), they were armed land grabbers and professional THIEVES – **Exodus 20:15, Habakkuk.** Constance Briscoe was JAILED for a lesser offence. Facts are sacred and cannot be overstated.

Karen Kwamboka: OUR OWN MONEY. OUR OWN NIGERIA, SHELL'S DOCILE CASH COW SINCE 1956 (OLOIBIRI). GDC WAS ESTABLISHED IN 1956.

Unlike PUTIN'S RUSSIA, there are no oil wells or gas fields in TOMMY ROBINSON'S LUTON and where the pure white mother and father of Paul Robert Ayers, the Senior Vice President of the Association of Her Majesty's District Judges, a closeted RACIST functional semi-illiterate crooked pure white imbecile, albeit our Senior District Judge in Bedford, a crooked hereditary RACIST pure white bastard. were born.

"Find the truth and tell it." Harold Pinter (1930-2008)

Yinka Bamgbelu: An undeclared interracial war: Treating one's pure white RACIST ENEMIES with respect - to their face, and cursing them behind their back, is COWARDICE.

"Treating one's adversaries with respect is striking soft in a battle." Dr Samuel Johnson (1709-1784).

Karen Kwamboka: BEDFORD, ENGLAND: Paul Robert Ayers, the Senior Vice President of the Association of Her Majesty's District Judges, a closeted RACIST functional semi-illiterate crooked pure white imbecile, albeit our Senior District Judge in Bedford, a crooked hereditary RACIST pure white bastard, and a brainless hereditary RACIST pure white bastard: The land on which his pure white mother and father were born yields only FOOD, he is verifiably a functional semi-illiterate, unlike PUTIN'S RUSSIA, there are no oil wells or gas fields in bland, colourless, and almost lifeless NORFOLK/NORWICH (Coastal Dole/the Departure Lounge of Life) and where his pure white father and mother were born, he is relatively very RICH, and he DISHONESTLY implied that he did not know that the pure white ancestors of his pure white father and mother were THIEVES – **Exodus 20:15,** extremely nasty and merciless racist murderers, **Exodus 20:13**, and owners of stolen children of defenceless poor people (AFRICANS) – **Habakkuk.**

Yinka Bamgbelu: Our own NIGERIAN BABIES with gigantic oil wells and gas fields near their huts eat only 1.5/day in our own NIGERIA, three, only three, but three too many very bellyful, verifiably crooked, brainless, and hereditary RACIST pure white bastards whose pure white mothers and fathers have never seen CRUDE OIL, and whose pure white ancestors, including the pure white Italian Jewish ancestors of Benjamin Disraeli (1804-1881), were fed like battery hens with gigantic yields of millions of stolen children of defenceless poor people, including the AFRICAN ancestors of the impure Black (43% Nigerian) and impure White, (57% European) – Duchess of Sussex.

Karen Kwamboka: The centuries-old unspoken myth that Christ-granted talents are related to the universally acknowledged irrefutably SUPERIOR SKIN COLOUR that the very fortunate wearer neither made nor chose is not the mother of all WARS, but it is the mother of all RACIST SCAMS.

"The Mother of all Wars." President Hussein, not Barack, but the real one, Hussein (1937-2006).

Yinka Bamgbelu: BEDFORD, ENGLAND: Paul Robert Ayers, the Senior Vice President of the Association of Her Majesty's District Judges, a closeted RACIST functional semi-illiterate crooked pure white imbecile, albeit our Senior District Judge in Bedford, a crooked hereditary RACIST pure white bastard, and a brainless hereditary RACIST pure white bastard, it is absolutely impossible to use facts and evidence to disprove the TRUTH, which is that it is absolutely impossible for you and your pure white type to COMPETE on a colour-blind level intellectual playing field without resorting to RACIST CRIMINALITY: Persecutory Negrophobia guarded by Negrophobic Perjury – **Habakkuk 1:4.**

Karen Kwamboka: The YANKS will always act in the best interest of the YANKS. To make America Great Again, the best interest of Americans must come first. Had SWEDEN and FINLAND done proper research, they might have remained NEUTRAL, as without the YANKS, NATO is PURIFIED FROTH.

Yinka Bamgbelu: Hereditary RACIST pure white bastards (predominantly but not exclusively pure white) control formal education, but they do not control informal education and genetic mix. Formal and informal education will polish what genetic mix presents to them.

Karen Kwamboka: BEDFORD, ENGLAND: Paul Robert Ayers, the Senior Vice President of the Association of Her Majesty's District Judges, a closeted RACIST functional semi-illiterate crooked pure white imbecile, albeit our Senior District Judge in Bedford, a crooked hereditary RACIST pure white bastard, and a brainless hereditary RACIST pure white bastard, apart from creating cushy salaried jobs for pure white Freemason Judges (predominantly but not exclusively pure white) who FAILED in practice, loads did, what do pure white IMBECILES (predominantly but not exclusively pure white) need very expensive administration of English Law for?

Yinka Bamgbelu: BEDFORD, ENGLAND: Paul Robert Ayers, the Senior Vice President of the Association of Her Majesty's District Judges, a closeted RACIST functional semi-illiterate crooked pure white imbecile, albeit our Senior District Judge in Bedford, a crooked hereditary RACIST pure white bastard, and a brainless hereditary RACIST pure white bastard,, our opportunist RACIST pure white bastard of our Empire of STOLEN INHERITANCE - **Exodus 20:15, Habakkuk**, was granted the platform to display uneducated and unintelligent hereditary PREJUDICE.

CHAPTER TWENTY-ONE

Karen Kwamboka: An ignorant hereditary RACIST pure white bastard; an ultra-righteous descendant of THIEVES and owners of STOLEN CHILDREN of defenceless poor people (AFRICANS) – **Exodus 20:15, Habakkuk**. The only evidence of his brainlessly and baselessly self-awarded HIGHER IQ is the GIGANTIC STOLEN INHERITANCE that his pure white ancestors crossed the English Channel, not that long ago, without luggage or decent shoes to latch onto.

Yinka Bamgbelu: Delusional grandeur of their decaying and erasing perverted culture whose entire foundation was based on STEALING and sharing ill-gotten gains – **Exodus 20:15, Habakkuk.**

1833: Yields of MERCILESS RACIST EVIL were shared among scores of thousands of Merchants of Stolen Lives, and African descendants of the robbed were not given a cent when the loot was shared.

Karen Kwamboka: If hereditary pure white bastards (predominantly but not exclusively pure white) are superiorly created by Almighty God, as they vulgarly brag, why do they need RACIST CRIMINALITY to defeat self-educated AFRICANS?

Yinka Bamgbelu: TRUTHS disfavour hereditary RACIST pure white bastards (predominantly but not exclusively pure white), so they subjugate progressive colour-blind objectivity and stifle FREEDOM OF EXPRESSION because they don't want their mentally gentler white children (OECD) and the pure white IMBECILES they shepherd (predominantly but not exclusively pure white) to know the TRUTH, which is that only the universally acknowledged irrefutably SUPERIOR SKIN COLOUR that they neither made nor chose and Almighty God are truly good – **Mark 10:18.**

Karen Kwamboka: BEDFORD, ENGLAND: Paul Robert Ayers, the Senior Vice President of the Association of Her Majesty's District Judges, a closeted RACIST functional semi-illiterate crooked pure white imbecile, albeit our Senior District Judge in Bedford, and a crooked hereditary RACIST pure white bastard, NIGERIA (oil/gas) is by far more relevant to the economic survival of all your mentally gentler white children (OECD) that Freemasons' Kempston. You are a LEECH. The pure white ancestors of your pure white father and mother were

THIEVES and owners of stolen children of defenceless poor people, including the AFRICAN ancestors of the impure Black/impure White (<43% Nigerian) great grandchildren of the Duke of Edinburgh of Blessed Memory, Prince Phillip (1921-2021).

Philippians 1:21: Phillip was a 33rd Degree Freemason, Scottish Rite.

Yinka Bamgbelu: BEDFORD, ENGLAND: Paul Robert Ayers, the Senior Vice President of the Association of Her Majesty's District Judges, a closeted RACIST functional semi-illiterate crooked pure white imbecile, albeit our Senior District Judge in Bedford, and a crooked hereditary RACIST pure white bastard, apart from DEBT-COLLECTION, what was in bland, colourless, and almost lifeless NORFOLK/NORWICH (Coastal Dole/the Departure Lounge of Life) for Freemason Solicitors to do?

Karen Kwamboka: RACIST descendants of THIEVES and owners of stolen children of defenceless poor people (AFRICANS); their hairs stand on end when they are challenged by AFRICANS. We and our type are the ones opportunist RACIST pure white bastards (predominantly but not exclusively pure white) – would beat up without the support of the YANKS.

Yinka Bamgbelu: "Jews are intelligent and creative, Chinese are intelligent but not creative, Indians are servile, and Africans are Morons." Antichrist indiscreet White Supremacist, Professor James Watson (1928-2025, **Psalm 39:5, Psalm 144:4)** paraphrased.

Karen Kwamboka: Hereditary RACIST pure white bastards (predominantly but not exclusively pure white) FU*K all the time, and when they do GENIUS JEWS are their go-to-people, their JIM WILL FIX IT.

Yinka Bamgbelu: 'The pure white man, not the Jew, is the devil.' Brother Khalid Abdul Mohammad paraphrased.

Several millions of Jews are pure white.

"The white man is not only practicing Racism and Zionism, and with the prostitution ring, the so-called Jew man with the Jew woman all over the world to make a few dollars, he is also practicing sexism. He's a racist, he's a Zionist, an imperialist. He's a no-good bastard. He's not a devil, but the white man is the Devil." Brother Khalid Abdul Mohammad (1948-2001, San Francisco State University, May 21, 1997.

Karen Kwamboka: Our intellectually IMPOTENT pure white nonentity of our own Empire of STOLEN INHERITANCE - **Exodus 20:15, Habakkuk,** ultra-righteously sat on a very expensive highchair (throne - **Revelation 3:21**) that his own pure white mother and father could not afford, and which the pure white IMBECILES (predominantly but not exclusively pure white) who sat before him could not and did not buy, and the hypocritical opportunist RACIST pure white bastard Judge SINNERS – **John 8:7, Matthew 7:1-6.** OYINBO OLE/ODE: A RACIST DESCENDANT OF THIEVES – **Exodus 20:15, Habakkuk.**

Yinka Bamgbelu: FAKE SUPERPOWERS. FLAT TRACK BULLIES. WITHOUT THE YANKS, NATO IS FROTH.

Paul Robert Ayers, the Senior Vice President of the Association of Her Majesty's District Judges, a closeted RACIST functional semi-illiterate crooked pure white imbecile, albeit our Senior District Judge in Bedford, a crooked hereditary RACIST pure white bastard, a brainless hereditary RACIST pure white bastard. A RACIST descendant of THIEVES and owners of stolen children of poor people (AFRICANS). No brain. Poor natural resources. Several centuries of stealing and slavery preceded their HUGE STOLEN INHERITANCE. The most important part of the matter is MONEY, and it is not the yield of the Christ-granted talent of the opportunist RACIST pure white bastard, and unlike PUTIN'S RUSSIA, there are no oil wells or gas fields in Tommy Robinson's LUTON and where the pure white mother and father of the deluded one-dimensionally educated opportunist RACIST pure white bastard was born. Poly-educated pure white rubbish; perception is grander than reality. He should stay here; it is safer than NIGERIA – **Exodus 21:23-27.**

Karen Kwamboka: They don't want their own mentally gentler white children (OECD) and the PURE WHITE IMBECILES they shepherd (predominantly but not exclusively pure white) to know the truth, which is that apart from our INFERIOR SKIN COLOUR and our more inferior accent when speaking an alien language, we are also properly created by Almighty God, and to conceal this TRUTH, and to save face, hereditary RACIST pure white bastards (predominantly but not exclusively pure white) resort to RACIST CRIMINALITY, and they steal yields of our own people's (NIGERIANS) Christ-granted talents, secure in the knowledge that all Judges will be PURE WHITE and their hope is that they would be hereditary RACIST pure white bastards too – **Habakkuk 1:4.**

Yinka Bamgbelu: GDC: British Soldier, Stephanie Twidale (TD), unrelentingly lied under oath and on record – **Habakkuk 1:4.** Constance Briscoe was JAILED for a lesser offence. "The truth allows no choice." Dr Samuel Johnson (1709-1784). If our British Soldier, a RACIST Negrophobic Perjurer, is as brave as she vulgarly brags, the hereditary RACIST pure white bastard should join the Russian Army as a mercenary and help PUTIN to evict Zelensky from the whole of Donbas.

Karen Kwamboka: Sir Keir Starmer, Knight of the Most Excellent Order of our Empire of Stolen Inheritance- **Exodus 20:15, Habakkuk,** why is it progressive sound logic to use NUCLEAR BOMBS to guard the continuing propagation of pure white IMBECILES (predominantly but not exclusively pure white)?

Yinka Bamgbelu: There are no RULES in their Godforsaken RACIST HELL HOLE; their LAW is what defenders of faiths, and dissenters of the faith – **John 14:6** (Freemasons) want, and absolutely everything else is DECEIT - **Habakkuk 1:4.**

Karen Kwamboka: ACCURATE SEERS: **Psalm 39:5, Psalm 144:4.** They are not the only creation of Almighty God, and they are not immortal, and the universally acknowledged irrefutably superior skin colour that the fortunate wearer neither made nor chose is not the only wonder of our world. Skin colour is a great creation of Almighty God, but it is not the greatest – **Proverbs 20:15.**

Conflict of interest: Elon Musk believes in a creator, but that cannot stop his absolutely inevitable infinite sojourn in Al Jahannam - **Mark 10:25**. An ignorant closeted white supremacist mere traveller passing through this transient reality - **Psalm 39:5, 144:4.**

Yinka Bamgbelu: They foresaw that a functional semi-illiterate pure white bastard will be a Senior District Judge in Bedford, so they embarked on armed robbery and dispossession raids in AFRICA, and wherever armed hereditary RACIST pure white bastards mercilessly slaughtered defenceless AFRICANS, they dispossessed them, and whenever they ROBBED our direct ancestors, they took possession – **Exodus 20:15, Habakkuk.**

Karen Kwamboka: The only countries hereditary RACIST pure white bastards (predominantly but not exclusively pure white) will beat up without the support of the YANKS are in AFRICA: Flat track bullies. Fake Superpowers. Delusional grandeur of the stolen past – **Exodus 20:15, Habakkuk.**

Yinka Bamgbelu: 1940: Without the support of the YANKS, France surrendered within 6/52.

In the same position as UKRAINE, but without the support of the YANKS, Great Britain would surrender with 6/7.

Karen Kwamboka: 666. It will take <6 hours to convert Europe to NUCLEAR ASH.

Yinka Bamgbelu: A brainless hereditary RACIST pure white bastard ultra-righteously sat on a HIGHCHAIR that his pure white father and mother could not afford, and which the pure white IMBECILES who sat before him (predominantly but not exclusively pure white) could not, and did not buy, and the slimily hypocritical pure white bastard, a closeted RACIST descendant of THIEVES – **Exodus 20:15**, extremely nasty evil RACIST KILLERS – **Exodus 20:13**, and owners of stolen children of defenceless poor people (AFRICANS) Judges SINNERS – **Habakkuk.**

Karen Kwamboka: Our IMBECILE Freemason Senior Judge of our Empire of Stolen Inheritance – **Exodus 20:15, Habakkuk**. If we are not very smart, the sixth largest economy on earth, why are we very RICH? Shepherds did not bring any of the millions of stolen AFRICAN CHILDREN back home to Great Britain, evil greedy RACIST pure white bastards carried other people's stolen children to their stolen new world and sold them to greedy, racist, and evil pure white European Christian Slave Merchants.

Yinka Bamgbelu: BEDFORD, ENGLAND: Paul Robert Ayers, the Senior Vice President of the Association of Her Majesty's District Judges, a closeted RACIST functional semi-illiterate crooked pure white imbecile, albeit our Senior District Judge in Bedford, and a crooked hereditary RACIST pure white bastard, it is not the TRUTH that daily dialogues with pure white IMBECILES (predominantly but not exclusively pure white adults with the basic skills of a child) is a proper job that is worthwhile and manly – **Proverbs 17:16.**

Karen Kwamboka: "They may not have been well written from a grammatical point of view but I am confident I had not forgotten any of the facts." Geraint Evans, England's Class Senior Postgraduate Tutor, Oxford.

Yinka Bamgbelu: Part of the gains of several continuous centuries of STEALING and SLAVERY is that a scatter-head, crooked, and indiscreetly RACIST pure white Welsh imbecile was our Senior Postgraduate Tutor, Oxford. Ignorant descendants of THIEVES and owners of stolen children of defenceless poor people (AFRICANS). Their motley assemblies of exotic cultures paid GERAINT EVANS, a functional semi-illiterate, crooked, and indiscreetly

RACIST pure white Welsh bastard -the SALARY of a postgraduate Tutor, Oxford.

Karen Kwamboka: Their indiscreetly RACIST culture that paid a crooked and unashamedly functional semi-illiterate pure white WELSH IMBECILE the salary of a Senior Postgraduate Tutor, Oxford. is worse than COMMUNISM, and it is affordable only because of gigantic yields of several centuries of ancestral theft (Maafa, 1445-1888).

Yinka Bamgbelu: Those who know the TRUTH obey the least.

"Those who know the least obey the best." George Farquhar (1677-1707).

Karen Kwamboka: BEDFORD, ENGLAND, Paul Robert Ayers, the Senior Vice President of the Association of Her Majesty's District Judges, a closeted RACIST functional semi-illiterate crooked pure white imbecile, albeit our Senior District Judge in Bedford, and a crooked hereditary RACIST pure white bastard, you are worthy only because you are PURE WHITE, and you are relatively RICH only because the pure white ancestors of your pure white mother and father were THIEVES, had you been BLACK and 10X as smart, you will not be a Senior Judge in our Great Britain.

Yinka Bamgbelu: Based on cogent, irrefutable, and available evidence, our own NIGERIA (oil/gas) is by far more relevant to the economic survival Geraint Evans, England's Class Senior Postgraduate Tutor, Oxford, than Nick Griffin's Llanerfyl Powys. No brain. Poor natural resources. Several centuries of stealing and slavery preceded their huge stolen inheritance – **Exodus 20:15, Habakkuk.** They are THIEVES. The only part of our own AFRICA they truly love is our own MONEY (natural resources), and absolutely everything else is crude and cruel deceit. They hate us, and we know.

Yinka Bamgbelu: Their QUASI-COMMUNIST CULTURE that is sustained by yields of several centuries of ANCESTRAL THEFT is doomed, as it is unsustainable: OYINBO OLE/ODE.

Karen Kwamboka: Those we could report crooked hereditary white supremacist Freemason bastards to are hereditary white supremacist Freemason bastards too.

Yinka Bamgbelu: BEDFORD, ENGLAND: GDC: Freemason, Brother Richard Willian Hill fabricated reports and unrelentingly lied under oath – **Habakkuk 1:4.** Cultural decay preceded by cultural erasure. Persecutory

Negrophobia guarded by Negrophobic Perjury: Constance Briscoe was JAILED for a lesser offence.

They love fighting: We and our type are the ones hereditary RACIST pure white bastards (predominantly but not exclusively pure white)

would beat up without the support of the YANKS

1940: Without the support of the YANKS.

Karen Kwamboka: France had one of the strongest Armed Forces in the World but surrendered in < 6/52.

In the same geographical position as Ukraine, but without the support of the YANKS, desertion, especially among ethnic minorities, would be extremely high, and Great Britain would surrender in < 6/7.

Yinka Bamgbelu: Innately wicked pure white bastards (predominantly but not exclusively pure white). They seek to know everything, so that they can seamlessly use their RACIST JUSTICE SYSTEM to destroy our own people, and only our people – **Habakkuk 1:4.**

Karen Kwamboka: OXFORD, ENGLAND: GDC, British Soldier, Stephanie Twidale (TD) unrelentingly lied under oath and on record - **Habakkuk 1:4**. The pure white ancestors of her pure white father and mother were incompetent RACIST liars too; they were THIEVES and owners of stolen and destroyed lives of children of defenceless poor people (AFRICANS).

Constance Briscoe was JAILED for a lesser offence: White Privilege. “White supremacy is real, and it needs to be shattered.” Dr Cornel West.

Yinka Bamgbelu: “Pardon him Theodotus: He is barbarian and thinks that the cultures of his tribe and Island are the laws of nature.” George Bernard Shaw (1856-1950).

Decayed and erased culture whose entire foundation is SLAVERY, COLONISATION, NEO-COLONIALISM

ETCETERA - is FU*KED – **Exodus 20:15.**

Karen Kwamboka: Poly-educated RACIST pure white RUBBISH. A righteous semi-illiterate pure white son of a pure white plebeian hoe. No brain. Poor natural resources. Stealing and SLAVERY preceded their GIGANTIC stolen inheritance. Constance Briscoe was JAILED for a lesser offence

Yinka Bamgbelu: BEDFORD, ENGLAND: Based on cogent, irrefutable, and available evidence, Bedford's District Judge, unrelentingly lied under oath and on record (approved Judgement) - **Habakkuk 1:4**. His pure white skin concealed his impure dark black brain. Perception is grander than reality.

CONSTANCE BRISCOE WAS JAILED FOR A LESSER OFFENCE.

Delusional grandeur of the STOLEN past – **Exodus 20:15, Habakkuk:** A 5th Rate Military Power impersonates a superpower.

Karen Kwamboka: BEDFORD, ENGLAND: Paul Robert Ayers, the Senior Vice President of the Association of Her Majesty's District Judges, a closeted RACIST functional semi-illiterate crooked pure white imbecile, albeit our Senior District Judge in Bedford, and a crooked hereditary RACIST pure white bastard, you are RICH only because the pure white ancestors of your pure white mother and father were THIEVES and owners of stolen children of defenceless poor people (AFRICANS) – **Exodus 20:15, Habakkuk**, and you are worthy only because you are PURE WHITE, and apart from those, you are nothing, PURIFIED FROTH.

Yinka Bamgbelu: BEDFORD, ENGLAND: Paul Robert Ayers, the Senior Vice President of the Association of Her Majesty's District Judges, a closeted RACIST functional semi-illiterate crooked pure white imbecile, albeit our Senior District Judge in Bedford, and a crooked hereditary RACIST pure white bastard, it is absolutely impossible for your Christ-granted talent and yields of the land on which your pure white mother and father were born to sustain your HIGH STANDARD of living. No brain. Poor natural resources. Several centuries of STEALING and SLAVERY (yields of several centuries of ancestral theft) preceded their GIGANTIC STOLEN INHERITANCE – **Exodus 20:15, Habakkuk.** Facts are sacred and cannot be overstated.

Karen Kwamboka: BEDFORD, ENGLAND: Paul Robert Ayers, the Senior Vice President of the Association of Her Majesty's District Judges, a closeted RACIST functional semi-illiterate crooked pure white imbecile, albeit our Senior District Judge in Bedford, and a crooked hereditary RACIST pure white bastard, unlike PUTIN'S RUSSIA, there are no oil wells or gas fields in bland, colourless, and almost lifeless Tommy Robinson's Luton and where your own pure white father and mother were born: OYINBO OLE/ODE: A RACIST DESCENDANT OF ULTRA-RIGHTEOUS PURE WHITE THIEVES AND OWNERS OF STOLEN HUMAN BEINGS.

Yinka Bamgbelu: Stealing is hereditary. Those who carried and sold millions of stolen human beings stole everything. The theft of human beings, including poor children, is the ne plus ultra of stealing. If the pure white ancestors of one's pure white father and

Karen Kwamboka: "Those who have robbed have also lied." Dr Samuel Johnson(1709-1784)

Stealing is GENETIC, so it cannot be a personal fault. RUSSIA should stop moaning. Where were RUSSIANS, in 1884,when their pure white European Christian kindred partitioned AFRICA and looted her?

Yinka Bamgbelu: European Racist descendants of THIEVES and owners of stolen AFRICANS should use the money they stole from RUSSIA to pay part of the interest of the Quadrillions of dollars they stole from AFRICA.

EXODUS 20:15, HABAKKUK: STEALING IS HEREDITARY AND IT IS IMMORTAL:

"All have taken what had other owners and all have had recourse to arms rather than quit the prey onto which they were fastened." Dr Samuel Johnson (1709-1784).

Karen Kwamboka: BEDFORD, ENGLAND: GDC, Freemason, Brother Richard William Hill fabricated reports and unrelentingly lied under oath and on record – **Habakkuk 1:4.**

BEDFORD, ENGLAND: District Judge unrelentingly lied under oath and on record – **Habakkuk 1:4** (approved Judgement). An opportunist RACIST pure white bastard was granted the platform to display uncontrollable hereditary prejudice. Then, all Judges were pure white FREEMASONS, and most of them were thicker than a gross of planks.

Constance Briscoe was JAILED for a lesser offence.

BEDFORD, ENGLAND: GDC, Sue Gregory, OBE, Officer of the Most Excellent Order of our Empire of Stolen Inheritance – **Exodus 20:15, Habakkuk,** unrelentingly lied under implied oath and on record – **Habakkuk 1:4.**

Yinka Bamgbelu: Hereditary RACIST pure white bastards (predominantly but not exclusively pure white) were not deterred by His Justice (**John 5:22**) because they did not believe in His exceptionalism - **John 14:6.**

BEDFORD, ENGLAND: Pure White Senior District Judge Paul Robert Ayers, our own NIGERIA (oil/gas) is by far more relevant to the economic survival of all your own mentally gentler white children (OECD) than TOMMY ROBINSON'S LUTON.

The Quality of human beings in your Country is very poor. Your Country is SHIT, and you are worse than SHIT.

"Sometimes people don't want to hear the truth because they don't want their illusions destroyed." Friedrich Nietzsche (1844-1900).

Karen Kwamboka: LATENT BUT VERY POTENT RACE WAR: AFRICA, NOT UKRAINE, NEEDS RUSSIA'S STOLEN BILLIONS.

Hereditary RACIST pure white bastards, direct descendants of THIEVES and owners of stolen children of defenceless poor AFRICANS should pay equitable, fair, and just reparation and settle several centuries of accruing interest.

Yinka Bamgbelu: Ignorant descendants of THIEVES: Gigantic yields of millions of stolen and destroyed lives decommissioned natural selection, reversed progressive evolution, and made it affordable for millions of IMBECILES to breed more millions of IMBECILES.

Karen Kwamboka: "Cultural erasure." President Trump.

Whose culture? Their culture whose entire foundation is RACIAL and FRAUD. Gigantic yields of several centuries of ancestral theft is the pillar on which their indiscreetly RACIST culture rests.

Yinka Bamgbelu: CULTURAL ERASURE: The erasure of unsustainable cultures fed like battery hens with yields of several centuries of ancestral theft, SLAVERY (Maafa, 1445-1888) is progressive.

Karen Kwamboka: Cultural erasure preceded by several decades of cultural decay. One of the huge gains of several centuries of STEALING and SLAVERY is that GERAINT EVANS, a functional semi-illiterate, crooked, and indiscreetly RACIST pure white Welsh bastard was paid the SALARY of the senior postgraduate Tutor, Oxford.

Yinka Bamgbelu: Cultural decay preceded cultural erasure. Then, in the Valleys, including in NICK GRIFFIN'S Llanerfyl Powys, there were scores of thousands of white pigs, white sheep, Welsh people and a few foreigners, and all the white pigs and white sheep, but not all Welsh people and foreigners, were incestuously conceived and, expectedly, all the white pigs and white sheep, but not all Welsh people and foreigners, were excessively stupid.

"There is no sin except stupidity." Wilde (1854-1900).

Karen Kwamboka: CULTURAL ERASURE: Their law is equal for Blacks and Whites, but its administration is not – **Habakkuk 1:4.** There is homogeneity in the administration of their law, and it is the impregnable secure mask of merciless RACIST EVIL, but there is no homogenous culture, and the motley assemblies of exotic cultures are FU*KED, irreparably FU*KED, as they have foreseeably succumbed to INCEST, weakening of their common genetic pool, and resultant physical and/or mental wonkiness, and hereditary white supremacist Freemason Senior Judges, and others, who make loads of money from unashamed mediocrity and confusion PROP SHIT UP – in pursuant of unfair ECONOMIC GAIN: Conflict interest.

"A government that robs Peter to pay Paul can always depend on the support of Paul." George Bernard Shaw (1856-1950).

Yinka Bamgbelu: "How Europe underdeveloped Africa." Dr Walter Rodney (1942-1980).

REVERSED ROBIN HOOD: Their decayed and erasing culture whose entire foundation is STEALING and sharing stolen money among IMBECILES – **Exodus 20:15, Habakkuk,** is unsustainable.

Karen Kwamboka: Paul Robert Ayers, the Senior Vice President of the Association of Her Majesty's District Judges, a closeted RACIST functional semi-illiterate crooked pure white imbecile, albeit our Senior District Judge in Bedford, and a crooked hereditary RACIST pure white bastard, you are RICH only because the pure white ancestors of your pure white mother and father were THIEVES – **Exodus 20:15, Habakkuk.**

Yinka Bamgbelu: RACIST ECONOMIC CANNIBALS: SLAVE-MERCHANTS MUTATED TO INSATIABLY GREEDY AFRICA'S NATURAL RESOURCES THIEVES – **EXODUS 20:15, HABAKKUK.** SUBSTITUTION IS FRAUDULENT EMANCIPATION

Karen Kwamboka: Ignorant hereditary RACIST pure white bastards desired everything in Europe, and they desired everything in AFRICA, so when SLAVERY (MAAFA, 1445-1888) became unprofitable, in 1884, insatiably greedy pure white bastard European Christians partitioned AFRICA and looted her – **Exodus 20:15, Habakkuk**.

Yinka Bamgbelu: Habakkuk 2:5: Pure white European Christians were greedier that the grave, and like death, hereditary RACIST pure white bastard THIEVES – **Exodus 20:15**, Evil Racist Murderers – **Exodus 20:13**, and owners of stolen children of defenceless poor people (AFRICANS), were never satisfied - **Habakkuk.**

Karen Kwamboka: RACISTS' ECONOMIC CANNIBALISM: EUROPE'S TRADE SURPLUS WITH AFRICA, 16th -19th CENTURY, >18 BILLION GOLD FRANCS

Yinka Bamgbelu: Hereditary RACIST pure white bastards want all NIGERIANS to be one-dimensionally educated BORN-AGAIN CHRISTIANS who have been systematically brainwashed to believe that FREEMASONS are the New Truly Good God - **Mark 10:18.**

Karen Kwamboka: Matthew 12:27: Reporting crooked pure white RACIST Freemason bastards to crooked pure white RACIST pure white bastard Freemason Judges - is akin to reporting DEVILS to DEMONS, an exercise in futility is a baren exercise.

Yinka Bamgbelu: BEDFORD, ENGLAND: GDC, Freemason, Brother Richard Hill fabricated reports and unrelentingly lied under oath – **Habakkuk 1:4.** Hereditary RACIST pure white bastards will investigate allegations of RACIAL HATRED against their own pure white kindred, and when they find they are based on TRUTHS, opportunist RACIST pure white bastards will criminally bury RACIST EVIL, secure in the knowledge that all Judges will be PURE WHITE and their hope is that they would be hereditary RACIST pure white bastards too – **Habakkuk 1:4**. No brain. Poor natural resources. Several continuous centuries of STEALING and SLAVERY preceded their huge stolen inheritance (gigantic yields of several continuous centuries of ancestral theft – **Exodus 20:15, Habakkuk**). Facts are sacred and cannot be overstated.

Karen Kwamboka: By 1800: Britain imported over £100 million in goods from AFRICA (equivalent to >$6 trillion in today's money), larger than GDP of >$3 trillion <$4trillion, in exchange for exported European made guns, bullets, and other implements of the commerce in STOLEN LIVES – **Habakkuk.**

Yinka Bamgbelu: 'Europe is being destroyed because leaders are weak.' President Trump

A RACIST son of a plebeian Scottish domestic servant, whose Scottish ancestors were neck-deep in SLAVERY, expect yields of transparent virtue to seamlessly replace gigantic yields of several centuries of ancestral theft – **Exodus 20:15, Habakkuk.**

Karen Kwamboka: President Trump, you are not a THIEF, but the direct Scottish ancestors of Mary Anne Macleod (1912-2000) were industrial scale PROFESSIONAL THIEVES - **Exodus 20:15, Habakkuk.** Scots were disproportionately active in the barbarously RACIST traffic in millions of stolen children of defenceless poor people, including the AFRICAN ancestors of the impure White (57% Caucasian European) and impure Black (43% Nigerian) Duchess of Sussex.

Yinka Bamgbelu: PRESIDENT TRUMP: A RACIST GENETIC SCOT.

"There are a few more impressive sights in the world than a Scotsman on the make." Sir James Matthew Barrie (1860 – 1937).

1800: Scots were >5% < 10% of Britain's population, but owned almost 50% of Jamaican plantations

1820: Scots owned close to 50% of SLAVES.

Karen Kwamboka: If RACIST PURE WHITE BASTARDS (predominantly but not exclusively pure white), TRUMP'S POODLES, are as brave as they vulgarly brag, they must DIRECTLY use overwhelming extreme violence to evict PUTIN from Crimea, he used extreme overwhelming violence to convert Avdiivka and Bakhmut from bricks to rubble and stole them – **Exodus 20:15**. A 5th Rate Military Force. A Fake Superpower. Delusional grandeur of the stolen past – **Habakkuk.** BULLIES: We (AFRICANS) and our type are the ones hereditary RACIST pure white bastards (predominantly but not exclusively PURE WHITE) would beat up without the support of the YANKS. Perception is grander than reality.

CHAPTER TWENTY-TWO

Yinka Bamgbelu: **Ecclesiastes 3:1-8.**

Now is the time to fight back against OPPORTUNIST RACIST pure white bastards – **Habakkuk 1:4.**

"Now it is time to stand up and fight back…There are no good crackers, and if you find one, kill him before he changes." Brother Khalid Abdul Mohammad (1948- 2001), West Chester University, PA, February 17, 1992.

Karen Kwamboka: Stealing from others what others stole from others is not stealing because robbing a robber yields of his robbery should not be stealing - **Exodus 20:15**. BEDFORD, ENGLAND: Pure White Senior District Judge Paul Robert Ayers, our own Senior Vice President of the Association of Her Majesty's District Judges, the pure white ancestors of your pure white father and mother were THIEVES and owners of stolen lives, including the African ancestors of our Mulatto Duchess of Sussex (impure White/impure Black, 43% Nigerian) – **Exodus 20:15, Habakkuk**. Facts are sacred and cannot be overstated.

Yinka Bamgbelu: Their ancestors were THIEVES - **Exodus 20:15, Habakkuk.** SLAVERY did not precede European civilisation, but it rebuilt everything it succeeded and paid for everything it preceded. Holland actively participated in MAAFA (1445-1888): Rembrandt (1603-1699) was born and died during SLAVERY. OYINBO OLE.

Karen Kwamboka: Vincent van Gogh (1853-1890): His ancestors were PROFESSIONAL THIEVES – **Exodus 20:15**, Racist Murderers – **Exodus 20:13,** and owners of stolen children of defenceless poor people (AFRICANS), and all his patrons were merchants of stolen lives and/or millions of those who benefited directly or indirectly in the extortionately profitable evil commerce in carrying and selling millions of stolen children of defenceless poor people (AFRICANS) – **Habakkuk.**

"The truth allows no choice." Dr Samuel Johnson (1709-1784).

Yinka Bamgbelu: Millions of stolen children of defenceless poor people (AFRICANS) were forcibly and criminally transported, across the Atlantic, by pure white European Christians, from 1445-1888 (MAAFA), with profits of RACIST CRIMINALITY (God's Law – **Exodus 20:13, Exodus 20:15**) fuelling European Golden Age.

Karen Kwamboka: "The fact is, that civilisation requires slaves. The Greeks were quite right there. Unless there are slaves to do the ugly, horrible, uninteresting work, culture and contemplation become almost impossible...." Wilde (1854-1900).

OYINBO OLE: RACIST DESCENDANTS OF THIEVES – **EXODUS 20:15, HABAKKUK.**

Yinka Bamgbelu: New Herod. **Matthew 2:16:** Hereditary RACIST pure white bastards see molecules and destroy all SELF-EDUCATED NIGERIANS, from shit hole Africa, who see quarks.

OXFORD, ENGLAND: GDC, A Mere DMF, Mrs Helen Falcon, MBE, Member of the Most Excellent Order of our Empire of Stolen Inheritance - **Exodus 20:15, Habakkuk.**

Karen Kwamboka: Mrs Helen Falcon, MBE: Our crooked, hereditary RACIST, and homunculus RACIST COUGAR of our own Empire of Stolen inheritance. A DISHONEST typical pure white ugly British Cougar (a libido killer). If one's skin colour is SUPERIOR, but if one's intellect is not, and if the ancestors of one's mother and father were THIEVES, Racist Killers, and owners of stolen children of defenceless poor people (AFRICANS), it is plainly deductible that Freedom of Expression is not one's friend.

Yinka Bamgbelu: Hereditary RACIST pure white bastards (predominantly but not exclusively pure white) LIED to their own mentally gentler WHITE CHILDREN (OECD) and the pure white imbeciles they shepherd (predominantly but not exclusively pure white) that they are ULTRA-RIGHTEOUS GENIUSES, highly civilised, and super-enlightened, and they do everything legally: Ruled Based Procedures, Precedent, Statute Etcetera, including RACIAL HATRED and FRAUD – **Habakkuk 1:4.** OYINBO OLE: They hate us, and we know. They destroy all SELF-EDUCATED NIGERIANS who know that they are brainless hereditary RACIST pure white bastards.

Karen Kwamboka: Their irreparably CORRUPT Fish and Chips Justice System is overseen by the BUILDERS for the benefit of IMBECILES.

New Herod, **Matthew 14:** John was Jailed only because he spoke, and the intolerant LUNATIC JEW removed his head solely to prevent him from speaking.

"Freedom of Expression is the cornerstone of our democracy." Lord Rees-Mogg

Yinka Bamgbelu: BEDFORD, ENGLAND: Pure White Senior District Judge Paul Robert Ayers, our own Senior Vice President of the Association of Her Majesty's District Judges, it is ABSOLUTELY IMPOSSIBLE for you and all your pure white type, including Mrs Helen Falcon (MBE), to COMPETE on a colour-blind level intellectual playing field without resorting to RACIST CRIMINALITY. Your country is SHIT. You are worse than SHIT - **Habakkuk 1:4.** You are worthy ONLY because you are pure white. You are relatively RICH only because the pure white ancestors of your own pure white father and mother were THIEVES – **Exodus 20:15**, extremely nasty and merciless RACIST KILLERS – **Exodus 20:13**, and owners of stolen children of defenceless people (AFRICANS) – **Habakkuk.**

"Find the truth and tell it." Harold Pinter (1930-2008).

Karen Kwamboka: Our IMBECILE Freemason Senior Judge of our Empire of Stolen Inheritance - **Exodus 20:15, Habakkuk**. BEDFORD, ENGLAND: District Judge, if you could disprove the TRUTH, which is that your own pure white kindred, Mrs Helen Falcon, MBE, unrelentingly lied under oath and on record – **Habakkuk 1:4,** you will concomitantly disprove the TRUTH, which is that you and your pure white type, including Mrs Helen Falcon (MBE) – are not INFERIOR creations of Almighty God. They are bastard RACIST BULLIES. They hate us, and we know. Everything about them is SUPERIOR except their intellect.

Yinka Bamgbelu: Proverbs 9:10, Proverbs 31:30: Sincerity is a prime attribute of CHRIST. Modesty is subservient to sincerity, so sincere immodesty is sincerer than insincere Modesty.

Karen Kwamboka: 1976-2022: A brainless hereditary RACIST pure white bastard; a properly schooled impostor, an expert of deception, and a waste of money fake Senior District Judge. Poly-educated pure white RUBBISH. He should stay here; it is safer than NIGERIA – **Exodus 21:23-27.**

Yinka Bamgbelu: TRUTHS disfavour hereditary RACIST pure white bastards (predominantly but not exclusively pure white), so they subjugate them. For their indiscreetly crooked, unashamedly MEDIOCRE, vindictive, potently weaponised, and institutionally RACIST Fish and Chips Justice to work as designed, they must be SUPERIOR, but they are not, so to conceal TRUTHS and to save face, hereditary RACIST pure white bastards resort to RACIST CRIMINALITY, secure in the knowledge that all Judges will be pure white and their hope is that they would be hereditary RACIST pure white bastards too. No brain. Poor natural resources. Several centuries of stealing and slavery preceded their huge stolen inheritance (gigantic yields of several centuries of ancestral theft – **Exodus 20:15, Habakkuk).** Ignorant hereditary RACIST pure white bastards were granted the platform to display hereditary prejudice.

Karen Kwamboka: "We won't die for Ukraine." French Protesters.

Gambari pa Fulani, Hausa ni Hausa nje.

If pure white people believe that their own pure white kindred are not worth dying for, why should NIGERIAN descendants of SLAVES and/or victims of several centuries of RACIST ECONOMIC CANNIBALISM fight and die in Pure White People's War in Eastern Europe, constructively in pursuant of the continuing propagation of the PHILOSOPHY that treats one RACE superior and BLACKS inferior-Bob Marley (1945-1981)?

Yinka Bamgbelu: There is no law in their Godforsaken RACIST HELL HOLE; their law is what FREEMASONS want, absolutely everything else is DECEIT. One rule for Pure Whites, a different rule for NIGERIANS. OXFORD, ENGLAND: GDC, Pure White British Soldier, Stephanie Twidale (TD) unrelentingly lied under oath and record – **Habakkuk 1:4**. Constance Briscoe was JAILED for a lesser offence. "British Justice is RACIST must not be trusted by BLACKS." Peter Herbert (OBE).

Karen Kwamboka: RACIST BASTARDS love fighting and AFRICANS are their preferred opponents: Imagbon, 1892. If hereditary RACIST pure white bastards are as brave as they vulgarly brag, they must DIRECTLY use violence to evict PUTIN FROM CRIMEA. Flat track bullies. Trump's poodles. A 5th Rate Military Power impersonates a SUPERPOWER: Delusional grandeur of the Stolen Past – **Exodus 20:15, Habakkuk.**

Yinka Bamgbelu: Their Country is SHIT. They are worse than SHIT.

Some Judges have body odour.

"Britons stank." W.S.

Wole Soyinka, not William Shakespeare (1564-1616), should know because at least one of his wives was a Briton, and some of his concubines were also Britons.

Karen Kwamboka: Romans, 55BC, and Normans, 1066, stole from others what others stole from others.

"It was in 1066 that William the Conqueror occupied Britain, stole our land, and gained control of it by granting it to his Norman friends, thus the feudal system that we have not yet fully escaped." Tony Benn (1925-2014).

No one is good, not even one – **Psalm 53.**

Yinka Bamgbelu: Motivated by uncontrollable inter-racial envy and hereditary RACIAL HATRED, our misfortunes, nearly all, are intelligently designed by hereditary white supremacist members of the Freemasonry Quasi-Religion (Mediocre Mafia).

BEDFORD, ENGLAND: GDC, Freemason, Brother Richard William fabricated reports and unrelentingly lied under oath and on record – Habakkuk 1:4. Had he been Black, he would have been in trouble. Constance Briscoe was JAILED for a lesser offence.

Karen Kwamboka: How come Judges, nearly all, are pure white, and how come pure white Judges, nearly all, are UGLY?

President Trump implied that pure white people are the smartest: "We shall forge a colour-blind society based on merit."

"Trump's administration packed courts with mediocre pure white Judges." Kamala Harris paraphrased

Yinka Bamgbelu: In a direct open dialogue with Justice Ruth Bader Ginsburg (1933-2020), Lady Hale lamented funding. My Lady, what is the value of several layers of unashamed mediocrity and confusion?

In our own NIGERIA, a properly proof-read and approved Judgement by a properly educated NIGERIAN JUDGE must pass through several separate filters, including the transcript writers, the proof-readers, the court clerks, and the Judge.

Karen Kwamboka: Based on contacts, the Pure White Senior District Judge stank; he had a distinct body odour.

BEDFORD, ENGLAND: Pure White Senior District Judge Paul Robert Ayers, our own Senior Vice President of the Association of Her Majesty's District Judges, I was brought up to look down on you and your pure white type, but I don't. I am the product of my upbringing, but I am not responsible for it.

"The blame is his who chooses. God is blameless." Plato

Yinka Bamgbelu: "Lammy refuses to budge on jury trials." News

Their Fish and Chips Justice System that was created and sustained with yields of STEALING (Slavery and Colonisation) cannot be sustained with yields of virtue because STEALING is by far more efficient than honest work.

Karen Kwamboka: Tony Benn (1925-2014), a Quasi-Communist Multi-Millionaire son of a very, very RICH hereditary Viscount (Mark 10:25) - implied that he was a pure genetic Briton because he did not know the real names of his ancestors, where they came from, and when?

Yinka Bamgbelu: Saxe-Coburg, and Gotha family, genetic Germans, arbitrarily acquired a camouflage English name in 1917.

Karen Kwamboka: Gustav Leibson (1876-1947), a LATVIAN JEW, arbitrarily acquired a camouflage English name in 1925, and had he not, NIGEL LAWSON (1932-2023) would not have been our Chancellor Exchequer.

Yinka Bamgbelu: The real name of Ghislaine Maxwell's Dad was Ján Ludvík Hyman Binyamin Hoch (1923-1991), the Czechoslovakian Jew arbitrarily acquired a camouflage British identity in 1940.

Karen Kwamboka: BEDFORD, ENGLAND: Pure White Senior District Judge Paul Robert Ayers, our own Senior Vice President of the Association of Her Majesty's District Judges, what is the real name of your pure white father, where did he come from and when, and when did he arbitrarily acquire a camouflage English name? Or did the pure white ancestors of your pure white father and mother evolve from MAMI WATA?

Yinka Bamgbelu: A brainless hereditary RACIST pure white bastard. What do you have? You do not have anything that is the yield of transparent virtue. The pure white ancestors of your pure white mother and father were THIEVES. It is absolutely impossible for your Christ-granted talent to sustain your high standard of living, and unlike PUTIN'S RUSSIA, there are no oil wells or gas fields in bland, colourless, and almost lifeless Tommy Robinsons' LUTON and where the pure white mother and father of Bedford's District Judge were born. No brain. Poor natural resources. Several continuous centuries of stealing and slavery preceded their huge stolen inheritance (gigantic yields of several centuries of ancestral theft – **Habakkuk, Exodus 20:15**). Facts are sacred and cannot be overstated.

Karen Kwamboka: Flat track bullies of Africans, and insatiably greedy looters of AFRICA – **Habakkuk 2:5.** White supremacist descendants of PURE WHITE

THIEVES, very greedy European Economic Cannibals who carried and sold millions of stolen African children(Maafa,1445-1888),and partitioned AFRICA (1884) and looted her, should evict the YANKS from NATO, admit UKRAINE into EU and NATO, and invoke Article 5; everything else is PURIFIED BLUFF and a bloody waste of lives – **Exodus 20:13.**

Yinka Bamgbelu: CAMOUFLAGE ENGLISH NAMES, INSTRUMENTS OF ECONOMIC SURVIVAL.

Michael Portillo, Mohammed Al Fayed (1929-2023), and Ali Kemal (1867-1922) did not arbitrarily acquire camouflage English names. Had Ali Kemal been as rich as Mohammed Al Fayed, BORIS JOHNSON would have been Mohammed Ali, and Britons would not have appointed Mohammed as their Premier.

Karen Kwamboka: BEDFORD, ENGLAND: Pure White Senior District Judge Paul Robert Ayers, our own Senior Vice President of the Association of Her Majesty's District Judges, what is the real name of your own pure white father, where did he come from, when, and when did he arbitrarily acquire a camouflage English name? Or did your pure white RACIST ancestors evolve from MAMI WATA in the River Great Ouse?

Yinka Bamgbelu: Pure White Senior Bedford's District Judge Paul Robert Ayers, our own Senior Vice President of the Association of Her Majesty's District Judges, let me tell you, the pure white ancestors of your pure white father and mother were THIEVES, and a civilisation based on robbing poor people and using STOLEN money to facilitate the breeding of millions of IMBECILES is not sustainable.

Karen Kwamboka: "The rulers of the state are the only persons who ought to have the privilege of lying, either at home or abroad; they may be allowed to lie for the good of the state." Plat

Sir Charles Phillip Haddon-Cave (1925-1999), Hereditary White Supremacist Oxbridge-educated Colonialist Economic Cannibal, and a very rich man's son (Mark 10:25): Negroes, I admit that our barbarously RACIST EVIL traffic in millions of stolen children of defenceless poor people (AFRICANS) reversed AFRICA and AFRICANS, and I also agree that continuing Neo-Colonialism is a variant of SLAVERY, but Colonisation was mutually beneficial for the Natives and Pure White European Christians (EUROPEAN POWERS).

Yinka Bamgbelu: It is not the TRUTH that African Slaves and their descendants were granted equality under the English Law after the 1807 Act: OYINBO OLE/ODE.

Judges that we may report RACIST EVIL to are RACIST BASTARDS too – **Habakkuk 1:4.**

All semi-illiterate pure white FREEMASON JUDGES in Great Britain are RACISTS

Karen Kwamboka: It is plainly deductible that the pure white ancestors of the pure white father and mother of King's School and Oxbridge-educated rich man's son **(Mark 10:25)**, albeit England's Class Lord Justice, KC, were THIEVES – **Exodus 20:15**, insatiably greedy racist pure white bastards – who were greedier than the grave, and like death, the sadistically RACIST evil pure white bastards were never satisfied – **Habakkuk 2:5**, and they were VICIOUS RACIST KILLERS – **Exodus 20:13** – who were not deterred by His Justice (**John 5:22**) because the blood thirty crude and cruel evil pure white RACIST BASTARDS did not believe in His exceptionalism – **John 14:6**, and the sadistic savages were owners of stolen children of defenceless poor people (AFRICANS), including the pure Black Africa ancestors of the IMPURE (<43% Nigerian) great grandchildren of the Duke of Edinburgh of Blessed Memory, Prince Phillip (1921-2021).

Philippians 1:21: Phillip was a 33rd Degree Freemason (Scottish Rite).

Sir Charles Phillip Haddon-Cave (1925-1999), Hereditary White Supremacist Oxbridge-educated Colonialist Economic Cannibal, and a very rich man's son (Mark 10:25): What are you talking about, Negro? Why should anyone perceive a mere Negro, from shit hole Africa, as existentially threatening?

Karen Kwamboka: Because we know secrets their mentally gentler white children (OECD) and the pure white IMBECILES (predominantly but not exclusively pure white) they shepherd, must not know.

TWENTY-THREE

Sir Charles Phillip Haddon-Cave (1925-1999), Hereditary White Supremacist Oxbridge-educated Colonialist Economic Cannibal, and a very rich man's son (Mark 10:25): Secrets! Personal Secrets or State's Secrets? When I was the Colonial Governor of Hong Kong, like President Thomas Jefferson, I feared no TRUTH, and there was no TRUTH known to God that I used my privileged position to conceal from the YELLOW PEOPLE that I ruled.

Karen Kwamboka: Sir, all Racist descendants of ultra-righteous pure white THIEVES – **Exodus 20:15,** Merciless Racist Murderers – **Exodus 20:13,** and owners of stolen children of defenceless poor people (AFRICANS), are BASTARDS: No one is good, no even one – **Psalm 53.** Hereditary RACIST pure white bastards (predominantly but not exclusively pure white) tell incompetent RACIST LIES all the time, but they lie that they don't lie – **Psalm 144.**

"Lies are told all the time." Oxbridge-educated rich man's son (**Mark 10:25**), Sir Robert Michael Havers (1923-1992), Attorney General, 1980.

Psalm 116:11: Like all Judges, all Presidents are LIARS; they tell lies all the time, albeit selflessly in pursuant of the continuing propagation of imbeciles (adults with the basic skills of a child).

Yinka Bamgbelu: The pure white ancestors of King's School and Oxbridge-educated very rich man's son (**Mark 10:25**), Lord Justice Charles Anthony Haddon-Cave, KC, a very hardened indiscreet RACIST first son of Tasmania University, and Oxbridge, educated, Sir Charles Phillip Haddon-Cave (1925-1999), an insatiably greedy Colonialist Economic Cannibal, a grandson of Francis Haddon-Cave, born in Hobart in early 20th-century Australian settlement, a descendant of opium merchants of the Qing Dynasty (Opium War, 1839-1842), and a descendant armed land grabbers (THIEVES -**Exodus 20:15**), and genocidal evil RACIST pure white bastards who directly and indirectly caused the death of > 90% of Native Tasmanians, including children (Black Wars, 1827-1832) – RACIST MURDERERS – **Exodus 20:13**, mass emigrated to TASMANIA - uninvited; the Evil Racist Pure White Genocidal Bastards directly and indirectly killed almost all the Native Tasmanians - through imported diseases, over work, and violent land grab: The Palawa people were ethnically cleansed by evil racist pure white genocidal bastards - **Exodus 20:13.**

"Those who know the least obey the best." George Farqhar (1677-1707).

Karen Kwamboka: Sir Charles Phillip Haddon-Cave (1925-1999), Hereditary White Supremacist Oxbridge-educated Colonialist Economic Cannibal, and a very rich man's son (Mark 10:25), the pure white ancestors of your pure white father and mother were PROFESSIONAL THIEVES – **Exodus 20:15, Habakkuk.**

Yinka Bamgbelu: There will be an inevitable erasure of the culture that was built with yields of millions of stolen and destroyed lives of children of defenceless poor people (AFRICANS) because it cannot be sustained by yields of transparent virtue.

"Pardon him Theodotus: He is a barbarian and thinks that the culture of his tribe and Island are the laws of nature." George Bernard Shaw (1856-1950).

Karen Kwamboka: Their Country is SHIT, and they are worse than SHIT. Based on several decades of very proximate observations and direct experiences, the Quality of Human Beings, including Judges, in their Country is very poor (OECD).

Homogeneity in the administration of their law is a potent weapon of race war.

"Trump's administration packed courts with white Judges." Kamala Harris

"The 99% of the meetings I go to, I am the only non-white person in the room. But why are we so surprised when most of the senior positions in Scotland are filled exclusively by people who are White. Take my Portfolio alone, the Lord President, White. The Lord Justice Clerk, White. Every High Court Judge, White. The Lord Advocate, White. The Solicitor General, White. The Chief Constable, White. Every Deputy Chief Constable, White. Every Assistant Chief Constable, White. The head of the Law Society, White. The head of the faculty of advocates, White. Every Prison Governor, White. Not just Justice, the Chief Medical Officer, White. The Chief Nursing Officer, White. The Chief Veterinary Officer, White. The Chief Social Work Adviser, White. Almost every trade union in this country is headed by people who are White. In the Scottish Government, every director general is White, and every chair of every public body is White." A former Scottish First Minister.

Yinka Bamgbelu: They talk rot, and all the time. The entire foundation of their civilisation is STEALING and SHARING stolen money among pure white

IMBECILES. In 1833, Evil Racist Bastards shared billions of pounds (today's money) among scores of thousands of merchants of stolen lives.

Karen Kwamboka: "An immediate increase in the birth rate is needed." Elon Musk

The fellow, a weirdo, should donate sperm, and 14 could become 14,000, 000, 000; he can afford to feed them.

In 1833, greedy RACIST pure white bastards shared yields on stolen lives, about 50% of the Annual Budget, in exchange for freeing only about one million stolen Africans; many of the RACIST BASTARDS had interests in plantations in North America, where SLAVERY continued for several decades afterwards.

Yinka Bamgbelu: Charles Darwin (1809-1882) married his first cousin, and had ten, and not all of them were physically and/or mentally wonky. Why should Britons have babies they don't need and cannot afford? "An immediate increase in the birth rate is needed." Elon Musk

Karen Kwamboka: MASS MIGRATION IS THE BEST ANSWER: WHY FORCE EUROPEANS TO HAVE CHILDREN THEY DO NOT NEED AND/ OR CANNOT AFFORD?

"An immediate increase in the birth rate is needed." Elon Musk

Yinka Bamgbelu: "Competence and merit are among our greatest civilisational advantages ...We shall forge a colour-blind society based on merit." President Trump's National Security Strategy

Karen Kwamboka: Ignorant hereditary RACIST descendants of Pure White THIEVES. Their SHIT COUNTRY where a functional semi-illiterate pure white bastard was a Senior District Judge.

BEDFORD, ENGLAND: Pure White Senior District Judge Paul Robert Ayers, our own Senior Vice President of the Association of Her Majesty's District Judges, unlike PUTIN'S SIBERIA, there are no gas fields in John Foster's Brickhill, Freemasons' Kempston, and where your own pure white father and mother were born. No brain. Poor natural resources. Several centuries of stealing and slavery preceded their huge stolen inheritance (gigantic yields of several continuous centuries of ancestral theft – Maafa (1445-1888) – **Exodus 20:15, Habakkuk 2:6-9**.

Yinka Bamgbelu: TRUMP'S POODLES: "Continental Europe has been losing share of global GDP—down from 25 percent in 1990 to 14 percent today." President Trump's National Security Strategy

When the economic input of immigrant-workforce is subtracted, 14% will become < 9%. Descendants of THIEVES and owners of stolen lives should pay equitable, fair, and just reparation for SLAVERY, Colonisation, and continuing Neo-colonialism. Ignorant descendants of THIEVES – **Habakkuk 2: 6-9, Exodus 20:15.**

Karen Kwamboka: "Undermining of political liberty and sovereignty, mass migration, stifling of free speech, cratering birthrates, and loss of national identities and self-confidence." President Trump's National Security Strategy

Their RACIST CIVILISATION whose entire foundation is STEALING and SLAVERY is Antichrist and intellectually flawed. In 1833, insatiably greedy RACIST pure white bastards shared yields of millions of stolen and destroyed lives among scores of thousands of Merchants of Stolen Lives: OYINBO OLE/ ODE/BARAWO.

Yinka Bamgbelu: "Should merit be smothered, America's historic advantages in science, technology, industry, defence, and innovation will evaporate." President Trump's National Security Strategy, 2025.

If as they imply, it is the truth that they are superior creations of Almighty God, what do Pure White Racist Cretins (predominantly but not exclusively pure white) need RACIST CRIMINALITY for?

Karen Kwamboka: WHITE SUPREMACISTS' PROPAGANDA:

"Should competence be destroyed or systematically discouraged, complex systems that we take for granted—from infrastructure to national security to education and research—will cease to function." President Trump's National Security Strategy, 2025.

BRAINLESS, ELEMENTARY, AND SHALLOW NONSENSE!

"The supreme vice is shallowness." Wilde (1854-1900).

Yinka Bamgbelu: Slavery, segregation, apartheid, Colonisation, continuing Neo-Colonialism, etcetera, were not based on colour-blind merit: Pure white dominance desires a retrogressive atmosphere where substance is subservient to superfluous. The centuries-old unspoken myth that intellect is related to the universally acknowledged irrefutably superior skin colour that the very fortunate wearer neither made nor chose is the mother of all RACIST SCAMS.

Karen Kwamboka: BEDFORD, ENGLAND: Pure White Senior District Judge Paul Robert Ayers, our own Senior Vice President of the Association of Her Majesty's District Judges, you are a grossly overrated pure white rubbish. The most important part of the matter is MONEY, and it is not the yield of your land or talent. Unlike PUTIN'S SIBERIA, there are no gas fields where your own pure white father and mother were born. Our own MONEY, Nigeria (oil/gas) is by far more relevant to the economic survival of all your own mentally gentler white children (OECD), your own pure white mother, your pure white father, and your pure white spouse that Robert Hibbert (1769-1849) and Tommy Robinson's LUTON.

Yinka Bamgbelu: BEDFORD, ENGLAND: Pure White Senior District Judge Paul Robert Ayers, our own Senior Vice President of the Association of Her Majesty's District Judges, you have all the characteristics of the IMPUDENT FRUGAL SCOTTISH LEECH. Your pure white ancestors were THIEVES. You are worthy only because you are pure white, and you are RICH ONLY because for several centuries, the pure white ancestors were PROFESSIONAL THIEVES and owners of stolen lives.

"The impudence of an Irishman is the impudence of a fly, that buzzes about you, and you put it away, but it returns and flutters and teases you. The impudence of a Scotsman is the impudence of a leech, that fixes and sucks your blood." Dr Samuel Johnson (1709-1784).

Karen Kwamboka: "In our every principle and action, America and Americans must always come first." President Trump's National Security Strategy, 2025.

Pure White American Europeans must always come first, and absolutely everything else is DECEIT: The most 'plastic indiscreetly institutionally RACIST country' since before the beginning – **Genesis 1:3.**

Armed European Christians stole the land of Native Americans – **Exodus 20:15, Habakkuk 2:6-9.**

Yinka Bamgbelu: OYINBO OLE/ODE/BARAWO: "If aliens visit us, the outcome would be much as when Columbus landed in America, which didn't turn out well for the Native Americans." Stephen Hawking (1942-2018).

Insatiably Greedy Christian Alien Bastards, Armed European Christian THIEVES - **Exodus 20:15**, visited Africa too, and they are still there, and expectedly things did not turn out well for Africans.

"How Europe underdeveloped Africa." Dr Walter Rodney (1942-1980).

Karen Kwamboka: SEGREGATIONIST RACIST RITUALIST PURE WHITE FREEMASON BASTARDS:

Prince Hall Masons: Exclusion based solely on skin colour that the wearer neither made nor chose: Substance was subservient to superfluous; Apartheid by stealth.

Yinka Bamgbelu: They hate us, and we know. 1717: Their Racist Satanic Network emerged in the early 18th Century, at a height of European Christians' evil commerce in millions of stolen children of poor people, including the African ancestors of the QUASI-MULATTO, impure White/Impure Black/<43% Nigerian, niece and nephew of the Prince of Wales.

Karen Kwamboka: Antichrist Defenders of Faiths are Dissenters of the Faith - **John 14:6.**

Closeted Hereditary White Supremacist Bastards, Wolves in Sheep's Clothing: Innately Racist Ritualists constructively demand and accept Quasi-Protection Money (TITHE) from gullible Born-Again Christians through Churches of Christ.

Yinka Bamgbelu: Then, all Judges were pure white Freemasons, and most of them were thicker than a gross of planks.

Hereditary RACIST pure white bastards feel safer when all NIGERIANS, from shit hole Africa, are ignorant one-dimensionally educated Born-Again Christians who have been systematically brainwashed to believe that closeted white supremacist Freemason Bastards are the New Truly Good God – **Mark 10:18.**

Karen Kwamboka: Police Officers, and Judges of the Lowest Courts, including District Judges, are not recruited from the pool of the brightest people in any society.

"I emphasis the point." Pure White Senior Bedford's District Judge Paul Robert Ayers, our own Senior Vice President of the Association of Her Majesty's District Judges.

Poly-educated RACIST pure white bastard rubbish. Reckless gaffes and brainless Malapropism. An ignorant hereditary RACIST descendant of THIEVES and owners of stolen lives – **Exodus 21:23-27**. The opportunist RACIST pure white bastard should stay here; it is safer than NIGERIA.

"We shall deal with the racist bastards when we get out of prison." Comrade Robert Mugabe (1924-2019).

Yinka Bamgbelu: If the hereditary RACIST pure white bastard read his approved Judgement, he was a FOOL, and if he did not, he lied as he implied that he did - Habakkuk 1:4. The pure white ancestors of his pure white mother and father were incompetent RACIST LIARS TOO, they were THIEVES and owners of stolen children of defenceless poor people, including the African ancestors of the QUASI-MULATTO, impure White/impure Black/<43% Nigerian, grandniece and grandnephew of Major Andrew Mountbatten Windsor.

Karen Kwamboka: Brainless retrogressive hereditary RACIST pure white bastards arbitrarily created an artificial intellectual ceiling, and RACISTS self-awarded the monopoly of knowledge, and they stifled individual development and overall growth, and they dragged self-educated Nigerians, from shit hole Africa, down to their very low intellectual level. They hate us, and we know.

Yinka Bamgbelu: Reasoning and vision do not have finite boundaries. The fellow is who He says He is - **John 14:6**. The mind that the NIGERIAN, from shit hole Africa, did not choose is FINER than your indiscreetly crooked, VINDICTIVE, unashamedly mediocre, potently weaponised, and institutionally RACIST waste of money fish and chips JUSTICE SYSTEM, and he does not believe in any part of your SHIT, as no part of your SHIT is good, not even one – **Psalm 53,** and he has the overwhelming POWER to use cogent facts and irrefutable evidence to irreparably destroy you and every part of your SHIT. No brain. Poor natural resources. Several centuries of stealing and slavery preceded their huge stolen inheritance (gigantic yields of several continuous centuries of ancestral theft – Maafa, 1445-1888) **Exodus 20:15, Habakkuk 2:6-9**.

Karen Kwamboka: When the UKRAINIAN WAR inevitably ends, Europe, particularly Great Britain, would be greater losers than UKRAINE. European Fake Powers have been found out, and they have been immortally humiliated.

Africans were their preferred opponents. Their ancestors were the world champions at using GUNS to slaughter defenceless AFRICANS – **Exodus 20:13, Habakkuk 2:6-9.**

Yinka Bamgbelu: BEDFORD, ENGLAND: Pure White Senior District Judge Paul Robert Ayers, our own Senior Vice President of the Association of Her Majesty's District Judges, our brainless hereditary RACIST pure white bastard Senior Judge of our own Empire of Stolen Inheritance. The land on which he was born yields only FOOD, he is verifiably a functional semi-illiterate, he is RICH, and he dishonestly implied that he did not know that the pure white ancestors of his pure white mother and father were PROFESSIONAL THIEVES – **Exodus 20:15, Habakkuk 2:6-9**, extremely nasty RACIST KILLERS – **Exodus 20:13**, and owners of stolen children of defenceless poor people, including the African ancestors of the QUASI-MULATTO, impure White/impure Black/<43% Nigerian, great grandchildren of the Duke of Edinburgh of Blessed Memory, Prince Phillip (1921-2021).

Philippians 1:21: Phillip was a 33rd Degree Freemason, Scottish Rite.

Karen Kwamboka: CONFLICT OF INTEREST: Planted SHIT guards 'DEMO CRAZY': Under Apartheid, a pure white IMBECILE could vote, but MANDELA could not.

"We shall forge a colour-blind society based on merit." President Trump.

You fu*king can't have it both ways: The brightest talents – period.

"At the same time, we cannot allow meritocracy to be used as a justification to open America's labour market to the world in the name of finding "global talent" that undercuts American workers." President Trump's National Security Strategy, 2025

Karen Kwamboka: DELUSIONAL GRANDEUR OF THE STOLEN PAST - **EXODUS 20:15, HABAKKUK.**

A Deluded 5th Rate Military Power impersonates a SUPERPOWER.

Their Country is SHIT, and they are worse than SHIT, but they don't know. The Quality of Human Beings in their Godforsaken Racist Hell Hole, including some soldiers, is very poor (OECD).

OXFORD. ENGLAND: BDA/MPS/GDC/NHS, British Soldier, Stephanie Twidale (TD), unrelentingly lied under oath and on record - **Habakkuk 1:4**. Constance Briscoe was JAILED for a lesser offence.

Yinka Bamgbelu: President Trump, the Scottish ancestors of Mary Anne Macleod (1912-2000) were Racist Murderers, THIEVES, and owners of stolen children of defenceless poor people.

"Many Scots masters were considered among the most brutal, with life expectancy on their plantations averaging a mere four years. We worked them to death then simply imported more to keep the sugar and thus the money flowing. Unlike centuries of grief and murder, an apology cost nothing. So, what does Scotland have to say?" Herald Scotland: Ian Bell, 2013

Karen Kwamboka: **"**Who a country admits into its borders—in what numbers and from where—will inevitably define the future of that nation." President Trump's National Security Strategy, 2025.

Native Americans did not admit Armed European Christians, they forcibly admitted themselves.

Yinka Bamgbelu: Ignorant descendants of THIEVES - Habakkuk, **Exodus 20:15**, and beneficiaries barbarously RACIST mass migration of millions of stolen AFRICAN CHILDREN, including the ancestors of MULATTO (impure White/impure Black/43% Nigerian) Duchess of Sussex.

Karen Kwamboka: RACIST BASTARDS DO RACIAL HATRED, AND THEY CALL INDISCREET RACIST EVIL IMPARTIAL COLOUR-BLIND LAW

There is no LAW is their Godforsaken RACIST HELL HOLE; their Law is what hereditary white supremacist Freemason bastards want.

Skin colour that they neither made nor chose is universally acknowledged to be irrefutably superior, and their accent when speaking their own language is more superior, but their intellects are not, and their indiscreetly crooked, VINDICTIVE, unashamedly mediocre, potently weaponised, and institutionally RACIST waste of money fish and chips Justice System is fundamentally designed to conceal that truth – **Habakkuk 1:4**

Yinka Bamgbelu: Then, evil, racist, pure white European Christians, and insatiably greedy bastards, benefitted from involuntary mass migration of millions of stolen children of defenceless poor people (AFRICANS) – at gunpoint. They don't want to pay equitable, fair, and just REPARATION, and they do not want mass migration. Greedy bastards eat their own cakes, eat ours, and have everything: No brain. Poor natural resources. Several centuries of stealing and slavery preceded their huge stolen inheritance – **Exodus 20:15, Habakkuk.**

Karen Kwamboka: Habakkuk 2:5: Based on available evidence, they are greedier than the grave, and like death evil RACIST pure white bastards (predominantly but not exclusively pure white) CAN NEVER be satisfied: OYINBO OLE – **Exodus 20:15.**

Yinka Bamgbelu: They are brainless hereditary RACIST pure white bastards (predominantly but not exclusively pure white), and they know that we know, and they resort to RACIST CRIMINALITY to conceal truths. They oversee the administration of their law, and they use unbounded and accountable powers to oppress self-educated Nigerians, from shit hole Africa, who beat their type at every stratum of formal education. They hate us, and we know.

CHAPTER TWENTY-FOUR

Karen Kwamboka: Whenever our own King, the true Defender of our own Faith, only our own Faith, the Faith—**John 14:6**, not President Trump, gives us the wink, we shall deal with the hereditary Pure White supremacist Freemason Segregationist Cultist bastards (not Prince Hall's Masons), and we shall use only the sword of truth, not Jonathan Aitken's, but the Divine Sword of transparent truth that is aligned to the Divine Exceptionalism and Exclusivity of Christ (**John 14:6**), to uncover and irreversibly destroy their centuries-old, crooked, closeted hereditary white supremacist, vulgarly charitable (**Matthew 6:2-4**), and Antichrist SATANIC MUMBO JUMBO, and we are prepared to perish in the process: Mediocre Mafia, Experts of their Law (New Pharisees), **Luke 11:52,** New Good Samaritans (**Luke 10:25–37),** New Good Shepherd **(John 10:11–18**), New Truly Good God **(Mark 10:18**): Relatively Very, very, very Rich (**Mark 10:25**), Deluded, conceited, shallow and narrow half-educated school dropouts, and MF, and their superiors who have informal access to some very, very, very, very, very, very, powerful FREEMASON JUDGES, and wear vulgar pharisees' charitable works as cloaks of deceit – **Matthew 6:2-4**, and use very, very, very, expensive colourful aprons, with vulgar embroideries, to decorate the temples of their powerless and useless fertility tools, and lie that they don't lie—**Psalm 144,** and they deceive their own mentally gentler children (OECD) and the pure white imbeciles they shepherd (predominantly but not exclusively pure white) that only they and God Almighty are truly good—**Mark 10:18**, integrity, friendship, respect and charity—all for one, and one for all—**Habakkuk 1:4**, Defenders of Faiths, including all the motley assemblies of exotic faiths and religions associated with the 15 Holy Books in the House of Commons, and Dissenters of the Faith—**John 14:6**).

Yinka Bamgbelu: The New Pharisees, Fake Experts of their Indiscreetly Institutionally Racist Law (**Luke 11:52**): It is absolutely impossible for pure white supremacist King's School and Oxbridge educated very, very, very, very, very, very, very, very, very, rich man's son (**Mark 10:25**), Lord Justice Charles Anthony Haddon-Cave, King's Counsel (KC), KBE, a Racist first son of a very, very, very, rich Oxbridge-educated Tasmanian Colonialist Economic Cannibal, and a grandson of Francis Haddon-Cave, born in Hobart in early 20th-century Australian settlement, and a hereditary white supremacist descendant of DRUG LORDS (opium, merchants of the Qing Dynasty), and alleged 33rd

Freemason (Scottish Rite), and his homie, Eton and Oxbridge-educated very, very, very, rich men's son, Archbishop Justin Welby (**Mark 10:25**), and all the Closeted Hereditary White Supremacist Freemason Judges in Great Britain, and all the Freemasons at the Masonic Hall, New York City, 71 W 23rd Street #1003, New York, NY 10010, United States, and all the Freemasons at Clifton Masonic Hall, 1496 Van Houten Avenue, Clifton, NJ 07013, United States, and all the Freemasons at The House of the Temple, 1733 16th Street NW Town or City Washington, D.C, United States, and all the Freemasons at the Masonic Lodge, Holly Wood Forever Cemetery, 5970 Santa Monica Boulevard, Los Angeles, CA 90038, United States, and all the 33rd Degree Freemasons at the Masonic Hall, Rising Sun, 1 Mill Road, Wellingborough NN8 1PE, and all the Freemasons at the Acacia Rooms, 27 Rockingham Road, Corby NN17 1AD, and all the Freemasons at Hotspur Lodge №1626, Fern Avenue Masonic Hall, 75–83 Fern Avenue, Jesmond, Newcastle upon Tyne NE2 2RA, and all the Freemasons at King's College School Lodge, Southside Common, London SW19 4TT, and all the members of the Bedfordshire Masonic Centre, the Keep, Bedford Road, Kempston, MK42 8AH, and all the members of Freemasons' Hall, Sheaf Close, Northampton NN5 7UL, and all the members of Towcester Masonic Centre, Northampton Road, Towcester, NN12 6LD, Northamptonshire, and all the 33rd Degree Freemasons (Scottish Rite) at Freemasons' Hall, 96 George Street, Edinburgh EH2 3DH, and all the 33rd Degree Freemasons (Scottish Rite) at the Provincial Lodge of Glasgow, 54 Berkeley Street, Glasgow G3 7DS, all the 33rd Degree Masons (Scottish Rite), at the Mother Temple, the Grand Masonic Lodge, 60 Great Queen St, London WC2B 5AZ, to disprove the truth, which is that UN Experts told the TRUTH when they corroborated Sir, Sadiq Khan, KBE, the Mayor of London's public declaration that RACIAL HATRED is rife throughout most organisations across Britain: "Africans in Great Britain are the subject of structural, institutional, and systemic racism"—UN, and they will not disprove the truth, which is that AI recklessly and incompetently lied on record (immortal mendacity), and they will not disprove the truth, which is that our own Mediocre, Physically Ill-Favoured, and Mentally Wonky, Pure White Hereditary Racist, unashamedly functionally semi-illiterate, poly-educated poor man's son, a downmarket former debt-collector Solicitor in bland and colourless Norfolk/Norwich, (Coastal Dole/the Departure Lounge of Life), a mere lowlife 5th Rate Partner, and the Senior Vice President of the Association of Her Majesty's District Judges, Bedford's District Judge Paul Robert Ayers, 3, St Paul's Square, MK 40 1SQ, maliciously lied or he was recklessly confused (Alzheimer's disease/Atypical Dementia) when he explicitly stated that the name of the Defendant on the approved Judgement is the name of the Defendant in the hearings before the approved Judgement, and Senior Judge, albeit England's Class, further maliciously lied or he was pathologically recklessly confused (Alzheimer's disease/Dementia), when he explicitly stated that the NIGERIAN, from shithole Africa, was invited to, and took part in, a hearing at Bedford County Court, May House, 29, Goldington Road, Bedford, MK40 3NN, on Monday, 1st July 2013, and they cannot disprove the truth, which is that Pure White Victoria Harrison, NHS Consultant, Northamptonshire PCT, unrelentingly lied under implied oath and/or record—**Habakkuk 1:4**, or she was pathologically confused (Alzheimer's disease/Atypical Dementia), and they shan't disprove the truth, which is that OXFORD, ENGLAND: NHS/GDCD/MPS/BDA, Pure White British Soldier, Territorial Defence, Stephanie Twidale (TD), unrelentingly lied under oath and on record—**Habakkuk 1:4**, and they cannot disprove the truth, which is that Pure White Kevin Atkinson, dentist, Scottish Kev, Sterling Kev, Morcott Parish Councillor, alleged Freemason, and England's Class Scottish Postgraduate Tutor, Oxford, unrelentingly LIED under oath and on record—**Habakkuk 1:4**, and they will never disprove the truth, which is that GDC/NHS, Freemason, Brother, Richard William Hill (NHS Postgraduate Tutor), fabricated reports and unrelentingly lied under oath and on record—**Habakkuk 1:4,** a very, very, dishonest white man, a closeted hereditary white supremacist NHS Postgraduate Tutor of our Empire of Stolen Inheritance—**Habakkuk,** and they will never be able to use cogent facts and irrefutable evidence to support the belief of all vulgarly charitable, Antichrist, and hereditary racist Pure White Freemasons (not Prince Hall) in the world, which is that very, very, very, vulgarly Charitable, Antichrist, and hereditary White Supremacist Freemasonry Quasi-Religion (Mediocre Mafia, New Pharisees **(Luke 11:52**), New Good Samaritans (**Luke 10: 25–37**), New Good Shepherd (**John 10: 11- 18**), New God (conceited and deluded White Supremacist bastards believe that only they and Almighty God are truly good—**Mark 10:18)**, Defenders of Faiths, including all the motley assemblies of exotic faiths and religions associated with the 15 Holy Books in the House of Commons, and Dissenters of the Faith—**John 14:6) -** is not an intellectually flawed SATANIC MUMBO JUMBO—centuries-old closeted hereditary white supremacists' scam, and they will not prove the belief of Dissenters of the Faith **(John 14:6),** which is that reasoning and vision have finite boundaries. If reasoning and vision have finite boundaries, the fellow must have LIED, in the Council, before Romans and Jews, when He, purportedly, disclosed pictures His unbounded painted, and He must have also lied when He audaciously stated that He was Divinely Extraordinarily Exceptional—**John**

14:6. If the fellow told Jews and Gentiles the truth—in the Council, we are all FORKED, as His Knights attack all Kings and Queens simultaneously, and only Queens can escape, and everything that is not aligned to the exceptionalism of the Christ **(John 14:6)**—is irreversibly doomed and heading straight for the ROCKS.

Karen Kwamboka: Ignorant hereditary RACIST pure white bastards (predominantly but not exclusively pure white), and ultra-righteous descents of Racists, thieves, and owners of stolen lives. "It does no harm to throw the occasional man overboard, but it does not do much good if you are steering full speed ahead for the rocks." Sir Ian Gilmour (1926–2007), Queen's Counsel (QC), Eton, and Oxford-educated rich man's son (**Mark 10:25**).

Yinka Bamgbelu: "Sorry, I am a free speech absolutist." Elon Musk.

BEDFORD, ENGLAND: Pure White Senior District Judge Paul Robert Ayers, the pure white ancestors of your pure white father and mother were PROFESSIONAL THIEVES – Habakkuk 2:6-9, Exodus 20:15: Extremely nasty and merciless evil RACIST KILLERS - Exodus 20:13, nastier than Yevgeny Prigozhin (1961-2023) and Hitler (1889-1945), and just by the by, several years of NAZI HOLOCAUST (1939-1945), was a mere storm in a teacup in comparison to several continuous centuries of BLACK HOLOCAUST – Maafa (1445-1888). An ignorant one-dimensionally educated descendant of armed robbers, armed land grabbers, gun runners, drug dealers (opium merchants), and owners of stolen children of defenceless poor people, including the African ancestors of the QUASI-MULATTO, impure White/impure Black/<43% Nigerian, grandniece and grandnephew of the Duke of York.

Karen Kwamboka: Our own IMBECILE Freemason Senior Judge of our own Empire of Stolen Inheritance – **Exodus 20:15, Habakkuk 2:6-9:** "It is incumbent upon the court and all those professionals involved to conclude court proceedings as quickly as possible. This hopefully ensures that a child has stability, love and affection and the parents working together to ensure that he has the best opportunity of developing academically and emotional." Pure White Senior District Judge Paul Robert Ayers, our own Senior Vice President of the Association of Her Majesty's District Judges – proofed and approved judgement.

****

Case No: 2YL06820
Bedford County Court
May House
29 Goldington Road
Bedford
MK40 3NN
Monday, 1st July 2013

B E F O R E:

DISTRICT JUDGE AYERS

DOBERN PROPERTY LIMITED

(Claimants)

v.

DR. ABIODUN OLA BAMGBELU

(Defendant)

-

Transcript from an Official Court Tape Recording.
Transcript prepared by:
MK Transcribing Services
29 The Concourse, Brunel Business Centre,
Bletchley, Milton Keynes, MK2 2ES
Tel: 01908-640067 Fax: 01908-365958
DX 100031 Bletchley
Official Court Tape Transcribers.

MR. PURKIS appeared on behalf of THE CLAIMANTS.
THE DEFENDANT appeared in PERSON.

JUDGMENT
(As approved)

BRAINLESS CROOKED RACIST NONSENSE.

Yinka Bamgbelu: Irreparable Civilisation Degradation: Bedford County Court, May House,29, Goldington Road, Bedford, MK40 3NN, is a block of flats.

QUASI-COMMUNISM: Apart from creating cushy salaried jobs for Pure White Solicitors and Barristers (predominantly but not exclusively pure white) who FAILED in practice (loads did), what do pure white IMBECILES (predominantly but not exclusively pure white) need very expensive administration of English Law for?

Karen Kwamboka: Our own NIGERIAN BABIES with huge oil wells and gigantic gas fields near their huts eat only 1.5/day in our own NIGERIA, a brainless hereditary RACIST pure white bastard whose pure white father and mother have never seen CRUDE OIL was our Senior District Judge in BEDFORD – **Habakkuk 1:4.**

Yinka Bamgbelu: When it became apparent to JEWS and GENTILES that the fellow was who He said He was – **John 14:6**, He was kidnapped and KILLED – **Matthew 27:32-56.** Our own MESSIAH was not punished for speaking but was KILLED solely to prevent HIM from speaking – **Exodus 20:13.**

"Freedom of Expression is a basic right." Lady Hale.

Karen Kwamboka: If Genetic Pure White Supremacist Briton, President Trump, could disprove the TRUTH, which is that his own pure white kindred, Pure White Senior Bedford's District Judge Paul Robert Ayers, our own Senior Vice President of the Association of Her Majesty's District Judges, unrelentingly LIED under oath (approved Judgement) when he stated that the NIGERIAN was invited to, and took part in, a hearing at Bedford County Court, May House, 29, Goldington Road, Bedford, MK40 3NN, on Monday, 1st July 2013, he will confirm the belief of scores of millions of pure white Britons, which is that SEXED UP LEGAL TRANSCRIPTS do not exist in the administration of English Law – **Habakkuk 1:4**. A corrupt JUSTICE SYSTEM that is overseen by Pure White Freemasons for the benefit of Pure White Imbeciles.

Yinka Bamgbelu: BEDFORD, ENGLAND: GDC, Freemason, Brother Richard William Hill fabricated reports and unrelentingly lied under oath – **Habakkuk 1:4.** Hereditary RACIST pure white bastards (predominantly but not exclusively pure white) will investigate allegations of RACIST CRIMES against their own pure white kindred, and when they find that they are based on TRUTHS, opportunist RACIST pure white bastard will CRIMINALLY BURY RACIST EVIL – **Habakkuk 1:4.** Constance Briscoe was JAILED for a lesser offence.

Karen Kwamboka: Integrity, friendship, respect, and charity: All for one, and one for all. Their people are everywhere and they control almost everything in their Godforsaken Racist Hell Hole: Half-educated school dropout GED type, and their SUPERIORS - who have informal access to some very POWERFUL Pure White Crooked Freemason Judges – **Habakkuk 1:4.**

Yinka Bamgbelu: They don't want their own mentally gentler WHITE CHILDREN (OECD) and the pure white imbeciles they shepherd (predominantly but not exclusively pure white) to know the TRUTH, which is that apart from our own INFERIOR SKIN COLOUR, which we neither made nor chose, and our more inferior accent when speaking a foreign language, we are human beings too, and we are also properly created by Almighty God, and to conceal this TRUTHS, hereditary RACIST pure white bastards (predominantly but not exclusively pure white) resort to RACIST CRIMINALITY, and they steal yields of our own people's Christ-granted talents, and their overwhelming leverage is the certainty that all Judges will be PURE WHITE and their hope is that they would be hereditary RACIST pure white bastards too – **Habakkuk 1:4.**

Karen Kwamboka: If as they vulgarly imply, hereditary RACIST pure white bastards (predominantly but not exclusively pure white) are truly superiorly created by Almighty God, why do RACIST pure white cretins – **Proverbs 17:16** (predominantly but not exclusively pure white) need RACIST CRIMINALITY to defeat self-educated NIGERIANS, from shit hole Africa, in open debates?

BEDFORD, ENGLAND: Based on cogent, irrefutable, and available evidence, GDC, Sue Gregory (OBE), our own Officer of the Most Excellent Order of our own Empire of Stolen Inheritance – **Habakkuk 2:6-9, Exodus 20:15,** unrelentingly lied under implied oath and on record – **Habakkuk 1:4.** Constance Briscoe was JAILED for a lesser offence: Apartheid by stealth. Facts are sacred and cannot be overstated.

Yinka Bamgbelu: Based on several decades of very proximate observations and direct experiences, homogeneity in the administration of their LAW is an impregnable secure mask of merciless RACIST EVIL, and a very potent weapon of RACE WAR.

RACIAL BIAS AND THE BENCH

Criminal Bar Association

https://www.criminalbar.com › uploads › 2023/02

In fact, there are currently no Black judges in the High. Court, Court of Appeal or Supreme Court. Not one. As Judge Peter Herbert stated: "The judiciary is ...

Karen Kwamboka: Pure White, King's School and Oxbridge-educated very rich man's son (**Mark 10:25**), Lord Justice Haddon-Cave, KC, a RACIST first son of a Tasmanian Colonialist Economic Cannibal, which part Old Bailey (1907), and Royal Courts of Justice (1882), was not STOLEN, or which part did Sir Charles Phillip Haddon-Cave (1925–1999) buy, or which part preceded SLAVERY?

Karen Kwamboka: OYINBO OLE/ODE/BARAWO: A RACIST DESCENDANT OF PURE WHITE THIEVES – **EXODUS 20:15, HABAKKUK 2:6-9.**

RACIST descendants of thieves and owners of stolen lives. It is their brainless and baseless self-awarded birth right to be intellectually superior to NIGERIANS, from shit hole Africa, and when they are not, they resort to RACIST CRIMINALITY: New Herod, **Matthew 2:16.**

Their 5th Rate Military Power impersonates a SUPERPOWER: Delusional Grandeur of the Stolen Past - **Exodus 20:15, Habakkuk 2:6-9.**

The YANKS are NATO, and absolutely everything else is an auxiliary bluff.

Their Country is SHIT, and they are worse than SHIT. The Quality of Human Beings in their Godforsaken Racist Hell Hole, including some Soldiers - is very poor (OECD).

Habakkuk 1:4: "The British Justice System is Racist and should not be trusted by ethnic minorities." Peter Herbert (OBE).

Their hairs stand on end when they are challenged by self-educated NIGERIANS, from shit hole Africa; we and our type are the ones hereditary

RACIST pure white bastards (predominantly but not exclusively pure white) would beat up without the support of the YANKS: Flat Track Bullies.

Imagbon, 1892.

Benin, 1897.

If hereditary RACIST pure white bastards (predominantly but not exclusively pure white) are brave as they vulgarly brag, they must directly use extreme overwhelming violence to evict PUTIN from Crimea, he used extreme overwhelming violence to convert Bakhmut and Avdiivka from bricks to rubble and stole them – **Exodus 20:15.**

OXFORD, ENGLAND: GDC, Pure White British Soldier, Stephanie Twidale (TD) unrelentingly lied under oath and on record – **Habakkuk 1:4**. Constance Briscoe was JAILED for a lesser offence. They hate Negurs, and we know. Facts are sacred and cannot be overstated.

Yinka Bamgbelu: The Father judges no one, He has given all judgment to the Son—**John 5:22**. Pure White Kings School and Oxbridge-educated Posh Very Rich Man's Son (**Mark 10:25),** Lord Charles Anthony Justice Haddon-Cave, KC, a RACIST first son of a Tasmanian Colonialist Economic Cannibal, if the SINLESS FATHER Judges no one, what MORAL RIGHT does a descendant of EVIL RACIST PURE WHITE BASTARDS, extremely nasty murderers, genocidal pure white racist killers – **Exodus 20:13**, who directly or indirectly KILLED >97 % of Native Tasmanians (Black Wars, 1824-1835).

"The white man is the devil." Elijah Mohammad (1897-1975).

Karen Kwamboka: Exodus 20:13: Pure White Kings School and Oxbridge-educated Posh Very Rich Man's Son (**Mark 10:25),** Lord Charles Anthony Justice Haddon-Cave, KC, a RACIST first son of a Tasmanian Colonialist Economic Cannibal, your own father, Sir Philip Haddon-Cave (1925-1999), a Colonialist Economic Cannibal, was born in Hobart to settlers whose era saw the near-extinction of Aboriginal Tasmanians through EXTREME RACIST VIOLENCE and land grab, in the 1800s. An ignorant hereditary RACIST descendant of THIEVES – **Exodus 20:15**. No brain. Poor natural resources. Several centuries of stealing and SLAVERY preceded their huge stolen inheritance (gigantic yields of several continuous centuries of ancestral theft) – **Habakkuk 2:6-9.** Abuse of temporary power is the fullest definition of RACIST EVIL

An opportunist RACIST pure white bastard was granted the platform to display hereditary prejudice.

"Those who have the power to do wrong with impunity seldom wait long for the will." Dr Samuel Johnson (1709-1784).

Yinka Bamgbelu: Racist bullies do not deserve anyone's sympathy when they are bullied by Trump.

Based on cogent, irrefutable, and available evidence, SEXED UP LEGAL TRANSCRIPTS are very, very, very, very, very, very, very, common in the administration of English Law – **Habakkuk 1:4**.

Karen Kwamboka: It is blatant DISHONESTY and/or RECKLESS RACIST CONFUSION (recklessness is malice) that the Negro was invited to, and took part in, a hearing at Bedford County Court, May House, 29, Goldington Road, Bedford, MK40 3NN, on Monday, 1st July 2013. The Pure White Racist Bastard, albeit England's Class Senior District Judge LIED – **Habakkuk 1:4**. The pure white ancestors of his pure white father and mother were incompetent RACIST LIARS too, they were THIEVES and owners of stolen children of defenceless poor people, including the African ancestors of the MULATTO Duchess of Sussex, impure White/impure Black/<43% Nigerian. Constance Briscoe was JAILED for a lesser offence: One rule for pure White, and a different rule for BLACKS: Apartheid by stealth – **Habakkuk 1:4.**

Yinka Bamgbelu: OYINBO OLE/ODE/BARAWO: A whole people, all pure white RACIST, and Aryan - versus a single NEGRO, only one NIGERIAN, from shit hole Africa.

They are obsessed with me. They fear the untamed minds of self-educated NIGERIANS, from shit hole Africa, more than PUTIN'S POISONS. It is me that evil RACIST pure white bastards want, but it is my daughter they got. They hate us, and we know. They should stay here; it is safer than NIGERIA – Exodus 21:23-27.

Karen Kwamboka: OYINBO OLE/ODE/BARAWO: If their intellects were as SUPERIOR as their universally acknowledged irrefutably SUPERIOR SKIN COLOUR, which they neither made nor chose, and their more SUPERIOR ACCENT when speaking their own language, why did hereditary RACIST pure white bastards (predominantly but not exclusively pure white) resort incompetent RACIST MENDACITY to persecute a lowly, supposedly, INFERIOR NEGRO – Infra Dignitatem – a mere NIGERIAN from shithole Africa?

Yinka Bamgbelu: They hate us, and we know; we hate them more, but they didn't know; their overwhelming leverage is that all Judges are PURE WHITE, and they have unbounded and unaccountable 'LEGAL POWERS', and we are powerless and have been robbed to penniless since their armed ancestors found ours, in the AFRICAN BUSH – in the 15th Century.

OYINBO OLE/ODE/BARAWO: "How Europe underdeveloped Africa." Dr Walter Rodney (1942-1980).

Karen Kwamboka: OYINBO OLE/ODE/BARAWO: Based on several decades of very, very, very, very, very, proximate observations and direct experiences, there is no IMPARTIAL LAW in their Godforsaken RACIST HELL HOLE; their Law is what Antichrist hereditary white supremacist FREEMASONS want, and absolutely everything else is DECEIT – **Habakkuk 1:4.**

CHAPTER TWENTY-FIVE

Yinka Bamgbelu: OYINBO OLE/ODE/BARAWO: TRUTHS disfavour hereditary RACIST pure white bastards (predominantly but not exclusively pure white), so they deceive their own mentally gentler white children (OECD) and the pure white imbeciles they shepherd (predominantly but not exclusively pure white) that they are ULTRA-RIGHTEOUS GENIUSES who do everything, absolutely everything, LEGALLY: Rules based procedures, precedent ,statute etcetera, including RACIAL HATRED and FRAUD—**Habakkuk 1:4.**

Karen Kwamboka: OYINBO OLE/ODE/BARAWO: They are not the only creation of Almighty God, and they are not IMMORTAL, and the universally acknowledged irrefutably SUPERIOR SKIN COLOUR that the very, very, very, very, very, fortunate wearer neither made nor chose is not the only wonder of our world. No brain. Poor natural resources. Several centuries of STEALING and SLAVERY preceded their huge stolen inheritance—**Habakkuk, Exodus 20:15**. Skin colour is a GREAT creation of Almighty God, but it is not the GREATEST—**Proverbs 20:15.**

Yinka Bamgbelu: BEDFORD,ENGLAND: Pure White Senior District Judge Paul Robert Ayers, our own Senior Vice President of the Association of Her Majesty's District Judges, if you could disprove the TRUTH, which is that GDC, Freemason, Brother Richard William Hill, England's Class Senior Postgraduate Tutor, Bedfordshire, fabricated reports and unrelentingly lied under oath and on record—**Habakkuk 1:4,** you will confirm that belief of scores of millions of Charlie Kirk (1993–2025), which is that President Trump meant it when he stated: "We shall forge a colour-blind society based on merit." You will also confirm the belief of all PURE WHITE FREEMASON JUDGES in Great Britain, which is that Homogeneity in the administration of English Law is not a weapon a ASYMMETRIC RACE WAR.

"Trump's administration packed Courts with white Judges." Kamala Harris

Karen Kwamboka: OYINBO OLE/ODE/BARAWO: AN IGNORANT HEREDITARY RACIST DESCENDANT OF ULTRA-RIGHTEOUS PURE WHITE THIEVES—**HABAKKUK, EXODUS 20:15.** A CLOSETED TOMMY MORRISON'S SYMPATHISER: HIS BRAIN IS HIS VERY, VERY, VERY, VERY, SOFT UNDERBELLY.

Yinka Bamgbelu: BEDFORD, ENGLAND: Pure White Senior District Judge Paul Robert Ayers, the Senior Vice President of the Association of Her Majesty's District Judges, it is impossible, absolutely impossible, for you and your pure white type, including ALL CLOSETED TOMMY MORRISON SYMPATHISERS, and GDC, Freemason, Brother Richard William Hill, England's Class Senior Postgraduate Tutor, Bedfordshire, to progressively compete on a colour-blind level playing field without resorting to RACIST CRIMINALITY. You are inferior. Only your universally acknowledged irrefutably SUPERIOR SKIN COLOUR and GOD are truly good—**Mark 10:18,** and you neither made nor chose it, and you will be considerably diminished as a human being without it, and you know it. Sincere immodesty is sincerer than insincere modesty.

Sincerity is a prime attribute of our own MESSIAH: "Jesus is the bedrock of my faith." HM (1926-2022).

Karen Kwamboka: "I have seen evil, and it has the face of Mark Fuhrman." Johnnie Cochran (1937–2005).

I saw SATAN, in propria persona: Stephanie Twidale, British Soldier (TD), and Mason, Richard Hill, England's Class NHS Postgrad Tutor, Bedfordshire—direct descendants of SATAN – **John 8:44, John 10:10.**

Yinka Bamgbelu: Habakkuk 1:4: It is absolutely impossible to compete on a colour-blind level intellectual playing field without resorting to RACIST CRIMINALITY. OYINBO OLE/ODE/BARAWO: There is a significant decline in educational standards; continuing decline may make it incompatible with the competent administration of English law.

Children in the UK hitting educational targets at 5, in descending order:

1. Asian (Indian)

2. Asian (Any other Asian)

3. White (British)

4. White (Irish)

5. Mixed (any other)

6. Mixed (white and black African)

7. Chinese

8. Mixed (White and black Caribbean)

9. Black (African heritage)

10. Asian (Any other Asian)

11. Black (Caribbean heritage)

12. Black (other)

13. Asian (Bangladeshi)

14. White (Any other white)

15. Any other ethnic group

16. Asian (Pakistani)

17. White (Traveller of Irish heritage)

18. White (Gypsy/Roma)

Source: Centre Forum, 2016.

Children in the UK hitting educational targets at 16, in descending order:

1. Chinese

2. Asian (Indian)

3. Asian (Any other Asian)

4. Mixed (White and Asian)

5. White (Irish)

6. Mixed (Any other)

7. Any other ethnic group

8. Asian (Bangladeshi)

9. Parent/pupil preferred not to say

10. Mixed (White and black African)

11. White (Any other white)

12. Black (African heritage)

13. White (British)

14. Asian (Pakistani)

15. Black (other)

16. Mixed (White and black Caribbean)

17. Black (Caribbean heritage)

18. White (Traveller of Irish heritage)

19. White (Gypsy/ Roma)

Source: Centre Forum, 2016.

Karen Kwamboka: Brainless hereditary RACIST pure white bastards (predominantly but not exclusively pure white). They were all PURE WHITE. Homogeneity in the administration of their LAW is a weapon of WAR, RACE WAR.

Yinka Bamgbelu: Irreversible GENETIC DAMAGE is the most enduring residue of insatiably greedy Pure White European Christians' Commerce in millions of Stolen African children of defenceless poor people, including the African ancestors of our Quasi-Mulatto Duchess of Sussex, impure White/ impure Black/43% Nigerian – **Habakkuk**.

Karen Kwamboka: Envy is a thief: It is natural (human nature) that Pure White Judges in Great Britain would be envious if their own mentally gentler pure white children (OECD) underperform in Academic Tests.

2023/24 UK government statistics,88.6% of Chinese pupils achieved grade 4+ in English and Maths GCSEs, versus 65.1% nationally and lower for pure white British children.

If Yellow Parents of Yellow Children (Chinese) who were first on the list of children meeting academic targets at age 16 were granted the basic right to choose for their own Yellow Children, they would not choose Pure White Britons, who were 13th on the list of c

Karen Kwamboka: When it becomes mandatory for Judges to HANDWRITE detailed legal and factual reasons for their decisions, functional semi-illiterate scatter-head closeted white supremacist Antichrist Freemason Judges would be found out – **Habakkuk 1:4.**

Then, there, Judges, nearly all, were members of the Antichrist Racist Freemasonry Quasi-Religion (Mediocre Mafia) and most of them were THICKER than a gross of planks.

Antichrist Racist Freemasonry Quasi-Religion (Mediocre Mafia) teaches its members secret voodoo handshakes, not grammar, the former is considerably easier to master.

https://www.youtube.com/watch?v=BlpH4hG7m1A.

Based on several decades of very proximate observations and direct experiences, their Country is SHIT, and they are worse than SHIT. The pattern of Merciless Racist Evil is the same almost everywhere in their Godforsaken Racist Hell Hole, and the Quality of Human Beings, including some Judges, in their Shit Country, is very poor.

"Sometimes people don't want to hear the truth because they don't want their illusions destroyed." Friedrich Nietzsche (1844-1900).

Facts are sacred and cannot be overstated.

Yinka Bamgbelu: Our own NIGERIA, Shell's docile since 1956 (OLOIBIRI). GDC was established in 1956. Our own NIGERIA BABIES with huge oil wells and gigantic gas fields near their huts eat only 1.5/day in our own NIGERIA, a very bellyful opportunist RACIST pure white bastard, a mere Poly-educated former debt-collector Solicitor in Norwich (5th Rate Partner), whose pure white father and mother have never seen CRUDE OIL, and whose pure white ancestors, the Pure White ancestors of Tommy Robinson, and Robert Hibbert (1769-1849) of LUTON, were fed like battery hens with gigantic yields of millions of stolen children of defenceless poor people, including the African ancestors of the QUASI-MULATTO, impure White, impure Black, <43% Nigerian, grandniece and grandnephew of Major Andrew Mountbatten Windsor – **Habakkuk.**

Karen Kwamboka: According to Centre Forum. Org, at age 5, white British children were third on the list of those hitting academic targets, and only in about a decade, at age 16, the white British majority had descended to 13th on the list of those hitting academic targets. If the descent continues, and the average white

British majority falls to Gypsies class on the list of those meeting academic targets, then dominance based upon population alone (they tyranny of the pure white majority) will not be justifiable, and one- man-one-vote may have to be revisited, as human beings are, clearly, not equally created by Almighty God. If the descent in educational standards continues, the finest filtration of white British majority may not be the best available, and only the best available is desirable.

Yinka Bamgbelu: Subjectivity contaminates transparent, colour-blind, and measurable objectivity, and it will always favour Pure White People: White Privilege.

"At the same time, we cannot allow meritocracy to be used as a justification to open America's labour market to the world in the name of finding "global talent" that undercuts American workers." President Trump's National Security Strategy, 2025

Karen Kwamboka: 'The judiciary, medical profession, media and government were all dominated by white middle classes.' Sir Bernard Hogan, Howe, Police Chief

The argument about aborigine of the land could substantially be untrue, certainly genetically, and it should be subservient to objective merit and the best interest of the whole people.

Yinka Bamgbelu: 'It was in 1066 that William the Conqueror occupied Britain, stole our land and gained control by granting it to his Norman friends, thus creating a feudal system we have not yet fully escaped.' Multi-millionaire Socialist Rich Man's Son (Mark 10:25), Tony Benn (1925-2014).

Karen Kwamboka: Normans stole from others what others had stolen from others. Genetically pure aboriginal Britons are extinct. Unelected, not merit based, closet racist, satanic network will not remove mediocrity and confusion.

Yinka Bamgbelu: Hereditary RACIST pure white bastards (predominantly but not exclusively pure white). They are the best in everything where objectivity is subservient to subjectivity. SUPERIORITY is their brainlessly and baselessly self-awarded inviolable birth right, so they must always win, even if they were THICKER than a gross of planks. Skin colour that the very fortunate wearer neither made nor chose is universally acknowledged to be irrefutably SUPERIOR, but their intellects are not, and their unashamedly MEDIOCRE, indiscreetly crooked, VINDICTIVE, potently weaponised, and institutionally RACIST waste of money Justice System is fundamentally designed to conceal that truth – **Habakkuk 1:4**. Facts are sacred and cannot be overstated. No brain. Poor natural resources. Several continuous centuries of stealing and SLAVERY preceded their huge stolen inheritance (gigantic yields of several continuous centuries of ancestral theft, Maafa, 1445-1888) – **Habakkuk 2:6-9, Exodus 20:15**. Unlike PUTIN'S SIBERIA, there are no gas fields in Bedfordshire and where the pure white mother and father of Pure White Senior Bedford's District Judge Paul Robert Ayers, our own Senior Vice President of the Association of Her Majesty's District Judges, were born. Poly-educated opportunist RACIST pure white rubbish. An ignorant hereditary RACIST pure white bastard was granted the platform to display hereditary prejudice. Superior skin colour, a huge stolen inheritance, and what else? Before Slavery, what?

"Those who know the least obey the best." George Farquhar (1677-1707).

Then, there was only subsistence feudal agriculture.

"Agriculture not only gives riches to a nation, but the only one she can call her own." Dr Samuel Johnson (1709-1784).

Karen Kwamboka: If you disagree with the Antichrist Racist Freemasons (Mediocre Mafia), especially if you are a mere Negro, from shit hole Africa, the closeted racist bastards will kill you, albeit hands-off.

Yinka Bamgbelu: Hereditary RACIST pure white bastards (predominantly but not exclusively pure white) should rewrite their own law: 'Freedom of Expression for dull adults with the basic skills of a child (imbeciles)' should replace 'Freedom of Expression for all'.

Karen Kwamboka: Unlike her little brother, who was regularly taken to Bedfordshire Masonic Centre, the Keep, MK42 8AH, with neither the knowledge nor the consent of Negro father of the Negro child, age saved the child's sister from the Extremely Nasty Closeted-Racist-Dylan–Roof-Freemason-Judge. She thanks her stars that the incontrovertibly functional semi-illiterate pure white bastard, an innately racist pure white man did not have anything to do with her education.

In her GCSE, she gained the following grades:

English Language A*
English Literature A*

Mathematics A*
Additional Mathematics A*
Physics A*
Chemistry A*
Biology A*
History A*
Latin A
Spanish A
Advanced Level Mathematics A

Yinka Bamgbelu: Only two years later, irrespective of unrelenting RACIST TYRANNY towards her father, she gained Six A-Grades in Her A/Level and has since gained a First-Class Science Degree from one of the topmost Universities in the World. Envy is a thief. They hate us, and we know. We hate them more, but they don't know. They are very powerful. We are absolutely powerless, and we have been robbed to penniless since their armed ancestors found ours – in the African bush in the 15th Century (1445-1888).

Karen Kwamboka: Hereditary RACIST pure white bastards (predominantly but not exclusively pure white) dress up interracial intellectual envy, and opportunist RACIST pure white bastards call RACIST EVIL something else.

Yinka Bamgbelu: The academic height that the pure white father and mother of our own indiscreetly opportunist RACIST Pure White Bastard, albeit England's Class Senior District Judge Paul Robert Ayers, our own Senior Vice President of the Association of Her Majesty's District Judges, CANNOT know, and which the Christ-granted talents of all his own mentally gentler white children (OECD), grandchildren, and great grandchildren will not exploit – **Proverbs 17:16.** Genetic Mix is the Holy Grail, and there is considerably more to it than superior skin colour that the very fortunate wearer neither made nor chose.

Karen Kwamboka: Collective superfluous superiority (skin colour and accent), the refuge of the intellectually disfavoured. Skin colour is a great creation of Almighty God, but it is not the greatest – **Proverbs 20:15**.

Yinka Bamgbelu: The centuries-old unspoken myth that intellect is related to their universally acknowledged irrefutably superior skin colour that they neither made nor chose – is the mother of all RACIST SCAMS.

Karen Kwamboka: Hereditary RACIST PURE WHITE BASTARDS are very desperate to conceal the truth, which is that the centuries-old unspoken myth that Christ-granted talent is related to the universally acknowledged irrefutably SUPERIOR SKIN COLOUR that the very fortunate wearer neither made nor chose is the mother of all RACIST SCAMS.

Yinka Bamgbelu: Envy is a thief.

Indiscreet envy.

"Envy is weak." Yul Brynner (1920-1985).

If according to Government Statistics, Nigerian Children were above Pure White British Children on the list of those meeting academic targets at age 16, why should Pure White British Judges be happy about that, and why should Nigerians allow a Pure White Alleged Genetic Gypsy Senior Judge, with an arbitrarily acquired camouflage English name have a say in the education of their Nigerian children – when pure white Gypsy were last on the list of those meeting academic targets at age 16?

Karen Kwamboka: BEDFORD, ENGLAND: Pure White Senior District Judge Paul Robert Ayers, our own Senior Vice President of the Association of Her Majesty's District Judges, a brainless hereditary RACIST pure white bastard ultra-righteously sat of the BONES of Stolen Children of Defenceless Poor AFRICANS, and more bones than the millions of skulls at the doorstep of Pol Pot (1925-1998), and the Opportunist RACIST pure white bastard who spent almost three times more years as an apprentice Judge (Deputy District Judge, 1992-2000) than he spent at Poly studying 5th Rate Law, Judged SINNERS – Matthew 7:1-6, John 8:7. It is me they want, but it is my daughter evil RACIST pure white bastards got. They should stay here; it is safer than NIGERIA – **Exodus 21:23-27.**

Yinka Bamgbelu: Then, all Judges were pure white Freemasons and most of them were thicker than a gross of planks, and yields of millions of stolen and destroyed lives were used to build magnificent courts, and yields of merciless RACIST EVIL were used to pay the salaries of pure white Freemason Judges who sent pure white people who stole money to Great Prisons built with yields of Stolen lives - **Habakkuk**.

Karen Kwamboka: Sadistic and Racist Pure White Bastards: The deliberate irreparable genetic damage of slave children on European Christians' plantations: Several centuries of irreversible weakening of the common genetic pool is the most enduring residue of European Christians' extortionately profitable evil commerce in millions of stolen and destroyed children of defenceless poor people, including the African ancestors of the Quasi-Mulatto, impure White/ impure Black, <43% Nigerian, Grandniece and Grandnephew of Major Andrew Mountbatten Windsor

Yinka Bamgbelu: Trump's Poodles. Paper Tigers. A Fifth Rate Military Power impersonates a SUPERPOWER. Delusional Grandeur of the Stolen Past. Their Country is SHIT, and they are worse than SHIT. The Quality of Human Beings, including FREEMASONS, in their Godforsaken Racist Hell Hole is very, very, poor (OECD).

Karen Kwamboka: BEDFORD, ENGLAND: Pure White Senior District Judge Paul Robert Ayers, our own Senior Vice President of the Association of Her Majesty's District Judges, the most important part of the matter is genetic mix, and there is considerably more to it than skin colour and accent. If as they vulgarly brag, it is the truth that they are intellectually superiorly created by Almighty God, why do PURE WHITE CRETINS need RACIST CRIMINALITY?

Yinka Bamgbelu: **Exodus 20:5:** "Give me liberty or give me death." Patrick Henry (1736-1799).

The Racist Tyranny of the Pure White Majority.

When OPPORTUNIST RACIST PURE WHITE BASTARDS place insurmountable obstacles before Negurs, they constructively invite Negurs to bow or die. We shan't bow to RACIST MOTHER FU*KERS, and we are prepared to die, but not alone.

Karen Kwamboka: Skin colour that they neither made nor chose is universally acknowledged to be irrefutably SUPERIOR, and their posh accent when speaking their own language is even more SUPERIOR, but their intellects are not, and their indiscreetly crooked, unashamedly mediocre, VINDICTIVE, potently weaponised, and institutionally RACIST waste of money Fish and Chips Justice System – is fundamentally designed to conceal that truth – **Habakkuk 1:4.**

Yinka Bamgbelu: Slavery is not hereditary; we are not bound to accept SHIT infinitely. We need legal tools for self-defence, not white supremacist thugs in camouflage Police Uniform.

Give us the tools, and we have the courage and conviction to return their fire for nastier fire.

Karen Kwamboka: If as they vulgarly brag, Pure White CRETINS are superiorly created by Almighty God, why do they need RACIST CRIMINALITY to defeat self-educated Nigerians, from shithole Africa – in open debates

OXFORD, ENGLAND: GDC, Mrs Helen Falcon (MBE), our own Member of the Most Excellent Order of our own Empire of Stolen Inheritance (**Exodus 20:15, Habakkuk 2:6-9**) unrelentingly lied under oath and on record – **Habakkuk 1:4.** Constance Briscoe was JAILED for a lesser offence: Apartheid by stealth.

Yinka Bamgbelu: Cultural Degradation/Civilisation Erasure. The Quality of Human Beings, including crooked and indiscreetly RACIST Mrs Helen Falcon (MBE), in their Godforsaken Racist Hell Hole -is very poor; excessive stupidity is the norm.

"There is no sin except stupidity." Wilde

Based on available evidence, the pattern of Merciless Racist Evil is the same everywhere in their Godforsaken Racist Hell Hole.

Karen Kwamboka: BEDFORD, ENGLAND: GDC, Sue Gregory (OBE), our own Officer of the Most Excellent Order of our own Empire of Stolen Inheritance (**Exodus 20:15, Habakkuk 2:6-9**) unrelentingly lied under implied oath and on record – **Habakkuk 1:4.** Constance Briscoe was JAILED for a lesser offence: Apartheid by stealth.

Yinka Bamgbelu: His mother, the source of his Principal X Chromosome, was bland, colourless, and unremarkable, so she is not part of the story of the properly schooled impostor and an expert of deception: Stolen Inheritance. Unearned Hereditary Advantages and Privileges. Undeserved Patronages. Haddon-Cave is the son of Sir Charles Philip Haddon-Cave, Chief Secretary of Hong Kong between 1981 and 1985, and elder brother of Francis, who was called to the Hong Kong bar in 1999. He is an uncle of the actresses Jessie Cave and Bebe Cave.

Karen Kwamboka: In the shoes of Trump, a genetic Briton, the selfless, but ruthless, far sighted, and practical Britons who stole North America, Australia, New Zealand, and almost every square inch of the defenceless world, would have stolen Canada, Greenland, and all defenceless land all over Planet Earth: Ignorant descendants of ultra-righteous pure white THIEVES – **Exodus 20:15, Habakkuk 2:6-9.**

Yinka Bamgbelu: Our world: The Serengeti of THIEVES – **Exodus 20:15, Habakkuk 2:6-9**: Once upon a time, a quarter of the land mass of the World belonged to Great Britain; she stole it.

"All have taken what had other owners and all have had recourse to arms rather than quit the prey onto which they were fastened." Dr Samuel Johnson (1709-1784).

Karen Kwamboka: Poly-educated (not Russell Group Inferior-Class Alternative Education -Proverbs 17:16) pure white son of a pure white plebeian hoe FAILED in practice, loads did, and from 1992-2022, the opportunist RACIST pure white bastard parked his LIABILITY at the public till, and sold unashamed mediocrity and confusion to the undiscerning – in exchange for very valuable considerations.

Yinka Bamgbelu: **Leviticus 19:33-34**: Hereditary RACIST Pure White Bastards overwhelm foreigners with RACIST LIES, and they kill our people, albeit hands-off.

Nigerian, Dr Richard Bamgboye, GP, only 56, and Indian Dentist, Dr Anand Kamath, only 42, were killed in Great Britain, albeit hands-off, with the mens rea hidden in the belly of the actus reus.

Karen Kwamboka: Envy is a thief. Badbelle: Indiscreet envy. "Envy is weak." Yul Brynner (1920-1985).

Hereditary RACIST pure white bastards are more familiar with Negroes of Afro-Caribbean Extraction, such David Lammy, Daine Abbott, and their type, direct descendants of plantation Negroes, Stolen African Children who were unnaturally selected, genetically reversed, deliberately bred for hard labour, and reared like cattle on stolen plantations.

Yinka Bamgbelu: Matthew 2:16: Hereditary RACIST pure white bastards are consumed by uncontrollable interracial intellectual envy, and they will destroy every Negro they cannot control: High Tech Lynching of Uppity Blacks - Clarence Thomas.

Karen Kwamboka: I can zip it but cannot lie; you are a PURE WHITE SHIT, and had you been Black, you will be worse than SHIT. A waste of money Fake Judge, within one of the dullest adult populations in the industrialised world (OECD), who FAILED in practice, loads did and parked his liability at the public till. You are worthy only because you are pure white, and you are rich only because, for several continuous centuries, your pure white ancestors were industrial-scale professional THIEVES – **Exodus 20:15, Habakkuk 2:6-9.**

Yinka Bamgbelu: New Herod, **Matthew 14:** They destroy all those they cannot control. Any Negro who disagrees with PURE WHITE RACIST

BASTARDS is a Lunatic. They are psychologically and intellectually insecure, and RACIST BASTARDS are more impervious to original thoughts than LUNATIC JIHADISTS.

Karen Kwamboka: Psalm 115:3/Proverbs 16:33: Ase eyi o wu ni Edumare. Varietas Fortunae.

Mary Anne Macleod (1912-2000), a plebeian domestic servant, the daughter of abjectly poor and wretched Scottish Crofters, was the mumsy of the Indisputable De Facto Ruler of our World, why Trump?

Yinka Bamgbelu: 1976-2022: The brain that you inherited from your pure white father and mother is not good. An ignorant hereditary RACIST pure white bastard studied 5th Rate Law at Poly. 1976-1992, he was a Solicitor in Norwich, and when he FAILED, loads did, the brainless opportunist RACIST pure white bastard was an apprentice Judge (Deputy District Judge) for nine years (1992-2000) because he kept FAILING the promotion exams.

Karen Kwamboka: The Legal Trade is Dying, and it is not in the Intensive Care Unit, it is in a Hospice receiving palliation; palliation is SUICIDE, albeit a slow one.

Based on several decades of very proximate observations and direct experiences, their indiscreetly crooked, unashamedly mediocre, VINDICTIVE, potently weaponised, and institutionally RACIST waste of money fish and chips Justice System is FU*KED, irreparably FU*KED, as it has foreseeably succumbed to INCEST, weakening of the common genetic pool, with associated physical and/or mental wonkiness, and hereditary white supremacist Freemason Judges, and others, who make loads of money from unashamed mediocrity and confusion prop shit up: Conflict of interest.

“A government that robs Peter to pay Paul can always depend on the support of Paul.” George Bernard Shaw (1856-1950).

Yinka Bamgbelu: Our own IMBECILE Freemason Senior Judge of our own Empire of Stolen Inheritance - **Exodus 20:15, Habakkuk 2:6-9**. No brain. Poor natural resources. Several centuries of stealing and slavery preceded their huge stolen inheritance

“The best opportunity of developing academically and emotional.” Pure White Senior Bedford’s District Judge Paul Robert Ayers, our own Senior Vice President of the Association of Her Majesty’s District Judges.

Our unashamedly functional semi-illiterate brainless pure white bastard of our own Empire of STOLEN INHERITANCE - **Exodus 20:15, Habakkuk 2:6-9**, approved and immortalised what his pure white mother and father spoke, and which his poly-educated pure white supervisors in LUTON, including HHJ Perusko, authorised.

Based on cogent, irrefutable, and available evidence, HHJ Perusko studied Law at Poly (not Russell Group Second-Class Alternative Education – Proverbs 17:16).

Facts are sacred: "The truth allows no choice." Dr Samuel Johnson (1709-1784).

Karen Kwamboka: The fellow, a Mother Fu*king Pure White Bastard, was a STORYTELLER.

"To survive, you must tell stories." Umberto Eco (1932-2016).

His approved Judgement is akin to the kind of STORIES his father used to tell when he returns home, at very odd hours, from his regular pub-crawl, Queen Victoria, Greene King, Nag's Head Etcetera, thoroughly stoned, hungry, angry, and very randy.

Yinka Bamgbelu: An opportunist RACIST pure white bastard was granted the platform to display hereditary prejudice. A brainless hereditary RACIST pure white bastard. The pure white ancestors of his pure white father and mother were THIEVES - **Exodus 20:15, Habakkuk 2:6-9**: Industrial-scale professional THIEVES, extremely nasty and MERCILESS RACIST KILLERS, nastier than Yevgeny Prigozhin (1961-2023), and Hitler (1889-1945), and just by the by, several years of NAZI HOLOCAUST (1939-1945) was a mere storm in a teacup in comparison to BLACK HOLOCAUST (Maafa, 1445-1888), armed land grabbers, gun runners, drug dealers (opium merchants of the Qing Dynasty), and owners of stolen children of defenceless poor people, including the African ancestors of the QUASI-MULATTO, impure White/impure Black/<43% Nigerian, grandniece and grandnephew of Major Andrew Mountbatten Windsor.

Karen Kwamboka: An intellectually impotent pure white nonentity. A RACIST descendant of ultra-righteous pure white THIEVES and owners of stolen children of defenceless poor AFRICANS. Unlike PUTIN's Siberia, there are no gas fields in bland, colourless, and almost lifeless Freemasons' Kempston and where the pure white father and mother of pure white Senior

Bedford's District Judge Paul Robert Ayers, our own Senior Vice President of the Association of Her Majesty's District Judges were born – Habakkuk. Ill-gotten gains: Our straight-faced ultra-righteous descendant of PURE WHITE THIEVES and owners of stolen lives.

Yinka Bamgbelu: If our own opportunist RACIST pure white bastard of our own Empire of Stolen Inheritance – **Exodus 20:15, Habakkuk 2:6-9**, read his own written Judgement that he approved, he was a FOOL, and if he did not, he LIED as he implied that he did. The pure white ancestors of his pure white father and mother were incompetent RACIST LIARS too; they were THIEVES and owners of stolen lives.

"Those who have robbed have also lied." Dr Samuel Johnson (1709-1784).

Karen Kwamboka: "Blue-eyed devils." Elijah Mohammad (1897-1975).

Based on several decades of study and proximate observations the direct descendants of the father of RACIST LIES – **John 8:44, John 10:10**, their pure white ancestors were not only DEVILS, but they were also a very nasty Racist Murderers, THIEVES, and a very wealthy Merchants of Stolen and Destroyed Lives – **Habakkuk**

Yinka Bamgbelu: Based on several decades of very proximate observations and direct experiences, they are innately very bad human beings. Like Babies, Trump, Xi, Putin, Kim, MBS Etcetera, they constructively demand that everyone must love them unconditionally, and they expect everyone to see everything only from their perspective (UNIPOLARITY), and they expect everyone to say and/or write only what they love to hear.

Karen Kwamboka: "All men are created equal." Abraham Lincoln (1809-1865).

Armed European Christians used guns to mercilessly slaughter, dispossess, rob, and take possession, and after they had stolen everything that had other owners, they dishonestly claimed that their victims were equal.

Yinka Bamgbelu: Flat track bullies.

Imagbon, 1892.

Benin, 1897.

Hereditary Racist Pure White Bastards (predominantly but not exclusively pure white) loved armed conflicts and Africans carrying sticks and stones were their preferred opponents.

Karen Kwamboka: If hereditary Racist Pure White Bastards (predominantly but not exclusively pure white) as brave as they vulgarly brag, they must directly use GUNS to evict Putin from Mariupol, he stole it with guns – **Exodus 20:15.**

Yinka Bamgbelu: BEDFORD, ENGLAND: Pure White Senior District Judge Paul Robert Ayers, our own Senior Vice President of the Association of Her Majesty's District Judges, the most important part of the matter is MONEY, and it is not the yield of your talent, and unlike PUTIN'S SIBERIA, there are no gas fields in Bedfordshire and where your own pure white mother and father were born.

Karen Kwamboka: Imperial Reversal. Ignorant descendants of ultra-righteous and very highly civilised PURE WHITE THIEVES – Exodus 20:15, Habakkuk 2:6-9, and owners of stolen lives. Varietas Fortunae: A very hardened unapologetic RACIST BASTARD, the son of a mere plebeian domestic servant, treats Great Britain like a domestic servant; In his very powerful shoes, Great Britain did worse, Sea Wolves looted and pillaged almost every square inch of the defenceless World.

Mo kuku ti ri omo oba to deru ri,mo si tun ti ri iwofa to di alaso.

Yinka Bamgbelu: Based on cogent, irrefutable, and available evidence, then, Britons, including Scots, were THIEVES and owners of stolen lives, including the African ancestors of the QUASI-MULATTO, impure White/impure Black/<43% Nigerian, grandniece and grandnephew of the Duke of Edinburgh.

Karen Kwamboka: Imperial Reversal: Verietas Fortunae. Their insatiably greedy RACIST BASTARD ancestors were worse than Trump; in Trump's very powerful shoes, they trampled on the defenceless world – with absolute impunity; they were THIEVES – **Exodus 20:15, Habakkuk 2:6-9.** Would Ukraine have been involved in a direct conflict with Russia with only the support of Europeans (without the support of the YANKS)?

Yinka Bamgbelu: The Negro did not clean; he paid others, including pure white people to clean. To conceal colour-blind intellectual inferiority, hereditary white supremacist bastards always declare that Negroes are dirty, both physically and/or morally.

RACIST CRIMINALITY, RACISTS' CURE FOR DIRTINESS AND LUNACY.

Karen Kwamboka: Only excessively stupid Negurs expect descendants of THIEVES and owners of stolen lives to voluntarily relinquish several centuries-old stolen advantageous positions in exchange for NOTHING

"To the American founding fathers, the 'truth that all men are created equal' was 'self-evident'. It'd better be, for it certainly can't be proved. True equality can only exist in heaven; on earth, the belief that all men are created equal is wishful thinking. For men are created unequal in strength, intelligence, character – well, in everything. Earthly inequality is thus a natural order of things, and it can only be distorted by unnatural means. Even then it won't disappear; it'll be replaced by a worse type of inequality or else camouflaged by demagoguery." ALEXANDER BOOT 2011.

Yinka Bamgbelu: The Irreversible fall of Great Britain: Survival desires excision, but it is impossible in a metastasised Malignant Melanoma. Only palliation is possible, but it is SUICIDE, albeit a slow one. Their Country is SHIT, and they are worse than SHIT, and the Quality of human beings in their Godforsaken Racist Hell Hole is generally very poor (OECD).

Karen Kwamboka: You are very powerful, but excessively stupid. I do not want to have anything to do with you; you are an existential threat

"Treating your adversary with respect is striking soft in a battle." Dr Samuel Johnson

BRAINLESS SHALLOW NONSENSE

Avoid Powerful Enemies, even Christ did. When Christ was kidnapped, He became very gentle, as He accurately foresaw bodily suffering, the Ne plus ultra of suffering.

Yinka Bamgbelu: Two Meal Tickets:**2 Thessalonians 3:6-10**: Which one our PUTRID TUBES did our Born-Again Christian tell Pure White Senior Bedford's District Judge Paul Robert Ayers, our own Senior Vice President of the Association of Her Majesty's District Judges, and Freemasons' at Brickhill Baptist Church - she used to work for 0.5M?

"You will bow; you can't beat the system." Our Born-Again Christian.

I shan't – **Exodus 20:15**. I know who will – **1 John 4:4, Romans 11.**

Karen Kwamboka: Two Meal Tickets: **2 Thessalonians 3:6-10:** Then, all Judges were PURE WHITE FREEMASONS, and most of them were thicker than a gross of planks, and they sent their daughters to university to gain tangible qualifications, so that they could eat their own food, but also to use their PUTRID TUBES to ensnare fellow university students who would become their main meal ticket (Odogwu) or their Second Meal Ticket.

Yinka Bamgbelu: "There is no sin except stupidity." Wilde (1854-1900).

Then, in our own tribe in the African bush, prior to the Second Coming of European Christians, when they came with GUNS and the Holy Book (Bible), excessively stupid people were castrated before they could breed and multiply excessive stupidity.

Karen Kwamboka: "To deny or belittle this good is, in this dangerous century when the resources and pretensions of power continue to enlarge, a desperate error of intellectual abstraction. More than this, it is a self-fulfilling error, which encourages us to give up the struggle against bad laws and class bound procedures and to disarm ourselves before power. It is to throw away a whole inheritance of struggle about the law and within the forms of law, whose continuity can never be fractured without bringing men and women into immediate danger." - E. P Thompson (1923-1994).

"Give me liberty or give me death." Patrick Henry (1736-1799).